The law was one of the most potent sources of authority and stability in early modern England. Historians have, however, argued over whether the discretion and flexibility embodied in the judicial system was used as a method of social control. By focusing their attention on felonies and on the actions of the protagonists in judicial decisions they have tended to ignore rich sources of information concerning attitudes towards and experiences of the law. Misdemeanour prosecutions affected many more people (and a broader social range of participants) than felony prosecutions, and in their choice of methods of prosecution both victims and justices of the peace exercised considerably greater flexibility in responding to petty crimes than they did with felonies. This book examines the day-to-day operation of the criminal justice system in Middlesex from the point of view of both plaintiffs and defendants, and offers an assessment of the social significance of the law in preindustrial England.

The book includes important discussions of the different methods, both formal and informal, of prosecuting petty crimes; of the importance of status, gender, and individual justices of the peace in shaping access to the law; of the attempts by the Societies for the Reformation of Manners from 1690 to manipulate the judicial system in order to enforce systematically the laws against vice; and of the contrasting prosecutorial strategies adopted in rural Middlesex and in different parts of London. The book is based on a careful statistical analysis of thousands of recognizances, indictments, and house of correction commitments, and will be of interest and importance to all social, legal, and urban historians of the early modern period.

Cambridge Studies in Early Modern British History

PROSECUTION AND PUNISHMENT

Cambridge Studies in Early Modern British History

Series editors

ANTHONY FLETCHER

Professor of Modern History, University of Durham

JOHN GUY

Richard L. Turner Professor in the Humanities and Professor of History, University of Rochester, NY

AND JOHN MORRILL

Lecturer in History, University of Cambridge, and Fellow and Tutor of Selwyn College

This is a series of monographs and studies covering many aspects of the history of the British Isles between the late fifteenth century and the early eighteenth century. It includes the work of established scholars and pioneering work by a new generation of scholars. It includes both reviews and revisions of major topics and books which open up new historical terrain or which reveal startling new perspectives on familiar subjects. All the volumes set detailed research into broader perspectives and the books are intended for the use of students as well as of their teachers.

For a list of titles in the series, see end of book.

PROSECUTION AND PUNISHMENT

Petty crime and the law in London and rural Middlesex, *c.* 1660–1725

ROBERT B. SHOEMAKER

Lecturer in History, University of Sheffield

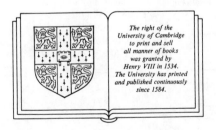

The right of the
University of Cambridge
to print and sell
all manner of books
was granted by
Henry VIII in 1534.
The University has printed
and published continuously
since 1584.

CAMBRIDGE UNIVERSITY PRESS

Cambridge

New York   Port Chester

Melbourne   Sydney

Published by the Press Syndicate of the University of Cambridge
The Pitt Building, Trumpington Street, Cambridge CB2 1RP
40 West 20th Street, New York, NY 10011–4211 USA
10 Stamford Road, Oakleigh, Melbourne 3166, Australia

First published 1991

Printed in Great Britain at the
University Press, Cambridge

British Library cataloguing in publication data
Shoemaker, Robert B., 1956–
Prosecution and punishment: petty crime and the law in
London and rural Middlesex, c. 1660–1725. – (Cambridge
studies in early modern British history)
1. England. Criminal law, History
I. Title
344.20509
Library of Congress cataloguing in publication data
Shoemaker, Robert Brink.
Prosecution and punishment: petty crime and the law in London and
rural Middlesex, c. 1660–1725 / Robert B. Shoemaker.
p.   cm. – (Cambridge studies in early modern British history)
Revision of the author's thesis (Ph. D.) – Stanford, 1986, under
title: Crime, courts, and community.
Includes bibliographical references (p.) and index.
ISBN 0–521–40082–1 (hard)
1. Criminal justice, Administration of – England – Middlesex –
History. 2. Criminal statistics – England – Middlesex – History.
3. Prosecution – England – Middlesex – History. 4. Middlesex
(England) – Social conditions. 5. Criminal justice, Administration
of – England – London – History. 6. Criminal statistics – England –
London – History. 7. Prosecution – England – London – History.
8. London (England) – Social conditions. I. Title. II. Series.
KD7876.S47 1991
345.421′205042–dc20
[344.212055042] 90–2580 CIP
ISBN 0 521 40082 1 hardback

CE

For Clara and David Shoemaker

CONTENTS

ILLUSTRATIONS

TABLES

ACKNOWLEDGMENTS

This book started its life many years ago as a Ph.D. dissertation at Stanford University, and when writing the dissertation I received generous financial support from the Mrs. Giles Whiting Foundation, the Josephine de Karman Fellowship Trust, and the Harris and Weter Funds administered by the History Department at Stanford. A summer grant from the National Endowment for the Humanities helped fund the research necessary to transform the dissertation into a book.

In many ways this book is the product of a collective effort, and I would like to thank several people for assistance beyond the call of duty. The bulk of the research was carried out at the Greater London Record Office, where Richard Samways, Harriet Jones and the rest of the staff patiently responded to my persistent questions and requests for documents. I would also like to acknowledge the help and advice I received from the staffs of the Stanford University Library, Huntington Library, British Library, Guildhall Library, Westminster Public Library, Bodleian Library, Public Record Office, and Corporation of London Record Office, as well as the computer centers of Stanford University and the University of London. As the dissertation research progressed I benefited from the suggestions of Tim Harris, Don Spaeth, and Norma Landau. Professor Landau's provocative questions concerning the nature of judicial procedures, both when I first met her in the archives and later in the form of detailed comments on drafts of the early chapters of the dissertation, helped focus my interests on the relationships between different legal procedures and on the role of individual justices of the peace in shaping patterns of prosecutions. Not only did her comments stimulate my thinking on a number of issues, but they saved me from several errors, and I am very grateful for her help. I was fortunate to have had Paul Seaver as dissertation supervisor. Not only did he patiently guide the dissertation to completion, but he continued to provide insightful suggestions, friendly encouragement, and constant support long after I left the protective confines of graduate school.

In completely rewriting the dissertation I have accumulated many more debts. John Beattie, Tom Green, John Langbein, and Jim Sharpe read the

xiv

finished dissertation and offered several helpful suggestions for revising and restructuring the manuscript. Laird Easton cast a critical editor's eye over early versions of several chapters, and Joanna Innes has given useful advice and criticism on many occasions. I am also grateful for suggestions and comments I have received from Tony Claydon, Tim Hitchcock, Mark Jenner, Peter King, Nick Rogers, John Styles, and Tim Wales. Most of these arose during conversations which took place at the Institute of Historical Research at the University of London. With its research library, active seminar schedule, and crowded tearoom, the Institute provided a welcome base for an unaffiliated scholar like myself.

The field of criminal justice history has yielded a rich harvest of research and publications in the last fifteen years; my substantial debts to the historians who came before me are acknowledged in the footnotes. I owe a special note of thanks, however, to those who have shared the products of their unpublished work with me, particularly Joanna Innes, Norma Landau, and Peter King. Chapters 9 and 10 especially are based on foundations laid by the hard work of others: my work on the reformation of manners campaign owes much to the doctoral theses of Andrew Craig and Tina Beth Isaacs, and the prosecution rates presented in chapter 10 were calculated using demographic and socio-economic statistics compiled by Beatrice Shearer and James Alexander from the hearth tax and four shillings in the pound tax respectively. Without the generosity of these historians in allowing me to make use of their findings, these chapters could never have been written.

Three other academics contributed much more personally to this project. My wife and fellow historian, Wendy Bracewell, provided a healthy mix of advice, encouragement and distractions which kept me sane. My parents, both emeritus professors of chemistry, made this all possible through their encouragement and support of my intellectual interests. It is to them that I dedicate this book.

Kentish Town, London

ABBREVIATIONS AND CONVENTIONS

All dates are in the old style, but with the new year beginning on January 1.

The spelling, capitalization, and punctuation in quotations from manuscript sources have been modernized.

All cited works were published in London unless otherwise noted.

The following abbreviated forms have been used in the footnotes:

PUBLISHED WORKS

Albion's Fatal Tree, ed. Hay *et al*: *Albion's Fatal Tree: Crime and Society in Eighteenth-Century England*, ed. Douglas Hay, Peter Linebaugh, John G. Rule, E. P. Thompson, and Cal Winslow (Harmondsworth, 1975)

Beattie, *Crime and the Courts*: John Beattie, *Crime and the Courts in England 1660–1800* (Princeton, 1986)

Beattie, "Pattern of crime": John Beattie, "The pattern of crime in England 1660–1800," *Past and Present* 62 (1974), 47–95

Bond, *Complete Guide*: John Bond, *A Complete Guide for Justices of the Peace* (3rd edn., 1707)

Boulton, *Neighbourhood and Society*: Jeremy Boulton, *Neighbourhood and Society: A London Suburb in the Seventeenth Century* (Cambridge, 1987)

Crime in England, ed. Cockburn: *Crime in England 1500–1800*, ed. J. S. Cockburn (Princeton, 1977)

CSPD: *Calendar of State Papers, Domestic*

Dalton, *Countrey Justice*: Michael Dalton, *The Countrey Justice, Containing the Practice of the Justices of the Peace out of their Sessions* (various editions)

Dowdell, *Quarter Sessions*: Eric George Dowdell, *A Hundred Years of Quarter Sessions* (Cambridge, 1932)

George, *London Life*: M. Dorothy George, *London Life in the Eighteenth Century* (1925; reprint edn. Harmondsworth, 1966)

Hawkins, *Pleas of the Crown*: William Hawkins, *A Treatise of Pleas of the Crown*, 2 vols. (1716)

Herrup, *The Common Peace*: Cynthia Herrup, *The Common Peace: Participation and the Criminal Law in Seventeenth-Century England* (Cambridge, 1987)

Ingram, *Church Courts*: Martin Ingram, *Church Courts, Sex and Marriage in England, 1570–1640* (Cambridge, 1987)

Innes, "Prisons for the poor": Joanna Innes, "Prisons for the poor: English bridewells, 1555–1800," in *Law, Labour, and Crime*, ed. Francis Snyder and Douglas Hay (1987), 42–122

King, "Crime, law and society": Peter King, "Crime, law and society in Essex, 1740–1820" (Ph.D. dissertation, Cambridge University, 1984)

Lambard, *Eirenarcha*: William Lambard, *Eirenarcha: or of the Office of the Justices of the Peace* (various editions)

Landau, *Justices of the Peace*: Norma Landau, *The Justices of the Peace 1679–1760* (Berkeley, 1984)

Middlesex Records, ed. Jeaffreson: *Middlesex County Records*, ed. J. C. Jeaffreson, 4 vols. (1886–1892)

Nelson, *Office and Authority*: William Nelson, *The Office and Authority of a Justice of a Peace* (various editions)

Office of the Clerk of the Peace: *The Office of the Clerk of the Assize ... together with the Office of the Clerk of the Peace* (1682)

Policing and Prosecution, ed. Hay and Snyder: *Policing and Prosecution in Britain 1750–1850*, ed. Douglas Hay and Francis Snyder (Oxford, 1989)

Sharpe, *Crime in Early Modern England*: J. A. Sharpe, *Crime in Early Modern England 1550–1750* (1984)

Sharpe, *Crime in Seventeenth-Century England*: J. A. Sharpe, *Crime in Seventeenth-Century England* (Cambridge, 1983)

Sharpe, " 'Such disagreement betwyx neighbours' ": J. A. Sharpe, " 'Such disagreement betwyx neighbours': litigation and human relations in early modern England," in *Disputes and Settlements. Law and Human Relations in the West*, ed. John Bossy (Cambridge, 1983), 167–87

Sheppard, *Sure Guide*: William Sheppard, *A Sure Guide for his Majesty's Justices of the Peace* (2nd edn., 1669)

Shoemaker, "Crime, Courts and Community": Robert B. Shoemaker, "Crime, Courts and Community: The Prosecution of Misdemeanors in Middlesex County, 1663–1723" (Ph.D. Dissertation, Stanford University, 1986)

Shoemaker, "London 'Mob' ": Robert B. Shoemaker, "The London 'mob' in the early eighteenth century," *Journal of British Studies* 26 (July 1987), 273–304

An Ungovernable People, ed. Brewer and Styles: *An Ungovernable People: the*

English and their Law in the Seventeenth and Eighteenth Centuries, ed. John Brewer and John Styles (1980)

Webb and Webb, *The Parish and the County*: Sidney and Beatrice Webb, *English Local Government from the Revolution to the Municipal Corporations Act: The Parish and the County* (1906)

ARCHIVAL SOURCES

BL   British Library

CLRO   Corporation of London Record Office

GLRO   Greater London Record Office

     MJ/   Middlesex sessions records

     WJ/   Westminster sessions records

          OC   Orders of the court

          SBB   Sessions book

          SBR   Sessions register

          SP   Sessions paper

          SR,   Sessions roll

               CP   Calendar of prisoners

               GDR   Gaol delivery recognizance

               HC   House of correction calendar

               I   Indictment number

               R   Recognizance number

PRO   Public Record Office

     KB   King's Bench records

     SP   State Papers

Part I

BACKGROUND

1

Introduction

Rooted in customary landholding practices and the unwritten constitution, the law played a central role in early-modern English society. It was given still greater prominence as a result of the civil war and the revolution of 1688. In the eighteenth century, Douglas Hay and E. P. Thompson have argued, the governing class was deprived of the full powers of the traditional bulwarks of social order – a strong monarchy and the church – and became dependent on the law as the primary instrument of its rule. Backed by a combination of the terror of threatened punishments, the mercy of pardons and partial verdicts, and the idea of equal treatment before the law, the ideology of the rule of law secured the consent of the governed.[1] Evidence of the pervasiveness of legal ideas comes most strikingly from rioters and others who challenged government policies, who often expressed their grievances in terms of the need for enforcement of specific laws.[2] If even the challengers to authority worked (at least partly) within the law, it appears that the law played a major role in limiting conflict and maintaining social stability in preindustrial England.

This argument is based primarily on evidence from the criminal law, and most historians working on the subject accept that the criminal justice system played an important role in maintaining social order. Recent debate has instead focused on how it functioned to achieve this end. Hay's assertion that the flexibility of the law allowed it to be used to discipline the lower classes through a mixture of ceremony, terror, and mercy dispensed by the ruling class has been countered with evidence that jury verdicts, sentencing decisions, and pardons were based upon "good-faith considerations of factors with which

---

[1] Douglas Hay, "Property, authority and the criminal law," in *Albion's Fatal Tree* ed. Hay *et al.*, pp. 17–63; and E. P. Thompson, "Patrician society, plebeian culture," *Journal of Social History* 7 (1974), pp. 382–405, and *Whigs and Hunters* (Harmondsworth, 1977), pp. 259–69. See also John Brewer and John Styles, "Introduction," *An Ungovernable People*, ed. Brewer and Styles, pp. 11–20; Anthony Fletcher and John Stevenson, "Introduction," *Order and Disorder in Early Modern England*, ed. Fletcher and Stevenson (Cambridge, 1985), pp. 25–26; Ingram, *Church Courts*, pp. 27–34.

[2] Brewer and Styles, "Introduction," pp. 16–17; Peter King, "Gleaners, farmers and the failure of legal sanctions in England 1750–1850," *Past and Present* 125 (1989), pp. 122–24.

ethical decision-makers ought to have been concerned."[3] Many historians now describe the law as a "multiple-use right" which accommodated complaints from, and depended upon the participation of, members of all social classes with the exception of the poor. Peter King has argued that quarter sessions prosecutions were dominated by a "broad group of farmers, tradesmen, and artisans ... using that court both to protect their property and to resolve the various types of dispute from which an assault case arose." Similarly, Cynthia Herrup asserts that "the obligation to participate in prosecutions went deep into the ranks of propertied society, assuring not only the involvement of a fair number of persons but also their interest in upholding deference to the law."[4] As Hay has recently conceded, both points of view have merit: the law served many purposes, both "as a generator of social symbols [and] a service institution for the prosecution of crime"; both as "promoting specific class interests ... [and] used by all social classes ..."[5]

Hay's critics have usefully broadened the scope of criminal justice history to include careful analysis of the process and results of formal prosecutions, but many fundamental questions concerning the social significance of the law in preindustrial England remain unanswered. We still know remarkably little about popular attitudes towards, and experiences of, the judicial system. This is a notoriously difficult subject, but one that is crucial for our understanding of the social impact of the law, for assertions about the accessibility of the law or the manipulation of justice for the purposes of "terror" or "mercy" mean little unless we can detect the impact of prosecutions and judicial decisions on the people they affected. Recent work has tended to focus on the attitudes of the protagonists in judicial decisions (jurors and judges), as opposed to the attitudes of the people who used the law as prosecutors and experienced the law as defendants (though the former have received some attention[6]). Our ignorance of this subject is greatest for the poorest sections of society, a substantial proportion of the population. How far down the social scale was the law truly accessible? How did those people with restricted access view the legal system? We also need to consider the consequences of the fact that popular consent to laws could be selective, in the sense that laws which

---

[3] John H. Langbein, "Albion's fatal flaws," *Past and Present* 98 (1982), pp. 96–120 (quote from p. 120). See also Peter King, "Decision-makers and decision-making in the English criminal law, 1750–1800," *Historical Journal* 27 (1984), pp. 25–58.

[4] Brewer and Styles, "Introduction," pp. 19–20; King, "Decision-makers," p. 32; Herrup, *The Common Peace*, p. 195.

[5] Douglas Hay, "The criminal prosecution in England and its historians," *Modern Law Review* 47 (1984), p. 21.

[6] Notably by Peter King ("Decision-makers" and "Crime, law and society," chap. 4); Cynthia Herrup (*The Common Peace*, chap. 4); Douglas Hay ("Prosecution and power: malicious prosecution in the English courts, 1750–1850," in *Policing and Prosecution*, ed. Hay and Snyder, pp. 343–95); and Ruth Paley ("Thief-takers in London in the age of the McDaniel gang, *c.* 1745–1754," *ibid.*, pp. 301–40).

conflicted with traditional customs and popular values often received no allegiance.[7]

More importantly, historians have yet to test Hay and Thompson's assertions that the criminal law was the most important institution for maintaining social stability in post-revolutionary England. Perhaps because historians of the criminal law have been unwilling to question a *raison d'être*, John Langbein's irreverent remark that the criminal justice system was no more important than a service industry such as refuse collection has not been taken seriously.[8] But if we are to understand the nature of social stability in preindustrial England it is clear that we need to assess the impact of the law and other sources of order more comprehensively. By focusing on the prosecution of felonies, historians have largely failed to assess the social importance of several other facets of the legal system, including misdemeanor prosecutions, civil cases, and suits prosecuted in the church courts.[9] More generally, social historians need to examine the role of other institutions, such as the family, the church, schools, and poor relief, in maintaining social order.[10]

This book takes a step towards a wider understanding of the social significance of the law by analyzing the prosecution of misdemeanors, an aspect of the law which had a broad social impact in terms of the numbers and status of people involved, the wide range of offences prosecuted, and the substantial degree of discretion and flexibility involved in the judicial process. Misdemeanor prosecutions can shed considerable light on popular experiences of, and attitudes towards, the law in the seventeenth and eighteenth centuries.

---

[7] Bob Bushaway, *By Rite: Custom, Ceremony and Community in England 1700–1880* (1982), chap. 6.

[8] Langbein, "Albion's fatal flaws," p. 120. For a satirical response to this argument, see Peter Linebaugh, "(Marxist) social history and (conservative) legal history: a reply to Professor Langbein," *New York University Law Review* 60 (1985), pp. 238–42. Peter King's recent article on gleaning, however, outlines some of the limitations of the powers of the "formal law," with respect to attempts to impose new definitions of property on the rural poor (King, "Gleaners, farmers and the failure of legal sanctions").

[9] With some notable exceptions: C. W. Brooks, "Interpersonal conflict and social tension: civil litigation in England, 1640–1830," in *The First Modern Society*, ed. A. L. Beier, *et al.* (Cambridge, 1989), pp. 357–99; David Sugarman and G. R. Rubin, eds., *Law, Economy and Society, 1750–1914: Essays in the History of English Law* (Abingdon, 1984); Ingram, *Church Courts*.

[10] Perry Anderson, *Arguments Within English Marxism* (1980), p. 200; Michael Ignatieff, "State, civil society, and total institutions: a critique of recent social histories of punishment," in *Crime and Justice: An Annual Review of Research*, ed. M. Tonry and N. Morris, vol. 3 (1981), pp. 182–87; Sugarman and Rubin, "Towards a new history of law and material society in England, 1750–1914," in *Law, Economy and Society*, pp. 62–67; Joanna Innes and John Styles, "The crime wave: recent writing on crime and criminal justice in eighteenth-century England," *Journal of British Studies* 25 (Oct. 1986), pp. 432–35; Fletcher and Stevenson, "Introduction," p. 31; J. C. D. Clark, *English Society 1688–1832* (Cambridge, 1985), p. 87.

I.I MISDEMEANORS AND SOCIETY IN PREINDUSTRIAL ENGLAND

The impact of misdemeanor prosecutions was felt in all corners of society. Perhaps nine times as many defendants were involved in misdemeanor prosecutions as in felony cases,[11] and they came from a wider range of social classes than other types of litigation. While the civil law increasingly arbitrated the financial disputes of the propertied[12] and the law of felonies was mainly used to prosecute thieves, who were disproportionately from the lower classes, defendants accused of misdemeanors came in significant numbers from all social classes. Misdemeanors, moreover, included a far more diverse collection of offences than felonies. The preindustrial definition of crime was far broader than our own, including offences we would label as sins, torts, or breaches of administrative regulations. While a narrow range of theft offences dominate the records of prosecuted felonies, misdemeanors include, in addition to property offences (theft, fraud, trespass), significant numbers of vice offences (keeping a disorderly or unlicensed alehouse, prostitution, gambling), regulatory offences (neglect of office, failure to repair the highway, selling goods underweight), poor law offences (idleness, vagrancy, bastardy) and offences against the peace (riot, assault, defamation). A study of the prosecution of misdemeanors illustrates the variety of social contexts from which people brought their grievances before the courts.

In contrast to felonies, a distinctive aspect of misdemeanor prosecutions is the large number of victimless offences, offences which directly harmed no one individual but indirectly could be said to harm the whole community. These include regulatory offences, poor law offences, and vice, and they were typically prosecuted by parish officials or informers. Private citizens were unlikely to assume the public burden of prosecuting victimless offences unless they were motivated by financial gain (part of the fine if the defendant was convicted) or religious zeal. As unpaid, part-time officials, parish officials often shared this reluctance to prosecute, but they were occasionally stimulated into apprehending or reporting the names of large numbers of offenders by pressure from neighbors, justices of the peace or the central government. Consequently, patterns of prosecutions for victimless offences, which fluctuate even more erratically than those for felonies or offences against the peace, were shaped by a combination of the attitudes of local and national governors and broader social and cultural changes.[13]

Discretion and flexibility were the hallmarks of the early modern criminal

[11] See below, Table 3.3. This calculation does not include summary convictions by fine for vice.
[12] Martin J. Ingram, "Communities and courts: law and disorder in early seventeenth-century Wiltshire," in *Crime in England*, ed. Cockburn, pp. 115–16; Brooks, "Civil litigation in England," pp. 396–97.
[13] Keith Wrightson, "Two concepts of order: justices, constables and jurymen in seventeenth-century England," in *An Ungovernable People*, ed. Brewer and Styles, pp. 21–46.

justice system, and, as patterns of prosecutions of victimless offences suggest, misdemeanor prosecutions provide abundant opportunities for observing discretion and flexibility in action. In contrast, plaintiffs and justices of the peace exercised considerably less flexibility in the prosecution of felonies. Justices were legally required to refer felony accusations to the quarter sessions or assizes courts, and victims could not legally conclude informal settlements with felons. Although recent research suggests that some cases were nonetheless settled informally, justices of the peace were under some pressure to refer felony accusations to the courts.[14] Felonies were often very serious crimes, and both community pressure and legal requirements encouraged formal prosecution by indictment.

Misdemeanors, on the other hand, were often rather trivial offences, and it is likely that a much smaller proportion of misdemeanors was prosecuted in comparison to felonies. While it is possible to argue that changes in prosecutions for theft (most thefts were felonies) reflect changes in the actual incidence of theft as inferred from economic conditions, it is impossible even to estimate the relationship between the number of prosecutions for most misdemeanor offences and the number of crimes which actually occurred.[15] For example, two of the most commonly prosecuted misdemeanors were assault and prostitution. In law, an assault could involve as little as a threatening gesture or placing a hand on another in anger.[16] Historians will obviously never know how many assaults took place; only a tiny proportion of such acts can ever have been prosecuted. Prostitution, like many other victimless offences, was even more erratically prosecuted. Because so many misdemeanors were not prosecuted, prosecution statistics are far more revealing of attitudes concerning the merits of resorting to the law than they are of changes in the actual incidence of crime.

Not only did victims and officials exercise greater discretion in choosing whether to prosecute misdemeanors, but they possessed greater flexibility in choosing a method of prosecution. While the indictment was the only legally recognized method of prosecuting felonies, misdemeanors could be (and were frequently) prosecuted using less formal procedures: plaintiffs could choose from informal mediation by a justice of the peace, binding over by recognizance, and summary conviction (with punishment by either fine or commitment to a house of correction).[17] These alternative procedures, which are only

---

[14] John Langbein, "Shaping the eighteenth-century criminal trial: a view from the Ryder sources," *The University of Chicago Law Review* 50:1 (1983), pp. 49–50; Beattie, *Crime and the Courts*, pp. 38–40; King, "Crime, law and society," chap. 4.

[15] See below, section 3.3.   [16] Dalton, *Countrey Justice* (1677), p. 282.

[17] In this study, I use the term "prosecute" to refer to all accusations reported by plaintiffs to a justice of the peace or to the grand jury at quarter sessions, whether the plaintiff sought informal mediation or a formal conviction.

now beginning to attract the attention of historians,[18] were used far more often than indictments for prosecuting misdemeanors. Since each procedure involved different facets of the law and resulted in contrasting social costs and consequences, the choice of a procedure was important, and it allowed plentiful opportunities for social considerations to influence legal strategies.[19] By examining these choices from the plaintiffs' point of view, this study seeks to illuminate people's motivations for bringing accusations and disputes before the courts. And by ascertaining the impact of prosecutions and punishments on defendants, the experiences and attitudes of those on the receiving end of the judicial system will be examined.

1.2 THE CONTEXTS: CITY AND COUNTRY IN MIDDLESEX, 1660–1725

How the judicial system was used in different social contexts reveals much about the social significance of the law. This study is based on records of the activities of justices of the peace in Middlesex, a county of contrasting environments. With its areas of relative social stability and instability, Middlesex offers the possibility of testing the hypothesis that the law contributed to social order in preindustrial England. Although geographically the county was still predominantly rural after the Restoration, about four-fifths of its population lived in the London metropolis.[20] Surrounding the City of London to the west, north, and east, the population of urban Middlesex far exceeded that of the City of London.[21] Rural Middlesex, with its market gardens and busy roads which supplied London with food and visitors, was undoubtedly less pastoral than most English counties, but its small villages and agricultural character

---

[18] J. A. Sharpe, "Enforcing the law in the seventeenth-century English village," in *Crime and the Law: the Social History of Crime in Western Europe since 1500*, ed. V. A. C. Gatrell *et al.* (1980); Joel Samaha, "The recognizance in Elizabethan law enforcement," *American Journal of Legal History* 25 (1981), pp. 189–204; Louis A. Knafla, "'Sin of all sorts swarmeth': criminal litigation in an English county in the early seventeenth century," in *Law, Litigants and the Legal Profession*, ed. E. W. Ives and A. H. Manchester (1983), pp. 50–67; Landau, *Justices of the Peace*, chap. 6; Innes, "Prisons for the poor," pp. 42–122; King, "Crime, law and society," chap. 6.

[19] In addition to providing evidence of prosecutorial attitudes and the flexibility of the law, these procedures merit closer investigation because they left more useful records than the indictments usually studied by historians of crime. While indictments reduce "complex human conflicts" to "the archaic language and fossilized categories of the criminal law" (Douglas Hay, "War, dearth and theft in the eighteenth century: the record of the English courts," *Past and Present* 95 (1982), p. 118), the language describing offences on recognizances and house of correction calendars, and in justices' notebooks, is more discursive and less constrained by legal categories. See below, section 3.2.

[20] Roger Finlay and Beatrice Shearer, "Population growth and suburban expansion," in *London 1500–1700*, ed. A. L. Beier and Roger Finlay (1986) Table 2, p. 42 (calculation based on the estimates from 1660, 1680 and 1700.)

[21] See below, section 1.3.

nevertheless contrasted sharply with the densely populated metropolis.[22] Within rural Middlesex, the rapidly growing parishes in the environs of the metropolis, whose proximity to the city generated both significant economic opportunities and social disruptions, should be distinguished from both the market gardening areas which extended along the rivers and the arable farming parishes in the northern and western regions of the county.[23] Within urban Middlesex, the population was socially segregated to a far greater extent than in the City.[24] While artisans and the laboring poor were concentrated in parishes east and north of the City of London, the gentry and nobility (along with the servants and tradesmen who catered to their needs) were concentrated in the west end.[25] By identifying the different prosecutorial strategies that emerged in these contrasting settings, some of the perceived advantages, and the probable social significance, of resorting to the law will be revealed.

How did approaches to the law differ between urban and rural Middlesex? Conventional wisdom suggests that crime was far less of a problem in rural England than in urban areas. John Beattie has suggested that crime occurred more frequently in London both because "targets and temptations were more abundant there" and, "above all, [because] poverty pressed with particular urgency in London ..."[26] It has also been suggested that there was less respect for judicial institutions in urban areas. According to Douglas Hay, social conditions in London undermined the ideological and social impact of the law: "resistance to the law, disrespect for its majesty, scorn for its justice were greater [in London]. Equally, judicial mercy in London was more often a bureaucratic lottery than a convincing expression of paternalism."[27] There are several grounds for questioning this model of the contrasting nature of crime and judicial authority in urban and rural areas. First, because of considerably shorter distances and more frequent meetings of the court, justices of the peace and the courts in London were more available than their rural counterparts. Higher prosecution rates in the metropolis may have been caused not (or not only) by higher urban crime rates but by the fact that plaintiffs were more willing to prosecute because the courts, prisons, and houses of correction were

22 Joan Thirsk, "The farming regions of England," in *The Agrarian History of England and Wales, IV, 1500–1640*, ed. Thirsk (Cambridge, 1967), p. 49; Alan Everitt, "The marketing of agricultural produce," *ibid.*, pp. 508–10.
23 L. Martindale, "Demography and land use in the late seventeenth and eighteenth centuries in Middlesex" (Ph.D. diss., London, 1968).
24 For the social topography of the City, see Roger Finlay, *Population and Metropolis* (Cambridge, 1981), pp. 77–81; R. W. Herlan, "Social articulation and the configuration of parochial poverty on the eve of the Restoration," *Guildhall Studies in London History* 2 (April 1976), p. 53; D. V. Glass, ed., *London Inhabitants Within the Walls 1695* (London Record Society, vol. 2, 1966), pp. xxii–xxiii; M. J. Power, "The social topography of Restoration London," in *London 1500–1700* ed. Beier and Finlay, pp. 206–22; Boulton, *Neighbourhood and Society*, p. 202.
25 M. J. Power, "The east and west in early-modern London," in *Wealth and Power In Tudor England: Essays Presented to S. T. Bindoff*, ed. E. W. Ives *et al.*, (1978), pp. 167–85.
26 Beattie, *Crime and the Courts*, p. 14.   27 Hay, "Property, authority," p. 55.

more accessible. Second, because personal relationships with other figures of authority such as resident gentry and the clergy may have been harder to establish in the city, justices of the peace may have played a *greater* role in mediating disputes than they did in the countryside.[28] In the large suburban parishes, only a small fraction of the residents can have attended church.[29] In many parishes there were few resident gentry, and in all the suburban parishes the large number of immigrants and the poor threatened to overwhelm informal methods of exercising authority. As exemplified in the phenomenon of "trading justices," urban justices of the peace clearly did establish rapport with local inhabitants.[30] Because of the larger number of cases coming before the courts, and the fact that the informal institutions of social control were weaker, the influence of the judicial system may have been greater in urban areas.

When thinking about crime and justice in London historians have relied on the commonly held, but unproven, idea that London life was, in contrast to rural life, essentially anonymous. Due to high levels of mortality and immigration, it is suggested, individuals had fewer family and community ties and their social contacts were more likely to be casual, transitory experiences.[31] These assertions, however, are based on weak theoretical models and insufficient research. The idealization of rural society as close-knit and unchanging, in contrast to the anonymity and mobility of urban areas, is based largely on nineteenth-century sociological models.[32] In contrast, a late sixteenth-century author took pride in what he perceived to be the virtues of urban life, arguing that when men are congregated into cities, they "are withdrawn from barbarous fer[oc]itie and force to a certain mildness of manners and to humanity and justice."[33]

The social history of preindustrial London has yet to be written. Recent research on sixteenth- and seventeenth-century London has, however, pointed to stable social relations and the existence of community ties. Jeremy Boulton has described early seventeenth-century Southwark as a set of "neighborhoods" where "local ties were the biggest single source of financial, emotional and

---

[28] This is suggested by Landau (*Justices of the Peace*, p. 201).

[29] It was claimed that the Stepney parish church could not hold one tenth of the parishioners (M. J. Power, "The urban development of east London, 1550–1700" [Ph.D. diss., London, 1971], p. 255).

[30] Landau, *Justices of the Peace*, p. 190, and below, section 8.4.

[31] E. A. Wrigley, "A simple model of London's importance in changing English society and economy 1650–1750," *Past and Present* 37 (1967), p. 51; Finlay and Shearer, "Population growth," p. 51; A. L. Beier, "Social problems in Elizabethan London," *Journal of Interdisciplinary History* 9:2 (1978), p. 217; and the sources cited by Boulton in *Neighbourhood and Society*, p. 206.

[32] Alan MacFarlane, *Reconstructing Historical Communities* (Cambridge, 1977), p. 1; C. J. Calhoun, "Community: toward a variable conceptualization for comparative research," *Social History* 5 (1980), p. 105.

[33] "An apology of the City of London" (1580) in John Stow, *The Survey of London* (2nd edn, 1603; Everyman, 1987), p. 483.

social support" for householders.[34] Even in the face of a disruptive force like the plague, Londoners displayed "social solidarity and collective defiance."[35] Other historians have noted that London possessed institutions unique to urban areas – the Lord Mayor and aldermen, apprenticeship, the guilds, the ward system of local government – which effectively cemented social bonds, relieved economic distress, resolved conflicts, and maintained public order.[36]

Much of this evidence, however, is derived from the late sixteenth and early seventeenth centuries and from parishes within the City of London, when and where the institutions encouraging social stability were strongest. In many respects, the middle decades of the seventeenth century constitute a turning point in the history of London; the demographic and socioeconomic changes London experienced during the second half of the century threatened to undermine whatever stability the metropolis had earlier possessed. After 1650, two of the institutions which historians believe contributed to social order in the City of London, the wardmote system of local government and the guilds, declined.[37] Moreover, by 1640 the population of the rapidly growing suburbs had exceeded that of the City of London; shortly thereafter, according to one estimate, the population of the City actually began to decline while the metropolis as a whole continued to grow. After mid-century, it was the suburbs which absorbed the thousands of immigrants who arrived from the country each year; between 1660 and 1700 the population of the suburbs north of the river increased by 76% to about 310,000, more than three times the population of the City.[38] The suburbs were not governed by the ward system, nor had the guilds ever had much impact outside the City.

Not enough is known about the extent of social instability in the suburban parishes, but it is clear that after the Restoration (if not before) population growth, poverty, and weak local government all presented potentially serious obstacles to the maintenance of order. Historians have been able to identify only a small proportion of the approximately 8,000 immigrants who moved to

[34] Boulton, *Neighbourhood and Society*, p. 291.
[35] Paul Slack, "Metropolitan government in crisis: the response to plague," in *London 1500–1700* ed. Beier and Finlay, p. 75.
[36] S. R. Smith, "The London apprentices as seventeenth-century adolescents," *Past and Present* 61 (1973), pp. 156–57; Steve Rappaport, *Worlds within Worlds: Structures of Life in Sixteenth-Century London* (Cambridge, 1989); Valerie Pearl, "Change and stability in seventeenth-century London," *London Journal* 5 (1979), pp. 8–27, and "Social policy in early modern London," in *History and Imagination. Essays in Honour of H. R. Trevor-Roper* (1981), pp. 115–31. See also Ian Archer, "Governors and governed in late sixteenth-century London, *c.* 1560–1603: studies in the achievement of stability" (Ph.D. diss., Oxford, 1988).
[37] Pearl, "Change and stability," pp. 25–27; J. R. Kellett, "The breakdown of gild and corporation control over the handicraft and retail trades in London," *Economic History Review*, 2nd series, 10 (1958), pp. 384–89. The weak impact of the guilds in Middlesex is documented in Dowdell, *Quarter Sessions*, pp. 175–76; A. L. Beier, "Engine of manufacture: the trades of London," in *London 1500–1700*, ed. Beier and Finlay, pp. 157–62.
[38] Finlay and Shearer, "Population growth," pp. 42, 45.

London each year during this period, most of whom settled in the suburban parishes.[39] While immigrants came from a wide range of socioeconomic and geographic backgrounds, recent research suggests that a significant proportion were teenagers or young adults and, increasingly, female. While the number of migrants taking up apprenticeships (virtually all apprentices were male) declined over the seventeenth century, the demand for female servants rose in the late seventeenth century with the growth of the west end as a center of fashionable living.[40]

Little is known about how immigrants adapted to urban life. It is possible, as Peter Burke has suggested, that immigrants lived in a "kind of cultural vacuum." While feelings of alienation or anonymity may have resulted from this situation, Burke suggests that "new forms of popular culture ... the culture of print, for example, or politics, or that of separatist congregations" may have filled the gap.[41] Peter Clark has pointed to the role played by alehouses, voluntary associations, lodging houses, and registry offices in helping new-comers cope with London life.[42] Some immigrants received advice and economic support from kin residing in the city.[43] Servants were assimilated into London life through the households in which they were employed, as well as by associating with other servants. Servants, however, were normally hired for only one year at a time and frequently faced periods of unemployment, perhaps without anywhere to turn for support but crime or prostitution.[44] Migration may thus have increased the level of poverty and unemployment in the metropolis. It is likely that a significant amount of migration was due to

---

[39] Wrigley, "Simple model," pp. 44–46.

[40] Peter Clark, "Migration in England during the late seventeenth and early eighteenth centuries," *Past and Present* 83 (1979), pp. 70–71; David Souden, "Migrants and the population structure of later seventeenth-century provincial cities and market towns," in *The Transformation of English Provincial Towns 1600–1800*, ed. Peter Clark (1981), pp. 142, 149–60; Finlay, *Population and Metropolis*, pp. 66–67, 140–41; Peter Earle, "The female labour market in London in the late seventeenth and early eighteenth centuries," *Economic History Review*, 2nd series, 42 (1989), pp. 333, 344; William F. Kahl, "Apprenticeship and the freedom of the London livery companies, 1690–1750," *Guildhall Miscellany* 1:7 (1956), p. 18; Lawrence Stone, "The residential development of the west end of London in the seventeenth century," in *After the Reformation. Essays in Honour of J. H. Hexter*, ed. Barbara C. Malament (Manchester, 1980), pp. 167–212.

[41] Peter Burke, "Popular culture in seventeenth-century London," in *Popular Culture in Seventeenth-Century England*, ed. Barry Reay (1985), p. 53. See also, Pearl, "Change and stability," p. 5; David Cressy, *Literacy and the Social Order: Reading and Writing in Tudor and Stuart England* (Cambridge, 1980), pp. 145, 147. For other aspects of urban life that helped immigrants adjust to living in London, see Beier and Finlay, "Introduction," *London 1500–1700*, pp. 21–23.

[42] Peter Clark, "Migrants in the city: the process of social adaptation in English towns, 1500–1800," in *Migration and Society in Early Modern England*, ed. P. Clark and David Souden (1987), pp. 267–91.

[43] V. B. Elliott, "Single women in the London marriage market: age, status, and mobility, 1598–1619," in *Marriage and Society. Studies in the Social History of Marriage*, ed. R. B. Outhwaite (New York, 1982), pp. 91–95; Boulton, *Neighbourhood and Society*, p. 259.

[44] See below, section 7.2.

economic hardship at home caused by factors such as the death of a parent, changing agricultural practices, or the operation of the settlement laws.[45] An anonymous author from the parish of St. Giles in the Fields complained in the 1720s that "one principal cause of the increase of our poor" was that "great numbers of idle people come out of the country, or from other parishes into this, and by continuing here, become at length chargeable."[46]

Whether or not immigration was a major cause, poverty became a serious problem in the metropolis in this period, particularly during the 1690s, when high bread prices, disruptions in trade, and government manipulation of the coinage combined to impoverish a large proportion of the lower class. Stephen MacFarlane has shown that expenditures on poor relief for the "able-bodied poor" in the City of London increased during the 1690s and 1700s; in one "outparish" of the City 29% of the inhabitants received at least "occasional" relief in 1711.[47] No equivalent calculations have been made for the urban Middlesex parishes, some of which must have experienced even greater poverty. In the hearth tax returns of the 1660s, about half of the households in the eastern and northern suburbs were classified as poor.[48] While this figure is based on a broader definition of the "poor" (householders who were exempted from paying the poor rate) than MacFarlane's figure of persons actually receiving poor relief, it suggests that the majority of Londoners in some parishes were vulnerable to distress, whether caused by individual factors such as sickness or old age, or by poor economic conditions. Throughout this period poverty was kept in the public eye by the presence of beggars on the streets, who were the subject of frequent complaints about their aggressive tactics of accosting pedestrians and knocking at people's doors.[49]

Poverty was of course not necessarily a disruptive force. In the City of London, the guilds and local government provided an extensive range of poor relief in the early seventeenth century in ways that cemented social bonds between the providers and the recipients.[50] In the late seventeenth century, however, the nature of poor relief, and of poverty itself, changed in London. The Act of Settlement of 1662 discouraged the immigrant poor from applying

---

[45] Elliott, "Single women in the London marriage market," p. 90; Finlay and Shearer, "Population growth," p. 53. George, *London Life*, pp. 116–17; Paul Slack, "Vagrants and vagrancy in England, 1598–1664," *Economic History Review*, 2nd series, 27 (1974), p. 377.

[46] *The Case of the Parish of St. Giles's in the Fields, as to their Poor, and a Workhouse Designed to be built for Employing them* [1722?], p. 3.

[47] Stephen MacFarlane, "Studies in poverty and poor relief in London at the end of the seventeenth century" (Ph.D. diss., Oxford, 1983), pp. 15, 110, 123, 126, 258–62, and "Social policy and the poor in the later seventeenth century," in *London 1500–1700*, ed. Beier and Finlay, pp. 253–54, 259–260.

[48] Power, "Social topography," p. 205.

[49] John Graunt, *Natural and Political Observations ... made upon the Bills of Mortality* (1662), p. 19; Dorothy Marshall, *The English Poor in the Eighteenth Century* (1926), pp. 231–35.

[50] Pearl, "Social policy," pp. 120–31.

for relief, for fear that they might be removed back to their parish of origin. With decreasing guild regulation of employment practices, employment was often arranged according to piecework, with the result that work was irregular and laborers became more vulnerable to trade depressions and seasonal fluctuations. Casual laborers unable to support themselves were unlikely to receive charity from the guilds.[51] By 1662, the churchwardens and overseers of the poor were unable to cope with the large number of poor inhabitants in the City's outermost parishes. According to John Graunt, "many of the poorer parishioners through neglect do perish, and many vicious persons get liberty to live as they please, for want of some heedful eye to overlook them."[52]

In the rapidly growing urban parishes in Middlesex, local government was even less capable of addressing poverty, or any other social problem. With the exception of the Westminster court of burgesses, the institutions of local government in the county – the parish, supervised by justices of the peace acting both individually and in petty and quarter sessions – were better suited to rural conditions than to those of the metropolis, where eleven parishes or hamlets had more than 5,000 inhabitants each in 1664.[53] Not only did the Middlesex justices possess limited powers, but as a group they demonstrated little interest in systematically attacking social problems.[54] Given the primitive administrative structure of both parochial government and quarter sessions, it is not surprising that corruption appears to have been a serious problem: socially inferior "trading justices" were accused of accepting bribes and fomenting quarrels among the poor, and "close" or "select" parish vestries, particularly in Westminster, were accused of inadequately relieving the poor and of running an inefficient nightly watch, despite the fact that large sums of money were raised for these purposes.[55] Although there are reasons to believe that these allegations of misconduct may have been exaggerated,[56] the fact that the complaints appeared plausible to contemporaries suggests that weak and inefficient government may have been widespread in urban Middlesex.

Fuelled by substantial demographic growth and other socioeconomic changes, the London suburbs in the late seventeenth and early eighteenth centuries faced

---

[51] Beier, "The trades of London," pp. 161–62; George, *London Life*, pp. 173–75, 187–190; Boulton, *Neighbourhood and Society*, p. 62.

[52] Graunt, *Observations*, p. 58.   [53] See below, appendix III.

[54] Dowdell, *Quarter Sessions*, pp. 190–92 and *passim*.

[55] For "trading justices," see below, sections 4.3 and 8.4. For select vestries, see Sidney and Beatrice Webb, *English Local Government from the Revolution to the Municipal Corporations Act: The Parish and the County* (1906), pp. 228–58; and Andrew Moreton [Daniel Defoe], *Parochial Tyranny: or, the House-keeper's Complaint Against the Insupportable Exactions, and Partial Assessments of Select Vestries, etc.* [1727].

[56] Landau, *Justices of the Peace*, pp. 184–204. Craig Rose has suggested to me that the attacks on close vestries, which were Tory controlled, may have been primarily motivated by political considerations.

a wide range of potentially disruptive problems. Nevertheless, it is important to recognize the forces – kin, employer, neighborhood, church – which promoted social ties and combated anonymity in the city. As M. D. George concluded, eighteenth-century London was characterized by "a seeming paradox" between its "extreme disorderliness" and "essential orderliness."[57] It is unwise to speculate on the extent of social instability, and consequently the extent of crime, in the metropolis until the precise dimensions of its social problems are better known. Yet, it is clear that contemporaries believed that London was becoming increasingly difficult to govern. In addition to the complaints about poverty, begging and misgovernment already cited, this attitude is manifest in the notoriously unsuccessful attempts by the crown and parliament to halt the growth of London in the seventeenth century.[58] With the lapsing of press censorship in 1695, there was greater public awareness of and debate concerning London's social problems.[59] This was the period when the word "mob," with its implications of irrational and disorderly plebeian behavior, was first used to describe rioting in London.[60] Complaints that London was experiencing a crime wave occurred frequently, particularly from 1688 through the 1690s, and from 1712 through the 1720s.[61]

These complaints are important, for they stimulated movements for social and judicial reform in the 1690s and early eighteenth century. Because all forms of deviance were thought to be related, fears about serious crime prompted concern about irreligion, immorality, and idleness, especially among the poor.[62] These concerns contributed to the founding of the Societies for the Reformation of Manners, the Society for the Promotion of Christian Knowledge, charity schools, corporations of the poor, and the parochial workhouse movement. On judicial matters these years witnessed the passage of statutes which expanded the number of felonies exempt from benefit of clergy and offered rewards for the conviction of the perpetrators of certain egregious felonies, the introduction of new types of punishments for convicted felons, and the adoption of new law enforcement strategies for misdemeanors, including adjustments to the night watch, the use of informers by the reformation of manners campaign, greater use of petty sessions by justices of

---

[57] George, *London Life*, p. 9.

[58] N. G. Brett-James, *The Growth of Stuart London* (1935), pp. 296–311.

[59] Lee Davison, Tim Hitchcock, Tim Keirn, and Robert Shoemaker, "The reactive state: governance and society from the Glorious Revolution to 1750," in *Reform and Regulation: The Response to Social and Economic Problems in England, 1689–1750* (forthcoming).

[60] William Sachse, "The mob and the Revolution of 1688," *Journal of British Studies* 4 (1964–65), p. 23 and n. 2; Shoemaker, "London 'mob'," p. 273.

[61] MacFarlane, "Social policy," pp. 260–61; Beattie, *Crime and the Courts*, pp. 216–17, 500–01, 516; and the royal proclamations for apprehending street robbers and other offenders listed in PRO, SP 35/17, no. 383.

[62] Beattie, *Crime and the Courts*, pp. 421–22, 494–96, 624–25.

the peace, and new foundations of and greater use of houses of correction.[63] These innovations introduce another important context for examining the social significance of the judicial system. To what extent did reformers manipulate the flexibility of the law in order to exercise greater control over the lives of those who were thought to be most prone to crime and immorality, the poor? By analyzing the reformers' prosecutorial strategies, it is possible both to determine the extent to which the law could be used to advance élite interests, and to assess the impact of such legal strategies on popular attitudes towards the law.

Despite our considerable ignorance about social conditions in seventeenth- and eighteenth-century London, three points emerge from recent research. First, conditions varied considerably, not only between urban and rural Middlesex but also within the metropolis. Second, despite the strong potential for disorder, forces for stability were present in the metropolis. Finally, regardless of their actual extent, *concern* about social problems in London was growing during this period. This book examines the contrasting prosecutorial strategies that were adopted in this complex environment, and asks whether the judicial system should be considered as one of the forces which contributed to maintaining social stability in the metropolis.

I.3 THE CONTOURS OF THIS STUDY

Any study based largely on institutional records must in some ways be shaped by the jurisdictional boundaries of that institution, in this case the Middlesex and Westminster courts of quarter sessions. By focusing on these courts, this study is limited to prosecutions which were initiated before justices of the peace in the county of Middlesex between 1660 and 1725. Fortunately, the records of both courts are virtually complete for this period.[64] The use of the Middlesex records, however, imposes three constraints on this study: the exclusion of petty offences prosecuted in other courts, the exclusion of the City of London and the suburbs south of the river, and the necessity of sampling. As explained in chapter 2, the relatively small numbers of misdemeanors prosecuted at King's Bench and in the manor and ecclesiastical courts are excluded from this study. The prosecution of crime in the City of London, which accounted for only about a quarter of London's population in 1680, merits a separate study; the institutions of justice and local government in the City differed in several important respects from those in Middlesex and thus the contexts in which crime was prosecuted – and judicial records were created – are not directly

---

[63] Beattie, *Crime and the Courts*, chap. 9; Shoemaker, "Crime, courts and community," pp. 243–44, 321–46; Joanna Innes, "Prisons for the poor," pp. 79–83; below, sections 3.1 and 9.1.
[64] K. Goodacre and E. Doris Mercer, *Guide to the Middlesex Sessions Records 1549–1889* (1965).

comparable. Misdemeanor prosecutions in London's southern suburbs, which contained about 15% of the population of the metropolis, have recently been studied by John Beattie. In 1680 the Middlesex sessions had jurisdiction over 60% of London's population, and this proportion probably increased over the ensuing decades.[65]

Because of the volume of quarter sessions records produced during the period of this study, only a small proportion could be carefully analyzed. Records of approximately 140,000 recognizances, 50,000 indictments, and 30,000 commitments to houses of correction have survived. As described in appendix I, a sampling strategy was devised which for statistical reasons favored intensive sampling of five sample periods of a total of seven years instead of a uniform sample from the entire period.[66] The proportions sampled within these years varied between 17 and 50%, and yielded large enough samples to permit confidence that the conclusions for the sample periods are statistically significant within the limits discussed in appendix I. In addition to this sample (referred to in the text as "the sample"), other less systematic samples of the sessions rolls were taken for specific purposes. In order to focus attention on how each procedure was used independently, cases in which one procedure was used in order to facilitate prosecution by another have generally been excluded from the analysis. Thus, recognizances which bound over defendants to appear in court to answer indictments, and defendants committed to houses of correction for want of sureties to enter into recognizances, have where possible been excluded.[67] The sample includes accusations (including *ignoramus* indictments) as well as convictions. Except where noted, the unit of analysis is the defendant, not the case.

This study is divided into three parts. Part I comprises this introduction and two chapters which set the stage for the in-depth analysis. Chapter 2, which describes the legal framework for prosecuting misdemeanors, demonstrates that plaintiffs, in consultation with justices of the peace, enjoyed considerable legal flexibility in their choice of a procedure for prosecution. The extent of this flexibility is demonstrated statistically in chapter 3, where patterns of prosecutions in Middlesex are analyzed according to type of crime and the procedure used for prosecution. Part II (chapters 4 to 7) examines how each of the procedures for prosecuting misdemeanors worked in practice, describing how cases were handled, the likely results of prosecutions, and the costs and benefits

[65] Finlay and Shearer, "Population growth," p. 45; Beattie, "Pattern of crime," pp. 47–95.

[66] For recognizances and indictments the years sampled were 1663–64, 1677, 1693, 1707 and May 1720 to April 1722. The less comprehensive survival of house of correction calendars dictated that a somewhat different set of years were sampled: see Table 7.1.

[67] In chapter 5, however, only defendants who were already indicted at the time they were bound over are excluded. The complex relationship between recognizances and indictments is explained in section 2.4.

of each procedure. These chapters seek to identify the social and legal parameters which shaped plaintiffs' choices as well as the likely consequences of prosecutions from the point of view of defendants. Part III is concerned with the social contexts of prosecutions. Focusing on the participants, chapter 8 describes the role of status and gender in determining the choice of a procedure and analyzes the role of official plaintiffs and justices of the peace in shaping patterns of prosecutions. The scope for a more aggressive use of the judicial system is assessed in chapter 9, which discusses the rise and fall of the reformation of manners campaign against vice in London. In chapter 10, the geographical distribution of prosecutions in Middlesex is analyzed in order to identify the particular social contexts in which different prosecutorial strategies were adopted. In chapter 11, the implications of these findings are assessed for our understanding of popular attitudes towards the law in preindustrial England.

2

Options for prosecution

With the extension of the jurisdiction of the royal courts in the twelfth and thirteenth centuries, violations of the king's peace that were not punishable by forfeiture of the offender's life and property became punishable by fines payable to the king. In the late fifteenth and early sixteenth centuries, these trespasses came to be called "misdemeanors."[1] Initially, wrongs that did not involve a breach of the peace were not covered by the criminal law, but numerous regulatory offences (especially violations of economic regulations, failures to fulfill community obligations, and neglects of duties by local officials) were added by statute over several centuries, so that by the sixteenth century a wide range of local government was "carried on through the forms of the criminal trial." Further development of the law of misdemeanors came from the Star Chamber, which created or refined several offences concerned with "sophisticated wrongdoing" such as perjury, forgery, fraud, extortion and sedition, offences which survived the abolition of the Star Chamber in 1641. The creation and modification of offences by statute continued through the seventeenth and eighteenth centuries, particularly in the area of moral and poor law offences.[2] By the late seventeenth century, therefore, the body of misdemeanor crimes had been enlarged far beyond offences against the peace.

A number of the courts that had possessed the power to judge violations of this disparate body of common and statute law in the middle ages, such as the sheriffs' courts and most courts belonging to private jurisdictions, had been superseded by royal justice before 1500.[3] Nonetheless, in the early modern period several different courts were entitled to try misdemeanors: notably, the manor courts, the church courts, and quarter sessions. Courts leet of manors could hear and determine most common law misdemeanors, but not statutory

---

[1] B. H. Putnam, ed., *Proceedings Before the Justices of the Peace in the Fourteenth and Fifteenth Centuries* (1938), p. cliv; *Oxford English Dictionary*.

[2] S. F. C. Milsom, *Historical Foundations of the Common Law* (2nd edn, 1981), pp. 404–25, 426–27; J. P. Dawson, *A History of Lay Judges* (Cambridge, Mass., 1960), p. 140; T. G. Barnes, "Star chamber and the sophistication of the criminal law," *Criminal Law Review* (1977), pp. 316–26; William Holdsworth, *A History of English Law* (1923–72), vol. 4, pp. 512–21.

[3] Holdsworth, *History of English Law*, vol. 1, p. 285.

offences.[4] By canon law, church courts could hear a narrow range of criminal offences including breaches of the peace that occurred in church or within the churchyard, sexual offences, drunkenness, blasphemy, working on the Sabbath, non-attendance at church, and defamation if the words implied that the victim had committed an offence triable by the church courts and not at common law.[5] In contrast, justices of the peace possessed jurisdiction over virtually the entire range of misdemeanors. Created in the fourteenth century, justices were initially given the power "to hear and determine felonies and trespasses done against the peace ... "[6] In subsequent centuries their powers were continually extended by statute not only with the expansion of the criminal law but also with the creation of a wide range of new administrative responsibilities.[7]

In contrast to the steadily expanding volume of business heard by justices of the peace, the criminal business of the church courts and manor courts declined in the seventeenth century. The church courts were abolished during the Civil War, and their powers were circumscribed when they were reinstated at the Restoration and seriously weakened by the Declaration of Indulgence of 1687 and the Toleration Act of 1689.[8] Although there has been little detailed research on the post-Restoration church courts, it is clear that certain types of immorality were still prosecuted in some courts between 1660 and 1689.[9] In the Consistory Court of London, for example, cases of fornication, bastardy, keeping disorderly alehouses, allowing tippling on the Sabbath, opening shops on the Sabbath, nonattendance at church and failure to receive the sacrament were brought by visitations, and numerous cases of defamation were prosecuted as "instance" cases. However, far more cases of bastardy, defamation, and keeping disorderly alehouses were prosecuted by recognizance or indictment at quarter sessions. Only for Sabbath offences did prosecutions in the church courts outnumber those brought before justices of the peace. After 1689, the criminal business of the Consistory Court was virtually confined to instance cases, and only with defamation did the work of this court overlap

---

[4] William Sheppard, *The Court Keeper's Guide; or a Plain and Familiar Treatise for Keeping of Courts Leet and Courts Baron* (6th edn, 1676), pp. 11–19.
[5] Henry Conset, *The Practice of the Spiritual or Ecclesiastical Courts* (2nd edn, 1700), pp. 17–18.
[6] 18 Edw. 3 c. 2.
[7] Esther Moir, *The Justices of the Peace* (Harmondsworth, 1969), chaps. 1–4; Putnam, *Proceedings*, pp. xix–xxxv. In one respect the powers of justices were weakened, however, when the Marian bail statutes discouraged the justices from hearing felonies by requiring them to certify documents concerning felonies to the gaol delivery or assize courts. In practice, however, justices throughout the country continued to hear cases of petty larceny, a non-capital felony, at sessions (John H. Langbein, *Prosecuting Crime in the Renaissance* [Cambridge, Mass., 1974], pp. 104–12).
[8] Ingram, *Church Courts*, pp. 372–74.
[9] Tina Beth Isaacs, "The Anglican hierarchy and the reformation of manners 1688–1738," *Journal of Ecclesiastical History* 33 (1982), p. 395; G. V. Bennett, "Conflict in the church," in *Britain after the Glorious Revolution 1689–1714*, ed. Geoffrey Holmes (1969), p. 157.

with that of the justices.[10] Despite the religious orientation of the reformation of manners campaign (which began in 1690), the reformers completely bypassed the church courts and initiated all their prosecutions before justices of the peace. Not only had the church courts been weakened by Toleration, but the reformers complained that initiating church court prosecutions was a "long and tedious" process and, in the case of fornication, the punishments (penance or a fine) were "in no sort adequate to the crime."[11]

The decline of the manorial courts occurred over a much longer period, and was subject to significant exceptions. For several reasons, many courts leet lost most of their business to quarter sessions in the sixteenth and seventeenth centuries. Courts leet could not hear many statutory offences, they met half as often as quarter sessions, their procedures were more cumbersome, and justices were able to hear prosecutions for some offences much more conveniently by summary jurisdiction.[12] Nevertheless, some courts were very active in this period: the court in Prescot, Lancashire, heard 1,252 cases of assault between 1615 and 1660.[13] Few records survive of courts leet for Middlesex during this period, but existing records suggest that even the most active courts heard a narrow range of criminal business. The rural courts whose records have been examined confined their activities to nuisances and other regulatory offences.[14] The court leet of the urban manor of the Liberty of the Savoy, on the other hand, heard several cases of bawdy houses, gaming houses and disorderly or unlicensed alehouses, but no other misdemeanors. As a liberty of the crown, the Savoy may have been atypical. It had no parish officers and its court leet

---

[10] GLRO, DL/C/144, 329, 625, 626. In the 1660s, the number of cases of fornication prosecuted in the two courts was roughly equal. Poor record survival prohibits a similar quantitative analysis of cases brought before the Archdeaconry of Middlesex, but surviving churchwardens' presentments from 1671 and 1689 reveal a similar preoccupation with church-related offences (non-attendance at church and working on the Sabbath) and contain only scattered cases of other misdemeanors (GLRO, AM/1). Tina Isaacs examined about one thousand church-wardens' presentments from parishes in the City of London between 1690 and 1740, and discovered that almost all reported *omnia bene* (all is well) ("Moral crime, moral reform, and the state in eighteenth-century England: a study of piety and politics" [Ph.D. diss., University of Rochester, 1979], p. 113).

[11] Isaacs, "Anglican hierarchy," p. 394; "A charge given by Hugh Hare, Esq., J.P., at the general quarter sessions for the county of Surrey, holden at Dorking, 5 April 1692," *Surrey Archaeological Collections* 12 (1895), p. 127; Whitelocke Bulstrode, *The Third Charge of Whitlocke [sic] Bulstrode, Esq.; to the Grand-Jury, and other Juries of the County of Middlesex* (1723), p. 11.

[12] Sharpe, *Crime in Early Modern England*, pp. 83–85; *The Jurisdiction of the Court-Leet: Exemplified in the Articles which the Jury or Inquest for the King in that Court is Charged* (1791), pp. xx–xxi.

[13] W. J. King, "Untapped resources for social historians: court leet records," *Journal of Social History* 15 (1982), p. 699.

[14] The two courts sampled were Isleworth Syon manor (comprising the parishes of East Bedfont and Hatton) and Hornsey manor: GLRO, Accession 1379/23; W. B. and Frank Marcham, *Court Rolls for the Bishop of London's Manor of Hornsey, 1603–1701* (1929), pp. 134–253.

filled a vacuum of local authority.[15] The Westminster court of burgesses, whose powers were similar to those of a manorial court, was also active during this period. In 1707 it heard sixty-eight cases of failure to repair the streets, fifty-six cases of selling in false measures, and twenty-five other regulatory cases as well as seventeen cases of disorderly, bawdy, or gaming houses.[16] In comparison, in the same year there were only five prosecutions for all these offences at the Westminster quarter sessions (four disorderly alehouses and one gaming house). In the first half of the eighteenth century, however, the burgesses came under attack from the increasingly assertive Westminster justices and parish vestries; according to the Webbs, by mid century the court had lost most of its powers and had been "flattened into a mere formality."[17]

Unlike in other counties, in Middlesex misdemeanors could also be tried as cases of first instance by indictment at King's Bench, since the court sat in the county.[18] A substantial number of Middlesex defendants were indicted at King's Bench, particularly for assault, riot, highway offences, and keeping gaming houses and disorderly alehouses. In 1720–21, about 300 defendants per year were indicted at King's Bench, about one-quarter the total number of defendants indicted at the Middlesex and Westminster sessions in those years. Only with gaming houses and riots, however, did the number of defendants indicted at King's Bench approach or exceed the number of those indicted at sessions, and when recognizances to appear at quarter sessions are added to the calculation it is clear that far more cases of each offence were heard at sessions than at King's Bench.[19] Why prosecutors chose to prefer indictments at King's Bench instead of sessions is unclear, though there were several possible advantages.[20]

Despite competition for certain (primarily victimless) offences from these courts, from the Restoration the Middlesex and Westminster justices of the peace, acting both inside and outside quarter sessions, dominated the business of prosecuting misdemeanor crime in Middlesex, and it is on the work of the justices that this investigation is primarily focused. Compared to other counties (with the anomalous exception of King's Bench), it appears that the criminal jurisdictions of the justices' rival courts declined more quickly in Middlesex. It is possible that it was the Middlesex justices' prominent role in governing

---

[15] Joseph Ritson, *A Digest of the Proceedings of the Court Leet of the Manor and Liberty of the Savoy* (1789), pp. 12–14; Sydney and Beatrice Webb, *English Local Government from the Revolution to the Municipal Corporations Act: The Manor and the Borough* (1908), p. 96.

[16] Westminster City Archives, WCB 3.

[17] Webbs, *Manor and the Borough*, pp. 215–29. See also below, section 9.2.

[18] J. H. Baker, "Criminal courts and procedure at common law 1550–1800," in *Crime in England*, ed. Cockburn, pp. 26–27.

[19] These calculations are based on a comparison of the sessions indictment sample findings from 1720–22 with the indictments filed at four meetings of King's Bench, between Easter term 1720 and Hilary term 1721: PRO, KB 10/17.

[20] See below, section 9.1.

London's rapidly growing suburbs which hastened the decline of both the manor and ecclesiastical courts in this county.

Victims, parish officials, and other plaintiffs who wished to prosecute alleged petty offenders before justices of the peace could initiate their prosecutions in one of two ways: either they could consult a justice of the peace outside sessions or they could prefer an indictment directly at sessions. The major disadvantage of the second course of action was that until and unless the indictment was approved by the grand jury the defendant remained unaffected by the prosecution. Because justices of the peace acting outside sessions had more legal options available to them for bringing immediate pressure on the defendant, most potential prosecutors consulted them first.[21] If the justice thought that the complaint had some merit, he could initiate one of three courses of action. Ignoring formal legal procedures, the justice (in consultation with the plaintiff) could attempt to mediate the dispute informally by exercising the influence and authority he possessed as a result of his office and his social standing in the community. Or, using the powers granted in the first clause of his commission, the justice could bind the defendant (and occasionally the prosecutor) over by recognizance to keep the peace (or be of good behavior) and to appear at the next sessions to answer the charge. (Regardless of whether or not a recognizance was issued, plaintiffs retained the option of filing an indictment at sessions.) Finally, on the authority of a growing number of statutes, the justice could issue summary convictions for certain offences on the spot and sentence the offenders to pay a fine, to be whipped, or to be committed to a house of correction. Because each of these procedures entailed different individual and social costs to the defendant, the plaintiff, and the justice, the choice of a procedure for prosecution was important. This chapter will outline the legal constraints that shaped this decision, particularly the range of offences which could be legally tried by each procedure.

2.1 INFORMAL MEDIATION BY JUSTICES

In cases of felony, justices were required by the Marian bail statutes to ensure that a formal prosecution of the accused would take place by committing the defendant to jail or by binding him over to appear in court, and by binding over any material witnesses to testify. It was in fact illegal for victims to "compound" a felony by accepting damages from the perpetrator in return for a promise not to prosecute the crime. There were no such laws in the case of petty offences, but informal judicial mediation of misdemeanors was of uncertain legality. William Lambard, author of *Eirenarcha*, a sixteenth-century

---

[21] See below, section 2.4, for a discussion of the number and types of cases in which prosecutors filed an indictment as their first step of legal action.

handbook for justices upon which many later manuals were based, encouraged
the justice of the peace

to occupy himself also in pacifying the suits and controversies, that do arise amongst his
neighbours: Yea, rather I wish him to be as well ... a compounder, as a commissioner
of the peace: and I think him so much the meeter to step in betwixt those that be at
variance, as (by reason of his learning, wisdom, authority, and wealth) he is like to
prevail more by his mediation and entreaty, than is another man.

Nevertheless, Lambard was aware that this opinion lacked a legal basis, and
based it on a justice's "common duty in charity" as opposed to his "proper
office in law."[22] Lambard's caution was echoed in the early seventeenth
century by the King's Bench judges, who ruled that justices could only facilitate informal agreements in cases of "petty quarrels between party and party,
or for the peace or petty trespasses, where the king is not to have a fine."[23]
Since most petty offences were punishable by a fine payable to the king, this
decision apparently left the justices little latitude for arranging informal
settlements.

Legal skepticism about the validity of informal settlements resulted not only
from the fear of losing revenue. By resolving a criminal accusation out of
court, a wrong done to a private individual was compensated, but the wrong
done to the public by breaking the peace was not. How could crimes be
prevented if offenders received no formal punishment for their crime? This was
particularly a problem in cases of theft because thieves were rewarded for their
misdeeds by victims who were willing to pay for the return of their goods.
Although compounding thefts, even petty thefts, was illegal, the practice
continued.[24] Because compounding rewarded thieves, informal settlements
were perceived to be one of the causes of the apparent increase in property
crime in the early eighteenth century.[25] Given the duties of their office, justices
must have been particularly sensitive to this charge that by compounding
offences they contributed to the perceived increase in serious crime. In 1722 the
Middlesex quarter sessions forbade the practice of compounding for two
serious misdemeanors, receiving stolen goods and assaulting women with
intent to rape, as well as for "other heinous and notorious offences."[26] Justices

---

[22] Lambard, *Eirenarcha* (1614), p. 10.
[23] Jean Latch, *Plusieurs tres-bons Cases, come ils estoyent adjudgees ... en la Court de Bank le Roy*
(1662), p. 49; William Noye, *Reports and Cases* [King's Bench and Common Pleas] (2nd edn,
1669), p. 103 (*Whinnel* vs. *Stroud*).
[24] Dalton, *Countrey Justice* (1635), p. 101; Gerald Howson, *It Takes a Thief. The Life and Times
of Jonathan Wild* [Formerly published as *Thief-Taker General* (1970)] (1987), chap. 1.
[25] Bernard Mandeville, *An Enquiry into the Causes of the Frequent Executions at Tyburn* (1725),
pp. 1–16; *Hanging, Not Punishment Enough, for Murtherers, High-way Men, and House
Breakers* (1701); reprint edn, 1812), pp. 15–17.
[26] MJ/SP/Dec. 1722, no. 54.

must have been wary of arranging informal settlements for any potentially serious offences.

2.2 RECOGNIZANCES

In cases where the parties were unable (or unwilling) to reach an informal settlement, or where the justice was unwilling to mediate because the offence was particularly serious, justices could bind the defendant over by recognizance to appear at the next meeting of quarter sessions. Recognizances were bonds which became payable to the crown if the person bound failed to satisfy certain specified conditions, in this case to appear in court and behave properly in the interim. Because they could be used to guarantee the appearance in court of indicted defendants, recognizances are often thought of as merely a useful appendage to the indictment. While this was often the case, two-thirds of all recognizances were issued against defendants who were never indicted for the crime.[27] Consequently, recognizances must be considered as a distinct legal procedure. Justices of the peace were empowered to use recognizances, either at their own initiative or at the request of a plaintiff, wherever they had the power to compel people to obey the law. In addition to guaranteeing the appearance in court of indicted defendants (and, in the case of felonies, their prosecutors), recognizances were most commonly used by justices to secure the appearance in court of persons who were accused of committing a variety of misdemeanors, to constrain people that the justices had reason to believe would break the peace or commit other offences, to prevent persons convicted of certain offences from further misbehaving, and as a preventive measure to oblige certain types of traders (especially alehouse keepers and middlemen in the food trade) to obey the law. This study excludes recognizances to prosecute and recognizances from the last two categories, and focuses on those which required the appearance at quarter sessions of defendants who were accused either of having committed a misdemeanor or of being inclined to do so.

Justices possessed considerable discretion in issuing recognizances, as to both the manner in which they were issued and the range of offenders who could be bound over. Typically, the defendant was joined on the recognizance by two sureties, each bound for half the sum of the principal, who guaranteed that the defendant would satisfy the condition listed on the recognizance. Except in cases where they were ordered to issue a recognizance by a warrant of *supplicavit* from Chancery or King's Bench, justices had complete freedom to determine the number and quality of the sureties (if any) a defendant was required to find, as well as the sums in which they were bound, subject only to the constraint that justices could be fined for allowing insufficient sureties if the defendant failed to appear in court.[28] If the defendant was unable to find

---

[27] See below, section 2.4.   [28] Dalton, *Countrey Justice* (1677), c.166, p. 437.

sureties, or the justice rejected them as insufficiently wealthy or respectable, the defendant was committed to prison until the sessions met or sufficient sureties were found.

Two different types of recognizances could be used against petty offenders, recognizances "for the peace" and recognizances "for good behavior." Together, they enabled the justices to bind over people suspected of committing (or of being inclined to commit) virtually any offence that could possibly be characterized as criminal. Recognizances for the peace could be used to bind over persons who had committed any breach of the peace or who threatened to commit bodily harm, as well as nightwalkers[29] and common disturbers of the peace. They were generally to be granted at the complaint of a plaintiff who made oath before a justice that he feared the defendant would physically hurt him, that the charge was not malicious, and that the danger was current. If the victim was no longer in danger of further harm, offenders could not be bound over by a recognizance for the peace.

Recognizances for good behavior could be used to discipline defendants who were accused of being a more general nuisance to society. By 34 Edw. 3 c. 1, justices had the power to take sureties for the good behavior of all persons "that be not of good fame," a term which came to be interpreted very broadly. According to William Hawkins, this recognizance was to be used against "all those whom [the justice] shall have just cause to suspect to be dangerous, quarrelsome, or scandalous, as of those who ... keep suspicious company, and of such as are generally suspected to be robbers ... " Although intended primarily to *prevent* crimes from occurring, recognizances for good behavior were also seen as a suitable method of prosecuting several types of petty offenders, including cheaters and cozeners, common disturbers, idle persons ("living well and having no estates, trades, or employment to support themselves"), people who abused officers of the peace, frequenters of bawdy or gaming houses, prostitutes, those who "tippled" in alehouses, and fathers of bastard children. Indeed, according to William Nelson, recognizances for good behavior could be issued against misbehavior "of any kind whatsoever," at the discretion of the issuing justice.[30] Nevertheless, the misbehavior was expected to be significant: recognizances for good behavior were not to be issued in response to mere "chiding words," such as calling someone a "knave."[31]

In theory, there were three major differences between recognizances for the peace and recognizances for good behavior. Not only could a wider range of

---

[29] Nightwalkers were people who slept in the day time and spent nights frequenting bawdy houses or in the company of suspected thieves (Bond, *Complete Guide*, p. 186).

[30] Nelson, *Office and Authority* (1715), pp. 88–90; Sheppard, *Sure Guide*, pp. 187–96; Dalton, *Countrey Justice*, pp. 263–66, 292–96; Bond, *Complete Guide*, p. 182.

[31] Judge Jenkins, *Eight Centuries of Reports ... Solemnly Adjudged in the Exchequer Chamber* 3rd edn (1771), p. 173; Henry Rolle, *Les Reports de Henry Rolle*, 3 vols. (1675–76), vol. 2, pp. 247–48.

suspicious activity justify a recognizance for good behavior, but persons so bound were expected to maintain a higher standard of behavior in order not to forfeit their recognizance. Whereas recognizances for the peace were forfeited if the defendant committed, or threatened to commit, a breach of the peace, a person bound for his good behavior was expected to "carry and demean himself well in his aport, gesture, and carriage, and in his company."[32] Because the circumstances under which recognizances for good behavior could be issued were so general, and because they exacted a higher standard of behavior from the defendant while bound, the conditions for issuing them were more stringent. According to the justices' manuals, these recognizances were normally to be granted by two or three justices acting together, or in open sessions, or at the testimony of more than one respectable witness.[33]

The distinction between these two types of recognizances was blurred, however, even in theory. As Dalton pointed out, the circumstances usually cited as sufficient to forfeit a recognizance for good behavior, such as traveling with an excessive number of companions, also constituted a violation of a recognizance to keep the peace.[34] In practice, Middlesex justices issued very few recognizances explicitly for good behavior, and most of these were issued by a single justice. Nevertheless, individual justices issued recognizances in a wide range of situations which were clearly outside the domain of recognizances for the peace, and which could only be legally justified as recognizances for good behavior.[35]

Disregarding legal niceties, justices used recognizances to address a broader range of social deviance than was possible by either indictment or summary conviction. Defendants bound over by recognizance could not, however, be punished without first being convicted on an indictment or under summary jurisdiction. A recognizance could require a defendant to appear at sessions and answer questions from the justices (and to obey the law in the interim), but by itself it could not be used to convict or punish the defendant, unless the process of binding over is itself considered a punishment.

2.3 INDICTMENTS

While justices were the key figures in determining whether or not to bind a defendant over by recognizance, the plaintiff normally decided whether or not

---

[32] Dalton, *Countrey Justice*, p. 290. See also Hawkins, *Pleas of the Crown*, vol. 1, p. 133.
[33] Dalton, *Countrey Justice* p. 291; Sheppard, *Sure Guide*, p. 192; Bond, *Complete Guide*, p. 182.
[34] Dalton, *Countrey Justice*, pp. 290–91.
[35] For the offences prosecuted by recognizance, see below, section 5.1. In Elizabethan Essex, however, the distinction between the two types of recognizances was maintained in practice (Joel Samaha, "The recognizance in Elizabethan law enforcement," *American Journal of Legal History* 25 [1981], pp. 193–201).

to attempt to file an indictment against the defendant.[36] Anyone who could afford the fees could ask the clerk of the peace at quarter sessions to draft a formal charge, written in Latin according to prescribed formulas, against a person alleged to have committed a misdemeanor. The accusation was then presented to the grand jury, which heard testimony from the plaintiff and any other witnesses for the prosecution. If a majority of twelve or more of its members on oath found it to be a "true bill," the charge became an indictment; if not, it was labelled *ignoramus* and no further action was taken. Defendants were then required to enter a plea to their indictments. Those who pleaded guilty were sentenced by the justices later in the same sessions. Trials of defendants who pleaded not guilty (by "traversing" their indictments) were normally postponed until the following sessions in order to allow the defendants time to prepare for the trial.[37] Defendants who were not in court during the sessions in which the indictment was approved by the grand jury were subject to writs of "process" which normally commanded them to enter into recognizances to appear at the next sessions to enter their pleas. Verdicts on traversed indictments were determined by a petty jury after hearing testimony by the plaintiff, witnesses, and defendant; justices determined the punishments, which were most frequently small fines but also included larger fines, whipping, the pillory, commitment to the house of correction, and transportation.

A broad range of both common law and statute law offences were indictable. According to William Hawkins,

all capital crimes whatsoever, and also all kinds of inferior crimes of a public nature, as misprisions, and all other contempts, all disturbances of the peace, all oppressions, and all other misdemeanors whatsoever of a publicly evil example against the common law, may be indicted; but no injuries of a private nature, unless they in some way concern the king.[38]

Private wrongs which could not be tried before justices included usury, failure to pay wages, making unreasonable distresses on one's tenants, and seducing an apprentice from his master.[39] For a variety of reasons a number of other offences could not be tried before justices of the peace at quarter sessions. By

---

[36] As noted above, in the case of serious misdemeanors, such as receiving stolen goods and assault with intent to rape, Middlesex justices were encouraged to force victims to prosecute indictments by binding them over by recognizance to attend sessions (MJ/SP/Dec. 1722, no. 61).

[37] Samuel Blackerby, *Cases in Law: Wherein Justices of the Peace Have a Jurisdiction . . . Being the second part of the Justice of Peace's Companion* (1717), p. 138; *Office of the Clerk of the Peace* (1682), p. 161.

[38] Hawkins, *Pleas of the Crown*, vol. 2, p. 210.

[39] Samuel and Nathaniel Blackerby, *The Second Part of the Justice of Peace his Companion; or, Cases in Law (Wherein Justices of Peace have a Jurisdiction)* (1734), pp. 218–19, 353; Thomas Leach, *Modern Reports*, 12 vols., 5th edn (1793–96), vol. 6, p. 288; William Salkeld, *Reports of Cases Adjudged in the Court of King's Bench*, 3 vols., 6th edn (1795), vol. 1, pp. 380, 389, and 406, and vol. 3, pp. 187–91; Sir Thomas Raymond, *Reports of divers special Cases, Adjudged in the Courts of King's Bench*, 3rd edn (1803), p. 205.

the commonly accepted interpretation of the Marian bail statutes, capital offences were tried at a gaol delivery sessions.[40] Other offences were excluded because of the legal definitions of "crimes of a public nature" and "disturbances of the peace" or the need for a specific offence as the subject of the indictment, or where other methods of conviction and punishment were dictated by statute.

Although any violation of the law could technically be interpreted as a violation of the peace, under the rubric of "disturbances of the peace" justices of the peace were only entitled to hear indictments for offences which involved "personal wrongs and open violence," such as assault, riot, and forcible entry, and other offences "as have a direct and immediate tendency to cause such breaches of the peace." Thus, insulting words were not indictable unless it was believed that they were likely to lead directly to the use of force or violence, such as a challenge to a duel, an insult to an officer of the peace in the execution of his office, and any insult to a justice of the peace.[41] Other insults had to be punished using other legal procedures: with a recognizance for good behavior or the peace, by a civil suit, or in the ecclesiastical courts.[42] The requirement that offences involve a potential breach of the peace, however, could be interpreted broadly. An indictment of overseers of the poor for refusing to raise funds for a Middlesex workhouse, for example, was upheld partly on the grounds that the employment of the poor "may be a means to prevent tumults."[43] Because of the implicit use of force, extortion was also indictable. Perjury and forgery, however, could not be tried before justices,[44] nor could cheating accomplished by simple lying. Cheating using an "artful device" such as false dice or false weights and measures, on the other hand, was indictable, since the use of false tokens increased the wrong, and thus, presumably, the likelihood of a breach of the peace when the victim discovered the crime.[45]

Many offences were indictable as nuisances, "an offence against the public, either by doing a thing which tends to the annoyance of all the king's subjects,

---

[40] Langbein, *Prosecuting Crime*, pp. 110–12.
[41] Blackerby and Blackerby, *Second Part*, pp. 213, 219, 339–40.
[42] *Ibid.*, pp. 339–40, 357; Salkeld, *Reports*, vol. 2, p. 697, and vol. 3, p. 190. Written scandalous words, on the other hand, such as a letter impugning the character of a woman the recipient is about to marry, were indictable, since the act of sending the letter was construed to be a breach of the peace (Blackerby and Blackerby, *Second Part*, pp. 198, 225). See also Thomas Siderfin, *Les Reports des divers special cases argue et adjudge en le court del Bank le Roy* (2nd edn, 1714), vol. 1, p. 271.
[43] [Whitelocke Bulstrode], *Laws Concerning the Poor*, 4th edn (1720), p. 168.
[44] Except for perjury on the statute of 5 Eliz. c. 9, where the statute explicitly gives justices jurisdiction over offences.
[45] Hawkins, *Pleas of the Crown*, vol. 2, pp. 40, 187; Leach, *Modern Reports*, vol. 6, p. 311; Joseph Shaw, *The Practical Justice of Peace: or, a Treatise Showing the Power and Authority of all its Branches*, 2 vols., (1728), vol. 2, p. 522. According to the King's Bench judges, bare lying was not indictable because "we are not to indict one man for making a fool of another" (Salkeld, *Reports*, vol. 1, p. 379).

or by neglecting to do a thing which the common good requires."[46] The second category included offences such as neglect of office, failing to serve on the night watch, and failing to repair the highway. The first category included actions such as obstructing the highway, keeping or slaughtering pigs within a city, erecting unlawful cottages, making, selling or throwing squibs, and certain types of blatant public immorality. The keepers of bawdy houses, gaming houses, and disorderly alehouses could be indicted, both because the houses were viewed as nuisances and because it was thought that they led to breaches of the peace.[47] As established by the famous case of Sir Charles Sedley, who stood naked on a balcony in Covent Garden and "acted all the postures of lust and buggery that could be imagined," "all lewdness, if open and scandalous, is of public nuisance, and indictable." Along the same lines, one could be indicted for frequenting bawdy houses and the related offence of nightwalking. On the other hand, except during the interregnum, adultery, prostitution, and solicitation of chastity by themselves were not indictable, since they were private wrongs and ecclesiastical offences.[48] The few indictments for adultery and prostitution which were filed in Middlesex during this period were all found *ignoramus*, quashed or removed by writ of *certiorari*.[49] The difficulty of using indictments for the prosecution of sexual offences clearly frustrated justices associated with the reformation of manners campaign.[50]

Two other categories of offences were not indictable. With a few exceptions, persons had to be indicted for specific actions, not for their general character or demeanor. One could not be indicted for being a common oppressor or a common disturber of the peace. However, a statute did authorize indictments for barretry, "the spreading of false rumours and calumnies, whereby discord and disquiet may grow among neighbours," as long as the prosecutor could prove "several repeated instances" of the offence.[51] Finally, in a series of decisions at King's Bench in the 1690s and early 1700s, it was ruled that

---

[46] Hawkins, *Pleas of the Crown*, p. 197.

[47] Shaw, *Practical Justice*, vol. 2, pp. 57–58; Blackerby and Blackerby, *Second Part*, pp. 18, 92, 174, 199; Hawkins, *Pleas of the Crown*, pp. 196, 198, 225. Keepers and frequenters of gaming houses could also be indicted under 33 Hen. 8 c. 9.

[48] *The Diary of Samuel Pepys*, ed. R. Latham and W. Matthews, 11 vols. (1970–1983), vol. 4, p. 209 (1 July 1663); Blackerby and Blackerby, *Second Part*, pp. 199, 221–23 (Blackerby argued, against prevailing opinion, that adultery *was* indictable at common law); Salkeld, *Reports*, vol. 1, p. 382; *A Report of all the Cases Determined by Sir John Holt* (1738), p. 597; Keith Thomas, "Puritans and Adultery: the Act of 1650 reconsidered," in *Puritans and Revolutionaries*, ed. D. Pennington and K. Thomas (Oxford, 1982), pp. 265–66. Since adultery was "a crime highly provoking [of] a breach of the peace," constables could arrest would-be fornicators and justices could bind them over with a recognizance for good behavior (Blackerby and Blackerby, *Second Part*, pp. 221–22).

[49] For example, see MJ/SR/1820,I. 51 (Sept. 1693); 1825, I. 44 (Dec. 1693).

[50] Bulstrode, *Third Charge*, pp. 10–11.

[51] Hawkins, *Pleas of the Crown*, vol. 2, pp. 226, 243; Blackerby and Blackerby, *Second Part*, pp. 199, 334.

statutory offences, such as keeping an alehouse without a licence, were not indictable when another method of conviction was prescribed (in this case summary conviction). Consequently, indictments for this offence virtually disappeared from the Middlesex sessions rolls after 1713.[52]

The rules defining indictable offences were thus far more detailed than those prescribing the types of offences suitable for binding over. Whereas recognizances for good behavior were targeted towards a broad range of suspicious behavior, indictments, with the exception of the offence of barretry, were primarily reserved for specific illegal actions or omissions of duty. Nevertheless, under the rubric of "disturbances against the peace" and nuisances, a wide range of petty offences were indictable at common law or by statute.

2.4 THE RELATIONSHIP BETWEEN RECOGNIZANCES AND INDICTMENTS

Because many petty offences could be prosecuted by both procedures and because recognizances were often used to require defendants to attend sessions to try indictments, many defendants were both indicted and bound over by recognizance for the same offence. According to the clerical notations on recognizances tabulated in Table 2.1, 28% of the defendants who were bound over to appear at quarter sessions were also indicted. This figure should be increased by about 5% to account for the fact that the clerks did not always record the existence of indictments on the relevant recognizance.[53] Thus, about one-third of the defendants bound over by recognizance were also indicted for the same offence. Somewhat less than half of these defendants had already been indicted at a previous sessions when their recognizance was issued, and slightly more than half were indicted at the next sessions after the recognizance was issued. Few were indicted at a sessions subsequent to the one at which the defendant was first required to appear by recognizance.

Where defendants were both indicted and bound over by recognizance, the

---

[52] *The English and Empire Digest* 14, pt. 1 (1977), pp. 262–63. For Middlesex indictments for this offence, see below, section 6.1 and Table 6.2.

[53] A careful comparison of the names of all the defendants who were indicted at one meeting of the court in 1723 with the names on all the recognizances in that roll and the surrounding rolls revealed that ten out of the fifty-seven defendants who were both indicted and bound over had recognizances that provide no evidence that they were ever indicted. This missing notation is often explained by the fact that the indictment was never tried, it was found *ignoramus* by the grand jury, or the case was removed by writ of *certiorari* to King's Bench. Although these defendants were bound over to appear at the sessions in which these indictments were filed, they most likely did not appear until the next sessions, by which time the indictment was no longer pending: MJ/SR/2402 (April 1723), 2399, 2402, 2404, 2407 (Feb.–July 1723). This case study suggests that for every forty-seven recognizances for indicted defendants which include a notation that the defendant was indicted, ten, or 21%, were not annotated. Consequently, the number of recognizances actually linked to indictments was 21% higher than the figure of 25% derived from the clerical notations.

Table 2.1 Relative timing of recognizances and indictments: recognizance sample[a]

Offence[c]	Never indicted %	Previously indicted %	Indicted next sessions[b] %	Indicted timing unknown %	N (100%)
Peace					
Keep the peace	85.8	2.0	10.8	1.4	296
Assault	70.3	7.3	20.4	1.9	626
Riot	62.7	19.3	16.3	1.8	166
Common disturber/defamation	81.9	3.4	13.4	1.3	149
Vice					
Alehouse offences	58.1	37.2	2.3	2.3	43
Sexual offences	91.4	3.1	5.5	—	128
Property					
Theft	64.6	1.7	8.8	24.9	181
Fraud	63.4	14.6	15.9	6.1	82
Regulatory					
Neglect of office	65.6	6.3	28.1	—	32
Other regulatory offences	73.0	14.9	12.2	—	74
Other					
Other[d]	86.2	1.2	8.8	3.8	260
Unknown[e]	53.6	33.0	8.6	4.8	291
Total	72.4	10.1	13.3	4.1	2328

a Several sessions were excluded from this table because disposition evidence was incomplete. See note a to Table 5.1.

b Indicted at the next sessions after the recognizance was issued.

c As described on the recognizance. As noted in section 3.2, offences were often described in different terms on indictments.

d Includes offences for which there were fewer than ten defendants indicted in the recognizance sample: master-servant disputes; loose, idle and disorderly conduct; bastardy; drunkenness; gaming; trespass and damage; and disaffection.

e The large number of cases in this category in which the defendant was indicted previously results from the fact that when defendants were bound over to attend sessions and answer their indictments, their recognizances often did not specify the nature of the offence.

purpose of the recognizance depended on both the nature of the offence and whether it was issued before or after the indictment was filed. Three types of conflicts prompted plaintiffs to bind defendants over by recognizance and subsequently indict them at sessions. If the offence was minor, such as scandalous words, the prosecutor probably did not initially intend to indict the defendant and only did so if the defendant refused to negotiate an informal settlement or caused further trouble. Similarly, recognizances to keep the peace (where no other offence was mentioned) were clearly meant to prevent an indictable offence from occurring, and in fact only a small proportion of the plaintiffs in these cases subsequently filed an indictment. As Table 2.1 demonstrates, when indictments were filed against defendants who were bound over to keep the peace, they were most likely to be filed after the recognizance. In the case of serious offences against the peace, on the other hand, such as assaults involving injury, it was likely that the victim (and the justice) would want to indict the defendant as soon as possible. In these situations, however, it was also necessary to have the defendant immediately bound by a recognizance to keep the peace in order to prevent further injury in the period before sessions met. Prosecutors who intended to file indictments for other serious offences, such as neglect or abuse of office, may have bound their defendants over by recognizance first as a means of expediting the prosecution of the indictment by requiring the defendant to appear in court. In the case of theft, magistrates were legally required by the Marian bail statutes to bind over all suspects immediately. Thus defendants were bound over before they were indicted both when the offence was minor (and it was hoped an indictment would not be necessary) and when, because of the gravity of the offence, it was necessary to keep track of the defendant, ensure his good behavior, and try the indictment expeditiously.

When the recognizance was issued after the indictment was approved by the grand jury, it served a less complicated function, simply that of requiring the defendant to appear in court and answer an indictment. Three types of offences were particularly likely to result in recognizances after defendants were indicted: alehouse offences, regulatory offences, and riots.[54] Indictments for alehouse offences and regulatory offences were probably based on constables' presentments, but since these offences were not particularly threatening to the plaintiffs (the constables), the defendants had not previously been bound over to keep the peace. In any case, in order to prevent informal settlements, defendants accused of offences against penal statutes, such as keeping an alehouse without a licence or failing to perform statutory labor on the highways, could not legally be bound over until they were indicted. (As

---

[54] This conclusion is based on limited evidence: as discussed in note e to Table 2.1, a large proportion (about 40%) of the recognizances in this category did not specify the offence for which the defendant was indicted.

contemporaries acknowledged, and Table 2.1 attests, this requirement was not always followed in practice.)[55] Rioting was a more threatening offence, but owing to the expense and trouble of obtaining recognizances typically only ringleaders were initially bound over to keep the peace. The remaining defendants (an indictment for riot required at least three defendants) were summoned by recognizance to answer the indictment at a later date.

Plaintiffs could choose to prosecute by recognizance alone, by indictment alone, or with both procedures together. If both procedures were used, plaintiffs could usually choose which to use first. Since there were distinct advantages and disadvantages to each procedure, these choices depended very much on the individual circumstances of each case. However, both recognizances and indictments shared one disadvantage: the defendant (unless unable to find sureties) remained at liberty until he or she appeared at sessions, up to three months after the crime was committed. For some offences, plaintiffs could obtain more immediate results by trying to convince a justice to convict the defendant summarily.

2.5 SUMMARY CONVICTION

Where empowered by statute for specific offences, justices of the peace, acting individually or in pairs, could convict defendants summarily without a jury and without referring the case to quarter sessions. Convictions could be based on the justice's own view, or on the testimony (depending on the offence) of one or two witnesses under oath. The number of statutes authorizing summary convictions by justices increased significantly during the seventeenth and eighteenth centuries, though because many new statutes simply redefined offences already punishable summarily the number of offences subject to summary jurisdiction did not expand quite so quickly.[56] The justices' powers applied to a broad range of offences which were punishable by whipping, fine, or commitment to a house of correction. Although some summary offences were newly created, most could also be prosecuted by indictment and/or recognizance. Because of their procedural simplicity, however, summary convictions were increasingly used as an alternative to the more formal traditional legal procedures during this period.

It is impossible to list all the offences that were punishable by summary conviction at this time. Most convictions in the seventeenth and eighteenth centuries can be placed in one of seven categories: vice (as defined by

---

[55] Lambard, *Eirenarcha* (1599 edn), p. 191; Dalton, *Countrey Justice*, pp. 462–63; William Sheppard, *The Justice of the Peace, His Clerk's Cabinet* (1660), pp. 6, 90.

[56] Joanna Innes, "Statute law and summary justice in early modern England" (unpublished paper, May, 1986).

contemporaries), vagrancy and idleness, disobedient servants,[57] certain types of petty theft and embezzlement,[58] violations of the game laws,[59] attending conventicles and other religious offences,[60] and violations of a miscellany of economic and administrative regulations.[61] The powers of summary jurisdiction were most extensive over "victimless offences" such as vice, vagrancy and idleness. One justice could convict offenders of drunkenness,[62] selling ale without a licence,[63] permitting tippling in an alehouse,[64] working or engaging in unlawful pastimes on Sunday,[65] and profane swearing and cursing.[66] Two justices could punish the parents of bastard children.[67] Violators of the laws against vagrancy, begging, and idleness who could be convicted by one justice included poor people who returned to a parish from which they had been removed by the settlement laws, persons who had no means of subsistence and refused to work, "idle and disorderly" persons, beggars, traveling peddlers, fortune tellers, and other "rogues and vagabonds." Two justices were necessary for convictions of those who left (or threatened to leave) their wives and/or children without support and thus in need of parochial relief.[68]

The earliest statutes authorizing summary convictions prescribed punishments by whipping and/or a fine, occasionally with the payment of damages to the victim. Whipping was reserved for the parents of bastard children (if the child was chargeable to the parish the mother was to be committed to the house of correction); persons stealing wood, or fruit or vegetables while growing, if they were unable to pay the damages; and rogues and vagabonds about to be passed to their place of settlement. Offences punishable by fine included several types of vice, attending conventicles, failure to attend church, embezzlement, and violations of economic and administrative regulations. Those who were unable to pay their fines were set in the stocks, whipped, or, as prescribed by some of the later statutes, incarcerated for a short period in a jail or house of correction.[69]

---

[57] Although justices often discharged delinquent servants without punishment, two justices could punish servants for leaving service without licence or for assaulting their masters: 5 Eliz. c. 4.

[58] Cutting grain growing in the fields, cutting trees or stealing wood, and stealing from orchards or gardens (43 Eliz. c. 7, 15 Car. 2 c. 2). For embezzlement, see John Styles, "Embezzlement, industry and the law in England, 1500–1800," in *Manufacture in Town and Country Before the Factory*, ed. M. Berg, P. Hudson, and M. Sonenscher (Cambridge, 1983), pp. 189–99, 209–10.

[59] P. B. Munsche, *Gentlemen and Poachers: The English Game Laws 1671–1831* (Cambridge, 1981), pp. 77, 185–86.

[60] For conventicles, see 16 Car. 2 c. 4 (expired July 1667); 22 Car. 2 c. 1 (partially repealed in 1689).

[61] P.S., *A Help to Magistrates* (1721), pp. 6–13.   [62] 4 Jac. 1 c. 5; 21 Jac. 1 c. 7.

[63] 3 Car. 1 c. 3.

[64] 1 Jac. 1 c. 9; 21 Jac. 1 c. 7; 1 Car. 1 c. 4.   [65] 1 Car. 1 c. 1; 3 Car. 1 c. 1; 29 Car. 2 c. 7.

[66] 21 Jac. 1 c. 20; 6 and 7 Wm. 3 c. 11.

[67] 18 Eliz. c. 3; 7 Jac. 1 c. 4. In addition, fathers were expected to provide support for the child.

[68] 39 Eliz. c. 4 (which gave constables the authority to whip many offenders without first bringing them before a justice); 43 Eliz. c. 2; 7 Jac. 1 c. 4; 21 Jac. 1 c. 28; 12 Anne c. 23.

[69] Styles, "Embezzlement," pp. 193–94; Innes, "Prisons for the poor," p. 87.

The introduction of houses of correction in the late sixteenth and early seventeenth centuries both added a significant new form of punishment for petty offences and was the occasion for increasing the scope of offences punishable by justices of the peace outside quarter sessions. Specifically intended as a place where poor offenders would be both punished and reformed, prisoners in houses of correction were to be both whipped and set to hard labor.[70] The statutes that created these houses, however, failed to specify with any precision the range of offences punishable therein, nor were the powers of justices acting out of sessions to commit prisoners and order them to be punished specifically defined. Although justices apparently enjoyed considerable latitude in their use of these new institutions, the extent of their powers remained uncertain throughout the seventeenth and early eighteenth centuries.

William Sheppard, author of several legal treatises and manuals for justices published in the mid-seventeenth century, adopted the most conservative interpretation of the justices' powers. Sheppard claimed that, unless specifically permitted by statute, commitments to the house of correction required a previous conviction at sessions:

All those that may be sent thither, must be convicted of the crimes for which they are to be sent thither; and there must be a way for it, and in most of them it must be by indictment, and cannot be otherwise and therefore the work, in those cases, may not be done, but in the quarter sessions.

Sheppard's careful wording evokes the ambiguity of the law, and Sheppard himself was aware that his interpretation was disputed.[71] Most other authors of manuals believed that justices outside sessions had the power to commit a broad range of offenders to houses of correction, but Sheppard's view that justices did not have the power to convict and punish prisoners outside sessions unless explicitly authorized by statute had more support.[72] These authorities believed individual justices could use houses of correction for custodial, but not punitive, purposes. In 1666, the King's Bench judges ruled that in the specific case of idle persons who lived above their station (without a legitimate means of support), offenders could be committed by an individual justice to a house of correction to be put to hard labor, but they could not be punished (whipped) until the case was tried at sessions.[73] This commitment could only have been based on the "idle and disorderly" clause of 7 Jac. 1 c. 4, one of the statutes

[70] Innes, "Prisons for the poor," pp. 42–77.
[71] Sheppard, *Sure Guide*, 1663 edn, pp. 290–92, and 1669 edn, pp. 268–70. Sheppard's interpretation was supported by two later authorities: "A charge given by Hugh Hare," pp. 127–28; and Nelson, *Office and Authority* (1715), pp. 353–54. In general, Sheppard adopted a cautious approach concerning the extent of the justices' powers (Nancy Matthews, *William Sheppard: Cromwell's Law Reformer* [Cambridge, 1985], p. 130).
[72] Dalton, *Countrey Justice*, p. 514. This point was embodied in 17 Geo. 2 c. 5 s. 32.
[73] Siderfin, *Reports des divers special cases*, vol. 1, p. 281.

which ordered that houses of correction be established in every county. As it was upon this clause that most commitments to houses of correction were based, this case appeared to limit severely the justices' powers of ordering punishments of offenders outside sessions.

To be punished, one had to be convicted of an offence, but did a mere commitment to a house of correction on the basis of 7 Jac. 1 c. 4 by a justice acting outside sessions constitute a conviction? Several authors of manuals for justices appear to have believed that a commitment on this statute did constitute a conviction.[74] There were apparently no other rulings on this issue before or during the period of this study, but on hearing an appeal of a commitment for "idle and disorderly" behavior in 1731, Justice Probyn ruled that such commitments were authorized by the statute, and "the statute makes the conviction."[75] It is likely that this ruling merely gave approval to existing practice, since throughout the period of this study individual justices ordered that the "idle and disorderly" prisoners they committed should be whipped (and also discharged) before sessions met.[76]

There was also uncertainty about the types of offenders which could be committed to houses of correction by justices acting outside sessions. According to 7 Jac. 1 c. 4, houses of correction were to "be used for the keeping, correcting, and setting to work of . . . rogues, vagabonds, sturdy beggars, and other idle and disorderly persons." While previous statutes had authorized justices acting outside sessions to punish most of these offences, this statute added a crucial new category of offenders, "idle and disorderly persons," without further clarification. Although "idle" had been used in previous statutes to refer to persons who could not support themselves and refused to work, this new phrase came to be interpreted much more broadly. Coke argued that it gave "a general and large power" to justices to commit offenders, including those who had a legitimate means of supporting themselves.[77] A few decisions by the Assize and King's Bench judges narrowed this category to exclude rogues and vagabonds (who were instead to be whipped and passed to their place of birth or last settlement), persons apprehended in brothels and disorderly houses (unless they were apprehended at an "unseasonable hour"), and servants who were merely "saucy" to their masters.[78] Since the high court

---

[74] Bond, *Complete Guide*, pp. 17, 24–25, 167–68, 195; Dalton, *Countrey Justice*, pp. 513–14; Nelson, *Office and Authority*, p. 354 (sample *mittimus*). See also S. C. [Samuel Carter], *Legal Provisions for the Poor* (1710), pp. 189–90.

[75] Leach, *Modern Reports*, vol. 11, p. 415.   [76] See below, section 7.3.

[77] Edward Coke, *The Second Part of the Institutes of the Laws of England* (1642), p. 730.

[78] Edward Bulstrode, *The Reports of Edward Bulstrode*, 3 vols., 2nd edn (1688), vol. 2, p. 357; *Report of all the Cases Determined by Sir John Holt*, p. 406; Leach, *Modern Reports*, vol. 8, p. 45, and vol. 12, p. 566; Robert, Lord Raymond, *Reports of Cases Argued and Adjudged in the Court of King's Bench*, 3 vols., 4th edn (1790–92), vol. I, p. 699; Innes, "Prisons for the poor," p. 86. By 12 Anne c. 23, rogues and vagabonds could be put to hard labor in a house of correction before being passed to their parish of last settlement or parish of birth.

judges generally confined their review of summary convictions to issues of legal procedure, not issues of fact, however, they had few opportunities to determine what types of "idle and disorderly" persons *could* be committed to houses of correction.

Some manuals for justices suggested that the term could include a broad range of offences. In addition to categories of offenders explicitly mentioned by statutes, such as servants who ran away from their masters and persons who refused to work and who could not support themselves, Michael Dalton, author of one of the most influential manuals for justices, advised justices to commit five categories of the "thriftless" poor to houses of correction:

1. The riotous and prodigal person, that consumes all with play, or drinking, etc.
2. The dissolute person, as the strumpet, pilferer, etc.
3. The slothful person, that refuses to work.
4. All such as willfully spoil or embezzle their work, etc.
5. The vagabond that will abide in no service or place.

Elsewhere Dalton added servants and apprentices who misbehaved and apprentices who "purloined" goods worth less than twelve pence from their masters. Dalton cited no legal authorities to support this advice, but it is likely that he believed that these offenders were examples of the "idle and disorderly persons" referred to in 7 Jac. 1 c. 4.[79] Although some authors adopted a more cautious approach, Dalton's broad interpretation of "idle and disorderly" conduct was clearly influential; his advice was repeated in another early eighteenth-century justices' manual and it was also copied by a Buckinghamshire justice into his commonplace book in 1705.[80]

In practice, justices acted according to the broadest possible interpretation of their powers.[81] Justices may have been encouraged to act in this manner by the fact that their commitments were unlikely to be reviewed by the higher courts, and when commitments were reviewed the judges confined their attention to determining whether the warrant cited an appropriate statute.[82] Thus, Dalton advised justices that the "safest" method of writing a *mittimus* was to state that the offender was "an idle and disorderly person," thus grounding the commitment firmly on 7 Jac. 1 c. 4.[83] It was unnecessary (and inadvisable) for the justice to justify his interpretation of this phrase by describing the offending behavior in more detail. From about 1735, however, the higher courts

---

[79] Dalton, *Countrey Justice*, pp. 119, 150, 170, 514.

[80] Bond, *Complete Guide*, pp. 167–68, 195; BL, Harley 5137, p. 385. See also Innes, "Prisons for the poor," pp. 70–71. For a more cautious approach, see Nelson, *Office and Authority*, pp. 38–39, 46, 352–53.

[81] See below, chap. 7.

[82] R. J. Sharpe, *The Law of Habeas Corpus* (Oxford, 1976), p. 26; Baker, "Criminal courts and procedure at common law," pp. 24–25.

[83] Dalton, *Countrey Justice*, p. 113. The sample *mittimuses* included in this and other manuals for justices contained formulaic descriptions of the offender as an "idle and disorderly person" (*ibid.*, pp. 513–14; Nelson, *Office and Authority*, p. 354).

expanded their review of summary convictions to include the evidence on which the conviction was based; over the course of the eighteenth century both the manner and the substance of summary convictions became subject to increasing legal scrutiny.[84]

2.6 FLEXIBILITY IN THE CHOICE OF A PROCEDURE

The procedures available to potential plaintiffs and justices of the peace for prosecuting misdemeanors differed considerably in terms of the types of offences which could be prosecuted, the method of determining the guilt of the offender, and the nature of the available punishments. With the exception of informal mediation by justices, where all but the most serious offences could be heard, each procedure was intended to be suitable for a different type of offence: indictments were for specific wrongful acts, recognizances focused on suspicious and threatening behavior, and houses of correction were for persons of bad character. Despite these differences in approach, however, there was considerable overlap in the specific offences that could be prosecuted by each procedure, and this choice of legal procedures gave potential plaintiffs considerable flexibility when determining their strategies for prosecution.

A relatively conservative interpretation of the law suggests that only a few offences could be prosecuted by all of the procedures under discussion: nightwalking, frequenting bawdy houses (at an unseasonable time of night), and certain types of petty theft. Nevertheless, virtually all petty offences could be prosecuted by two procedures, and many could be prosecuted by three. A wide range of offences could be prosecuted by indictment, recognizance and informal mediation: all offences against the peace, except assault with intent to rape; barretry; keeping bawdy houses, disorderly alehouses, and gaming houses; gaming; insults to officers of the peace; and fraud involving the use of false tokens. Other offences could be prosecuted by all procedures except an indictment: drunkenness, misbehavior of servants, and idle and disorderly behavior.

The vague or ambiguous definitions of many of these offences, however, gave prosecutors greater flexibility in their choice of a procedure than is immediately apparent. Ultimately, whether an offence could be tried by a particular procedure depended on how loosely justices of the peace or members of grand juries were willing to interpret the legal definitions of offences punishable by that procedure. Despite the increasing specificity of the criminal law during this period,[85] there was ample scope for flexibility, and in practice many offences were interpreted very broadly. As we shall see, indictments for

---

[84] Landau, *Justices of the Peace*, pp. 346–52; below, section 7.4.
[85] Innes, "Statute law and summary justice"; Barbara Shapiro, *Probability and Certainty in Seventeenth-Century England* (Princeton, 1983), pp. 168 ff.

assault, recognizances for the peace and commitments to houses of correction for loose, idle and disorderly behavior, to name only the most obvious examples, were used to prosecute a wide variety of criminal and quasi-criminal behavior. Even the evidence of recorded prosecutions, to which we now turn, demonstrates that legal requirements were frequently stretched or evaded by plaintiffs and justices who sought to prosecute their cases by the procedures most suited to their interests.

3

Patterns of prosecutions

Plaintiffs, in consultation with justices of the peace, were confronted with a choice of procedures for prosecuting petty crimes. Each of the procedures will be examined in Part II; this chapter will give a brief overview of the patterns of prosecutions which resulted from plaintiffs' choices. The motivations for prosecution suggested by these patterns will be examined more thoroughly in the ensuing chapters.

3.1 THE CHOICE OF PROCEDURE

How often were each of the procedures used for prosecuting petty crimes? Any comparison of criminal prosecutions initiated by different legal procedures is hampered by conflicting patterns of record keeping and record survival. While virtually all the indictments and recognizances from this period have survived, records of summary convictions were kept much less systematically and records of cases informally mediated by justices of the peace are extremely rare. Nevertheless, a few surviving justices' notebooks document the entire range of judicial business which individual justices heard outside sessions. These notebooks make it possible to formulate rough estimates of the proportions of criminal accusations prosecuted by each procedure. Although no comprehensive notebook survives from urban Middlesex for the period of this study,[1] the notebook kept by Henry Norris, a Middlesex justice who lived in Hackney, between 1730 and 1741 provides an unusually detailed record of the criminal business heard by a justice out of sessions (Table 3.1). Of the cases for which the final disposition is known, Norris settled a large proportion, 38%, informally. It is possible that an even larger number of cases were settled informally, since Norris failed to record the disposition of almost half the cases

[1] A few minor notebooks have survived, but none is comprehensive: Wiltshire Record Office, Accession 118, "Notebook of recognizances and informations taken before Edward Smyth, J.P., 1664–1666" (Southwark); Swiss Cottage Library, A/SF/30 (journal of William Woodhouse containing several depositions concerning felonies, Kentish Town); Hampshire Record Office, Coventry MS, 1M53/1373–74 (notebooks kept by James Dewy, 1692–1703, Westminster).

brought before him.[2] Informal settlements account for an even greater proportion, between 48 and 58%, of the cases heard by William Hunt, a Wiltshire
justice who kept an equally detailed notebook in the 1740s (Table 3.2).[3] On the
other hand, while 34% of the cases heard by Norris resulted in further legal
action (issuing a recognizance or committing the defendant to prison), only 8%
of Hunt's cases were continued.

One reason that Norris settled fewer cases informally, and referred more
cases for further legal action, may be that he lived in a more urban location
than Hunt. Hackney had more than 3,500 inhabitants in the 1730s and was
little more than a mile away from London, while Hunt lived in West Lavington,
a rural village in Wiltshire with around 600 inhabitants.[4] Norma Landau's
analysis of the notebooks kept by ten justices in eighteenth-century Kent, most
of whom lived in rural areas, shows that a recognizance was issued in less than
10% of the cases in which the justices issued a warrant. On the other hand, a
recognizance was issued in 21% of the cases heard by Norris for which the final
disposition is known.[5] Landau suggests that urban justices issued recognizances against a higher portion of the defendants who appeared before them
because these justices heard more serious crimes than rural justices.[6] Norris'
notebook, however, shows that he was more inclined than Hunt to encourage
further legal action for all types of offences. It is more likely that justices living
in or near London issued recognizances more often because the Middlesex and
Westminster courts were more accessible than rural courts: the Middlesex
sessions met more often (eight times a year, whereas most county sessions, and
the Westminster court, met quarterly), and most people in London lived within
only two miles of a courthouse.[7] Even in Hackney, however, almost two-fifths
of justice Norris' criminal business was settled informally.

---

[2] Cases in which the disposition was unknown were left out of the calculation of the proportion of
cases prosecuted by each procedure in Norris' notebook. Since warrants were issued in most of
these cases, it is likely that many of the persons apprehended on these warrants were brought
before other justices. Any further legal action on these cases would then not be recorded in
Norris' notebook. It is possible, however, that many of these cases were dropped by plaintiffs
who were no longer interested in pursuing the prosecution, and it may be the case that some were
also informally settled.

[3] The exact figure for the proportion of cases that were informally mediated depends on how the
category of cases in which Hunt issued "orders" is interpreted. See note b to Table 3.2 and
below, chap. 4.

[4] For Hackney, see George, *London Life*, pp. 408–12 (figures for the number of houses multiplied
by 5.4 to obtain a figure for the entire population). For West Lavington, see *The Compton
Census of 1676: A Critical Edition*, ed. Anne Whiteman (1986), p. 122 (figure for communicants
multiplied by 1.67). I am grateful to Donald Spaeth for this reference.

[5] Landau, *Justices of the Peace*, p. 192. Landau's figures are not strictly compatible with mine since
the latter include a small number of cases in which a warrant was not issued. Eliminating such
cases would only increase the difference between Norris and the Kent justices. Both figures
include recognizances to prosecute. Landau notes that eighteenth-century rural justices issued far
fewer recognizances than their pre-Restoration counterparts (pp. 192–93).

[6] *Ibid.*, pp. 177 and 179.   [7] See below, sections 10.1 and 10.2.

Table 3.1 Criminal accusations heard by Henry Norris, February 1730–July 1741[a]

Offence	Agreed	Summary conviction[b]	Further legal action[c]	Dismissed[d]	Disposition unknown[e]	TOTAL
Vice						
Swearing/cursing	0	5	0	0	1	6
Drunkenness	0	4	0	0	0	4
Other	1	3	1	0	0	5
TOTAL N	1	12	1	0	1	15
% of known dispositions	7%	86%	7%	—	*	
Theft, property disputes						
Wood, fruit, vegetables	3	9	0	0	3	15
Other items[f]	1	5	19	9	16	50
Damaging property	2	1	1	0	3	7
Other	2	0	0	0	1	3
TOTAL N	8	15	20	9	23	75
% of known dispositions	15%	29%	38%	17%	*	
Offences against the peace						
Assault	43	1	27	5	110	186
Other	7	0	5	1	8	21
TOTAL N	50	1	32	6	118	207
% of known dispositions	56%	1%	36%	7%	*	
Other offences[g]	6	3	4	1	15	29
% of known dispositions	43%	21%	29%	7%	*	
TOTAL N	65	31	57	16	157	326
%	38%	18%	34%	9%	*	

a Source: GLRO, M79/X/I, checked against the minutes of the Hackney petty sessions, which Norris attended: P79/JN1/214. The unit of analysis is the case, not the defendant.

b Includes convictions with a fine or whipping as punishment, as well as commitments to the house of correction.

c Includes defendants who were bound over by recognizance to attend quarter sessions (and cases in which the prosecutor was bound over by recognizance to prosecute), defendants who were committed to New Prison for want of sureties, and defendants who were committed to Newgate prison to await trial.

d Cases dismissed because of insufficient evidence, or because the plaintiff did not appear before Norris to testify against the defendant.

e In the majority of these cases a warrant was issued against the defendant but the defendant was apparently never brought before justice Norris to answer the complaint.

f Includes cases in which the stolen items were not identified.

g Includes eight poor law cases (bastardy, refusing to work, leaving family members chargeable to the parish) and eleven disputes between apprentices and servants and their masters or mistresses.

Table 3.2 *Criminal accusations heard by William Hunt, April 1744–May 1748[a]*

Offence	Agreed	Ordered[b]	Summary conviction[c]	Further action[d]	Dismissed[e]	Disp. unknown[f]	TOTAL
Vice							
Alehouse offences	1	1	7	1	4	0	14
Other	0	0	3	0	1	0	4
TOTAL N	1	1	10	1	5	0	18
% of known dispositions	6%	6%	56%	6%	28%	*	
Theft, property disputes							
Wood, fruit, vegetables	19	5	39	0	6	2	71
Other items	6	1	3	4	9	1	24
Damaging property	8	2	1	0	1	1	13
Fraud/detaining property	12	3	0	0	3	1	19
TOTAL N	45	11	43	4	19	5	127
% of known dispositions	37%	9%	35%	3%	16%	*	
Offences against the peace							
Assault	58	4	1	9	6	3	81
Other	7	1	0	1	2	1	12
TOTAL N	65	5	1	10	8	4	93
% of known dispositions	73%	6%	1%	11%	9%	*	
Poor law[g]							
Bastardy	8	3	1	7	1	0	20
Failure to maintain wife	4	1	0	0	0	0	5
Other	0	0	2	0	1	0	3
TOTAL N	12	4	3	7	2	0	28
% of known dispositions	43%	14%	10%	25%	7%	*	
Employment disputes							
Failure to pay wages	9	3	0	0	0	0	12
Other complaint vs. master	0	1	0	0	0	0	1
Complaint vs. servant	3	3	0	0	0	0	6
TOTAL N	12	7	0	0	0	0	19

Other offences

Hunting	0	0	7	0	2	9
Miscellaneous	10	2	1	1	0	16
TOTAL N	10	2	8	1	2	25
% of known dispositions	43%	9%	35%	4%	9%	*
TOTAL N	145	30	65	23	36	310
% of known dispositions	48%	10%	22%	8%	12%	*

^a Source: *The Justicing Notebook of William Hunt, 1744–1749*, ed. Elizabeth Crittall, Wiltshire Record Society vol. 37 (Devizes, Wiltshire, 1982). Cases recorded after May 1748 (nos. 568–77) have not been included in this analysis because after this date Hunt appears to have ceased to record all the criminal accusations he heard, and only recorded convictions. The unit of analysis is the case, not the defendant.

^b Hunt "ordered" the defendant to perform a specific penalty, such as the payment of damages to the plaintiff or wages to a servant. These orders do not appear to constitute legal convictions, yet the language of the diary suggests that Hunt believed they had legal authority, and were not merely examples of informal mediation.

^c Includes convictions with a fine or whipping as punishment, and commitments to the house of correction.

^d Includes defendants who were bound over by recognizance, either to attend quarter sessions or to indemnify the parish against the cost of maintaining a bastard child; and defendants who were committed to prison, either for want of sureties or to await trial at quarter sessions or assizes.

^e Cases were dismissed because of insufficient evidence, or because the plaintiff did not appear before Hunt to testify against the defendant.

^f In five of these cases a warrant was issued against the defendant but the defendant was apparently never brought before justice Hunt to answer the complaint.

^g Settlement cases and orders to enter into service are excluded from this table.

About a fifth of the cases heard by both justices resulted in a summary conviction, primarily for alehouse offences, swearing and cursing, petty theft from
woods, gardens and orchards, and violations of the game laws. If a notebook
survived from a truly urban justice, it is likely that there would have been
more summary convictions, but for a somewhat different list of offences.
Because of their proximity to houses of correction, urban justices committed
more people for loose, idle, and disorderly conduct, vagrancy, prostitution,
and petty theft. As suggested by the activities of the Lord Mayor of London
and the Westminster justices who attended the St. Margaret's petty sessions,
the summary convictions with fines made by urban justices were primarily for
vice (drunkenness, swearing, and profaning the Sabbath).[8] Between 1664 and
1688, urban justices were probably also more active than their rural counterparts in convicting people for attending conventicles.[9] Although numerous
other offences were punishable by summary conviction, with punishment
either by whipping or by fine, few are likely to have been prosecuted frequently.[10]

Until more justices' notebooks from the metropolis are discovered, it will be
impossible to determine the relative importance of informal mediation compared to summary convictions and other formal legal actions among the
criminal business heard by urban justices. The evidence of justices' notebooks
from rural areas, however, suggests that a substantial proportion, between a
third and two thirds, of criminal accusations reported to justices were resolved
informally. Since many of the cases in these notebooks that resulted in further

---

[8] CLRO, Lord Mayor's Waiting Book, vol. 3 (1664–68) and Mansion House Charge Book,
   vols. 7–8 (1686–1695); Westminster City Archives, St. Margaret's petty sessions minutes
   (1719–1723).
[9] Anthony Fletcher, "The enforcement of the conventicle acts 1664–1769," in *Toleration and
   Persecution*, ed. W. Sheils (Studies in Church History, vol. 22, 1984), p. 245.
[10] Offenders punishable by whipping included the parents of bastard children (if the child was
   chargeable to the parish the mother was to be committed to the house of correction), persons
   stealing wood or fruit if they were unable to pay the damages assessed by the justice, and rogues
   and vagabonds about to be passed to their place of settlement. In the notebooks of Henry Norris
   and William Hunt, however, whipping was only occasionally administered for petty thefts of
   wood and vegetables and never for bastardy or vagrancy. In the early seventeenth century, on the
   other hand, many parents of bastard children were whipped. See Walter J. King, "Punishments
   for bastardy in early seventeenth-century England," *Albion* 10:2 (Summer 1978), pp. 130–51;
   Alison D. Wall, *Riot, Bastardy and Other Social Problems: The Role of Constables and Justices
   of the Peace, 1580–1625* (Wiltshire Monographs No. 1, Trowbridge, 1980), pp. 18, 20; Ingram,
   Church Courts, pp. 338–40. Although passing vagrants was big business in Middlesex (see
   MJ/SBB/803, p. 49 [July 1722]), it is likely that many were not whipped. See Joanna Innes,
   "Social problems: poverty and marginality in eighteenth-century England" (unpublished
   typescript, summer 1985), pp. 78–79.
      Besides the offences punishable by fine already discussed, scattered evidence survives of
   summary convictions for various regulatory offences such as hawking and peddling goods
   without a licence, forestalling, using false or unsealed measures, and not repairing or cleansing
   the highway.

legal action were felonies, an even higher proportion of misdemeanor cases was resolved informally. Informal mediation was clearly the most popular method of resolving misdemeanor accusations in rural areas. While it may have occurred less frequently in parts of London where the courts were more accessible, it seems likely that a significant proportion of urban criminal business was also heard informally.[11] Although cases of informal mediation were rarely recorded, their importance should not be forgotten as this study moves on to examine the judicial records on which any study of criminal accusations must be based.

With a few minor exceptions, it is possible to calculate the exact number of criminal accusations which led to the issuing of a recognizance or the filing of an indictment during the period.[12] House of correction calendars are less complete, but they survive in virtually continuous series from 1680 in Westminster and from 1712 in Middlesex. Few systematic records of other summary convictions survive, but it is possible to estimate the number of persons convicted by fine for attending conventicles in the 1660s and 1680s, and the number of prosecutions for vice (profaning the Sabbath, swearing and cursing, and drunkenness) initiated by the Societies for the Reformation of Manners in the early eighteenth century. Of the three procedures (recognizances, indictments, and summary conviction), recognizances were clearly the most popular: the number of recognizances issued annually was nearly equal to the total of indictments and commitments to houses of correction combined (Table 3.3). The estimated annual averages for houses of correction are somewhat inflated, as they derive primarily from the latter half of the period, when commitments increased significantly. Nevertheless, they represent convictions, not just accusations; defendants committed to houses of correction considerably outnumbered defendants *convicted* on indictments. When summary convictions by fine are added to the house of correction commitments, Table 3.3 demonstrates how significant summary jurisdiction had become by the late seventeenth century, making indictments the least used procedure for prosecuting petty crime. Even when felony indictments are also considered, summary prosecutions still outnumber indictments. As Peter King has recently argued, the fact that far more people experienced the criminal law through summary jurisdiction (or, one should add, informal mediation or recognizances) than trial by indictment has important implications for our understanding of

---

[11] See below, section 4.3.
[12] In addition to the missing evidence noted in the list of sources for Table 3.3, it is possible that some recognizances which were released before sessions were never returned to sessions (see below, section 5.2).

Table 3.3   *Annual numbers of defendants prosecuted*

	Middlesex		Westminster			Total defendants
	Years covered	Average per year	Years covered	Average per year	Defendants per document	
Recognizances	(1661–1725)	1,598	(1661–1725)	557	1.11	2,392
Indictments	(1661–1725)	620	(1661–1725)	164	1.55	1,215
Commitments to houses of correction	(1712–21)	698	(1680–1721)	495	N/A	1,193
Summary convictions by fine (vice)	(1708–09, 1715–18, 1720–24)	unknown		unknown	N/A	659
(conventicles)	(1682–86)	171	(1682–86)	103	N/A	274
Felony indictments	(1699–1725)	unknown		unknown	N/A	508

Note: With the exception of commitments to houses of correction, these figures are of *accusations*, and include prosecutions that did not result in convictions. Since the unit of analysis for recognizances and indictments is the case, the totals in the right-hand column have been multiplied by the average number of defendants per document in the samples.

Sources:

Recognizances: MJ/SBB/189–836 (1661–1725), supplemented by sessions rolls where books are missing. For three years, information on the number of recognizances was unavailable for one meeting of the court and the missing number was extrapolated from the other sessions of that year.

Indictments: MJ/SBP/5–12 (1661–1725), and WJ/SBP/1 (1661–1678), supplemented by sessions rolls for Westminster indictments from 1679. Information was unavailable for three Westminster sessions and the missing numbers were extrapolated. *Ignoramus* indictments for Westminster are not included.

Commitments to houses of correction: MJ/SR/1571–2376 (1680–1721). Rolls were missing or unfit for seven sessions; the missing numbers were extrapolated. Calendars are unavailable in a continuous series for Middlesex until 1712.

Summary convictions by fine (vice): Based on the reports of the Societies for the Reformation of Manners as tabulated in Table 9.1. The figures have been reduced by 39% to account for the fact that the Societies' figures are for all of London, and the population of urban Middlesex was approximately 61% of that of the metropolis as a whole: Roger Finlay and Beatrice Shearer, "Population growth and suburban expansion," in *London 1500–1700*, ed. A. L. Beier and Roger Finlay (1986), Table 3.

Summary convictions by fine (conventicles): T.J.G. Harris, "Politics of the London crowd in the reign of Charles II" (Ph.D. diss., Cambridge University, 1985), Table 1:1, p. 276, cases for Middlesex only. I have allocated convictions with unknown geographical origins proportionally according to the distribution of known cases.

Felony indictments: Peter Linebaugh, "Tyburn: a study of crime and the laboring poor in London during the first half of the eighteenth century," (Ph.D. diss., Warwick University, 1975), appendix I.

popular experiences of, and attitudes towards, the law in preindustrial England.[13]

3.2 TYPES OF CRIME

As discussed in chapter 2, the choice of a procedure was to a certain degree constrained by legal considerations. Yet for most offences, prosecutors had a choice of procedures, and the resulting patterns of prosecutions reveal some of the perceived advantages and disadvantages of each. Before examining this evidence, however, it is first necessary to consider the evidential problems raised when comparing the records of different legal procedures.

The documents generated by each procedure describe offences using different terminologies, which were shaped by legal constraints specific to each procedure. Records of summary convictions by fine, for example, normally describe the offence with only a word or a phrase, such as "swearing," "drunkenness," and "profaning the Sabbath," which justified punishing the offence summarily under a specific statute. With a far more demanding system of judicial review, indictments had to describe the offence in Latin according to prescribed rules. Yet since they tended to be written according to proven formulas, the descriptions of offences on indictments are as cryptic as those on certificates of summary convictions by fine. In contrast, although offences listed on recognizances and house of correction calendars also tend to be formulaic, they occasionally provide more detailed accounts of the offending behavior.

A comparison of the descriptions of offences on indictments and recognizances illustrates the difficulty of interpreting formulaic descriptions of offences on indictments. The standard indictment for assault, which gives no indication of the circumstances surrounding the crime, accounted for 79% of 321 indictments for assault in the sample (excluding riotous assault); the remaining indictments included evidence that violence or a weapon was used, or that an additional offence was committed.[14] Recognizance evidence suggests, however, that these figures severely underestimate the number of such complicating factors involved in indicted assaults. In a subsample of recognizances and indictments pertaining to the same case, the recognizances indicate that ten of twenty-eight (36%) assaults described according to the standard formula on the indictments in fact involved violence, the use of a weapon, or an additional offence.[15] A defendant indicted for a simple assault in 1723, for example, was described on the recognizance as having assaulted and wounded

---

[13] Peter King, "Crime, law and society in Essex, 1740–1820" (Ph.D. diss., Cambridge, 1984), p. 278. We will return to this point in the conclusion.

[14] This figure is based on only four years of the sample, 1663–4 and May 1720–April 1722.

[15] The subsample of 89 linked recognizances and indictments is from 1664 and 1723.

the plaintiff with a burning faggot.[16] Similarly, indictments for assault often failed to include the fact that the incident occurred during a riot.[17]

In addition to not consistently mentioning complicating factors which were occasionally included in the Latin charge, indictments for assault could not possibly include the wealth of detail found on some recognizances. Michael Ireland and Richard Franklyn, for example, were indicted in 1722 for assaulting Katherine Hanscomb. On their recognizances, Ireland was accused of "assaulting and taking up her clothes and exposing her nakedness," and Franklyn was charged with "assaulting and throwing water upon her."[18] A married couple who were indicted in 1664 for an assault had, according to the recognizance, violently assaulted two scavengers who were collecting their rates and stole the ratebook.[19] Thus, offences listed on indictments simply as assaults could include symbolic acts of defamation or attempts to obstruct the collection of taxes. Because as little as a threatening gesture, or merely placing a hand on another in anger, could be indicted as an assault,[20] a wide variety of altercations were recorded on indictments under this rubric. Similarly, recognizances reveal contrasting circumstances surrounding identical indictments for keeping a disorderly alehouse.[21]

While recognizances and indictments frequently described the same incident using different language and in varying degrees of detail, they normally described broadly similar offences. Only three of the eighty-nine offences in the linked indictment–recognizance subsample were described in completely different terms on the two documents.[22] These findings suggest that comparisons between crimes prosecuted by different legal procedures are viable if they rest on broad categories of offences (such as "offences against the peace"), and avoid making detailed distinctions (such as between assault and violent assault, or between assault and riot).

Because they documented complaints, not formal convictions,[23] descriptions of crimes on house of correction calendars and recognizances tend to be more detailed. Nevertheless, many descriptions of offences in these records are formulaic. Offenders on house of correction calendars were often described as "loose [or lewd], idle, and disorderly persons" in order to justify the commitment under 7 Jac. 1 c. 4, a statute which required the building of houses of correction. Similarly, recognizances were often worded so as to fit the requirements of a recognizance "for the peace" or (less frequently) "for good

---

[16] MJ/SR/2402, I. 65, R. 85 (April 1723); see also I. 8 and R. 70.
[17] For example, see MJ/SR/2208, I. 48, R. 15 (April 1713) and I. 19, 20, 21 and R. 210. For other offences which led to indictments for assault, see below, section 6.1.
[18] MJ/SR/2379, I. 40, R. 99 (Jan. 1722).   [19] MJ/SR/1296, I. 3, R. 6 (Dec. 1664).
[20] Dalton, *Countrey Justice*, (1677), p. 282.
[21] Shoemaker, "Crime, courts, and community," pp. 256–57.
[22] For the offences, see *ibid.*, p. 256, n. 18.
[23] Commitments to houses of correction can be interpreted as convictions: see above, section 2.5.

behavior"; many followed the wording of the sample recognizances included in most manuals for justices.[24]

Like indictments for assault, formulaic recognizances and commitments to houses of correction obscure valuable details concerning offences. Defendants charged with "loose, idle and disorderly" conduct were in fact accused of having committed a broad range of petty offences, including prostitution, petty theft, and insubordination to masters.[25] Similarly, recognizances "for the peace," which were ostensibly issued to prevent crimes from occurring rather than to punish past behavior, appear to have been used to bind over defendants who were already accused of having committed a variety of specific offences, such as defamation or riot, at the time the recognizance was issued.[26] Other recognizances and entries in house of correction calendars, however, provide some of the most detailed descriptions available of the objectionable behavior that led to misdemeanor prosecutions. Perhaps because these documents were rarely subject to judicial review, justices felt less compelled to use legal terminology and were more apt to use common language to describe offences. House of correction calendars are full of brief descriptions of incidents of prostitution, theft, and disobedience to masters, to name only the most common offences. There were enough specific offences on the calendars, in fact, to account for over ninety separate codes in the computerized sample. The even greater details of offences recorded on recognizances necessitated over 340 computer codes for this study.[27]

Descriptions of offences prosecuted by each of the procedures thus vary considerably in the amount of information they provide. Because difficulties arise when tabulating cases which are described in such contrasting degrees of detail, it is necessary to be cautious when comparing the number of prosecutions for specific offences by different procedures. The more general the category of offence analyzed (such as "offences against the peace"), the more likely it is that such comparisons will reflect real differences in the distribution of offences prosecuted by each procedure.

Despite these limitations, the records amply illustrate the flexibility enjoyed by prosecutors of petty crime. Table 3.4 lists the types of crime prosecuted using each procedure. Most types of offences were prosecuted by at least three procedures, although few offences were frequently prosecuted by more than two. Prosecutors of petty theft exercised the most flexibility: evidence survives of a significant number of prosecutions in all five columns. Estimates of the

---

[24] See above, section 2.2.   [25] See below, section 7.1.

[26] This is evident from comparing the dates of the offences on recognizances and indictments for the same incidents.

[27] Throughout this study, cases are categorized according to the most specific offence indicated. Thus, a defendant accused of being loose, idle and disorderly and a common pilferer is included under theft, not under loose, idle and disorderly conduct.

annual numbers of prosecutions of offences by recognizance, indictment, and commitment to houses of correction are provided for 1720–22 in Table 3.5. Although there was considerable overlap, each procedure was most commonly used for a somewhat different range of offences. From the choices documented in these tables, the relative advantages of each of the procedures begin to appear.

Informal mediation was used primarily for offences against the peace and property offences. The notebooks of William Hunt and Henry Norris reveal that between 56 and 73% of the disputes involving assault, riot and defamation that were brought before them were settled informally. Because these disputes typically occurred between individuals who were acquainted with one another, informal settlements were feasible. For the same reason, disputes between masters and their servants or apprentices were often informally mediated, although impatient masters often committed their charges to houses of correction for a quick spell of corporal punishment. Property offences were also often handled informally, both by informal mediation and by recognizance, particularly when the offence concerned a relatively minor dispute over ownership or damage.[28] Nevertheless, most types of property offences were viewed very seriously in preindustrial England, and it is not surprising that many thefts, frauds, and trespasses resulted in formal prosecutions by indictment or summary conviction. Compared to offences against the peace, considerably smaller proportions of the property offences brought before justices Hunt and Norris were settled informally.

Recognizances, the least formal of the other procedures, were typically used for a wide range of primarily minor offences. By far the most common type of offence prosecuted by recognizance was offences against the peace, which account for over two thirds of all recognizances. In addition to property offences, which were prosecuted by several of the procedures, recognizances were also used for bastardy and certain other sexual offences, gambling, and, in small numbers, for several other offences. Fathers of chargeable bastard children were typically bound over by recognizance, either in order to require them to appear in court and receive orders concerning the child's support, or as a means of indemnifying the parish from the expense of maintaining the child.[29] Other sexual offenders prosecuted by recognizance include adulterers, prostitutes, clients, and brothel keepers, but by far the most commonly prosecuted sexual offenders, prostitutes, were usually committed to houses of correction. This pattern reflects not only the double standard of sexual

---

[28] *Justicing Notebook of William Hunt 1744–49*, ed. Elizabeth Crittall, Wiltshire Record Society, vol. 37 (Devizes, 1982), pp. 13–14; below, sections 4.1 and 5.1.

[29] The latter type of recognizance is not normally found in the quarter sessions rolls, but is recorded in justices' notebooks. In many cases, however, fathers simply paid the parish for the upkeep of the child without being bound over (Nicholas Rogers, "Carnal knowledge: illegitimacy in eighteenth-century Westminster," *Journal of Social History* 23 [1989], p. 360, n. 31).

Table 3.4   *Types of crime prosecuted by each procedure*[a]

	Informal mediation by justices[b]	Recognizance (non-indicted)[c]	Indictment[c]	House of correction[d]	Summary conviction with fine[e]
Peace					
Keep the peace	**	***	—	—	—
Assault	***	***	***	**	—
Riot	—	**	***	**	—
Common disturber/defamation	—	**	**	**	—
Poor Law					
Complaints vs. apprentices/servants	*	*	*	**	—
Complaints vs. masters	**	*	—	—	—
Loose, idle, disorderly person	—	**	*	***	—
Vagrancy	—	*	*	**	unknown
Bastardy	**	**	—	*	—
Vice					
Alehouse offences (proprietors)	*	*	**	**	unknown
Drunkenness	—	**	—	***	*
Prostitution	*	**	*	**	—
Adultery	—	*	*	*	—
Gaming	—	*	**	—	—
Cursing and swearing	—	—	—	—	**
Profaning the Sabbath	—	—	—	—	***

Property					
Theft	**	**	**	***	unknown
Fraud	*	**	**	*	—
Trespassing/damage	**	*	**	*	—
Regulatory					
Neglect of office	—	*	**	—	—
Other regulatory offences	*	**	***	—	unknown
Other					
Disaffection	—	*	**	*	***

[a] Key to symbols:

—   No prosecutions discovered using this procedure.

*   Rarely prosecuted. Up to 2% of the sample of prosecutions by this procedure were for this offence.

**   Commonly prosecuted. Between 3% and 9% of the sample of prosecutions.

***   Frequently prosecuted. 10% or more of the sample of prosecutions.

[b]   Based on the total number of cases settled informally by justices Norris and Hunt (Tables 3.1 and 3.2).

[c]   From the basic sample. Does not include recognizances for cases where an indictment was issued.

[d]   From the basic sample. Because their commitments were not the result of summary jurisdiction, the following defendants were excluded: defendants committed for want of sureties to attend sessions, defendants committed by the bench at sessions, and defendants committed for "safe keeping."

[e]   Based on certificates of conviction kept in the sessions records, and on the records of the Societies for the Reformation of Manners.

Table 3.5   *Offences prosecuted by each procedure, 1720–22 sample: projected annual averages*

	Recognizances (non-indicted)[a]	Indictments[b]	Houses of correction[c]
Sample size:	17%	25%	33%
Offences against the peace			
Keep the peace[d]	183	—	—
Assault[d]	627	574	30
Riot	243	46	24
Common disturber/defamation	156	20	21
TOTAL	1209	640	75
Poor law			
Master–servant disputes	39	4	111
Vagrancy/loose, idle, disorderly[d]	15	2	183
Bastardy	42	0	3
TOTAL (including other poor law)	117	6	312
Vice			
Alehouse offences	18	76	0
Prostitution[e]	69	2	501
Gaming	63	44	12
TOTAL (including other vice)	174	122	546
Property			
Theft	96	78	351
Fraud	57	62	12
Trespass and damage	48	60	0
TOTAL	201	200	363
Regulatory			
Neglect of office	9	16	0
Nuisance	9	104	0
TOTAL (including other reg.)	24	152	0

Other			
Disaffection	6	4	6
Unknown, misc.	36	22	6
TOTAL	42	26	12
TOTAL	1767	1146	1308

[a] 1720–22 sample. Does not include recognizances for cases where an indictment was issued.

[b] 1720–22 sample.

[c] 1721 sample. As noted in note d to Table 3.4, does not include commitments which did not result from summary jurisdiction.

[d] These are residual categories: where another offence is mentioned the case is included in the more specific category.

[e] Includes nightwalkers and "lewd" persons.

behavior,[30] but also the fact that adulterers and prostitutes' clients may not have been regular offenders. As was the case with gambling, it is possible that the goal of the prosecution in these cases was to discourage further offences rather than to punish the transgression. It is also likely, however, that the high social status of many of these offenders kept them from being committed to houses of correction.[31]

Of the other offences prosecuted by recognizance, one of the most erratically prosecuted was religious disaffection. In most years, only a very small number of people were bound over for this type of offence, but in 1683 over two hundred people were bound over for attending conventicles and in 1715 a similar number of suspected "papists" were bound over for refusing to take the oaths of allegiance, supremacy and abjuration to the new regime.[32] Given the large number of people involved in these unusual waves of prosecutions, it is likely that the justices hoped to convince the offenders to mend their ways without having to go to the trouble and expense of prosecuting them formally (though some of the conventiclers in 1683 were indicted). In other years, prosecutors of religious offenders sought formal convictions. Conventiclers were indicted, or, after the 1664 Conventicle Act, convicted summarily and fined. In April 1681, fifty-one people were indicted for recusancy.

Although indictments were used for serious offences like religious disaffection and property crimes, the majority of indictments were used for less serious ones: offences against the peace (especially assaults), regulatory offences, and vice. As discussed in section 6.1, indictments for assault were often used by prosecutors to fight a variety of civil disputes as well as to prosecute physical attacks. Defendants accused of statutory offences such as failing to serve on the night watch could only be prosecuted by indictment. These and other nuisance offences, such as obstructing the highway, were typically the result of constables' presentments, which became indictments when they were approved by the grand jury.

Vice, significantly, was also generally unsuitable for informal prosecution by mediation or recognizance. As discussed in chapter 4, since plaintiffs in cases of vice (who were often public officials) usually did not know their defendants, they were unlikely to accept informal settlements. (As we have seen, the one offence where plaintiffs and defendants were likely to know each other, adultery, was occasionally dealt with by recognizance.) Many prosecutions for vice, therefore, were by indictment or summary jurisdiction. The choice depended principally on the legal status of the offence. Proprietors of houses

---

[30] Keith Thomas, "The double standard," *Journal of the History of Ideas* 20 (1959), pp. 195–216. Neither prostitution nor adultery was an indictable offence. See above, section 2.3.

[31] See below, section 8.1.

[32] This statement is based on a 20% sample of the Middlesex recognizances in 1683 and the Westminster recognizances in 1715.

which encouraged vice, such as brothels, gaming houses, and disorderly and unlicensed alehouses, could be indicted for having created a nuisance. The number of indictments in 1721 (documented in Table 3.5) was low however, because a series of decisions at King's Bench in the 1690s and early 1700s ruled that statutory offences punishable by summary conviction with a fine, such as keeping an alehouse without a licence, could not also be prosecuted by indictment.[33] Three minor offences, drunkenness, cursing and swearing, and profaning the Sabbath, were also punishable by the quick and inexpensive method of summary conviction with a fine. Because of the ambiguous legal status of prostitution, prostitutes could not be prosecuted either by indictment or summary conviction with a fine, but they were frequently committed to houses of correction as nightwalkers or "loose [or lewd], idle, and disorderly persons."

In addition to prostitution, the offences most commonly punished in houses of correction were "loose, idle, and disorderly" conduct and petty theft. The vague definition of the former allowed a wide range of deviant behavior to be punished.[34] The most common complaint, besides prostitution, was probably failure to find work or vagrancy, and it is not surprising that few of the accused were prosecuted by informal mediation or recognizance. Persons accused of these offences were by definition without established residences or jobs and therefore could not be trusted to abide by informal settlements. Defendants committed to houses of correction for petty theft may also have been without work or established residence; otherwise it is difficult to explain why they should have been treated differently from the petty thieves whose cases were handled by informal mediation or recognizance.

In sum, the profiles of offences prosecuted by each procedure suggest the contexts for which each procedure was most suited. Both informal procedures, informal mediation by justices and recognizances, were used primarily for offences against the peace, which were typically disputes between parties who knew each other. Although indictments were also used for offences against the peace, they were also commonly used for vice, serious crimes such as religious disaffection and property offences, statutory offences not punishable by summary conviction, and regulatory offences included on constables' presentments. Houses of correction, on the other hand, were primarily used for victimless offences and petty thefts, which were often committed by persons without fixed habitation or employment. There was, however, a considerable degree of overlap in the range of offences prosecuted by each procedure: assaults, riots, cases of defamation and disturbing, prostitution, petty thefts, frauds, cases of trespass and damage, and certain regulatory offences were all commonly prosecuted by more than one procedure. The choice of a legal

---

[33] See above, section 2.3.   [34] See below, section 7.1.

procedure was clearly not influenced solely by the nature of the offence, but also by other aspects of the case, such as the desired outcome of the prosecution (punishment or reformation) and the relationship between the defendant and the plaintiff. These themes will be examined in greater detail in Part II.

3.3 YEAR-TO-YEAR FLUCTUATIONS[35]

More evidence concerning the motivations of prosecutors can be inferred from an analysis of the considerable year-to-year variations in the number of cases prosecuted by each procedure. Graphs of the annual totals of prosecutions by each procedure reveal that each series was characterized by dramatic fluctuations rather than linear growth (Figures 1, 2, and 3). Middlesex recognizances peaked not at the end of the period but in the early 1680s, and then entered into a long decline from which they did not begin to recover until 1705. Westminster recognizances peaked in 1715 and then decreased substantially to the end of the period. Commitments to the Westminster house of correction peaked in 1690 and 1691 at a level just below that of their highest year, 1717. The long term decline of the Westminster indictments from the 1670s was interrupted by a dramatic peak in 1685, and the Middlesex indictments peaked in the 1690s. The causes of these and other substantial fluctuations are manifold: levels of prosecutions were shaped by the shifting mixture of offences prosecuted, and the number of prosecutions of each type of crime was determined both by changes in the number of crimes actually committed and by varying levels of prosecutorial initiative. An analysis of these fluctuations suggests that it is prosecutorial initiative – the decision whether or not to prosecute taken by a potential prosecutor, often in consultation with a justice of the peace – that was the most important factor in shaping levels of Middlesex prosecutions.[36]

Broadly conceived, misdemeanors can be divided into three categories of offences: property offences, offences against the peace, and victimless offences (vice, regulatory offences, religious and political disaffection, and certain types of poor law offences). For only property offences is it possible to consider whether prosecutions responded to changes in the actual number of crimes

[35] In addition to the basic sample and Figures 1, 2 and 3, the conclusions in this section are drawn from samples of the following years, in which prosecutions were abnormally high or low:
   Middlesex recognizances: 1683, 1704 (20% sample)
   Westminster recognizances: 1715 (20% sample)
   Middlesex indictments: 1698 (100% sample)
   Middlesex house of correction: 1717, 1720 (33% sample)
   Westminster house of correction: 1690 (100% sample of the three surviving sessions rolls), 1702 (33% sample).

[36] Comparison of Figures 1, 2 and 3 reveals that the trends for the three procedures generally fluctuate in tandem. It is thus unlikely that year-to-year fluctuations were caused by a transfer of business from one procedure to another.

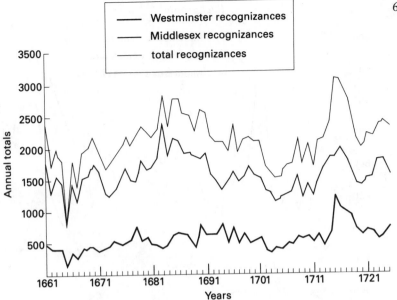

Figure 1 Annual totals of Middlesex and Westminster recognizances
Source: see Table 3.3.

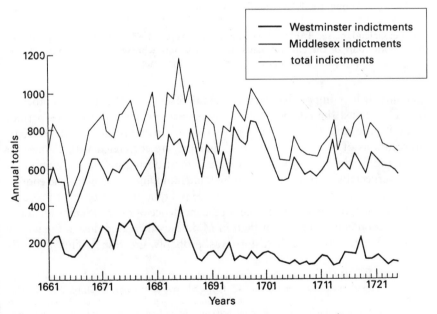

Figure 2 Annual totals of Middlesex and Westminster indictments
Source: see Table 3.3.

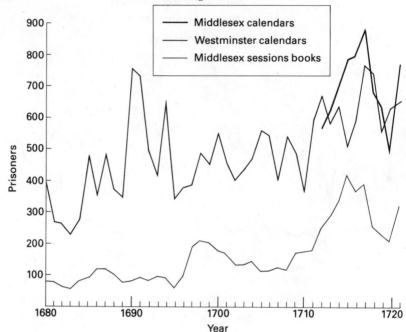

Figure 3 Annual totals of commitments to houses of correction: Middlesex and
Westminster

Source: Calendars: see Table 3.3. Session books: MJ/SBB/370–396. The sessions books
record only part of the commitments: those prisoners who were in the house of correction at the time sessions met.

committed; it is impossible even to speculate on how the actual number of
offences against the peace or victimless offences changed during this period.
John Beattie and Douglas Hay have recently demonstrated that levels of
prosecutions of theft in preindustrial England are correlated with changes in
economic conditions; prosecutions were highest during periods of high grain
prices (especially in rural areas) and high unemployment following the ends of
wars (in urban areas). Thus, Beattie and Hay argue that patterns of prosecutions for theft mirrored real changes in the incidence of theft.[37] Similarly, house
of correction commitments for theft in Middlesex increased during the winter
months when economic hardship was probably greatest.[38] This thesis is

---

[37] Beattie, *Crime and the Courts*, chap. 5; Douglas Hay, "War, dearth and theft in the eighteenth
century: the record of the English courts," *Past and Present* 95 (May 1982), pp. 117–60. This
approach has been questioned, however, by King, ("Crime, law and society," chap. 2), and
Joanna Innes and John Styles ("The crime wave: recent writing on crime and criminal justice in
eighteenth-century England," *Journal of British Studies* 25 [Oct. 1986], section 3).
[38] For the seasonality of hardship, see Boulton, *Neighbourhood and Society*, pp. 49–59.

difficult to test against year-to-year patterns of misdemeanor prosecutions without tabulating prosecutions by type of crime over a long period, a task which was not possible given the large number of prosecutions in Middlesex. Nonetheless, a sample of Middlesex indictments during their highest year, 1698, demonstrates that changing levels of property offences did contribute to the high levels of Middlesex indictments in the late 1690s, when high bread prices combined with peacetime unemployment and shortages of coin to cause extreme hardship.[39] The number of defendants indicted for property offences (unlawfully taking goods, fraud, receiving stolen goods, trespass and damage) in 1698 was double that of normal years, and accounted for about a quarter of the increase in the number of defendants indicted over a normal year. In constrast, in the relatively prosperous year of 1681, property offences fell to about a third of their normal level.[40] Although a sample of Middlesex house of correction commitments from the difficult year of 1697 included only an average number of commitments for theft, in a sample of another difficult year, 1717 (shortly after the end of the War of the Spanish Succession), commitments for theft were 39% above normal and accounted for over one third of all commitments. The subsequent low level of house of correction commitments for theft in 1720 (commitments were 20% below normal) was not, however, caused by improved economic conditions. The decline is probably attributable in part to the introduction of an alternative punishment – transportation – which encouraged the transfer of cases of small-scale theft from summary jurisdiction to indictments for grand larceny.[41] Prosecutions of property offences occasionally fluctuated according to the presence or absence of economic distress, but they by no means invariably did so.

Both offences against the peace and victimless offences played a far more important role in shaping overall levels of misdemeanor prosecutions. Offences against the peace (assault, riot, common disturber, defamation) account for over half of all recognizances and indictments; changes in the number of prosecutions for these offences contributed significantly to the year-to-year fluctuations in total prosecutions. Prosecutions of offences against the peace by recognizance in Middlesex varied from as few as the estimated 640 recognizances in 1704 to an estimated 1,230 in 1683, respectively the lowest and the highest years for recognizances in the period. Similarly, the number of defendants indicted for offences against the peace varied from 312.5 per year in the 1663–64 sample to 675 in 1698, the peak year of Middlesex indictments. Given the manifold causes of offences against the peace, it is impossible to explain these fluctuations. Typically, prosecutions resulted from personal

---

[39] Stephen MacFarlane, "Social policy and the poor in the later seventeenth century," in *London 1500–1700*, ed. A. L. Beier and Roger Finlay (1986), p. 259.
[40] Similarly, the number of people committed to the Westminster house of correction in 1680 for theft was the lowest of the six sample years.
[41] See below, section 7.1.

tensions between two (or more) individuals arising out of private disputes over issues such as sexual conduct or property transactions,[42] and it is difficult to explain why such tensions would lead to prosecutions more frequently in some years than in others.

Some assaults and riots, however, resulted from political and religious conflict. Two of the sample years with high prosecutions for offences against the peace occurred during periods of political instability: in 1683, during the final years of Charles II's reign, and in 1715, immediately following the Hanoverian accession. These were years of widespread protest and disorder – and of low tolerance of such activities – and the quarter sessions rolls for these years include examples of politically motivated assaults and riots. In April 1715, for example, a Tory rioter was bound over and indicted for assaulting a householder who refused to put candles in his windows to mark the anniversary of Queen Anne's coronation.[43] However, such cases account for only a small fraction of the offences against the peace in these years, and it is unlikely that a significant portion of the remaining vaguely described assaults and riots were related to political and religious conflicts.[44] Other years in which offences against the peace peaked, such as 1677 and 1698, were not periods of significant political conflict; there were many, many other reasons for committing, and prosecuting, offences against the peace. Even in 1683, political motivations were not paramount. In October, members of the grand jury complained that "many bills [indictments] which come before us are for assault and battery, and for the most part [are] among poor people, and their offences arise from scolding, backbiting, and reproaching ..."[45] The sessions rolls include examples of assaults prompted by this type of verbal sparring, but because so few cases are described in any detail, and because assaults occurred in so many other contexts, it is impossible to generalize about the causes of changing patterns of prosecutions of offences against the peace.

Patterns of prosecutions of victimless crimes are less difficult to explain since they often resulted from concerted campaigns to prosecute specific offences. Since offences such as vice, regulatory offences, and religious disaffection typically did not directly harm specific individuals, they were rarely prosecuted

---

[42] See below, section 6.1; Shoemaker, "London 'mob'," pp. 277–80.

[43] MJ/SR/2248, I.14 and unnumbered R. (Westminster sessions, April 1715), cited by Nicholas Rogers, "Popular protest in early Hanoverian London," *Past and Present* 79 (1978), p. 72. See also Tim Harris, *London Crowds in the Reign of Charles II* (Cambridge, 1987), pp. 172–88.

[44] Similarly, the relatively high numbers of assaults and riots (both on recognizances and, in the case of assaults, indictments) in the 1720–22 sample, a period of concern about Jacobite plots and the collapse of the South Sea Bubble, included few examples of politically motivated offences. For a contrasting interpretation, based on Surrey evidence, see Beattie, "Pattern of crime," pp. 66–73. A significant amount of politically inspired violence was not prosecuted (James L. Fitts, "Newcastle's mob," *Albion* 5 [1973], pp. 44–47; Shoemaker, "Crime, courts, and community," pp. 521–23).

[45] MJ/SBB/408, p. 47 (Oct. 1683).

by private citizens.[46] Instead, victimless offences were usually prosecuted by public officials, or public-spirited informers, often in organized campaigns stimulated by justices of the peace. Such campaigns could substantially affect the overall distribution and level of prosecuted offences. Thus, the peak years of recognizances in Middlesex (1683) and Westminster (1715) experienced exceptionally high numbers of recognizances for religious disaffection (conventiclers in 1683, suspected papists who refused to take the oaths of allegiance, supremacy, and abjuration in 1715). In addition, in 1715 more than double the normal number of people were bound over by recognizance in Westminster for vice (mostly for offences involving prostitution).

Victimless offences played an even greater role in shaping patterns of prosecutions by indictment. In October 1683, in a concerted campaign against encroachments in Wapping, 147 indictments for obstructing the highway with stalls or buildings were filed. These indictments accounted for half of the indictments that sessions, and 19% of all Middlesex indictments in 1683. Thus, the peak in Middlesex indictments in that year is largely explained by one burst of regulatory activity. Similarly, the sudden peak in Westminister indictments in 1718 (documented in Figure 2) was due to a campaign against gaming houses. Of 251 indictments that year, 67 (27%) were filed at the July sessions for keeping unlawful games such as "ninepinns" and "shovel board." The high level of indictments in 1698 was caused in part by more than double the normal number of defendants indicted for vice, primarily for keeping alehouses without a licence. In other years, the indictment totals were inflated by campaigns against recusancy, nuisances, and gaming.[47]

Victimless offences were still more common on the calendars of houses of correction, where "loose, idle, and disorderly" conduct and prostitution account for about half of all commitments. Because the level of commitments for these offences was dependent upon the activities of a relatively small number of informers and officers of the peace, total numbers of commitments to houses of correction fluctuated even more wildly than recognizances and indictments (Figure 3). Supporters of the Societies for the Reformation of Manners were often behind these prosecutions, and from 1690 fluctuations in commitments to houses of correction can occasionally be linked with changing activities of the reformers. After the initial burst of enthusiasm in 1690 and 1691, the Societies came under attack, and one very active justice, Ralph Hartley, was

---

[46] See below, section 8.3.

[47] The most extreme example of this phenomenon occurs on the July 1702 Westminster sessions roll, which includes 181 indictments for subdividing houses and letting the rooms, all of which were found *ignoramus*: MJ/SR/1992 (these indictments were not included in any of the tables and graphs). For other examples of prosecution waves of victimless offences, see Sharpe, *Crime in Seventeenth-Century England*, pp. 193–98; Keith Wrightson, "Two concepts of order: justices, constables and jurymen in seventeenth-century England," in *An Ungovernable People*, ed. Brewer and Styles, pp. 21–46 and 299–307.

ejected from the Middlesex commission of the peace.[48] The demoralization of the reformers caused by Hartley's ejection is evident in the sharp decline in commitments to the Westminster house of correction in 1692 and 1693. From 1700, the societies published annual accounts of the number of prostitutes and "lewd and disorderly" people they apprehended, and a comparison of the Societies' reports with the Westminster and Middlesex calendars (where available) reveals that peaks in the reformers' efforts coincided with peaks in total house of correction commitments in 1708 and 1717. Similarly, the significant decline in cases reported by the Societies in 1720 is reflected in commitments to both the Middlesex and Westminster houses of correction. The importance of victimless offences in causing these fluctuations is confirmed by sample evidence: while the number of commitments for victimless offences peaked at the Middlesex house of correction in 1717 at almost 450, it reached its nadir in 1720, when less than 200 were incarcerated. The reformers' efforts to prosecute offences by summary conviction with punishment by fine also fluctuated considerably. While accusations averaged about 2,000 per year in 1708 and 1709, the reformers made only between 714 and 959 accusations a year between 1716 and 1724.[49]

Whether directed against vice, nuisances, or political or religious disaffection, regulatory campaigns usually depended on the extraordinary zeal of a few prosecutors, either informers or unpaid parish officials, often working with energetic justices of the peace. Although the results of their efforts, visible in bulging sessions rolls, were often impressive, these prosecution waves were also typically short-lived, leaving their marks as occasional peaks in the annual totals of prosecutions, especially prosecutions by indictment and summary conviction.

Levels of misdemeanor prosecutions for different types of crime were thus shaped by a combination of largely independent variables, including economic conditions and the presence or absence of zealous constables and informers. It is thus surprising that levels of prosecutions for different categories of offences often moved in tandem. During the peak years of Middlesex and Westminster recognizances (1683 and 1715 respectively), for example, there were significant increases in prosecutions not only for religious disaffection, but also, in 1683, for property offences, regulatory offences, and offences against the peace and in 1715 for offences against the peace. Similarly, the peak year of Middlesex indictments, 1698, witnessed significant increases in prosecutions for offences against the peace, property offences, and vice. This phenomenon is less visible with commitments to houses of correction, but the peak years of commitments in 1717 (Middlesex) and 1721 (Westminster) were caused by high levels of prosecutions for both victimless offences *and* theft, and the low year of 1720

[48] See below, section 9.3.
[49] For the number of prosecutions initiated by the reformers, see below, Table 9.1.

Table 3.6　Numbers of recognizances issued by Middlesex justices of the peace

	1664	1677	1683[a]	1693	1704[b]	1707	1721
No. of justices in sample	45	42	45	50	50	51	57
No. of justices issuing more than an estimated 50 recogs. per year[c]	8	8	12	9	6	6	9
% of total recogs.	(65%)	(68%)	(74%)	(55%)	(59%)	(54%)	(57%)
No. of justices issuing 15–49 recogs. per year	12	14	11	16	8	12	17
% of total recogs.	(20%)	(23%)	(12%)	(32%)	(18%)	(27%)	(27%)
No of justices issuing 1–14 recogs. per year	25	20	22	25	36	33	31
% of total recogs.	(11%)	(8%)	(6%)	(11%)	(21%)	(16%)	(15%)
% of recognizances issued by justices in groups	(5%)	—	(7%)	(1%)	(3%)	(3%)	(1%)
Sample size (100%)	315	307	475	299	233	263	281
Sample proportion	20%	20%	20%	20%	20%	20%	17%
Most active justice:	Robert Jegon	John Underwood	Abraham Bayley	Robert Constable	Roger Smith	Roger Smith	Matthew Hewitt
Estimated no. of recognizances he issued:	250	215	375	160	195	225	198
% of total recogs.	(16%)	(14%)	(16%)	(11%)	(17%)	(17%)	(12%)

[a]　Year of most recognizances between 1661 and 1725

[b]　Year of least recognizances between 1661 and 1725.

[c]　Estimates calculated by multiplying sample total by inverse of sample proportion. For example, where the sample proportion is 20%, a justice responsible for 12 recognizances in the sample is estimated to have issued 60 recognizances per year.

(Middlesex) witnessed deficits in both categories of offences. These patterns suggest that a factor unrelated to specific offences played an important role in shaping patterns of prosecutions. That factor is the availability and energy of active justices of the peace.

Initiating a prosecution, especially by recognizance or commitment to a house of correction, depended upon a plaintiff finding a justice of the peace who was willing to hear the case. Low levels of prosecutions in some rural districts have been attributed to the fact that few justices lived in the area.[50] Even in urban areas, finding a justice willing to act presented more of a problem than appears at first sight, since only a fraction of the justices on the commission actually heard judicial business. In 1699, of the approximately 200 justices on the Middlesex commission, only 79 issued recognizances.[51] Sample evidence suggests that truly active justices were far rarer: judicial business was concentrated in the hands of a small group of active justices who issued, on average, more than one recognizance a week. Although such active justices rarely amounted to more than a fifth of the justices in the samples who issued recognizances, they routinely accounted for over half of all the recognizances issued (Table 3.6).[52] Even this statistic, however, fails to document the extraordinary activity of the most active justices in the sample: Abraham Bayley, whose estimated 375 recognizances in 1683 constituted 16% of the Middlesex recognizances that year, or the Westminster justice William Conne, whose 290 recognizances constituted 23% of the Westminster recognizances in 1715.[53] Similar concentrations of business in the hands of a few justices occurred with commitments to houses of correction and summary convictions with punishment by fine.[54]

Plaintiffs thus appear to have relied on a small number of active justices for initiating their prosecutions. Why some justices adopted such an active approach to their office will be discussed in chapter 8. For the moment it is sufficient to note that, as demonstrated in Table 3.6, levels of prosecutions were

---

[50] King, "Crime, law and society," pp. 48–49.

[51] Many of the justices on the commission probably did not even bother to take out their *dedimus*, which gave them the authority to act (Landau, *Justices of the Peace*, pp. 320–21). Excluding honorary justices, there were 129 Middlesex justices in 1680 and 212 in 1702 (*ibid.*, Appendix A). Although many justices were on both, the Middlesex and Westminster commissions were distinct. There were 66 Westminster justices in 1680 and 264 in 1721: S. N., Esq., *A Catalogue of the Names of All His Majesties Justices of the Peace ... According to the Late Alterations* (1680); GLRO, WJP/L/10.

[52] Similar concentrations of judicial activity have been found in other counties (Beattie, *Crime and the Courts*, p. 61; King, "Crime, law and society," p. 238).

[53] Unless otherwise noted, calculations concerning the number of recognizances issued by justices in the following discussion are based on a 20% sample.

[54] For houses of correction, see Appendix II. For summary convictions with punishment by fine, see GLRO, WC/R1 (profane cursing and swearing); Bodleian Library, Rawlinson MS D1396–1404 (working on the Sabbath); and Bertram Osborne, *Justices of the Peace 1361–1848* (Shaftesbury, Dorset, 1960), pp. 138, 155 (conventicles).

strongly influenced by the number of very active justices practicing in Middlesex, and that the supply of active justices was shaped by the frequent alterations in the county commissions of the peace which took place during the "age of party," particularly between 1679 and 1720. Lionel Glassey, who has recently chronicled these waves of politically inspired appointments and purges, has warned historians not to overestimate the impact of these changes on the justices' work of local administration.[55] Perhaps because Middlesex and Westminster were situated at the center of the national political scene, however, patterns of judicial business were dramatically influenced by alterations in their commissions of the peace. The appointment of Bayley as a justice in 1681 as part of an attempt to remodel the Middlesex bench during the exclusion crisis, for example, was largely responsible for the dramatic increase in the number of recognizances issued in Middlesex between 1681 and 1683. Bayley's 375 recognizances in 1683 constituted 55% of the increase between 1681 and 1683.[56] In 1711, Charles Peter was appointed a Westminster justice as part of Lord Keeper Harcourt's alterations to the commissions of the peace. Two years later, commitments to the Westminster house of correction had increased by 81%, and Peter's estimated 237 commitments in 1712, primarily for prostitution, account for 78% of that increase. In December of that year, however, for reasons that are unclear Peter was left out of the Westminster commission.[57] Consequently, commitments to the Westminster house of correction fell by 38% in 1713.

Bayley and Peter provide the most dramatic examples, but they were not the only active justices whose addition to or elimination from the commissions of the peace influenced patterns of prosecutions. Purges during the exclusion crisis, for example, eliminated four active Middlesex and Westminster justices who had together issued 18% of the recognizances in 1677. Similarly, the 33% decline in Middlesex recognizances from 1699 to their lowest level in the entire period in 1704 (Figure 1) can be attributed to a series of purges of mainly Whig justices initiated from the summer of 1700 by Lord Chancellor Wright, as well as a high mortality rate on the commission.[58] Of the forty-eight justices left out in those years because they had died, nine had issued a total of 379 recognizances in 1699, 22% of the total. Of the sixty-three living justices in Middlesex who were put out of the commission, ten had accounted for 256 recognizances in 1699, 15% of the total. A further cause of decline was a decrease in the number of recognizances issued by justices of the peace who remained on the commission. The twenty-four justices who issued recognizances in both 1699

[55] Lionel K. J. Glassey, *Politics and the Appointment of Justices of the Peace* (Oxford, 1979), pp. 267–69. For a contrary view see Landau, *Justices of the Peace*, p. 234. For the alterations generally, also see Landau, chap. 3.
[56] For Bayley's appointment, see PRO, C231/8, 16 March 1681.
[57] PRO, C234/25, Feb. 1711 and Dec. 1712. The 1712 estimate is based on a 33% sample.
[58] For lists of the justices left out between 1700 and 1704, see House of Lords Records Office, Main Papers, 20 March 1704. The 1699 recognizance figures are based on a 100% sample.

Table 3.7 *Impact of purges to the Westminster commission of the peace, December 1715–March 1719*[a]

Date left out	Justice	No. of recognizances in 1715 sample[b]
December 1715	John Chamberlayne	17
	Thomas Burdus	2
	Edward Hawkes	24
March 1719	Michael Crake	26
	Thomas Moody	3
		—
		72 (29% of 1715 sample)

[a] Not including justices who died. Source for changes to the commission of the peace: PRO, C234/25.
[b] Twenty percent sample of the Westminster recognizances for that year.

and 1704 issued 26% fewer in 1704 than they did in 1699. There may thus have been a grain of truth in contemporary complaints that the nature and scale of the alterations of the commissions at that time had brought the magistracy as a whole into disrepute, in part because many of the recent appointees allegedly lacked the appropriate social qualifications.[59] Certainly the newly appointed justices did little to take over the business previously conducted by their dead or absent predecessors. Few of the new justices were active, at least initially, in issuing recognizances. When the Whigs achieved power after the Hanoverian accession, the tables were turned: purges of Tory justices partly account for the 51% decline in Westminster recognizances between 1715 and 1720. Five of the living justices left out between December 1715 and March 1719 accounted for 29% of the recognizances issued in 1715 (Table 3.7).[60]

Because the purges were largely motivated by political reasons and there is no evidence that they were targeted at the small number of judicially active justices, not all purges had a significant impact on levels of prosecutions. Thus, the purges engineered by Lord Chancellor Harcourt between 1711 and 1714 netted no Westminster justices who had issued recognizances in 1707, although he did leave out two justices who were active in making commitments to houses of correction (one was Charles Peter). And although Lord Chancellor Cowper's purges between late 1715 and 1718 had a significant effect on levels of Westminster recognizances, his initial purges in 1714 and 1715 left out few active justices and failed to prevent 1715 from becoming the peak year for Westminster recognizances during the entire period.

Although many more justices were appointed than were purged,[61] the new justices, who were appointed largely for political reasons, were in general even less likely to be active than their predecessors. This trend is documented in Table 3.6, which shows that the number of barely active justices (those issuing less than fifteen recognizances a year), and the proportion of judicial business they accounted for, increased during the period. The number of very active justices, on the other hand, did not increase significantly. Nevertheless, major additions to the commissions sometimes included men who subsequently became energetic justices. Between 1673 and 1679, for example, dozens of new justices were added to the Middlesex and Westminster commissions, and fifteen of those added between 1673 and 1677 issued an estimated 750 recognizances in 1677, which amounted to 36% of the recognizances issued that year and more than accounted for the increase in the annual total of Middlesex and Westminster recognizances issued between 1673 and 1677. Similarly, justices added to the Middlesex commission during the exclusion

[59] Glassey, *Politics and Appointment*, pp. 160–62; *Journals of the House of Lords* 17 (30 March 1704); Osborne, *Justices of the Peace*, pp. 153–54.
[60] For the justices left out, see PRO, C234/25, 27 Dec. 1715 to 25 March 1719.
[61] Landau, *Justices of the Peace*, p. 85.

Table 3.8 Impact of additions to the Middlesex commission of the peace, 1678–83[a]

Date added	Justice	No. of recognizances in 1683 sample[b]
January 1678	Thomas Orby	1
March 1678	William Bridgeman[c]	1
January 1680	John Elwes [Ellwayes]	4
	William Blucke	1
May 1680	John Perry	20
January 1681	George Treby, Recorder of London	2
March 1681	Abraham Bayley	75
	John Balsh	9
April 1682	Hugh Middleton	1
	Tho Done[c]	5
October 1682	Robert Hastings	17
January 1683	Charles Hinton	1
May 1683	Edward Guise[d]	19
	Charles Osborne	8
October 1683	Thomas Jenner, Recorder of London	1
		165 (35% of 1683 sample)

[a] Sources for changes to the commission of the peace: PRO, C231/7–8; Historical Manuscripts Commission, Eleventh Report, Appendix, Part II, *The Manuscripts of the House of Lords 1678–1688*, pp. 184–85.

[b] Twenty percent sample of the Middlesex recognizances for 1683.

[c] Appointed to the Westminster commission.

[d] Appointed to the Westminster commission in April.

crisis fuelled a dramatic growth in Middlesex recognizances, making 1683 the highest year in the period (Figure 1 and Table 3.8). While Abraham Bayley was the primary cause of the increase, he issued only 16% of the recognizances in 1683. Fourteen other justices appointed between 1678 and 1683 accounted for another 19% of the 1683 recognizances (about 450). Since less than 10% of the recognizances issued that year were for identifiably political or religious offences (primarily for attending conventicles), the 1683 peak in Middlesex recognizances was apparently caused not so much by the religious and political tensions of those years as by the zeal of recently appointed justices.

Additions of new justices on the accession of both William III and George I also had a significant impact on judicial business. Although levels of recognizances in Middlesex and Westminster declined immediately after the Revolution of 1688, a wave of appointments in 1689 and the early 1690s[62] halted the decline. Justices appointed between 1689 and 1693 accounted for an incredible 46% of the recognizances issued in 1693. At the Westminster house of correction, levels of commitments skyrocketed in 1690 with the appointment of two enthusiastic new justices allied to the reformation of manners campaign, Robert Fielding and John Ward. Between them, Fielding and Ward were responsible for over half the commitments in the first half of the year. Although their activities soon ceased, justices appointed since the Revolution were responsible for 45% of the Westminster house of correction commitments in 1693.[63]

Similarly, the appointment of 121 new Westminster justices by Lord Chancellor Cowper within a year of the accession of George I[64] caused a dramatic increase in recognizances in 1715. Seventeen of these new justices issued an estimated 690 recognizances in 1715, 56% of the recognizances issued that year. Since the number of recognizances in 1715 was 606 more than in 1714, Cowper's justices must take the credit for making 1715 the highest year of Westminster recognizances in the period of this study. Like the peak in Middlesex recognizances in 1683, the cause of this increase must be primarily attributed to an influx of new justices, not to political and religious tensions. A quarter of the recognizances issued by the new justices were for political or religious offences (primarily for refusing to take the oaths of allegiance to the new regime), but the vast majority of the recognizances issued by the new justices were for offences against the peace. Cowper's additions also affected levels of prosecutions in Middlesex: it is highly probable that some of the 178 justices added in 1714 and 1715 were responsible for the peak of Middlesex

---

[62] PRO, C231/8; GLRO, WJP/L/1.
[63] The estimates of judicial activity in this paragraph are based on a 100% sample of the Westminster house of correction calendars for the first half of 1690, and a 50% sample of the calendars for 1693.
[64] PRO, C234/25; WJP/L3–4.

recognizances in 1716. Four years later, these justices were still playing a major role in the county's judicial business: they accounted for 26% of the recognizances in the 1720–22 sample and 30% of the commitments in the 1721 house of correction sample.[65] In 1718, Thomas Parker became Lord Chancellor and a new wave of appointments followed.[66] Between 1719 and 1721 he added seventy-nine new justices to the Westminster commission, including nine who issued 31% of the recognizances issued in 1721. In addition, fifteen of these justices made 22% of the commitments to the Westminster house of correction in 1721, thereby more than accounting for the increase in commitments over the two previous years.

The frequent manipulations of the commissions of the peace during the late seventeenth and early eighteenth centuries can thus be shown to have had a dramatic impact on the year-to-year fluctuations in the volume of criminal business heard by justices of the peace. (Although it is more difficult to prove, it is likely that these changes also affected the number of indictments which were filed.[67]) We cannot measure, however, the precise effect the removal or addition of justices had on the inclination of potential plaintiffs to prosecute. When their local justice was removed from the commission, did potential prosecutors bring their case before another, less familiar justice, who perhaps lived further away? Or, did they abandon their impulse to prosecute and attempt to resolve the dispute by some other method? Similarly, it is difficult to determine whether new justices actively sought business, possibly by encouraging disputants to prosecute, though contemporaries certainly thought that some justices, known as "trading justices" did so.[68] Although we cannot answer these questions directly, the preceding evidence strongly suggests that in many cases the availability of a specific justice determined whether or not an offence was prosecuted. The immediate decline in prosecutions when certain justices were removed from the commission certainly suggests that criminal business was not directly transferable from one justice to another. It is also very likely that zealous justices did actively encourage prosecutions. How else could a justice like William Conne or Charles Peter be responsible for hundreds of prosecutions within months of taking office?

---

[65] BL, Stowe MS. 228, f. 205; GLRO, MJP/L/1–2. The 1720–22 figure is based on a 17% sample of the recognizances issued between May 1720 and April 1722; the 1721 house of correction evidence is based on a 33% sample.

[66] PRO, C234/25; GLRO, WJP/L/9–10.

[67] Although their participation was not essential, individual justices of the peace also facilitated indictments by binding over defendants to appear at sessions to plead to their indictments. Since such judicial activity is not conveniently recorded, it is difficult to measure the impact of the efforts of individual justices on the number of indictments issued. The graph of indictments in Figure 2 follows a similar trend to that of recognizances in Figure 1, however, which suggests that many of the conclusions regarding recognizances in this section also apply to indictments.

[68] See below, section 8.4.

Levels of prosecutions were shaped by several factors, including the availability of cooperative justices and, for victimless offences, the enthusiasm of constables and informers. It is impossible to measure the precise importance of these factors, however, because with the possible exception of property offences (which on occasion appear to increase during periods of economic distress), neither the total number of crimes which actually occurred nor the propensity of private prosecutors to prosecute can be estimated. Thus, it is impossible to determine whether changing patterns of prosecutions should be explained in terms of changes in the number of crimes actually committed, shifts in the eagerness of plaintiffs to prosecute, alterations in the commissions of the peace, or some combination of these factors. The evidence presented here, however, strongly suggests that the most important factors which shaped year-to-year fluctuations in the number of misdemeanor prosecutions are the number of active justices of the peace who were available to facilitate (or encourage) prosecutions, and, in the case of victimless offences, the zeal of informers and parish officers in reporting and prosecuting offenders. Patterns of misdemeanor prosecutions thus demonstrate the considerable degree of flexibility possessed by justices of the peace and potential plaintiffs in choosing whether or not to prosecute petty crimes.

As we have seen, those who chose to prosecute possessed further flexibility, in the form of the choice of a procedure for prosecution (for most offences). It is now necessary to examine this choice in greater detail. Part II will identify the advantages and disadvantages of each procedure, from the point of view of not only plaintiffs and justices but also defendants.

Part II

PROCEDURES FOR PROSECUTION

4

Informal mediation by justices of the peace

Most criminal prosecutions began when a plaintiff reported the offence to a justice of the peace, and a significant proportion of such accusations were resolved informally by the justice without further legal action. Although prosecutions resulting in informal settlements are the most poorly documented of all prosecutions, the nature and importance of informal mediation by justices of the peace is apparent from justices' notebooks and other records. Tables 3.1 and 3.2 document that justices Norris and Hunt were able to mediate informally a broad range of offences including assault, petty theft, poor law offences, and disputes between employers and their employees. Nevertheless, informal mediation was not suitable for every type of offence and offender, and particularly in an urban environment there were several obstacles to informal settlements.

4.1 TYPES OF SETTLEMENTS

The term "informal mediation" includes several different methods by which justices responded to criminal accusations; the common denominator of these is that the case was resolved without further legal action, whether in the form of a summary conviction or referral of the case to quarter sessions by a recognizance or commitment to prison. Upon hearing a criminal accusation, justices normally issued a warrant or a summons for the accused to appear before a justice. Once a constable apprehended the accused and notified the plaintiff, the parties were brought before a justice, not necessarily the same one who issued the original warrant, for a hearing. Since a few days often elapsed between the original warrant and the hearing, the parties occasionally reached a settlement on their own before the hearing.[1] Upon learning this, the justice would almost certainly discharge the defendant, unless, as noted below, he thought that the crime was a felony.

In most cases, on the appearance of the parties the justice held a hearing,

---

[1] GLRO, M79/X/I, 6 Dec. 1731 and 4 May 1732.

interrogating both of the parties involved. At this point, the justice often suggested or "recommended" that the parties reach an informal settlement, often by suggesting that the defendant pay some form of compensation for the wrong.[2] Different types of compensation were used, depending on the nature and circumstances of the offence and the offender. In some cases, defendants were simply requested to apologize, promise not to offend again, or make a "submission,"[3] either orally or in writing. After Sarah Bryant complained to justice Hunt in 1747 that William Lewis had illegally roamed "about her mother's house at unseasonable times of the night," the dispute was settled when "the defendant gave a note of hand never to molest the complainant again."[4] In the case of victimless offences, it was the justice who received the apologies. Joseph Ratcliffe, accused of allowing a puppet show to be performed in his alehouse, was forgiven by the justices at the Hackney petty sessions "upon his making a proper submission and begging pardon for what he hath done and promising never to be guilty for the future."[5] In cases of theft or damage to property defendants were usually required to return the stolen goods, repair the damaged property, or pay damages to the plaintiff. When a poor man broke fourteen panes of glass in 1682, the Middlesex justice ordered him to repair them.[6]

The payment of monetary damages was particularly common with offences against the peace, though the amount of compensation varied greatly, apparently not always according to the severity of the offence. Lesser offences were resolved with the payment of damages of as little as 16d. in a case of scandalous words and 2s. 6d. for unspecified "abuse."[7] Compensation for more serious crimes varied from only one shilling and the cost of "the cure of [the victim's] head" for a beating, 4s. for a violent assault in the face with a pick, and 7s. 6d. for "violently assaulting and beating ... and threatening to wrift [sic] [the defendant's] neck," to 13s. 6d. for a violent assault and forcible theft of an apron, and two guineas (£2 2s.) for beating the plaintiff "several times."[8] Given the brief entries in justices' notebooks, the differences between these sums are difficult to explain. It is likely that factors other than the severity of the crime were taken into account, such as the wealth of the defendant, the nature of the relationship between the defendant and the plaintiff, whether or not the plaintiff threatened to file a formal prosecution, and the attitude of the

---

[2] For example, see M79/X/I, 26 Jan. 1741.   [3] M79/X/I, 28 May 1735.
[4] *The Justicing Notebook of William Hunt 1744–49*, ed. Elizabeth Crittall, Wiltshire Record Society vol. 37 (Devizes 1982), case 422.
[5] GLRO, P79/JN1/214, 28 Feb. 1732; see also 19 June 1732.
[6] MJ/SR/1616, R. 220 (Sept. 1682); see also MJ/SP/April 1712, no. 19.
[7] MJ/SR/1284, R. 105 (April 1664); *Justicing Notebook of William Hunt*, case 107.
[8] *Justicing Notebook of William Hunt*, cases 160, 413, 480, 497; M79/X/I, 25 June 1733. In one case heard by Hunt (case 402) both the defendant and the plaintiff entered into bonds of £100 "never to offend each other" again.

justice. Some justices and plaintiffs certainly drove a hard bargain; in a case of broken windows and assault in 1746, justice Hunt required the three defendants "to pay for the examination and the warrant, for the loss of the complainant's and witnesses' time, for my clerk's time and attendance, and likewise for mending the windows, the whole amounting to 18s. 4d."[9] It is possible that in cases like this the plaintiff was prepared to file (or had already filed) a civil suit for damages, and therefore his demand for monetary compensation was conditioned by what could be obtained at law.

Instead of merely recommending settlements, in some cases justices adopted a more assertive approach and "ordered" or "adjudged" defendants to agree to an informal settlement. Such cases account for 10% of the criminal accusations heard by William Hunt. Upon hearing a complaint against Robert Jones for assaulting and beating Henry Franklyn on the highway, justice Hunt wrote that "I found [Jones'] abuse so great that I adjudged the said Jones to pay Mr. Franklyn £4. 4s. and all charges of prosecution, which he did accordingly, and Mr. Franklyn forgave him."[10] In other cases Hunt "ordered" the defendant to compensate for the wrong in a specified manner. The term "ordered" underlines the ambiguous legal status of many decisions made by justices outside sessions, which can be interpreted either as informal settlements or as legally binding orders or summary convictions. When justices issued orders in poor law cases, disputes between servants and their masters, cases of failure to pay wages (in certain occupations), and petty thefts of wood, fruit or vegetables, their actions could be characterized as a form of summary jurisdiction authorized by statute. Some of these statutes encouraged relatively informal methods of resolving disputes. Thus, the statute of artificers advised justices to try to resolve conflicts between servants and apprentices and their masters privately, "according to the equity of the case."[11] In the case of petty thefts of wood, fruit, or vegetables, justices were given the flexibility to determine the amount of the fine (to be given to the poor) and the amount of compensation to be paid to the victim. In such cases, justice Hunt "adjusted the fines according to the circumstances of the offender and sometimes remitted them entirely."[12] Similarly, Sarah Chandler, who confessed to having gathered fallen fruit from a fenced-in garden, was dismissed by justice Norris with a reprimand at the plaintiff's request.[13]

The flexibility accorded to justices by statutes and the limitations of justices' notebooks as a source thus often make it difficult to distinguish between cases of informal mediation and summary convictions or legally binding orders.

---

[9] *Justicing Notebook of William Hunt*, case 343.
[10] *Justicing Notebook of William Hunt*, case 311. See also cases 109 and 239.
[11] 5 Eliz. c. 4, s. 5, 35; [Whitelocke Bulstrode], *Laws Concerning the Poor*, 4th edn (1720), p. 261. An example of this procedure is provided below.
[12] 43 Eliz. c. 7; 15 Car. 2 c. 2; *Justicing Notebook of William Hunt*, pp. 14–15.
[13] M79/X/I, 4 Sept. 1740. See also *Justicing Notebook of William Hunt*, case 322.

While this ambiguity presents problems of interpretation for the historian bent on categorizing cases, it was not an issue which concerned contemporary justices. It is significant that Hunt used the same language of "orders" to refer to his judgements in cases of assault, where justices clearly had no power to issue summary convictions, as for his convictions in cases of petty theft or damage to property, where he was acting by statutory authority. Thus, Hunt "ordered" Robert Martin to pay Elizabeth Whitley 1s. 6d. for an assault and "convicted" William Harroway and Anne Robbince of a violent assault and ordered them to pay for the warrant.[14] Because justices' legal powers were manifold and flexible, their actions in informal settlements often assumed a mantle of legal authority which they technically did not possess.

Defendants accepted justices' efforts at informal mediation, whether they took the form of suggestions of possible settlements or "orders," for several reasons. Most defendants (and plaintiffs) preferred to avoid the considerable trouble and expense of further legal action, and many wished to avoid the scandal of being publicly prosecuted in court. A millwright accused of a felony, "being tender of his good name ... and for avoiding the scandal," illegally paid £10 to the prosecutor to drop the charge.[15] Moreover, justices often possessed considerable influence over defendants. As individuals, justices typically were respected members of their communities. As justices of the peace, they possessed substantial supervisory powers in matters of local government (such as poor relief and taxation) which gave them additional power over their neighbors. Most importantly, if attempts at informal mediation failed justices always possessed the power to bind defendants over by recognizance to appear at quarter sessions or to commit them to a house of correction. After hearing a complaint against Henry Bedford for an assault in 1735, Henry Norris began to write out a recognizance for Bedford's appearance at sessions. Subsequently, he crossed out the recognizance and marked the case "agreed."[16] Similarly, after justice Hunt heard a complaint against five women for an assault, "their *mittimus* was made to the house of correction, but afterwards [they] were released by consent of the parties paying charges."[17] Through the threat of further legal action, defendants were induced to accept the informal settlements that justices proposed.

Plaintiffs benefitted from informal mediation in two ways. First, informal settlements often involved compensation for the victim, whereas formal prosecutions rarely did so. For the victim of an assault or broken windows, an

---

[14] *Justicing Notebook of William Hunt*, cases 170, 338.
[15] MJ/SR/1294, R.165 (Oct. 1664). For the costs of prosecution, see sections 5.4, 6.3 and 7.4.
[16] M79/X/I, 29 Aug. 1735. See also Bodleian Library, MS Rawlinson D1137, Diary of Sir Thomas Sclater, 5 Sept. 1668 and 4 Oct. 1670; P79/JN1/214, 23 April and 4 June 1733.
[17] *Justicing Notebook of William Hunt*, case 230.

informal settlement with compensation for medical expenses or the cost of repairing the window must have been far more attractive than a formal conviction with a fine payable to the king. Second, plaintiffs were spared the costs, both financial and emotional, of a formal prosecution. With regard to the latter, it has been argued that litigation during this period was regarded as "a breach of proper neighborly relations," and that litigants were under some pressure from justices and their neighbors to settle disputes informally.[18] When John Hare was apprehended by a constable in 1712 for assaulting and beating two women, "he by the constable and others offered to agree to it and make what reparation we [the victims] would in reason demand." When the victims refused to negotiate, the frustrated justice discharged Hare without punishment.[19] From the point of view of the community, informal settlements were desirable as a means of preserving social harmony.

Justices both expected and pressured disputants to settle informally because it enhanced their authority and reputation in the community. Informal mediation was one of the duties incumbent upon prominent members of the community, regardless of whether or not they were justices.[20] Since they had the flexibility to recommend a settlement which took into consideration the interests of both parties, justices could win local respect by reducing tensions in the community. Unlike a formal prosecution, with informal mediation both defendant and plaintiff could be found guilty. When Elizabeth North accused William Austen of assaulting her "divers times," the justices at a petty sessions in Hackney "made up the matter between [them] being both something in fault."[21] It was easier for justices to tailor punishments to the specific circumstances of the case when the defendant had not been formally convicted and a punishment was not prescribed by statute. Moreover, justices concerned about their popularity could use informal mediation to mitigate the enforcement of unpopular laws, such as those against conventicles and vice.[22] Justices could also use informal mediation to gain the loyalty of specific individuals or social groups. Contemporary writers commented that a justice's local reputation was contingent upon his being sympathetic to the common people. On hearing complaints it was alleged that some justices, seeking to profit from

---

[18] Sharpe, "'Such disagreement betwyx neighbors'," p. 175. See also J. A. Sharpe, "Enforcing the law in the seventeenth-century English village," in *Crime and the Law: The Social History of Crime in Western Europe since 1500*, ed. V. A. C. Gatrell *et al.* (1980), pp. 111–12; Martin J. Ingram, "Communities and courts: law and disorder in early seventeenth-century Wiltshire," in *Crime in England*, ed. Cockburn, pp. 117, 127.

[19] MJ/SP/April 1712, no. 30.

[20] Herrup, *Common Peace*, p. 54; Anthony Fletcher, *Reform in the Provinces* (1986), pp. 66–69.

[21] M79/X/I, 17 Feb. 1733. See also 10 June 1734 and 18 Dec. 1738.

[22] For conventicles, see *The Diary and Autobiography of Edmund Bohun Esq.* (1853), ed. S. Wilton Rix, p. 37. For vice, see below, section 9.2.

having men "always at [their] devotion," showed "sympathy ... to the inferior fellow."[23] In fact, informal mediation gave justices sufficient flexibility to win the favor of anyone who might be able to render them a service.

4.2 LIMITS OF MEDIATION

If informal mediation was to lead to successful resolutions of disputes, the cooperation of all three parties to the prosecution – the defendant, the plaintiff and the justice – was necessary. Whether defendants and plaintiffs were willing to agree to, and abide by, informal settlements depended on several factors, not the least whether they respected the justice who acted as mediator. Thomas Evans' insult to justice Samuel Blackerby in 1709, "calling him hell fire son of a bitch and saying he would not do him justice," suggests that Evans, who was accused of keeping a disorderly alehouse, was unwilling to negotiate an informal settlement with Blackerby. Equally disrespectful was the man who told justice John Gonson in 1721 that "he valued him no more than the dirt under his foot."[24] Clearly, these are isolated examples, and it is difficult to generalize about the extent of, or the conditions which prompted, the kind of disrespect for justices which hindered their attempts at informal mediation. Two situations in particular, however, appear to have encouraged such disrespect. First, justices who systematically enforced unpopular laws, such as the laws against vice, were likely to be unsuccessful mediators. Thus justices, such as John Gonson, who supported the reformation of manners campaign were often the target of insults or riots.[25] Second, it was alleged that the frequent politically motivated alterations in the commissions of the peace during the age of party lowered the social status, qualifications, and general reputation of justices of the peace.[26] Samuel Blackerby, for example, was a lawyer who had only recently been appointed to the Westminster commission, and he may have lacked the social authority necessary to mediate disputes.

More commonly, informal mediation collapsed because the defendant proved recalcitrant. When Mary Cole called Alice Joell in 1664 a "pocky whore and common whore to footmen," Joell went before justice Thomas Swalowe, who summoned Cole and "friendly composed" the dispute by ordering Cole to pay Joell 16d. for the injury. The next day, however, Cole

---

[23] Timothy Nourse, *Campania Foelix; or, a Discourse of the Benefits and Improvements of Husbandry* (1700), p. 264. See also *Justice of Peace, his Calling: a Moral Essay* (1684), p. 113. Peter King has argued that justices' decisions in poor relief cases and disputes over conditions of work often favored the poor ("Crime, law, and society," pp. 279, 286).

[24] MJ/SR/2136, R. 19 (Sept. 1709); 2374, R. 181 (Oct. 1721). See also MJ/SR/1282, R. 5 (Feb. 1664).

[25] MJ/SR/2373, R. 103 (Westminster sessions, Oct. 1721); Nicholas Rogers, "Popular protest in early Hanoverian London," *Past and Present* 79 (1978), pp. 91–92 and n.82. Gonson is depicted in Plate 3.

[26] See above, section 3.3.

repeated the offensive words, adding "that for sixteen pence more she could at any time call her ... or any of them whores again." Consequently, Cole was bound over by recognizance to appear at quarter sessions.[27] Although plaintiffs and justices were often willing to consent to an informal agreement for a first offence, if further offences occurred they were likely to initiate a formal prosecution. Some victims, however, were willing to put up with repeated offences before finally resorting to quarter sessions. Thirteen neighbors finally petitioned the court to take action against Richard Bradbery and his wife Sisley for frequently breaking the peace and making slanderous speeches, after having "often borne with them from time to time hoping to see some amendment of their lives, but we find it otherwise ..."[28] As Edmund Bohun complained, some offenders who had no intention of compromising with plaintiffs took advantage of their tolerance and patience in order to avoid punishment: "there may be some who may be compelled though they cannot be persuaded, and who have no greater pleasure than to concoct delays; by means of which ... they may defeat the innocent."[29]

In order to avoid such insincere defendants, plaintiffs were less willing to consent to informal mediation if the defendant was known to have committed other offences or was considered to have a bad character. In 1700 Timothy Nourse claimed that "there are many stubborn, cross-grained rogues ... to reform these by soft admonitions and persuasive methods, is all one as to polish and civilize a wolf by reading of moral lectures."[30] Thus, the Suffolk justice Abraham Oakes was unwilling to accept the apologies of John Farrant, a delinquent servant, who promised that he would return to service and "be more diligent." Oakes claimed that Farrant had "an ill character ... by reason he has known the said Farrant to do penance in the parish church for his crimes and misbehavior," and committed him to the house of correction.[31]

Plaintiffs were also less willing to consent to informal mediation for offences where the legitimacy of the law was itself in dispute. In rural areas, the game laws, enclosure laws, and laws against wood stealing and gleaning were unpopular because it was believed that they infringed upon common rights.[32] In both rural and urban areas, disagreements arose between 1664 and 1688 over the conventicle laws and between 1690 and 1738 over the prosecution of

---

[27] MJ/SR/1284, R.105 (April 1664). See also MJ/SR/1293, R.66 (Westminster sessions, Oct. 1664).
[28] GLRO, Acc. 203/11 (undated).   [29] *Diary of Edmund Bohun*, p. 10.
[30] Nourse, *Campania Foelix*, pp. 273–74.
[31] PRO, KB 1/2, Hilary 8 Geo. I, 60, 62.
[32] Douglas Hay, "Poaching and the game laws in Cannock Chase," in *Albion's Fatal Tree*, ed. Hay *et al.*, pp. 189–253; P. B. Munsche, *Gentlemen and Poachers: The English Game Laws 1671–1831* (Cambridge, 1981), pp. 107–09 (though Munsche argues that the most significant opposition to the laws occurred after the mid-eighteenth century); Bob Bushaway, *By Rite: Custom, Ceremony, and Community in England 1700–1880* (1982), chap. 6; Peter King, "Gleaners, farmers and the failure of legal sanctions in England 1750–1850," *Past and Present* 125 (1989), pp. 116–50.

vice.[33] Where plaintiffs and defendants differed on the legitimacy of a law, plaintiffs were unlikely to trust defendants to abide by an informal settlement. Only two of the forty-one cases of vice and hunting offences heard by William Hunt and Henry Norris, for which the disposition is known, were settled by an informal agreement. Only 26% of the cases of wood stealing brought before justice Hunt were resolved informally, compared to 65% of all other offences. At the St. Margaret's petty sessions on June 26, 1723, which was conducted by two justices active in the reformation of manners campaign, only one out of eighteen alehouse keepers summoned to attend for permitting drinking during the time of divine service escaped punishment.[34]

The difficulty with mediating accusations of vice informally lay not only with the lack of popular support for the laws against vice. The typical settlements resulting from informal mediation were unacceptable to the members of the Societies for the Reformation of Manners. A promise not to offend again would have meant little, given the high rate of recidivism for vice[35] and the fact that informers were often not personally acquainted with their victims. Because of the damaging charges of hypocrisy and corruption levelled against the reformers,[36] informers were not allowed to accept informal payments of damages. Such payments could be interpreted as punishment and compensation for past wrongs, but they could also be interpreted (as they often were) as bribes to prevent prosecutions. More fundamentally, the reformers questioned whether private informal settlements properly punished defendants for wrongs done to society as a whole. As the reformers phrased this problem, for offences "against God and the public laws ... 'tis not in a private man's power to forgive the injury to the public, as he may do a pecuniary debt that is owing to himself."[37] The reformers feared that an accumulation of unpunished sins would result in divine punishment for the whole country.[38]

While plaintiffs were unwilling to accept informal settlements for offences

---

[33] For opposition to the conventicle laws, see Tim Harris, *London Crowds in the Reign of Charles II* (Cambridge, 1987), chap. 4. For opposition to attempts to enforce the laws against vice, see below, chap. 9.

[34] See above, Tables 3.1 and 3.2. Westminster City Archives, St. Margaret's Westminster petty sessions minutes.

[35] See below, section 7.4.

[36] For example, see Daniel Defoe, *Reformation of Manners, A Satyr* (1702), pp. 5–6; Daniel Dolins, *The Charge of Sir Daniel Dolins, Kt. to the Grand Jury and Other Juries of the County of Middlesex* (1725), pp. 25–28; *An Account of the Endeavours that have been used to Suppress Gaming Houses* (1722), pp. 8–9.

[37] John Shower, *A Sermon Preached to the Societies for the Reformation of Manners* (1698), p. 15. Shower thought that informal settlements were acceptable, however, for first or second offenders, those who were victims of "the frailty of human nature," friends of the prosecutor, and "persons of quality," for whom a conviction "would be likely to do more hurt than good" (pp. 41–45).

[38] D. W. R. Bahlman, *The Moral Revolution of 1688* (New Haven, 1957), pp. 10–14. The fact that individual crimes harmed not only the victim but society as well was also a problem in cases of theft, where compounding the crime was itself illegal. See above, section 2.1.

against controversial laws, justices of the peace were often unwilling to preside over informal settlements of felonies and other serious crimes. Because under the Marian bail statutes justices were required to forward cases of felony to quarter sessions or a court of gaol delivery, justices were reluctant to preside over informal agreements in such cases.[39] Although informal settlements of felony accusations did occur,[40] justices' notebooks show clearly that cases of theft (all thefts were felonies) were far less likely to be informally settled than offences against the peace.[41] Henry Norris was particularly careful not to discharge defendants in property cases until he was certain that there was insufficient evidence or that the case was not a felony.[42] Similarly, he was unwilling to allow an informal settlement in a case of violent assault until it was clear that the victim's wounds would be cured; if the victim had died, the defendant could have been charged with murder.[43] Justice Hunt, on the other hand, was far less cautious when he heard accusations of felonies and other serious offences. While Norris settled informally only one of the thirty-four cases of theft he heard which could not be determined by summary conviction, Hunt settled six of twenty-three.[44] A case of the night-time theft of "two wheels for spinning turns" in 1748, for example, was settled under Hunt's supervision by the payment of "9s. for damages and all expenses of prosecution" to the plaintiff.[45] Hunt even settled a case of attempted rape, by ordering the defendant to pay five guineas (£5 5s.) damages and enter into a bond of £100 never to molest the victim or her husband again.[46] Although attempted rape was not a felony, in Middlesex it was treated as a "heinous and notorious" offence which justices were prohibited from settling informally.[47] It is likely that the more litigious environment of the metropolis forced Middlesex justices, including Henry Norris, to act more cautiously than rural justices such as William Hunt.

In sum, despite its evident advantages, informal mediation could not succeed without the cooperation of all the parties involved. Disputes often resulted in a

---

[39] For the Marian statutes, see John H. Langbein, *Prosecuting Crime in the Renaissance: England, Germany, France* (Cambridge, Mass., 1974), Part One.

[40] King, "Crime, law and society," pp. 258, 262.

[41] Tables 3.1 and 3.2; John Beattie, "Judicial records and the measurement of crime in eighteenth-century England," in *Crime and Criminal Justice in Europe and Canada*, ed. Louis A. Knafla (Waterloo, Ontario, 1981), pp. 131–32, citing Elizabeth Silverthorne, ed., *Deposition Book of Richard Wyatt, J.P., 1767–1776*, Surrey Record Society, vol. 30 (Guildford, 1978).

[42] M79/X/I, 5 Oct. 1738, 30 May 1735. The latter case, described by Norris as "not appearing to be a felony," involved a man who had "run away" with a "dung fork" and spade belonging to the plaintiff.

[43] M79/X/I, 19 May 1737.

[44] These figures do not include cases in which the disposition is unknown.

[45] *Justicing Notebook of William Hunt*, case 485.   [46] *Ibid.*, case 239.

[47] MJ/SP/Dec. 1722, no. 54. One reason why the court treated cases of attempted rape so seriously may have been the fact that women often prosecuted their attackers for attempted rape even when a rape had actually occurred (Beattie, *Crime and the Courts*, pp. 129–30).

formal prosecution if the defendant proved recalcitrant, or if for any reason the plaintiff or the justice did not trust the defendant. Plaintiffs were particularly likely to press for the formal prosecution of offences where the legitimacy of the law itself was in question. Legal requirements, moreover, discouraged justices from facilitating informal settlements of felonies and other serious offences.

4.3 INFORMAL MEDIATION IN AN URBAN SETTING

Because of the paucity of surviving evidence, much of the preceding discussion has been based on the evidence of justices who lived and acted in rural areas. Although the conclusions must be largely speculative, it is necessary to consider how well informal mediation worked in the contrasting social environment of the metropolis. In the towns of Languedoc in the late eighteenth century, social mobility disrupted the traditional role of private mediators (such as the *seigneurs*) and disputants increasingly came to rely on the services of judges and other state officials as mediators.[48] Similarly, while several aspects of London life appear to have inhibited informal settlements, the evidence suggests that informal mediation by justices of the peace thrived. Henry Norris of Hackney, the most urban justice for whom a detailed notebook survives, settled informally 38% of the criminal accusations brought before him between 1730 and 1741.[49]

The range of disputes which justices were willing to mediate in London, however, was narrower than in the country. As we have seen, Norris was particularly reluctant to allow informal settlements in cases which might be indictable as felonies. Norris was clearly aware of the growing body of "Newgate" or "Old Bailey" solicitors who filed suits against justices who acted improperly. Thomas DeVeil warned justices in 1747 not to dismiss defendants, even at the request of the prosecutor, until they were certain that the offence was not a felony.[50] DeVeil also advised justices to be wary of interfering in property disputes, which were properly resolved in the civil courts, and disputes concerning unpaid wages, which were only within the justices' jurisdiction for servants in husbandry.[51] Although the legal status of justices' orders concerning unpaid wages in other occupations was uncertain, and the practice of issuing such orders clearly continued,[52] DeVeil's warnings were well

---

[48] Nicole Castan, "The arbitration of disputes under the 'ancien régime'," *Disputes and Settlements*, ed. Bossy, pp. 219–60.

[49] Table 3.1.   [50] Norris was particularly cautious about this: M79/X/I,15 and 19 May, 1732.

[51] Thomas DeVeil, *Observations on the Practice of a Justice of the Peace* (1747), pp. 1–16; William Holdsworth, *A History of English Law*, 12 vols. (1923–72), vol. 11, pp. 467–68.

[52] Thomas Leach, *Modern Reports*, 12 vols. 5th edn (1793–96), vol. 6, p. 204; Sir John Strange, *Reports of Adjudged Cases in the Courts of Chancery, King's Bench, Common Pleas, and Exchequer* (2 vols., 3rd edn, 1795), vol. 2, p. 1002; R. Keith Kelsall, "Wage regulation under the statute of artificers," in *Wage Regulation in Preindustrial England*, ed. W. E. Minchinton (Newton Abbot, 1972), pp. 136–37.

founded: more than one action was filed during this period against Middlesex justices for issuing improper orders concerning wages.[53] Given their ambiguous legal status, even informal settlements of wages cases left justices open to charges of acting outside their jurisdiction. Significantly, while justice Hunt heard twelve cases involving unpaid wages in Wiltshire, Norris heard only two in Middlesex. As suggested by Norris' apparent reluctance to hear wage disputes, the danger of being sued constricted the range of disputes London justices were willing to settle informally.[54]

Urban justices also faced the problem that their fellow justices occasionally interfered in cases they were trying to settle informally. At least forty justices heard criminal complaints in urban Middlesex (including Westminster) during each of the years sampled during this period. The concentration of justices was especially high in the west end: in Westminster in the early 1720s, about fifteen justices issued fifteen or more recognizances a year.[55] Finding another justice to intervene on a defendant's behalf with a counter prosecution, in lieu of accepting a justice's offer of an informal agreement, was not difficult. Justice John Robinson bound Elizabeth Caviller over to appear at sessions in 1664, because "when I had ordered a difference between her and a very poor creature her late servant, in spite of me she procured a warrant [from another j.p.] and committed the wench to Bridewell."[56] Complaints that justices interfered with each other's criminal business occurred frequently in Middlesex during this period.[57] Edward Chamberlayne, a justice who claimed to have facilitated many informal settlements, complained in 1696 about another justice who, jealous of Chamberlayne's authority in his parish, had directed "nothing but spite and malice and false stories" against him for two years.[58] Informal mediation was unlikely to succeed when fellow justices undermined each other's authority.

Finally, both justices and plaintiffs may have been reluctant to trust urban defendants to abide by informal settlements. Informal mediation worked best among people who knew each other, since the defendant's word could be trusted and if further trouble occurred the defendant could easily be appre-

---

[53] J. Harvey, *A Collection of Precedents Relating to the Office of a Justice of the Peace* (1730), pp. iv–vii; [Bulstrode], *Laws Concerning the Poor*, p. 264; Sir Thomas Jones, *Reports of Several Special Cases Adjudged in the Courts of King's Bench and Common Pleas* (2nd edn, 1729), p. 47. For suits against metropolitan justices, see also Landau, *Justices of the Peace*, p. 354.

[54] Concern about such litigation appears to have increased significantly in the early eighteenth century. While Middlesex justices frequently issued recognizances against employers who failed to pay wages in years sampled from the late seventeenth century, they issued none in the 1720–22 sample.

[55] This calculation is based on the 17% sample of recognizances issued between May 1720 and April 1722.

[56] MJ/SR/1286, R.134 (May 1664).   [57] Below, section 8.4.

[58] MJ/SP/Sept. 1696, no. 29. Chamberlayne was the author of *Angliae Notitia*, the guide to English social and political conditions that went through twenty editions between 1669 and 1702.

hended and punished. Eighty-two percent of the cases heard by justice Hunt in which the parties knew each other as husband/wife, master/servant, or house-holder/lodger were settled informally or by "order." When Anne Davis charged Elizabeth Kyte with the theft of three pewter dishes, justice Hunt persuaded them to settle the dispute informally, "they being all near rela-tions."[59] According to a supporter of the reformation of manners campaign, if the parties knew each other even accusations concerning vice could be inform-ally settled.[60] Cases in which the parties lived in the same parish were also more likely to be settled informally. In justice Hunt's notebook, 66% of the cases in which the parties lived in the same parish were settled informally or by "order," while the corresponding figure for parties who lived in different parishes was 58%. Similarly, Martin Ingram concluded that informal medi-ation in seventeenth-century Wiltshire "worked in favour of local people and against strangers."[61] Informal settlements between parties who lived in the same parish succeeded not only because the parties knew each other. Where a sense of neighborhood existed, local opinion could help enforce settlements. When John Boddington, an apprentice, affronted a gentlewoman in 1664, the Middlesex justice ordered him to acknowledge his fault "in the presence of the officer and neighbours before whom he had so abused her," thus enlisting community pressure to ensure the success of the informal settlement.[62]

While there is reason to believe that the anonymity of urban life in preindus-trial England has been overestimated, it is very probable that many London neighborhoods experienced a higher degree of geographical mobility than many rural parishes.[63] It seems likely that such mobility inhibited informal settlements, especially when one of the parties was a newcomer to the metro-polis who was poor and/or had few local connections and was thus less likely to trust or be trusted by others.

Despite the obstacles to informal settlements, there may, as suggested earlier, have been a greater demand for judicial mediation in cities than in rural areas, especially among the poor. Norma Landau has demonstrated that urban justices in eighteenth-century Kent heard more criminal accusations than rural justices. As in eighteenth-century Languedoc, Landau argues that because there were fewer people available to serve as non-judicial mediators in urban areas, both women and the poor were more likely to seek the help of

---

[59] *Justicing Notebook of William Hunt*, case 212. See also p. 12.
[60] Shower, *Sermon*, pp. 41–45.
[61] Ingram, "Communities and courts," p. 127.   [62] MJ/SR/1291, R.158 (Sept. 1664).
[63] See above, section 1.2. Jeremy Boulton's study of residential mobility in the Boroughside district of Southwark revealed rates of persistence only marginally lower than those that have been discovered for rural areas (*Neighbourhood and Society*, p. 217). The Boroughside, however, may have been atypical of urban parishes. Persistence in the Boroughside may have been encouraged by the relative wealth of its inhabitants and its strong local government, which was able to keep out poorer immigrants.

justices.[64] Unable to afford the cost of a formal prosecution, the urban poor were particularly likely to ask justices to intervene informally in their disputes, even if they had to pay a small fee for the service. Justice Edward Chamberlayne, whose complaint that a fellow justice had maliciously attacked him was cited above, boasted in the same letter that "all in our parish and in several adjacent parishes chose rather to make their addresses to me because I never treated any roughly and insultingly but endeavoured reconciliation and saving charges especially amongst the poorer sort in a mild way."[65] Chamberlayne, who lived on the periphery of the metropolis in Chelsea, was clearly confronted with frequent demands from the poor for informal judicial mediation.

Partly as a consequence of the demands of the urban poor for judicial mediation, the "trading justice" developed in the metropolis. Because eminent gentlemen refused to serve as justices in urban parishes where the poor created a substantial amount of judicial business, lesser men who depended on judicial fees for their livelihood were appointed to the commission of the peace. Although these justices were generally held in low esteem, it was noted in 1748 that "the common people ... apply to [trading justices] upon every trivial occasion, to gratify their own spleen and malice against their neighbours." Norma Landau has shown that trading justices in urban Kent made their living by charging fees for mediating disputes by issuing recognizances and then releasing them and by convicting defendants for profane swearing and cursing. Although there is no evidence that justices used these particular practices in Middlesex, it is possible that some metropolitan justices earned their income by issuing recognizances without releasing them.[66] Recognizance evidence certainly suggests that several Middlesex justices specialized in mediating the disputes in which they issued recognizances, though these justices did not hear only the disputes of the poor.[67] Disputes cannot strictly speaking be said to have been informally mediated when a formal legal document such as a recognizance was issued. Nevertheless, if the document was only issued as a means of charging a fee after a settlement had been reached and the plaintiff had no intention of using the document for its intended purpose, it can be said that the dispute was informally settled. Despite the obstacles posed by the

---

[64] Landau, *Justices of the Peace*, pp. 178, 194–203. Landau also argues that one institution for resolving disputes among women in rural areas, the skimmington (also known as ridings or charivaris), did not occur in urban areas. Riots which served a similar function to skimmingtons did occur, however, in eighteenth-century London (Shoemaker, "London 'mob'," pp. 278, 291–92).

[65] MJ/SP/Sept. 1696, no. 29.

[66] *Memoirs of the Life and Times of Sir Thomas DeVeil* (1748), p. 18; Landau, *Justices of the Peace*, pp. 184–90, 198–201. Middlesex justices did not release recognizances (below, section 5.2).

[67] See below, section 8.4

urban setting, informal judicial mediation persisted in London, but with a new dimension: some justices made it profitable.

Judicial mediation was most commonly used to settle minor criminal disputes between disputants who lived in the same area. Its desirability lay in its low cost, convenience, and flexibility, which allowed the justice to suggest a settlement which satisfied the demands of both parties. Informal mediation worked best, however, in parishes with stable social relations where residents knew each other, the justice's authority was well established and neighborhood opinion could help enforce a settlement. Except when practiced by "trading justices," it was less likely to be successful in urban neighborhoods, where frequent geographical mobility and competing justices undermined informal settlements. In any case, informal mediation often failed even in stable parishes. Plaintiffs were frequently unwilling to trust defendants, defendants were uncooperative, and plaintiffs and defendants often differed over the legitimacy of the law in question. Plaintiffs in these cases demanded further legal action. Unless the case was a felony, the most common next step was for the justice to bind the defendant over by recognizance to appear at sessions. The plaintiff could decide whether or not to file an indictment when sessions met.

5

Binding over by recognizance

It is only recently that historians have discerned the multifaceted role that the recognizance played in the prosecution of crime.[1] Because many recognizances required defendants to appear in court to answer indictments, most historians of crime have treated them as incidental to their central interest, trial by indictment.[2] Consequently, the different social and legal functions of recognizances and indictments have often been misunderstood. While most defendants indicted for petty offences were, at one time or another, bound over to ensure their appearance in court in order to enter a plea to an indictment or to stand trial, recognizances were much more frequently used as an *alternative* to filing an indictment. Although binding over by itself could not result in a formal conviction or court-ordered punishment, it often successfully resolved a dispute without further legal action; not much more than a fifth of the defendants bound over were subsequently indicted. Because the social costs and consequences of prosecution by recognizance alone differed considerably from those of prosecution by recognizance and indictment together, very different circumstances and motivations led to the choice of each procedure.[3] This chapter, therefore, excludes recognizances that were issued primarily for the purpose of requiring a defendant to appear in court to answer an existing indictment and concentrates on recognizances for defendants who had not been indicted at the time they were bound over. Prosecution by indictment will be considered in chapter 6.[4]

Like informal mediation, recognizances were used to address a wide variety of petty disputes and criminal accusations. And like mediation, recognizances

[1] Compare *Middlesex Records*, ed. Jeaffreson, vol. 1, p. xlviii, to Joel Samaha, "The recognizance in Elizabethan law enforcement," *American Journal of Legal History* 25 (1981), p. 189 and Landau, *Justices of the Peace*, chap. 6.
[2] The neglect of recognizances has also been encouraged by the preoccupation of historians with felonies, where bail was difficult to obtain and few defendants were bound over. In any case, recognizances to attend assizes have not survived for many counties (Beattie, *Crime and the Courts*, p. 22; Sharpe, *Crime in Seventeenth-Century England*, pp. 11–12).
[3] See above, section 2.4.
[4] As noted in section 2.2, besides requiring a defendant to appear at quarter sessions, recognizances were also used for other purposes which lie outside the scope of this study.

Table 5.1 Offences and dispositions of recognizances: defendants not previously indicted[a]

	Misc. &[b] unknown	Appeared and discharged	Delinquent[c]	Indicted	Total (N = 100%)
	%	%	%	%	
Peace					
Keep the peace	2	78	8	12	290
Assault	3	61	12	24	580
Riot	4.5	60	13	22	134
Common disturber/ defamation	3.5	72	9	15	144
Poor law					
Servant or apprentice disputes	5	63	12	21	43
Loose, idle, and disorderly person	8	62.5	21	8	24
Poor relief	31	44	20	5	75
Vice					
Sexual offences	3	65	26	6	124
Alehouse offences	7	67	18.5	7	27
Gaming	15	52	22	11	27
Property					
Theft	8	44	13.5	34	178
Trespassing/damage	15	67	7	11	27
Fraud	13	54	7	26	70
Regulatory					
Neglect of office	3	47	20	30	30
Nuisance	6	63.5	16	15	63
Unknown, Misc.[d]	8	58	14	20	256
TOTAL (%)	6%	62%	13%	19%	
(N)	125	1291	270	406	2092

a The following sessions were excluded from this table because disposition evidence was incomplete: all Westminster sessions for 1663, 1664, 1693, and 1721; the Westminster sessions for January 1677, October 1707, and January 1722; and the Middlesex sessions for March and April 1663 and February 1721.

b Including cases which were continued to a subsequent sessions when the outcome is unknown, and cases discharged by the general pardon of 1721.

c Includes cases which were marked as "did not appear" (193) and cases where the defendant (or a surety) appeared at a sessions subsequent to the one in which he or she was initially required to appear and the court respited the case indefinitely (77). Over the course of the period, fewer cases were marked with the former notation, and more were marked with the latter. Indicted defendants are not included in this column.

d Includes 11 defendants accused of drunkenness, 16 accused of disaffection, 34 accused of miscellaneous offences, and 195 for whom the offence is unknown.

appear to have frequently facilitated informal settlements of disputes. Although the recognizance technically postponed the hearing of the dispute until the defendant appeared before sessions, in practice the experience of being bound over often encouraged defendants to reach informal settlements with their prosecutors before sessions met. As we shall see, however, recognizances for certain types of offences and offenders often did not lead to satisfactory settlements of disputes.

5.1 OFFENCES

In terms of the range of offences which could be prosecuted, recognizances were the most flexible method of prosecuting misdemeanors, with the exception of informal mediation. Through the twin possibilities of recognizances for the peace and recognizances for good behavior, justices of the peace could issue recognizances against a wide variety of errant behavior.[5] As demonstrated in Table 5.1, recognizances were most frequently issued for offences against the peace such as assault, riot, and defamation, but significant numbers were also issued for sexual offences (particularly adultery and prostitution), theft, and, in certain years, political or religious disaffection.[6] Compared with prosecutions by indictment, few defendants were bound over for alehouse and nuisance offences (Tables 3.4 and 3.5) and, compared with the number of summary convictions, few persons were bound over for vagrancy; loose, idle, and disorderly conduct; prostitution; and other vice offences such as drunkenness, cursing and swearing, and profaning the Sabbath. Nevertheless, with the exception of vagrancy, cursing and swearing, and profaning the Sabbath, at least a few persons in the sample were bound over for each of these offences.

Indeed, the broad range of offences listed on recognizances defies categorization. Although the majority of recognizances were issued at the behest of plaintiffs who had been, or who feared they would be, victims of assaults or riots, many recognizances were issued in response to specific private wrongs that involved little or no physical force and were often not strictly speaking criminal. Defamatory words or actions, such as calling a woman "whore," which were punishable in the church courts or civil courts,[7] accounted for about sixty recognizances per year. Many persons were bound over for "white collar" offences such as fraud, deception, and failing to abide by agreements. Ingenious deceivers were bound over for counterfeiting documents (including a ticket for a turnpike and a warrant to discharge a prisoner[8]), perjury, extortion

---

[5] See above, section 2.2.   [6] See above, section 3.3

[7] Sharpe, *Crime in Seventeenth-Century England*, p. 157; see also his *Defamation and Sexual Slander in Early Modern England: The Church Courts at York* (University of York: Borthwick Papers, no. 58, 1980). Insulting words could not be indicted unless they were thought to incite a breach of the peace: see above, section 2.3.

[8] MJ/SR/1810, R. 62 (Feb. 1693); 2371, R. 72 (Aug. 1721).

by making false accusations (particularly regarding the paternity of bastard children), clipping coins, and uttering clipped or counterfeit currency. Persons who were given goods to hold or use in trust, such as pawnbrokers or pieceworkers, were bound over when they failed to return the goods.[9] Also bound over were those who violated agreements or contracts of service. Despite the fact that for most occupations justices did not have the power to order employers to pay delinquent wages,[10] they exerted pressure on dozens of employers by binding them over by recognizance for unpaid wages, particularly during years of economic difficulty such as 1693. A jeweller was bound over in 1677 for "refusing to serve [his employer] according to a contract made between them,"[11] while numerous masters, servants, and apprentices were bound over under the statute of artificers for failing to fulfill the terms of their contract of service or indenture. Another type of private wrong that resulted in recognizances was negligence which led to injury, such as driving a horse and cart recklessly or possessing a dog that attacked people.[12]

What might be termed "public wrongs" also led to the issuing of recognizances. Offences such as attending a conventicle and voicing, or printing and selling, seditious words subverted the authority of the monarch and the established church. A man from Holborn was bound over in 1721 for "selling impressions of medals representing the pretender and his wife under the name of king and queen of Great Britain."[13] People who interfered with the judicial system and the execution of the law were bound over for undermining the rule of law. These include officers who refused to serve, failed to execute warrants, or allowed prisoners to escape. Also bound over were private citizens who refused to assist an officer when commanded to do so, such as a carman who failed to obey a constable's command to "bring his cart and horses to carry certain persons called Quakers to prison, for that they themselves would not go [by] themselves."[14] Others were bound over for actively obstructing justice by such diverse tactics as hiding a woman from a headborough who was about to serve a warrant against her, refusing to permit one's house to be searched under a warrant for stolen goods, and impersonating an overseer of the poor at sessions in testimony concerning a settlement case.[15] Many more defendants were bound over for resisting the law more directly by physically assaulting officers in the execution of their office. Many "public wrongs" that occasioned the issuing of a recognizance injured the public in a different way: by tending to increase the number of people dependent on poor relief. These offences include having bastard children, failing to provide for wives and children, and dividing

---

[9] MJ/SR/1526, R. 7 (May 1677); 2086, R. 94 (Feb. 1707).   [10] See above, section 4.3.
[11] MJ/SR/1533, R. 128 (Oct. 1677).
[12] For example, see MJ/SR/2098, R. 112 (Westminster sessions, Oct. 1707); 2361, R. 141 (Feb. 1721).
[13] MJ/SR/2369, R. 218 (July 1721).   [14] MJ/SR/1291, R. 213 (Aug. 1664).
[15] MJ/SR/1533, R. 63 (Oct. 1677); 1524, R. 117 (April 1677); 1531, R. 316 (Sept. 1677).

up lodgings to accommodate "inmates." One man was accused in 1721 of bringing into St. Botolph Aldgate a pregnant woman who, together with her forthcoming child, was potentially chargeable to the parish.

Recognizances served many functions. In addition to ensuring the appearance at sessions of defendants who were accused of committing a wide variety of private and public wrongs, recognizances were intended to constrain defendants to obey the law in the future. Indeed, according to William Blackstone, preventing crimes was their primary purpose.[16] In many cases, the sole condition of the recognizance (in addition to requiring the defendant to appear in court) was that the defendant "keep the peace" or (more rarely) "be of good behaviour." About a seventh of the defendants bound over in the sample were bound over simply to "keep the peace," usually towards a specific person who had sworn that the defendant had threatened him or her with bodily harm (Table 5.1). The ease with which justices could be persuaded to issue such recognizances is suggested by the number of defendants who alleged that the prosecutions were vexatious. One wife swore the peace against her husband when he complained about her lewd living, and in other cases recognizances for the peace were issued as part of disputes over debts.[17]

In most cases, regardless of what was written on the recognizance, the motivations of plaintiffs for getting defendants bound over were almost certainly a mixture of complaints about past wrongs committed and concerns to prevent future misbehavior. Thus, defendants bound over to keep the peace must have misbehaved sufficiently before they were bound over to provoke the plaintiff to complain to a justice. Elizabeth Peters was bound over not only to keep the peace, but also for raising tumults about George Tailor "several times, cursing and abusing him in such manner that he cannot go quietly about his lawful business." While justice Robert Constable carefully recorded the complaint which led to this request for a recognizance for the peace, other justices simply described the purpose of most of their recognizances as "to keep the peace."[18] Equally, complaints about previous misconduct must often have been accompanied by fears that the defendant would commit further offences. Victims of violent assaults, for example, must have often been as fearful that they might be subjected to additional attacks as they were upset about the injuries they had already received. Anne Dickenson was bound over after she broke into Elizabeth Arputh's house, violently assaulted and wounded her, and destroyed her goods. According to the recognizance, Dickenson confessed the fact and said she would do so again, "whereby the said Elizabeth goes in fear of further damage by the said Anne Dickenson or by some others by her procurement."[19]

---

[16] William Blackstone, *Commentaries on the Laws of England*, 4 vols. (Oxford, 1765–69), vol. 4, p. 249.

[17] MJ/SP/April 1691, no. 25; Oct. 1708, no. 25; Jan. 1722, no. 6. See also April 1691, nos. 26 and 45; Aug. 1694, no. 7.

[18] MJ/SR/1820, R. 157 (Sept. 1693).　　　[19] MJ/SR/1273, R. 18 (Aug. 1663).

Because binding over was intended as much to prevent further misbehavior as to punish offences which had already occurred, recognizances could be used in cases where there was little or no proof that the defendant had committed a crime, but the defendant's general demeanor gave rise to suspicion. A woman was bound over in 1693 for entering a shop "with an intent to steal."[20] Persons apprehended late at night by the watch were often bound over if they were unable to "give a good account" of themselves. George Kemp was bound over in 1664 not only for beating his wife and making a disturbance, but also because he was accused of "being a person that liveth jolly, spending highly and goes in habit above his degree so that honest neighbours do much marvel how he gets what he hath."[21]

Behind many recognizances, therefore, lay a background of accumulated distrust and suspicion as well as specific offences. The short descriptions of plaintiffs' complaints at the bottom of recognizances rarely do justice to the complexity of their motives for requesting that defendants be bound over. In 1677, however, justice Thomas Hariot described the complaints against William Hewett in unusual detail. Hewett was bound over

to answer his almost daily ... sitting up late tippling to the great grief and impoverishment of his poor wife. And using obscene and scandalous speeches and actions to and with one Anne Hixon a woman of evil fame with whom by his own confession he hath a long time lived in incontinence and whoredom. And likewise abusing one Mr. Edward Morris, a person of good quality, in very gross languages and carriages.[22]

Recognizances were suitable for addressing all these complaints.

5.2 INFORMAL SETTLEMENTS

Why were recognizances used in such a wide variety of circumstances? Recognizances were perceived to work, in the sense that they led to resolutions of disputes. Since recognizances by themselves only punished defendants in the sense that they had to pay some fees and were required to appear in court, the plaintiffs who requested them clearly had goals other than to impose vengeance or punishment on the defendant. Instead, plaintiffs who prosecuted by recognizance hoped tensions would be reduced and specific wrongs compensated for. When the accusation involved damaged, stolen, or unreturned property, for example, recognizances were probably obtained primarily in order to secure the payment of damages or the return of the property. When the accusation involved vice and the plaintiff was a relation or employer of the defendant, the goal in obtaining a recognizance was the reformation of the defendant's behavior. Thus, when masters complained against alehouse keepers who

---

20 MJ/SR/1820, R. 86 (Sept. 1693).   21 MJ/SR/1284, R. 104 (March 1664).
22 MJ/SR/1531, R. 191 (Sept. 1677). Significantly, although Hewett's wife does not appear as the plaintiff, his conduct towards his wife formed part of Morris' complaint to the justice.

allowed their apprentices to drink or game in their houses, the plaintiffs were in all likelihood as interested in removing their servants and apprentices from sources of vice as in punishing the keepers.[23] In case of assault and riot, plaintiffs probably desired both payment of damages for injuries received (as occurred when cases of assault were informally mediated by justices)[24] and reformation of the defendant's behavior in order to prevent a further attack.

Recognizances often facilitated such informal settlements. As Table 5.1 demonstrates, 62% of the defendants bound over by recognizance were exonerated and discharged when they appeared at sessions. Occasional notes in the sessions records provide evidence that these cases had been informally settled before the defendant appeared in court.[25] On the recognizance for two men who were accused of "giving unhandsome language" to Sir James Smith, for example, a note was added that "Sir James Smith at the intercession of the neighbours has forgiven the said persons and desires that they shall be discharged."[26] As in the cases discussed in chapter 4, settlements were tailored to the nature of the offence. Unpaid wages were paid, apologies were received for insults, and overseers of the poor received security for the maintenance of bastard children. A man who had been chosen to serve as a constable and had refused agreed to take the oath and serve; a widow accused of "living incontinently" with a man was exonerated after the two were married; a couple charged with keeping a disorderly alehouse agreed to move out of the parish; and two carmen paid damages to a woman who had been injured when she was run over by their cart.[27] In return for the defendants' efforts to redress wrongs and reform behavior, plaintiffs agreed not to prosecute the cases further and defendants were discharged by the justices when they appeared at sessions.

While these examples provide evidence of how recognizances were settled outside the court, they do not indicate how many of the 62% of the cases in which defendants were exonerated and discharged were actually settled informally. Compared with some other counties, the number of recognizances formally marked as agreed in the Middlesex records is very low. In eighteenth-century Kent, justices simply wrote "concordantur" (agreed) at the base of the recognizance when the parties reached an informal settlement before sessions. This notation was found on half of the recognizances from urban areas in Kent in 1716–17 and 1721–23.[28] Evidence from seventeenth-century justices' notebooks reveals high proportions of recognizances marked as agreed in rural areas as well: one quarter of the recognizances issued by William Lambard

---

[23] MJ/SR/1282, R. 109 (Feb. 1664); 2361, R. 33 (Feb. 1721).   [24] See above, section 4.1.

[25] MJ/SP/July 1708, no. 43. For similar cases, see MJ/SP/Sept. 1707, no. 10; July 1711, no. 63; Feb. 1712, no. 32.

[26] MJ/SR/1294, R. 68 (Oct. 1664). See also MJ/SR/1275, R. 37 (Westminster sessions, Oct. 1663).

[27] MJ/SR/1533, R. 83 (Oct. 1677); 1815, R. 99 (May 1693); 2088, R. 3 (Westminster sessions, April 1707); MJ/SP/Feb. 1723, no. 26; Feb. 1721, no. 33.

[28] Landau, *Justices of the Peace*, pp. 186–88.

and Bostock Fuller in Kent and Surrey in the early seventeenth century, and two-thirds of those issued by William Bromley in Warwick in the 1690s, were discharged prior to sessions.[29]

The Middlesex justices, however, appear to have followed different procedures, procedures which obviated the need to record recognizances as agreed. Although justices' manuals differed on whether, in cases where the defendant and the plaintiff had settled their differences, defendants were required to appear in court to discharge their recognizances, the Middlesex court followed the prevailing trend of legal advice, which required all persons bound over by recognizance to appear in court.[30] Petitions to the court noting that cases had been agreed assumed that the defendants or their sureties still had to appear in court in order to get their recognizances discharged.[31] In 1693, a man was accused of fraud when he took 6s. from William Weston "to discharge a recognizance at the sessions at Hicks Hall without the appearance of the said William, by reason of which the said recognizance was forfeited …"[32] This tactic may have worked in other counties, but it was not acceptable in Middlesex.

Although all defendants were required to appear at the Middlesex court, the court had no time to consider each case individually, with an average of two hundred persons bound over to appear at each sessions. Consequently, the standard practice in Middlesex and Westminster appears to have been to

[29] *Ibid.*; [Bostock Fuller], "Notebook of a Surrey justice," ed. Granville Leveson-Gower, *Surrey Archaeological Collections* 9 (1888), pp. 161–232; [William Lambard] "An ephemeris of the certifiable causes of the peace, from June, 1580, till September, 1588," in *William Lambarde [sic] and Local Government*, ed. Conyers Read (Ithaca, New York, 1962), pp. 15–52; [William Bromley], *Warwick County Records Volume 9: Quarter Sessions Records Easter, 1690, to Michaelmas, 1696*, ed. H. C. Johnson and N. J. Williams (Warwick, 1964), pp. xxxvii–xlv. Bromley did not actually mark these recognizances as agreed or discharged, he just crossed them out.

[30] Legal opinion on this issue was in a state of transition during this period. Earlier manuals suggested that in some circumstances defendants could be discharged from the need to appear in court: Lambard, *Eirenarcha* (1614), pp. 110–11; Dalton, *Countrey Justice* (1618), pp. 146–47, 163. Following an order of King Charles to the assize judges of the western circuit in 1635, however, most manuals in the late seventeenth and early eighteenth centuries prohibited this practice (William Sheppard, *The Justice of the Peace his Clerk's Cabinet* [1660], p. 113; Dalton, *Countrey Justice* [1661], pp. 201–02, 462; P. S., *A Help to Magistrates* [1721], p. 52; Richard Burn, *The Justice of the Peace and Parish Officer*, 2 vols. [1755], vol. 2, pp. 437, 455). Nevertheless, legal opinion on this issue was clearly in a state of transition in this period, since some manuals for justices include both descriptions of the procedure for releasing recognizances and advice that the procedure was no longer acceptable (Sheppard, *Sure Guide* [1669], pp. 382–89; Nelson, *Office and Authority* [1715], pp. 94, 486; Joseph Shaw, *The Practical Justice of Peace: or, a Treatise Showing the Power and Authority of all its Branches*, 2 vols. [1733], vol. 2, pp. 103–04, 107–08). Moreover, on the authority of a King's Bench decision from the early seventeenth century, some manuals still advised justices that discharges were permitted before sessions in cases of petty quarrels, minor trespasses, and breaches of the peace that were not punishable by fine (William Noye, *Reports and Cases* [At King's Bench and Common Pleas], 2nd edn [1669], p. 103 [Whinnel vs. Stroud]; Landau, *Justices of the Peace*, p. 186, n. 30).

[31] MJ/SP/Oct. 1707, nos. 7, 46; Oct. 1720, no. 68 a and c.   [32] MJ/SR/1810, R. 17 (Feb. 1693).

discharge defendants automatically when they appeared in court if no further complaint was heard from the prosecutor or the issuing justice. It was thus unnecessary to inform the court routinely that recognizances were agreed; when cases were settled before sessions, the prosecutor simply did not attend.[33] Cases were continued to a subsequent sessions only when the plaintiff or justice reported to the court that the defendant continued to misbehave.[34] Next to the sessions book entry for a recognizance for unpaid wages in 1677, for example, is a note requesting that the defendant not be discharged until the plaintiff was paid.[35]

The relative dearth of evidence concerning informal settlements of recognizances in Middlesex is thus explained by the fact that informal out-of-court settlements were expected. Only when special circumstances prevented the defendant from appearing in court was it necessary to inform the court in writing that the case had been agreed. Defendants who appeared in court were automatically discharged unless the justices were informed that the dispute remained unresolved or, in rare cases, when the court thought the case was particularly serious. It would be unreasonable to conclude, however, that in all such cases the discharged defendants had resolved their differences with their plaintiffs. All that can be inferred from the records is that tensions between the parties had sufficiently subsided so that the prosecutor did not feel it was necessary or worth the effort to continue the prosecution, either by requesting the justices to respite the recognizance to a subsequent sessions or by filing an indictment. Nevertheless, as the written evidence of agreed cases suggests, in many cases recognizances did facilitate satisfactory resolutions of disputes.

In addition to defendants who were discharged without further legal action on their first appearance in court, other recognizances also led to diminished tensions between the parties. As discussed below, many of the continued cases (about 5% of all recognizances) also eventually resulted in the unconditional discharge of the defendant. It is also possible, despite unanimous legal advice that recognizances should be returned to sessions even if the plaintiff had withdrawn his complaint,[36] that some Middlesex justices followed the Kent

---

[33] An order of the Westminster court in 1723 reveals that the court did not expect prosecutors to appear unless they desired to prosecute the case further: WJ/SBB/815, p. 44 (Oct. 1723). The practice of discharging defendants if prosecutors failed to appear was recommended by some manuals for justices of the peace (*Office of the Clerk of the Peace*, p. 172), but others advised the court that it was preferable to defer such cases to the next sessions (Dalton, *Countrey Justice* [1677], p. 279).

[34] See below, section 5.3. Occasionally, the sessions books contain notes requiring that the justice or plaintiff be notified when the defendant appeared in court: MJ/SBB/509, R. 103 (Dec. 1693); 646, R. 19 (Feb. 1707); 649, R. 60 (May 1707).

[35] MJ/SBB/345, R. 2 (July 1677).

[36] Lambard, *Eirenarcha* (1614), p. 111; Sheppard, *Sure Guide*, p. 382; Dalton, *Countrey Justice* (1677), pp. 278, 280; Nelson, *Office and Authority* (1704), pp. 78–87. In 1664, a Surrey justice was convicted and fined in King's Bench for compounding and not returning recognizances as well as appropriating for his own use fines collected for unlicensed alehouses (Thomas Siderfin,

practice of not returning agreed recognizances.[37] Because unreturned recognizances remained with the justices, it is only possible to check whether agreed recognizances were returned when evidence of judicial activity outside sessions, such as justices' notebooks or petty sessions minutes, survives. Of the fifty-four defendants bound over by justices at the Brentford petty sessions in seven sample years, recognizances for only three of the defendants were not returned, and two of these cases are listed as agreed in the petty sessions minutes.[38] On the other hand, recognizances in agreed cases issued by Westminster justice James Dewy in the 1690s and early 1700s, Middlesex justice Phillip Wilshire in Poplar in 1723, Middlesex justice Henry Norris in Hackney in the 1730s and Surrey justice Edward Smyth in Southwark in the 1660s *were* returned to sessions.[39] Thus, agreed recognizances issued by urban justices were returned to the Middlesex sessions. The fact that the only evidence of non-returned recognizances comes from Brentford, ten miles from the courthouse in London, suggests that rural justices may have been less conscientious in returning agreed recognizances, though it should be noted that the vast majority of the Brentford recognizances, most of which did not lead to further legal action, were nonetheless returned. To the extent that agreed recognizances were not returned, the surviving records underestimate the number of satisfactory settlements achieved by recognizance.

Several aspects of the procedures for hearing recognizances explain why they facilitated so many out-of-court settlements. The time that elapsed between the issuing of recognizances and meetings of sessions provided a "cooling off period" which allowed tensions to subside and negotiations to take place. (Time between sessions averaged one and a half months for the Middlesex sessions and three months for the Westminster and most county sessions.) Of the twenty-six released recognizances in justice Bostock Fuller's notebook, fourteen were released within a month of when they were issued. If Fuller's experience in early seventeenth-century Surrey is indicative, the one and a half months that elapsed between Middlesex sessions provided sufficient time for

---

Les Reports des divers special cases argue et adjudge en le court del Bank le Roy [2nd edn, 1714], p. 192, R. vs. Sir Purbeck Temple).
[37] Landau, *Justices of the Peace*, p. 188.
[38] GLRO, Accession 890, checked against the relevant sessions books (where available). The years sampled were 1661–62, 1668, 1690, 1693, and 1710–11.
[39] For the agreed recognizances see Hampshire Record Office, 1M53/1373, entry for 27 Jan., 1701/2 (I am indebted to Mark Jenner for this reference); PRO, KB 1/2, Easter 9 Geo. I, no. 8; GLRO, M79/X/I, entries for 25 Jan. 1732/3 and 31 Dec. 1739; Wiltshire Record Office, Accession 118, "Notebook of recognizances and informations taken before Edward Smyth, J. P., 1664–66," entries for 17 Dec. 1664 and 9 Jan. 1664–5. Of the twenty-two recognizances recorded in James Dewy's notebooks, all but two, both of which bound men to appear and appeal against bastardy orders, were returned to the Middlesex or Westminster sessions (Hampshire Record Office, 1M53/1373–74).

many cases to be settled informally. If the time before sessions was too short to allow tensions to subside, the plaintiff could always request that the case be continued until the following sessions.

While bound, the defendant was under pressure to reach an accommodation with the plaintiff. If a satisfactory settlement was not achieved by the time sessions met, the court might require the defendant to appear again at the subsequent sessions, thereby putting him to further expense and inconvenience. Although an indictment was not likely, the threat remained: at least a fifth of the defendants who were not indicted at the time they were bound over were subsequently indicted (Table 5.1).[40] Since indicted defendants incurred higher court fees, the possibility of a further appearance in court, and a fine if convicted, this threat was not trivial. Furthermore, while bound over the defendant had to stay out of trouble: any breach of the peace could result in the forfeiture of the recognizance, in which case the sums in which the defendant and sureties were bound (usually from £10 to £50 per person) became debts to the crown.[41]

Defendants were frequently willing to negotiate because they often knew their plaintiffs and were accused of minor offences. According to Table 5.1, the two types of recognizances which were most likely to be discharged without further legal action were cases of defamation or being a common disturber and recognizances to keep the peace. Both categories of offences were minor, and typically occurred between people who knew each other. The very nature of the offence of being a common disturber dictated that the offender was well acquainted with his (or, more likely, her) neighbors. Recognizances to keep the peace were designed to prevent tensions from erupting into violence, and they appear to have worked. Because recognizances encouraged informal negotiations, they were most successful in contexts similar to those in which informal mediation by justices succeeded.[42]

Pressure to settle disputes also came from the two other parties involved in recognizances: the justices of the peace who issued them, and the sureties who, by assuming a financial risk, guaranteed that the defendant would abide by the conditions of the recognizance. While recognizances were probably issued only when justices' attempts to encourage informal agreements proved unsuccessful, after the recognizance was issued some justices continued to take an interest in the case. When defendants appeared at sessions, justices occasionally addressed the court concerning the merits of continuing the recognizance.[43] If the recognizance was in danger of forfeiture as a result of the non-appearance of

---

[40] As noted in section 2.4, the disposition evidence on recognizances (from which Table 5.1 is derived) slightly underestimates the real number of defendants who were both bound over and indicted.

[41] Nelson, *Office and Authority* (1715), p. 474; Bond, *Complete Guide* (1707), p. 213.

[42] See above, section 4.1.

[43] See below, section 5.3.

the defendant, justices took action to prevent this from occurring, especially if they knew that the parties had agreed or were about to reach a settlement.[44] Since these justices kept in touch with plaintiffs and defendants, it is likely that they continued to serve as mediators between them.

Justices of the peace also indirectly encouraged settlements through the appointment of individuals as sureties. Sureties provided a financial guarantee that the defendant would fulfill the obligations stated on the recognizance, which were usually to appear at the next sessions and to keep the peace (or to be of "good behavior") in the interim. If the defendant failed to fulfill the obligations, the recognizance was forfeited and the sums of money pledged by the sureties (typically from £10 to £40, depending on the severity of the crime) became debts to the crown. By assuming a financial liability, sureties found themselves in a potentially difficult position which required them to weigh their own financial interest in getting the recognizance discharged against the desires of the defendants who selected them, who may have wanted to avoid (or postpone) appearing in court.

Defendants normally nominated their own sureties (usually two), subject to the justice's approval. The evidence suggests that justices encouraged (through their veto power) the selection of people who were sufficiently detached from the defendant's immediate circle of acquaintances that they were effective in getting the recognizance (and hence their risk) discharged. For example, sureties were rarely related to defendants: only 5% of the 2,361 defendants in the sample had sureties who were married to them or who shared the same surname. While this figure does not include related sureties with different surnames, their inclusion could not substantially increase this low figure.[45] In addition, although defendants and sureties tended to come from similar positions in the social hierarchy, few defendants and sureties shared the same occupation. Of 128 male defendants bound over by recognizance to attend the April 1723 Middlesex sessions, only 28% had a surety with the same occupational or status label as their own. If the labels are divided into three broad status groups (gentlemen, tradesmen and craftsmen, laborers), it turns out that almost one quarter of the defendants chose both sureties from a different status group from their own. Half of the defendants, however, chose sureties whose occupations were different from their own but who, like themselves, fell within the broad social status group of tradesmen and

---

[44] MJ/SP/Sept. 1720, no. 34; Oct. 1720, no. 134; WJ/SP/Oct. 1719, no. 8.
[45] On the other hand, David Levine and Keith Wrightson found in an early-modern village (Terling, Essex) that 18% of defendants chose at least one kinsman as a surety and 6% chose two. Nevertheless, they note that in about half of the cases where kinsmen were not chosen as sureties, adult kinsmen were available in the village (*Poverty and Piety in an English Village: Terling, 1525–1700* [New York, 1979], pp. 101–02).

craftsmen.[46] Since one would expect defendants' closest acquaintances to be the men most willing to act as their sureties, it is remarkable how often defendants chose sureties from outside their immediate social and occupational environment. Similarly, a comparison of the residences of sureties and defendants suggests that they did not know each other as well as might be expected. Although it is an unfortunately large unit of analysis, the evidence concerning this question is available only at the parish level. Over half of the defendants had at least one surety who lived in a different parish, and almost one-third chose sureties who both lived in a different parish from themselves. About two-thirds of the second group, however, lived in parishes which were contiguous to the parish of at least one of their sureties.[47]

In sum, the evidence suggests that defendants and their sureties had reason to know each other, but they were not close friends. Few sureties were relatives, neighbors, employers, or co-workers of defendants, but many came from similar social environments and from a neighboring parish.[48] Of course, little is known about the social and geographical extent of Londoners' acquaintances during this period, and it would be wrong to underestimate the typical range of their contacts.[49] Nevertheless, given the fact that sureties voluntarily incurred a substantial financial risk, even the relatively small social and geographical distance which separated defendants from their sureties is remarkable. It suggests, although little is known about how justices influenced the selection of sureties, that justices actively encouraged the selection of people who were able to exert the maximum possible pressure on the defendant to fulfill the obligations of the recognizance. Sureties closely acquainted with the defendant could have conspired to evade the conditions of the recognizance by hiding from the authorities; because they were not closely acquainted, sureties were more likely to try to get their financial liability discharged by demanding that defendants fulfill their obligations.

There is some evidence that sureties worked hard to get defendants to appear at sessions in order to discharge their recognizances. Joshua Glassington, a surety for the appearance of Mary Kealing, testified to the court after she failed to show up that he had "made strict and diligent inquiry after her as well among her acquaintances as also at several of her late lodgings, and places of

---

[46] MJ/SR/2402 (April 1723); see also Shoemaker, "Crime, courts and community," Tables 9 and 10, pp. 154–55. These calculations exclude 154 male defendants whose occupation or social status was unidentified.

[47] These calculations include only cases in which the parish of residence of both the sureties and the defendants was known. See Shoemaker, "Crime, courts and community," Table 11, p. 155.

[48] Similar conclusions can be drawn concerning the relationships between sureties (Shoemaker, "Crime, courts and community," Table 12, p. 158).

[49] The best friend of Nehemiah Wallington, a London turner who lived in St. Clement Eastcheap in the center of the City in the 1630s and 1640s, for example, lived east of the City in Whitechapel (P. S. Seaver, *Wallington's World* [Stanford, California, 1985], p. 95).

above, and can hear nothing of the said Kealing."[50] When recognizances were in danger of being forfeited by the non-appearance of the defendant, sureties were notified in order to give them a chance to convince the defendant to attend sessions.[51] Not surprisingly, a surety's attempts to get a defendant to appear in court could cause conflict between them. Elizabeth Templar, a surety for the appearance of Katherine Barnes, complained that Barnes refused to appear, "beating and evil entreating your petitioner [Templar] when she requests her thereunto."[52] If a surety had reason to believe in advance that the defendant was not going to appear in court, he could take preventive action and cause the defendant to be brought before a justice of the peace and committed to prison, thereby discharging himself of his obligation.[53] Defendants in these circumstances, however, sometimes fought back: when John Bradford, "being apprehensive of coming into trouble" caused Francis Simpson to be arrested, Simpson procured a warrant for his own discharge and, Bradford complained, subsequently "ran away."[54] Relations between defendants and sureties, however, often had more positive consequences. Motivated by the desire to eliminate their financial risk, sureties often appeared in the court in lieu of the defendant in order to prevent the recognizance from being forfeited.[55] To the same end (of getting the recognizances discharged) it appears that sureties encouraged defendants to conclude informal settlements with their plaintiffs.[56] Because sureties were not close personal acquaintances of defendants, they must have been viable and frequently successful mediators between the parties.

More than any other factor, however, the success of informal settlements depended on the willingness of the defendant to respond to the plaintiff's complaint by compensating the plaintiff for his past misdeeds and reforming his behavior for the future. One of the most important reasons why recognizances succeeded in facilitating informal settlements is that, because the legal obligations defendants incurred were not burdensome, recognizances did not poison relations between defendants and their prosecutors. Defendants remained at liberty (with the significant exception of those who were unable to find sureties) and they rarely faced punishment or further legal action if they appeared in court. Compared with the impact of an indictment or a commitment to a house of correction, the experience of being bound over by recognizance was not onerous. Although some defendants did respond antago-

---

[50] MJ/SP/Oct. 1720, no. 30. See also MJ/SP/July 1719, no. 5a.

[51] MJ/SP/Oct. 1720, nos. 137, 141.

[52] MJ/SP/Oct. 1691, no. 4.

[53] Nelson, *Office and Authority* (1704), p. 64; MJ/SP/1709 no date, no. 8.

[54] MJ/SP/Oct. 1720, no. 65. See also MJ/SP/Jan. 1691, no. 10.

[55] Sureties often attended the October sessions in which delinquent recognizances were estreated, and convinced the court to discharge the recognizance by adjourning the case indefinitely: WJ/SBB/815, p. 44 (Oct. 1723).

[56] In one case, a surety notified the court in writing that the parties had agreed (WJ/SP/Oct. 1722, no. 16).

nistically, defendants were far less hostile to being bound over by recognizance than they were to being indicted or committed to a house of correction.

The best available indicator of defendants' attitudes towards legal procedures is the frequency with which they responded to them by initiating vexatious counter prosecutions against their prosecutors. The same day that Thomas Jefferys was bound over for threatening Mary Parrot by saying "it was no more [a] sin to pull her heart out of her body and broil it on the coals than to kick the dirt before him in the street," he was accused of insulting the justice by saying "if he could not have law here he would go where he could have law."[57] Although justices were advised to refuse to issue recognizances "if a man will require the peace because he is at variance, or in suit with his neighbour,"[58] a defendant seeking revenge for being bound over could sometimes convince another justice to require the plaintiff to enter into a recognizance as well. This tactic could be particularly effective if the plaintiff was unable to find sureties and was committed to prison until sessions met.[59] If such vexatious counter prosecutions had occurred with any frequency, the viability of the recognizance procedure would have been threatened. In Middlesex, however, counter prosecutions by recognizance were rare: of eighty-three defendants bound over to appear at the April and May sessions in 1713 for rioting, only two procured recognizances against their plaintiffs.[60] Despite the numerous incidents of justices interfering in each other's activities which arose among the large number of active justices living in urban Middlesex, no complaints were made against justices for issuing vexatious counter recognizances.[61]

Except for several cases in which plaintiffs were indicted,[62] no other types of vexatious litigation were commonly directed against the prosecutors of recognizances. Compared with the litigation carried out by indicted defendants against their prosecutors in a variety of courts,[63] the overall paucity of evidence of malicious prosecution initiated by defendants who were bound over is significant. Typically faced only with the inconvenience of an appearance in court, defendants bound over by recognizance were rarely inclined to escalate the dispute by pursuing further legal action. In fact, defendants on recogni-

---

[57] MJ/SR/2358, R. 71, 72 (Jan. 1721).   [58] Dalton, *Countrey Justice* (1677), p. 266.
[59] MJ/SP/Feb. 1723, no. 12.
[60] The search for relevant recognizances was conducted in the sessions roll in which the recognizance was found as well as the rolls for at least two sessions prior and two sessions subsequent to that sessions: MJ/SR/2203, 2205, 2208, 2210, 2212, 2214 (Jan–Sept. 1713). Of course, not all counter recognizances were vexatious; justices occasionally issued recognizances against both parties in quarrels and fights.
[61] See above, section 4.3, and below, section 8.4.
[62] Of the eighty-three defendants mentioned above who were bound over to appear at sessions in April and May 1713, five had indicted their plaintiffs by September.
[63] See below, section 6.3.

zances were often in a frame of mind which was conducive to negotiating informal settlements with their prosecutors.

In sum, recognizances encouraged and facilitated informal resolutions of disputes through coercion tempered by flexibility and leniency. Threats of more costly and time-consuming legal action should the dispute remain unresolved were mitigated by a "cooling off period," during which the defendant remained at liberty, between the issuing of a recognizance and its consideration by sessions. In this intervening period, justices of the peace and sureties served as mediators who encouraged defendants and prosecutors to settle their differences. Consequently, most defendants were discharged by the court at the first opportunity and only a fifth were indicted.[64] For these reasons, recognizances were the most popular legal procedure in urban Middlesex during this period.

5.3 UNSUCCESSFUL RECOGNIZANCES

Although the majority of defendants bound over by recognizance were discharged at their first appearance in court, close to a third of all recognizances did not lead to satisfactory conclusions: 19% of the defendants were subsequently indicted and at least a further 13% failed to appear at the first meeting of the court after the recognizance was issued.[65] Although many of the latter later appeared and were discharged, 71.5% of the delinquent defendants are recorded as having never appeared. Moreover, a small proportion of the defendants who did appear punctually in court had their cases continued to a subsequent sessions. An examination of the cases where defendants were not exonerated by the court at the first opportunity illustrates the limits of recognizances as a procedure for prosecuting crime.

Just under 5% of the defendants who appeared in court expecting to have their recognizances discharged were instead required to appear again at a subsequent meeting of the court. While cases could be deferred because the defendant or prosecutor was ill, overseas, or otherwise unable to attend the court, the most common reason for continuing a case was probably that the defendant continued to behave in an objectionable manner. When the case of Thomas Dryer, a bookseller who was bound over in 1721 for mistreatment of his wife and child, was heard in court, his wife petitioned that since he had been bound over he "threatened to use her worse and neglects to provide for your petitioner and her said child." The court agreed to continue the recognizance

---

[64] As noted above, this discussion does not include defendants who had already been indicted at the time they were bound over.

[65] Since the notation "appeared and discharged" was rarely dated, it is also likely that some of the defendants whose recognizances were so marked appeared at a later sessions.

to the next sessions.[66] In 1720, a justice wrote the following note on the bottom of a recognizance he returned to sessions: "I desire thy Footit [the defendant] may be continued on his good behavior for such time as the court shall think fit, for continuing in the sin of adultery."[67] Cases involving vice were frequently continued: 18.5% of the defendants accused of alehouse offences, and 11% of those accused of gaming, were continued. When Charles Greenwood, a gentleman who had been arrested in a gaming house in Covent Garden, appeared in court on his recognizance in April 1721, he unrepentantly told the court that he would "play as long as he hath a shilling in the world." After this impolitic remark, Greenwood was bound over for £200 to appear at the next meeting of the Middlesex sessions. Greenwood, however, did not turn up until the July sessions, when he successfully pleaded the King's pardon of July 1721.[68] For morals offences, binding over by recognizance, like informal mediation, was unlikely to effect any genuine change in the defendant's behavior.

Defendants accused of serious offences (political or religious disaffection and fraud) and poor law offences (primarily bastardy and failure to provide support for wives and children) were also frequently asked to reappear at a subsequent meeting of the court. In serious cases, the court was clearly hesitant to discharge defendants until the justices were certain that the defendant had reformed his behavior and/or was not going to be indicted. Similarly, in cases of failure to provide for a wife or child the court appears to have been reluctant to discharge defendants until it was informed by the overseer of the poor that arrangements had been made to provide for the dependants in question.[69] In bastardy cases, the recognizances of the reputed fathers were normally deferred until after the birth of the child. Silence from the plaintiff was not a sufficient reason to discharge defendants in poor law cases; the importance of ensuring the maintenance of potential paupers dictated caution.

Many defendants whose cases were continued were subsequently discharged and exonerated, often at the next sessions. The option of continuing recognizances to a future sessions was a useful means of handling difficult cases, and the fact that recognizances were continued cannot be interpreted as evidence that the procedure ultimately failed to resolve those disputes. Nevertheless, as the case of Charles Greenwood suggests, continued cases often resulted from the fact that binding over applied insufficient pressure on obstinate defendants.

More serious evidence of the limitations of recognizances is the fact that at least 13% of defendants failed to appear at the first sessions after they were bound over (these cases constitute the "delinquent" column in Table 5.1, and do not include defendants who were indicted). Unless they had a good excuse

---

66 WJ/SP/Oct. 1721, no. 2.   67 MJ/SR/2346, R. 2. See also MJ/SR/1286, R. 110 (April 1664).
68 MJ/SR/2364, R. 96 (April 1721); MJ/SBB/791, 792, 793 (April–July 1721).
69 MJ/SR/1534, R. 122, 167 (Dec. 1677); 2093, R. 75 (Westminster sessions, July 1707).

justifying their nonappearance, these defendants had technically forfeited their recognizances, and the sums in which they and their sureties were bound became debts to the king, which were known as estreats. Because recognizances were estreated only once a year, however, many delinquent defendants subsequently appeared in court and had their cases discharged before they were formally estreated. The threat of an estreat induced many defendants or their sureties to appear at the October sessions, after which recognizances were normally estreated.[70] Nevertheless, a significant proportion, between 8 and 12% of all Middlesex recognizances, and 10 and 15% of those in Westminster, were estreated each year. In addition, between 6 and 11% more recognizances were threatened with being estreated before they were discharged.[71]

Despite the courts' willingness to discharge defendants who appeared at the last minute, about a tenth of all recognizances were forfeited and estreated. Although this proportion remained relatively stable during the period of this study, it appears to have increased in the mid-eighteenth century with the advent of "people of low and desperate fortunes" serving as sureties, who, as Thomas DeVeil complained, "will swear anything to save the criminals, or their accomplices from going to jail, and are often not the persons they swear themselves to be, or [are] *common bail* to everybody for money."[72] Such people would not have entered into recognizances if they thought that they would be held financially liable in the event of the defendants forfeiting their recognizances. This complaint thus suggests that by the mid-eighteenth century estreating was no longer a sufficient threat to coerce defendants and their sureties into fulfilling the obligations on their recognizances. In fact, there is some evidence that penalties on estreated recognizances were inefficiently collected: in the late 1720s or 1730s the Middlesex sessions published *An Alphabetical List of Persons who are Reputed to be Common Bail, whose Recognizances, by Suffering the Same to be Forfeited, have been Divers Times*

---

[70] WJ/SP/Oct. 1722, no. 1; MJ/SBB/815, p. 44 (Westminster sessions, Oct. 1723). Formal lists of estreated recognizances were sent to the Exchequer in Westminster, which issued summons to sheriffs to levy the penalties (Michael Dalton, *Officium Vicecomitum. The Office and Authority of Sheriffs* [1670], pp. 328–29; Sir Geoffrey Gilbert, *A Treatise on the Court of Exchequer* [1758], pp. 131–32).

[71] These calculations include all the recognizances issued during the sample years for which an estreat book is available: MJ/EB/1–14, 22–25, 32–34, 49–57 (1689–97, 1702–03, 1707–08, 1720–25) and WJ/EB/4, 14–15, 32–33, 45–46, 56–58 (1663–64, 1677–78, 1693–94, 1707–08, 1720–23). Sessions affected by general pardons were excluded from these calculations. These figures include recognizances to answer existing indictments. Since these recognizances were about twice as likely to be estreated as all others, and those to answer indictments account for about 9% of all recognizances, these figures overestimate the proportion of all other recognizances that were estreated by about 10%.

Similarly, in early seventeenth-century East Sussex, 11% of the defendants bound over by recognizance forfeited their recognizances by failing to appear (Herrup, *The Common Peace*, p. 90).

[72] Thomas DeVeil, *Observations on the Practice of a Justice of the Peace* (1747), pp. 4–5.

Estreated into the Court of Exchequer. Since all but one of the 187 names was listed with a single street or parish address, and they were able to forfeit "divers" recognizances, it appears that little attempt was made to collect the forfeited bail.[73]

It is impossible to determine how frequently estreats were actually collected, since sheriffs' returns to the Exchequer have not survived.[74] Despite reports of inefficiency and corruption among sheriffs' subordinates and at the Exchequer,[75] it is likely that the defendants and sureties who forfeited recognizances had to pay at least part of their penalties in order to get their estreats discharged. In the early eighteenth century there is evidence that people feared having a recognizance estreated. In 1701, a writer complained that victims refused to report thefts to magistrates for fear of being bound over to prosecute and then forfeiting their recognizances.[76] A defendant attempted to discredit a prosecutor at a trial in 1720 by describing him as "a person of very ill repute, and had forfeited three recognizances, and under such circumstances as he could not safely stay in England."[77] Nevertheless, this prosecutor testified at the Old Bailey. The ample time which elapsed between the forfeiture of a recognizance and the arrival of the sheriff's collectors facilitated the escape of anyone who was willing to move out of the county. In fact, moving to another parish within the metropolis was probably all that was necessary to evade the collectors. The fear of forfeiting recognizances, therefore, was probably strongest among the older, more established and less mobile residents.

It is possible that the problem of persons serving as "common bail," noted by both DeVeil and the Middlesex justices (in their published list), concerned defendants who had the most to lose by appearing in court: defendants accused of felonies and other serious offences, not the types of minor offences typically prosecuted at quarter sessions. The offences for which sessions recognizances were most likely to be estreated were some of the most serious offences prosecuted at sessions – 16% of the defendants bound over for neglect or abuse of office (failure to execute office, extortion, allowing a prisoner to escape), and 14% of those accused of fraud (including forgery), had their recognizances estreated. In addition, the recognizances of indicted defendants, regardless of

---

[73] This publication was undated; references to the parishes of St. George Hanover Square and St. George the Martyr date this document no earlier than 1724. In the British Library catalogue it is listed as "[1730]": shelf mark 7754.c.13.

[74] *Reprint of Statutes, Rules and Schedules Governing the Disposal of Public Records by Destruction or Otherwise* (1914), pp. 164–71.

[75] T. G. Barnes, *Somerset 1625–1640* (Cambridge, Mass., 1961), pp. 135–42; T. E. Hartley, "Undersheriffs and bailiffs in some English Shrievalties, *c.* 1580 to *c.* 1625," *Bulletin of the Institute of Historical Research* 47 (1974), pp. 171–75.

[76] *Hanging, Not Punishment Enough, for Murtherers, High-Way Men, and House Breakers* (1701; reprint edn, 1812), p. 15.

[77] *The Proceedings on the King's Commissions of the Peace, Oyer and Terminer ... at Justice-Hall in the Old Bayly; on ... March, 1719[20]*, (1720), p. 6.

the offence, were twice as likely to be estreated as defendants who were not indicted at the time they were bound over. Since indicted defendants faced higher court costs and the possibility of a fine if they were convicted there was a greater incentive to forfeit their recognizances. Nevertheless, defendants in less serious cases also often forfeited their recognizances. Once again, persons accused of vice were particularly likely to fail to cooperate with the courts: 9.5% of alehouse offenders and 13% of sexual offenders (those accused of prostitution and adultery) forfeited their recognizances.[78] Many more vice offenders came close to forfeiting their recognizances: a quarter of those accused of sexual offences, 18.5% of those accused of alehouse offences, and 22% of those accused of keeping or frequenting gambling houses initially failed to appear in court.

Even prior to the 1730s, therefore, the problem of defendants who failed to appear in court to discharge their recognizances was a serious one for the Middlesex sessions. Justices and plaintiffs faced the distinct possibility that the defendant would never appear in court, though possibly at a substantial cost to the defendant if the estreat was collected. Even if the money was collected, however, the defendant suffered the penalty several months after the recognizance was forfeited, and the plaintiff benefitted little from such a punishment. And if the threat of an estreat eventually caused the defendant (or a surety) to turn up in court, the appearance was normally several sessions late. In the meantime, it is unlikely that the original dispute moved any closer to resolution.

Even when the defendant dutifully appeared in court, recognizances often failed to resolve disputes. For plaintiffs faced with defendants who were unwilling to reach an informal settlement or who refused to reform their behavior, the most common next step was to indict them. A substantial proportion, about a fifth of the defendants who had not been indicted at the time they were bound over, were subsequently indicted. At 34%, defendants accused of theft were most likely to be indicted (Table 5.1). Since informal settlements of felonies (including petty larceny) were illegal, plaintiffs were under pressure to initiate formal prosecutions. Regardless of legal requirements, however, it is clear that the most serious offences were the most likely to result in indictments. In addition to theft, these offences include fraud (26% of defendants bound over) and neglect or abuse of office (30%). Either because the defendants accused of these offences were unusually obstinate, or because plaintiffs believed recognizances were too lenient for such offences, defendants accused of serious offences were often prosecuted by indictment.

Recognizances for less serious offences, including loose, idle, and disorderly

[78] Martin Ingram has noted that those accused of sexual offences were likely to be younger, and hence more mobile, than other offenders (*Church Courts*, pp. 343 ff).

conduct, disturbing and defamation, and all types of vice, as well as recognizances to keep the peace, resulted in indictments much less frequently. Nevertheless, with the exception of two categories of offences which were largely unindictable, sexual and poor relief offences,[79] at least 7% of the defendants bound over for every category of offence in Table 5.1 were indicted. It is impossible to determine whether the plaintiffs had originally intended to file an indictment when the defendant was bound over, or only decided on one when it became apparent that the recognizance had not brought about any change in the defendant's behavior. For most petty offences, it is likely that plaintiffs regarded the filing of an indictment, a more formal and far more costly procedure, as a procedure of last resort, to be used only after it was clear that the recognizance had failed.[80] In any case, since defendants bound over by recognizance could not be effectively punished without being formally convicted, it is not surprising that a significant number of plaintiffs chose to file indictments after first getting the defendant bound over.

In sum, recognizances for two types of offences often failed to yield satisfactory results. Defendants accused of vice and particularly serious offences (such as theft and neglect of office) were most likely to be delinquent in fulfilling the conditions of their recognizances, or to be indicted by their plaintiffs, or both. Where a crime harmed no specific individual but instead violated moral standards, it is likely that recognizances often failed because the plaintiff and the defendant failed even to attempt to resolve their differences. The unpaid and part-time parish officers who were responsible for getting such defendants bound over were unlikely to keep track of their subsequent behavior. Without a vigilant plaintiff to complain when the defendant refused to mend his ways or failed to appear in court, defendants had fewer incentives to seek informal settlements or fulfill the requirements of their recognizances. In any case, since the parties typically held fundamentally opposing values, disputes over morals offences were not amenable to the kind of compromises often achieved with recognizances or informal mediation. For these offences, plaintiffs and justices frequently sought formal convictions and more serious punishments. As was the case with particularly serious offences, defendants accused of morals offences were typically indicted or committed to a house of correction.

---

[79] See above, section 2.3. Two poor law offences, subdividing houses and building cottages on less than four acres of land, were commonly indicted, but these were statutory offences for which defendants could not be bound over except for the purpose of requiring them to appear to answer an existing indictment: see above, section 2.4.

[80] See above, section 2.4.

5.4 OTHER LIMITATIONS

In addition to problems with recalcitrant defendants and forfeited recognizances, there were two other serious disincentives to prosecuting by recognizance: the costs, both financial and practical, of getting a defendant bound over, and the difficulty defendants encountered in finding sureties. Although defendants paid the bulk of the legal fees, plaintiffs paid one or two shillings for the warrant that brought the defendant before a justice in order for the recognizance to be issued.[81] At a time when the average weekly income of laborers and the lowest paid journeymen in London was between eight and twelve shillings a week,[82] this fee probably often exceeded their limited discretionary income.[83] For those who could afford it, a warrant was nevertheless expensive enough to constitute a serious disincentive to proceeding with the prosecution. For those who were unemployed or irregularly employed, warrants were probably unaffordable.[84] As suggested by the small number of recognizances issued in the poorest parishes of the metropolis, the cost of prosecuting by recognizance could be prohibitive.[85]

Recognizances put defendants to far greater expense. Defendants were required to pay 2s. or 2s. 4d. to the clerk of the justice who issued the recognizance, 2s. or 2s. 4d. to the clerk of the peace for each appearance in court (normally only one was necessary unless the case was continued) and 4d. to the crier when the case was discharged, for a minimum total of 4s. 4d.[86] Although in a few cases fees were reduced or eliminated entirely for the poor[87] clerical costs must have constituted a considerable financial burden for many lower class defendants, and these account for two-fifths of those bound over by

---

[81] According to justices' manuals, justices could charge 2s. for a warrant of the peace (*A Help to Magistrates*, p. 19; Nelson, *Office and Authority* [1715], p. 259). In January 1721, however, the Middlesex sessions ruled that no more than a shilling could be charged: MJ/SP/Jan. 1721, no. 77; MJ/OC/I, ff. 111–112d.

[82] George, *London Life*, p. 166 and p. 360, n. 8; E. W. Gilboy, *Wages in Eighteenth-Century England* (Cambridge, 1934), pp. 8–10, 13; John Rule, *The Experience of Labour in Eighteenth-Century Industry* (1981), pp. 62–64.

[83] An indication of how small the discretionary income of lower class families was is provided by the sample budgets in George, *London Life*, pp. 169–70.

[84] Stephen MacFarlane has shown that weekly pensions in the City of London at the end of the seventeenth century were typically only one or two shillings a week ("Studies in poverty and poor relief in London at the end of the seventeenth century" [Ph.D., Oxford University, 1983], p. 220).

[85] See below, section 10.1.

[86] MJ/SP/Jan. 1721, no. 77; MJ/OC/I, ff. 84d–85 (Oct. 1719); MJ/SBB, *passim*; *Office of the Clerk of the Peace*, pp. 247–54; Nelson, *Office and Authority* [1704], p. 225; Bond, *Complete Guide*, p. 93.

[87] This is evident from marginal notations in the sessions books (MJ/SBB).

recognizance.[88] Nonetheless, defendants (and plaintiffs) on indictments faced much higher costs.[89]

Many poor defendants, however, were never bound over by recognizance because they were unable to find sureties. Because the justice could be held liable if a surety was too poor to pay the penalty if his recognizance was forfeited,[90] justices examined potential sureties to see if they were worth more than the amount they would risk on the recognizance.[91] Since these sums were substantial (usually between £10 and £40), justices encouraged the selection of persons who "lived in tolerable credit, or at least were house-keepers."[92] Thus, Thomas Railton rejected a potential surety because he "seemed to be but poor by his habit" and demanded instead "housekeepers." Of the 379 sureties who guaranteed recognizances to appear at the Middlesex sessions in April 1723, 7% were gentlemen and 68% were tradesmen or craftsmen; only 3% were identified as laborers.[93]

It was the defendant's responsibility to locate acceptable sureties. This could be a particularly difficult task if the defendant was poor and had no socially respectable acquaintances, or if he had recently moved and had no local ties, especially since he was required to remain under arrest while potential sureties were located.[94] When justice William Booth ordered Richard Manley to find sureties in order to enter into a recognizance to answer a charge of beating his servant, Manley replied that he had "lately come to lodge at Clerkenwell where he was a stranger," and requested time to send for his friends from his former residence in Westminster. Although such a request would normally have been granted, in this case justice Booth maliciously refused. Manley was thus put in the situation of recent immigrants to the metropolis, and had to try to convince

[88] This calculation covers male defendants only, since women were identified on recognizance only by their marital status. "Lower class" defendants include laborers, lower social status craftsmen, and men who were too poor to risk bail on their recognizances. See below, Table 8.1.
[89] See below, section 6.3.
[90] Sheppard, *Sure Guide*, p. 189; Dalton, *Countrey Justice* (1677), p. 437 (Dalton advised justices to select "subsidymen"); Bond, *Complete Guide*, pp. 46, 212; MJ/GSP/1663, no. 2.
[91] *The Justicing Notebook of William Hunt 1744–49*, ed. Elizabeth Crittall, Wiltshire Record Society vol. 37 (Devizes, 1982), case 137; GLRO, M79/X/I, 2 Dec. 1737; *Office of the Clerk of the Peace*, p. 175. For serious offences, justices were advised to give the names of potential sureties to plaintiffs in order to encourage investigations of sureties' qualifications: MJ/OC/III, f. 29 (27 Aug. 1725); DeVeil, *Observations*, p. 5. A man was indicted in the City of London in 1693 for misrepresenting himself to the City Recorder as a housekeeper worth £40 so that he would be accepted as a surety for a woman accused of being a nightwalker: CLRO, sessions roll, Dec. 1693. Although it happened rarely in Middlesex, at their own discretion justices could bind defendants by recognizance without sureties. Justice Henry Norris bound over a man for the peace "in his own recognizance alone with the consent of the plaintiff" (M79/X/I, 2 Nov. 1731); the consent of the plaintiff was not legally necessary.
[92] *Memoirs of the Life and Times of Sir Thomas DeVeil* (1748), p. 35.
[93] Hertfordshire Record Office, D/EP/153, Rex vs. Wood; Shoemaker, "Crime, courts and community," Table 9, p. 154; the remaining sureties were victuallers (17%), widows (1%), officers (2%), and unidentified (2%).
[94] Bond, *Complete Guide*, p. 186.

people living nearby, "although of little acquaintance," to be his sureties.[95] While Manley, a gentleman, was successful, less socially respectable defendants with no local ties must have frequently been unable to find sureties, especially since defendants were typically given only a few hours to find them.[96] When James Tampsett, a linenweaver, was ordered to enter into a recognizance when attending the Kent quarter sessions in Maidstone, he was sixteen miles from his home and "altogether a stranger there and so had no friends nor acquaintances to assist him." Unable to find sureties, Tampsett, like all defendants in his situation, was to be committed to jail until he found sureties, or, failing that, until the next sessions. Instead, he chose to "withdraw himself from the court rather than to stay and be sent to jail."[97]

It is not surprising that Tampsett was anxious to avoid spending any time in jail. Prisoners were expected to pay their living expenses and, like most seventeenth- and early eighteenth-century prisons, conditions in the two Middlesex prisons were horrific unless one was able to pay extra for special treatment.[98] The prison for those awaiting the Middlesex sessions was New Prison, in Clerkenwell; prisoners awaited the Westminster sessions in the Gatehouse Prison, near Westminster Abbey. In New Prison, a room, clean sheets, and "a good bed" cost one shilling for the first night and three pence for each subsequent night. Those who could not pay these fees were crowded together in a separate part of the prison where conditions were at their worst. Since these prisoners had been unable to find sureties, they may not have had any friends or family living nearby to bring them food and clothing. Although some provision was made for the relief of destitute prisoners, it was clearly inadequate. As the Middlesex justices noted in 1720, "many persons who are committed to [New Prison] . . . wanting money, being destitute of friends, or falling sick, are in danger of perishing for want of help and succour."[99]

Given the power that the keeper had over his charges, it is not surprising that the prisoners complained of extortion. In 1672, the keeper of the Gatehouse was fined one hundred marks and removed from office for extorting fees and otherwise mistreating the prisoners.[100] In 1709, prisoners in New Prison claimed that the keeper monopolized the sale of food at unjust prices and

---

[95] Justice Booth's behavior in this case was the subject of a letter of complaint from the Middlesex bench to the Lord Chancellor: MJ/OC/I, ff. 84d–85 (Oct. 1719).

[96] DeVeil, *Observations*, pp. 5–6; GLRO, M79/X/I, 4 Nov. 1737 and 15 March 1739.

[97] Kent Archives Office, Q/SB/11/56 (undated, but with 1663 papers). I am indebted to Norma Landau for this reference.

[98] For prisons in Surrey during this period, see Beattie, *Crime and the Courts*, pp. 299–303. As Beattie points out, conditions no doubt varied depending on the extent of overcrowding; New Prison was most crowded at the end of our period, during the years of peace following 1714.

[99] MJ/SP/July 1720, no. 50. At New Prison the keeper was entitled to collect twelve pence from each of the wealthier prisoners for the relief of destitute prisoners.

[100] T. Raymond, *Reports of Divers Special Cases, Adjudged in the Courts of King's Bench, Common Pleas, and Exchequer* (1803), p. 216.

charged higher fees than were permitted by law. Two years later, a prisoner in the Gatehouse, Mary Pitt, complained that the keeper's wife threw her down the stairs because she did not have the money to pay for a bed. She was forced to bed down next to a corpse. Extortion was also practiced by prisoners: when Pitt was unable to pay "garnish money" (used to pay for necessities such as candles and fuel), the turnkey and other prisoners "took off her gown and threatened her." In 1719, when similar complaints were voiced against the keeper of the Gatehouse and some of his prisoners, the keeper was even accused of charging too much for gin.[101]

Paradoxically, since those committed to prison were likely to be poorer than those who found sureties, defendants who awaited sessions in prison paid considerably higher fees than those who were only bound over by recognizance. Prisoners were expected to pay the cost of having a constable convey them to jail (perhaps 4d.).[102] Upon their arrival, they were expected to pay "garnish money" (perhaps 5s., though Mary Pitt was expected to pay 7s. 6d.) in addition to their own living expenses, and upon their release they were charged discharge fees of between 5s. and 18s. 6d. If the defendant found sureties and was released before sessions, an additional 3s. or 3s. 4d. had to be paid to the justice of the peace for the discharge from prison and for entering into a recognizance.[103] Thus, a prisoner who was discharged before sessions was likely to pay at least 13s. 4d., almost six times as much as he would have paid if he had found sureties without first being committed to prison. Prisoners remaining until sessions saved the 3s. cost of the discharge and entering into a recognizance but waited up to seven weeks in New Prison; Westminster prisoners stayed as long as three months in the Gatehouse before sessions met. Even after they were discharged by the court, prisoners who failed to pay their court and prison fees endured further imprisonment until the fees were paid, although very poor prisoners were apparently discharged without paying.[104]

The high costs, both physical and financial, of a commitment to prison during this period explain why a number of illegal acts were committed in order to avoid imprisonment. As discussed above, potential sureties misre-

---

101 MJ/SBB/671, pp. 48, 68–71 (July 1709); British Library, Add. MS 38,856, ff. 140, 150, 153–56. See also James Whiston, *England's Calamities Discovered* (1696), pp. 10–16; Hepworth Dixon, *John Howard and the Prison World of Europe* (1849), pp. 9–22; Michael Ignatieff, *A Just Measure of Pain: The Penitentiary in the Industrial Revolution* (1978), pp. 33–39.

102 3 Jac. 1, c. 10; 13 and 14 Car. 2, c. 12. No evidence of the amount of these fees has been located, but presumably they were similar to the fees charged for an arrest by the sheriff's bailiffs or the jailer (both 4d.): Dalton, *Countrey Justice* (1677) p. 71; Whiston, *England's Calamities*, p. 37.

103 Add. MS 38,856, ff. 150, 153–56; MJ/SP/July 1720, no. 50; MJ/OC/I, ff. 84d–85 (Oct. 1719), ff. 111–112d (11 Jan. 1721); Beattie, *Crime and the Courts*, pp. 289–90.

104 For prisoners who were kept in prison for their fees, see MJ/SBB/710, p. 46 (Dec. 1712); MJ/SP/April 1722, no. 12; Herrup, *The Common Peace*, p. 162, n. 40. For examples of poor prisoners who were discharged without paying their fees, see *Universal Journal*, 6 May, 1724; Ignatieff, *A Just Measure of Pain*, p. 36. I am grateful for the advice I have received on this subject from John Langbein and Joanna Innes.

Table 5.2 Dispositions of prisoners accused of misdemeanors committed to New Prison and the Gatehouse

| Year | No. of sessions[a] | (Accused of felony)[b] | Average number of prisoners per sessions | | | | Total sample |
			Discharged before sessions[c]	Not discharged	Disposition unknown	Total per sessions	
1677	9	(7.6)	23.6	9.1	0.7	41.0	368
1693	2	(1.5)	15.0	4.0	—	20.5	41
1707	3	(7.0)	19.0	7.0	0.7	33.7	101
1721	8	(17.5)	26.5	8.6	1.4	54.0	432
TOTAL	22	(10.5)	23.2	8.2	0.9	42.8	942

a The small number of sessions in this table has three causes: the poor condition of many prison calendars because they were used as wrappers for the sessions rolls; many calendars only included prisoners who were not discharged before sessions; and dispositions are incomplete on some calendars. The following sessions are included in this table:
Middlesex: January, February, May, July, December 1677; January, February, October 1693; January, February, April, May, July, December 1721.
Westminster: All sessions 1677; April, July, October 1721.
b Includes defendants accused of petty larceny, defendants committed on suspicion of felony, and all prisoners who were subsequently committed to Newgate. Prisoners in this column are not included in subsequent columns.
c Prison keepers rarely specified whether prisoners were simply discharged without further legal action or whether upon discharge they entered into a recognizance to appear at sessions. Evidence from those calendars on which this information was recorded indicates that 82% of 184 discharged prisoners entered into a recognizance.

presented their financial status and trustworthiness in order to get defendants bailed. Similarly, justices of the peace occasionally bailed defendants accused of serious offences with insufficient bail, or, if they were already in prison, without consulting the justice who had committed them.[105] On the other hand, one Middlesex justice was indicted for prevailing with another justice *not* to grant bail to a prisoner, and then extorting money from the prisoner as a condition for his release.[106] Similarly, some plaintiffs abused the powers commitment to prison gave them over people who were unable to find sureties. Vexatious plaintiffs could get such people committed to prison simply by convincing a justice to order them to enter into a recognizance and, for a price, they were willing to withdraw the accusations and allow the prisoners to be discharged. When Mary Rogers was threatened with imprisonment on what she claimed was a malicious complaint of unlawfully detaining goods, the plaintiff told her he would drop the charges if she would pay him four guineas "satisfaction."[107] Similarly, one prisoner claimed that her prosecutor demanded a bond of fifty or one hundred pounds guaranteeing that she would not trouble her in the future as the price for dropping the charges and allowing her to be released.[108] In other cases, however, sympathetic plaintiffs requested that defendants be discharged from prison before sessions, apparently without entering into a recognizance or paying damages.[109] Because imprisonment was so onerous and prisoners could be released at a plaintiff's request, plaintiffs played a more active role in shaping the outcome of cases where defendants were imprisoned for want of sureties than in those where they were bound over by recognizance.

How frequently were defendants committed to prison for want of sureties? Since bail was legally permissible for all misdemeanors, defendants were only committed to prison if they were unable to find sureties. As Table 5.2 demonstrates, about forty defendants per sessions, or about 320 per year, were committed to the New Prison in Middlesex. About one quarter of these prisoners were accused of felonies, however, and were generally ineligible for bail.[110] More than two-thirds of the remaining prisoners were discharged before sessions met (typically after only a few days in prison), most often because they had found sureties and entered into a recognizance to appear at sessions. Thus, while an average of two hundred people were bound over to attend each sessions, only about eight defendants accused of misdemeanors

---

[105] Shoemaker, "Crime, courts and community," pp. 381–82.
[106] Thomas Leach, *Modern Reports*, 12 vols. (5th edn, 1793–96), vol. 6, p. 31.
[107] MJ/SP/May 1723, no. 16.   [108] MJ/SP/Dec. 1713, no. 7.
[109] GLRO, M79/X/I, 12 June 1732, 15 March 1739, 31 Dec. 1739.
[110] A significant number of these defendants, however, were bailed. For the laws concerning bail for accused felons, see Beattie, *Crime and the Courts*, p. 282.

actually remained in prison until sessions. Some of these prisoners, moreover, had only recently been committed and had not had much time to find sureties before sessions met.

The small number of defendants who were imprisoned for want of sureties, however, does not mean that defendants found sureties easy to obtain. Rather, it appears that the justices were unwilling to commit defendants to prison for minor offences. When justice Henry Hawley committed a man to Newgate in 1693 for stealing a magpie, the court ridiculed the action, stating that "it is a very simple weak thing of the justice of peace to commit the poor fellow for such a trifle." Instead, the justices suggested that the defendant, who was a soldier, should have been "sent to his captain, and ... run the gauntlet."[111] In other cases where sureties could not be found, justices appear to have committed the defendants to houses of correction for immediate punishment. Because prisoners so committed could be discharged after a short period of incarceration, houses of correction were an attractive alternative place of confinement for defendants accused of minor offences who were unable to find sureties. They were specifically designed as institutions for the punishment of poor offenders,[112] the kind of people who were likely to have trouble finding sureties. The corporal punishments (whipping and hard labor) satisfied justices and plaintiffs that the defendant had been punished, and defendants avoided a long and expensive stay in prison, which they could not afford. Thus, in effect, punishments were reduced to fit what were often very minor crimes.

As justices adopted this practice and commitments to houses of correction increased, the prisons suffered. Three times during the period of this study, in 1675, 1687, and 1720, the keeper of New Prison complained to the court that the income from his fees had decreased as the result of a reduction in the number of offenders committed to his prison. In 1687, Captain Thomas Jones complained that "for about twenty years past, cheats, nightwalkers, and suspicious and disorderly persons have been constantly brought by the watches, but now, for a whole week together, not one such nightwalker has been brought to the prison, whereby the perquisites and fees are so much reduced ..."[113] Since the offences Jones mentioned are frequently listed on house of correction calendars, it is likely that the missing prisoners were sent there. In 1675, the keeper complained that people "arrested on [the] watches for criminal causes" had been committed to the liberty prisons or house of correction instead of to his prison. In 1720, a statute legitimised the practice of committing minor offenders who were unable to find sureties and were

---

[111] *The Trial of John Foster for Stealing a Magpie* [1693].
[112] Innes, "Prisons for the poor," p.42.
[113] MJ/SBB/447, p. 38 (May 1687).

awaiting an appearance at sessions to houses of correction. This statute probably occasioned the keeper's complaint in December 1720.[114]

In response to this last complaint, a committee of justices examined the records of the house of correction and discovered that only about seven commitments per sessions for want of sureties had been made in the previous six months.[115] It would be wrong to conclude from this report, however, that defendants who were unable to find sureties were not committed to houses of correction. When making such commitments, justices typically phrased the charge against the defendant as an offence punishable by summary jurisdiction, thus eliminating the need for an appearance at sessions. Such prisoners were then listed on house of correction calendars as having been committed in order to receive punishment, not for want of sureties. The explanation of the small number of prisoners awaiting sessions in New Prison, therefore, appears to be the fact that many defendants who were unable to find sureties were committed to houses of correction for summary punishment. In both 1675 and 1687, when the keepers of New Prison complained of low numbers of prisoners, commitments to the Middlesex house of correction peaked.[116]

From his survey of recognizances issued in Elizabethan Colchester, Joel Samaha concluded that few defendants were committed to jail for want of sureties and that recognizances were frequently used to "control 'undesirable' and 'dangerous persons' ... the recognizance was a tool essentially aimed at strangers and the poor in the town."[117] In Middlesex at the turn of the eighteenth century, on the other hand, newcomers and persons living on the margins of respectable society were unlikely to have had sufficient social contacts to be able to find sureties, and instead were committed to prison to await sessions, or (more probably) to a house of correction for immediate punishment. Consequently, the offences with which the poor were typically accused appear relatively rarely on recognizances (or on prison calendars) when compared with house of correction calendars. In the early 1720s, an estimated 183 defendants accused of vagrancy and "loose, idle and disorderly" conduct were committed to the Middlesex and Westminster houses of correction each year, while only about 15 defendants per year were bound over by recognizance for this offence. Similarly, while about 501 defendants per year were committed to houses of correction for offences related to prostitution, only 69 were bound over by recognizance, and while 351 defendants were committed for petty theft, only 96 were bound over.[118] While there were other

---

[114] MJ/SBB/328, pp. 47–49 (Oct. 1675); 6 Geo. I c. 19; MJ/SBB/789, pp. 54–55 (Dec. 1720).

[115] MJ/SP/April 1721, no. 1.

[116] Figure 3.3. In 1720, on the other hand, the number of prisoners in both New Prison and the Middlesex house of correction appears to have been lower than in the surrounding years, and the keeper's complaint may have derived from his need to raise funds for the repair of the prison: MJ/SBB/789, pp. 54–55.

[117] Samaha, "The recognizance," pp. 197, 201.   [118] Above, Table 3.5.

reasons (discussed in chapter 7) why plaintiffs might want their defendants committed to houses of correction instead of being bound over, the desire to avoid long periods of imprisonment for poor defendants who were unable to find sureties appears to have been an important factor.

Defendants who could not enter into a recognizance faced the costly, painful, and probably humiliating consequences of incarceration, either in a prison or a house of correction. While manuals for justices of the peace characterized those without sureties as having "refused" to provide them, in practice sureties were simply unavailable to defendants who, either because of their poverty or because they had recently moved, had no respectable social contacts.

With the probable exception of informal mediation by justices, the recognizance was numerically the most popular legal procedure for the prosecution of petty crime in Middlesex. It was attractive to prosecutors and to justices because it was a convenient and frequently successful means of using the law to resolve a wide range of criminal accusations and interpersonal disputes relatively informally. Nevertheless, recognizances were not suitable for all types of offences and offenders. Because the only punishment experienced by defendants who were bound over was the cost and inconvenience of appearing at one (or, rarely, more than one) sessions, recognizances could not exert much pressure on obstinate offenders, nor could they inflict significant punishments in retribution for serious crimes. Indeed, the delays and questionable efficiency of the process of collecting penalties from defendants who forfeited their recognizances meant that hardened offenders could easily avoid any punishment at all. Recognizances were also largely unavailable to recent immigrants and the poor, both large sections of the metropolitan population. Potential prosecutors from the poorest parts of London often found it difficult to afford the expense of getting a defendant bound over, and poor defendants and immigrants often found it difficult to find respectable social contacts who could serve as sureties to guarantee their appearance at sessions.

As a result of these limitations, recognizances were ill-suited for many of the offences which were the subject of greatest public concern during this period: serious offences (such as theft), vice, and vagrancy. Because theft was a felony, accused thieves had restricted access to bail, but in any case victims of theft sought more serious punishments than binding over. For reasons discussed in chapter 9, the Societies for the Reformation of Manners used recognizances relatively rarely in their campaign against "loose, idle and disorderly" conduct, prostitution and several other types of vice. By definition, vagrants lacked the social connections necessary to enter into a recognizance. As a slow and lenient procedure which exerted little pressure on the defendant, recognizances were ideal for prosecuting offences against the peace and other offences where the parties knew each other. But for those offences that were the subject of public concern, plaintiffs sought more significant, and more efficiently executed, punishments, either by indicting their defendants or by having them committed to a house of correction.

6

Indictment at quarter sessions

The most formal method of prosecuting misdemeanors was to file an indictment at quarter sessions. Typically the primary source used by historians of crime in England, the indictment plays only a supporting role in this study. Yet it is an important role: despite its considerable costs it accounted for over a fifth of all misdemeanor prosecutions at the end of this period.[1] Why did prosecutors choose this cumbersome procedure instead of, or in addition to, a recognizance? Indictments put prosecutors to greater trouble than recognizances, but prosecutors could also gain more from the prosecution. Prosecutors seeking vengeance could enjoy the satisfaction of a formal conviction and punishment, while those seeking financial compensation for their injuries often reached lucrative out-of-court settlements with their defendants. Because prosecution by indictment involved both higher costs and bigger rewards, it was used in different contexts than the other procedures.

6.1 OFFENCES

The overall distributions of offences prosecuted by recognizances and indictments were quite similar: about half of the defendants were accused of offences against the peace, and property offences and vice each accounted for between 10 and 20% of prosecutions (Table 6.1).[2] Nevertheless, there were significant differences in the types of offences prosecuted by the two procedures. More poor law offences, sexual offences, and cases of disturbing and defamation were prosecuted by recognizance. Indictments were more commonly used to prosecute most types of regulatory offences as well as religious and political disaffection, alehouse offences, and trespass and damage to property. Even where an offence, such as assault, was frequently prosecuted by both procedures, the nature of the behavior which led to prosecution could differ markedly.

Legal reasons account for the lack of prosecutions by indictment for several

---

[1] Table 3.3. This calculation does not include summary convictions for conventicles.
[2] See also above, Table 5.1.

127

Table 6.1 *Indictment offences by year*[a]

	1663–64	1677	1693	1707	1720–22[b]
	%	%	%	%	%
Peace	40	42	42	59	50
Vice	14	16	13	16	13
Property	11	12	20	16	17
Regulatory	32	29	21	8	17
Disaffection	3	1	3	—	—
Misc. and unknown	1	1	1	1	4
TOTAL N (100%)	585	319	279	235	389

[a] The unit of analysis is the crime.
[b] May 1720–April 1722.

offences, including private wrongs, sexual offences, and living in a suspicious or immoral manner.[3] Close examination of the offences prosecuted by indictment, however, reveals that legal restrictions were often circumvented. Just as recognizances for "the peace" or for "good behavior" were used in a wide variety of circumstances, indictments for offences such as assault or forcible entry covered a broad range of wrongs. Although the wording on indictments was scrutinized by legal officials far more carefully than that on recognizances,[4] the formulaic language often concealed flexible interpretations of the law. Compared with recognizances, however, this flexibility was more often used with indictments to prosecute defendants involved in property disputes and other civil offences.

In law, an assault could involve as little as a threatening gesture, or merely placing a hand on another in anger, or as much as wounding with a sword.[5] In a case informally mediated by Henry Norris, an assault was proved by testimony that the defendant had laid hold of the victim's collar.[6] In the majority of indictments for assault, the formulaic descriptions of the offence render analysis of the nature of the offence impossible. Where additional information is available, however, it becomes clear that indictments for assault, and related crimes such as riot, rescue, and false imprisonment, were used against a wide range of essentially non-indictable behavior.[7] This is because any wrong could lead to an indictment if the defendant could be construed to have broken the

[3] See above, section 2.3.
[4] J. H. Baker, "The refinement of English criminal jurisprudence, 1500–1848," in *The Legal Profession and The Common Law: Historical Essays* (1986), pp. 305–10.
[5] Dalton, *Countrey Justice* (1677), p. 282.　　[6] GLRO, M79/X/I, 26 Jan. 1734.
[7] Additional evidence usually comes from recognizances related to the same case; few depositions survive for misdemeanors. For a discussion of the evidential problems surrounding the descriptions of crimes on indictments, see section 3.3.

peace. Many wrongs amounted to little more than some insulting words: a grand jury complained in 1683 that many indictments for assault arose from "scolding, backbiting, and reproaching one another."[8] Similarly, people who spoke scandalous words in the street, thereby causing a crowd to gather, were indicted for causing a rout.[9]

Indictments for assault also involved disputes about money and property. In 1663, when two men carried a poor boy across a parish boundary in order to prevent him from becoming chargeable to their parish, they were indicted for an assault.[10] Thomas DeVeil complained in 1747 that landlord–tenant disputes were often framed as criminal charges "under the colour of felonies, force, or assault."[11] Given the formulaic language of indictments, it is difficult to substantiate this complaint, but some similar cases have come to light. In 1721, two yeomen were indicted for breaking into a chamber and stealing a large amount of furniture, clothing, and bonds which were listed as belonging to the dead husband of the victim. The fact that the defendants were found not guilty suggests this indictment was filed as part of an inheritance dispute.[12] One reason that plaintiffs prosecuted such cases as indictments at quarter sessions may have been the fact that the court occasionally encouraged defendants to pay damages to their prosecutors.[13]

Other property disputes were prosecuted as indictments for fraud. To be indictable as a fraud, it was necessary that an "artful device" such as false tokens had been used, as opposed to simple lying,[14] but it is impossible to determine whether this requirement was always met. Alongside indictments for obtaining money by such ruses as falsely begging for prisoners in the Gatehouse by using a counterfeit badge, cutting out the pages of a book of accounts, cheating at gaming, and making false charges of rape and bastardy, are cases which appear to have involved little in the way of an artful device. Thus, a woman was indicted for failing to take some goods worth £28 to be pawned as she had promised, and a man sent to deliver a guinea (21s.) to another man was indicted when he "embezzled" the money for his own use. In a case of what

---

[8] MJ/SBB/408, p. 47 (Oct. 1683).

[9] A rout occurred when three or more people who had gathered together for the purpose of committing an unlawful act "moved forward to the execution of any such act" but did not actually commit the crime (Dalton, *Countrey Justice* [1618], p. 191). Henry Fielding noted that when making out warrants justices of the peace were inclined "to construe a little harmless scolding into a riot" (*Amelia* [1752], p. 12, cited by Landau, *Justices of the Peace*, p. 198).

[10] MJ/SR/1272, I. 41 (July, 1663).

[11] Thomas DeVeil, *Observations on the Practice of a Justice of the Peace* (1747), pp. 13–14.

[12] MJ/SR/2364, I. 32 (April 1721). See also MJ/SR/1822, *ignoramus* indictment (Oct. 1693). For examples of other criminal prosecutions where the element of force was essentially fictitious, see Martin J. Ingram, "Communities and courts: law and disorder in early seventeenth-century Wiltshire," in *Crime in England*, ed. Cockburn, pp. 119–22; T. G. Barnes, "Due process and slow process in the late Elizabethan-early Stuart Star Chamber," *American Journal of Legal History* 6 (1962), p. 226.

[13] See below, section 6.5. [14] See above, chap. 2, note 45.

Table 6.2 *Indictments: estimated annual averages of selected offences*[a]

	1663–64	1677	1693	1707	1720–22[b]
Peace					
Assault	224	309	216	249	362
Riot	44	54	105	147	16
Common disturber/defamation	24	39	33	21	14
Vice					
Alehouse w/o licence	31	27	21	21	0
Disorderly alehouse	51	72	60	54	68
Gaming	7.5	51	6	36	33
Property					
Petty larceny	14	15	3	3	8
Receiving stolen goods	0	0	33	18	24
Trespassing/damage	22.5	21	24	9	28
Fraud	22.5	24	72	66	40
Regulatory					
Not serving on watch	75	51	36	12	2
Not repairing highway	17.5	51	51	6	80
Keeping/slaughtering animals	17.5	9	12	3	0
Not serving as apprentice	22.5	24	9	6	0
Subdividing/cottages[c]	36	33	12	3	6
Disaffection					
Attending conventicle	17.5	0	0	0	0
Sampling proportion:	40%	33%	33%	33%	25%

[a] Method of calculation: sample counts divided by number of years in sample and multiplied by sampling proportion. The unit of analysis is the crime.
[b] May 1720–April 1722.
[c] Subdividing houses and erecting cottages on less than four acres of land.

appears to have been a conflict over conditions of employment, a widow was indicted in 1707 for fraudulently acquiring cloth under pretence of "putting out."[15] In an unusual indictment that same year, three women were indicted for fraudulently corrupting the plaintiff's daughter into prostitution and encouraging her to take and consume the goods of her father.[16] As these last four cases suggest, defendants were often indicted for fraud when, though the offence was tantamount to theft, they could not be indicted for forcibly removing the property. In addition, several people in the sample were indicted for "taking and carrying away goods," often worth considerably more than a shilling,

[15] MJ/SR/2378, I. 20 and calendar of prisoners (Westminster sessions, Jan. 1722); 1819, I. 2 (Feb. 1693); 1820, I. 48 (Sept. 1693); 2361, I. 38 (Feb. 1721); 1282, I. 19 (Feb. 1664); 2083, I. 16 (Westminster sessions, Jan. 1707); 2381, I. 12 (Feb. 1722); 2093, I. 12 (July 1707).
[16] MJ/SR/2089, I. 30 (April 1707).

under circumstances which were not regarded as felonious larceny. These cases include one indictment for taking forty pounds in weight of lead off a roof (worth 3s. 4d.) and another for unlawfully abducting a mare valued at £3 3s.[17] Either the mare was not taken in circumstances that amounted to theft, or the prosecutor did not wish to charge the defendant with horse theft, a non-clergyable capital offence. Thus, a wide range of property disputes led to indictments for property offences at quarter sessions.

It is possible that the number of indictments which addressed disputes typically heard in the civil courts increased during this period. Many offences, of course, do not neatly fit into categories like "criminal" and "civil"; most of the examples described above were probably both criminal and civil in nature. Nonetheless, the number of cases with an essentially civil dimension may have increased: the number of indictments for assault and fraud, offences which frequently involved civil complaints, was highest, judging by the sample years, during the second half of the period (Table 6.2). Concurrently, the number of civil suits tried at the Home Circuit assizes, King's Bench, and the Court of Common Pleas began to decline dramatically in the late seventeenth century.[18] As complaints by DeVeil and William Blackstone suggest, the practice of prosecuting civil cases at quarter sessions continued through at least the mid-eighteenth century.[19]

While offences against the peace and property offences were frequently prosecuted by informal mediation and recognizance as well as by indictment, one category of offences was prosecuted predominantly by indictment: regulatory offences, which include nuisances, cases of neglect of office, and violations of economic regulations. Offences in this category were primarily "victimless" offences, in the sense that the offence harmed the entire community instead of specific individuals, and prosecutions were initiated primarily by public officials. To the modern mind, the use of indictments, a procedure for prosecuting crime, for these essentially administrative problems seems an inappropriate and awkward method of governing a growing metropolis. It is thus not surprising that many of these offences ceased to be prosecuted by indictment in the early eighteenth century (Table 6.2).

The majority of nuisance offences involved acts of omission, particularly

---

[17] MJ/SR/2381, I. 36 (Feb. 1722); 2366, I. 17 (May 1721). Items attached to freehold property could not be subject to larceny (Hawkins, *Pleas of the Crown*, vol. 1, p. 93; Baker, "Refinement of English criminal jurisprudence," pp. 320–23).

[18] J. S. Cockburn, *A History of English Assizes 1558–1714* (Cambridge, 1972), pp. 138–39; C. W. Brooks, "Interpersonal conflict and social tension: civil litigation in England, 1640–1830," in *The First Modern Society*, ed. A. L. Beier *et al.*, (Cambridge, 1989), pp. 360–63. See also Beattie, "Pattern of crime," p. 70.

[19] William Blackstone, *Commentaries on the Laws of England*, 4 vols. (Oxford, 1765–69), vol. 4, pp. 356–57.

failure to repair streets or highways. A few indictments were also filed against individuals who created nuisances by keeping and/or slaughtering animals within the metropolis, dumping cartloads of filth on common land, keeping a bakehouse with ovens too close to other houses, and obstructing highways with stalls, baskets, or wheelbarrows offering goods for sale.[20] Indictments for nuisance thus provided local officials and the courts with a means of reducing disease and fire hazards and keeping roads clear for traffic, as well as keeping the roads repaired. Indictments for neglect of office provided a means of supervising local officeholders. Public officials were indicted for failing to perform such duties as executing a warrant, suppressing an affray, and levying penalties on inhabitants for not putting out candles in the street at night.[21] In addition, several officers were indicted for charging illegitimate or excessive fees. The most frequent type of neglect was committed by householders who failed to serve by rotation on the nightly watch (or hire a substitute).

Considering the scope of the relevant legislation, the number of defendants indicted for violating economic regulations is insignificant, accounting for only 4% of the sample. As Dowdell has observed, by the eighteenth century trade in urban Middlesex was "left mainly to look after itself."[22] A small and declining number of indictments were filed for selling goods in insufficient measures and for engrossing, forestalling, and regrating.[23] Up to two dozen men a year were accused of practicing a trade without having served a seven-year apprenticeship. Although Dowdell argued that the enforcement of this law by the City companies "practically ceased after 1675,"[24] there continued to be a few indictments in every sample year up to 1707. Nevertheless, the last conviction for this offence in the sample was in 1677. As new forms of labor organization emerged, so did new crimes: groups of craftsmen who pressed for higher wages or better conditions during this period were indicted for conspiracy or riot.[25]

Over the course of the late seventeenth and early eighteenth centuries, the distribution of offences prosecuted by indictment changed significantly (Table 6.2). Between the first and last sample periods the number of indictments for

[20] MJ/SR/1528, I. 97 (July 1677); 1534, I. 29 (Dec. 1677); 1275, I. 65 (Westminster sessions, July 1663); 1287, I. 29 (May 1664); 2374, I. 55 (Oct. 1721).

[21] MJ/SR/1268, I. 29 (April 1663); 1276, I. 12, 115 (Oct. 1663); 1282, I. 12 (Feb. 1664).

[22] Dowdell, *Quarter Sessions*, p. 189.

[23] These offences may also have been dealt with at any manorial courts that were still active in the metropolis. For an example from early seventeenth-century Southwark, see Boulton, *Neighbourhood and Society*, pp. 76–77, 264. Forestalling, regrating, engrossing, and selling wine at excessive prices were also occasionally prosecuted by information at quarter sessions, particularly during the 1660s (Dowdell, *Quarter Sessions*, pp. 165–66, 184).

[24] Dowdell, *Quarter Sessions*, p. 175. For the difficulty of enforcing this law, see J. R. Kellett, "The breakdown of gild and corporation control over the handicraft and retail trade in London," *Economic History Review*, 2nd series, 10 (1958), pp. 383–89.

[25] MJ/SR/2349, I. 80 (July 1720); 2351, R. 10, 11, 16, 18–20, 100, 130 (Sept. 1720); 2354, I. 58 (Oct. 1720); 2356, I. 60, 61 and related recognizances (Dec. 1720); Dowdell, *Quarter Sessions*,

assault and riot increased by 41%.[26] Although the number of indictments for most property offences remained stable or declined, those for fraud and receiving stolen goods increased significantly. As we have seen, a broad range of deviant behavior resulted in indictments for property and peace offences, and it is possible that prosecutions of essentially civil wrongs account for some of these increases (with the exception of receiving stolen goods[27]). Concurrently, as the result of a combination of the shifting priorities of prosecutors, changing legal requirements, and possibly greater use of King's Bench, indictments for several victimless offences appear to have declined markedly during this period. Prosecutions for such offences fluctuated considerably from year to year according to regulatory initiatives, but the general trend seems clear.[28] The Toleration Act and changing attitudes towards religious nonconformity, for example, led to the virtual disappearance of indictments for religious offences after 1689. Similarly, the declining number of indictments for many regulatory offences, including keeping cottages on less than four acres of land, subdividing houses, keeping or slaughtering animals within the metropolis, and practicing a trade without an apprenticeship, was caused by more *laissez-faire* attitudes towards economic regulation. On the other hand, the decline in indictments for not serving on the night watch was the result of new methods of local government (the use of a salaried nightly watch and local improvement acts).[29]

Indictments for some offences declined because summary conviction replaced indictments as the preferred method of prosecution. The disappearance of conventiclers from the sample after 1664, for example, is largely explained by the fact that a statute in that year made the offence punishable by summary conviction.[30] Similarly, a series of rulings at King's Bench in the 1690s and early 1700s that keeping an alehouse without a licence could only be punished summarily (as dictated by the relevant statutes) explains the total absence of indictments for this offence in the 1720–22 sample.[31] The concurrent decline in

pp. 154–55; *Middlesex Records*, ed. Jeaffreson, vol. 4, pp. xxvii–xxxiii, 60–65; Shoemaker, "London 'mob'," pp. 279–80; C. R. Dobson, *Masters and Journeymen; A Prehistory of Industrial Relations 1717–1800* (1980), pp. 32–33, 62, 126–27.

26 A further sample shows that indictments for riot increased consistently over the course of this period (Shoemaker, "London 'mob'," p. 274).

27 It was only in 1691 that the first effective statute against receiving stolen goods (3 and 4 Wm. and M. c. 9) was passed (Beattie, *Crime and the Courts*, pp. 189–90).

28 The evidence presented here, based on sample years, is confirmed (with one exception, noted below) by the more systematic investigations conducted by Dowdell (*Quarter Sessions*).

29 Dowdell, *Quarter Sessions*, chaps. 3, 4, 6. As a result of the growth of turnpike trusts and the increased use of summary conviction, indictments for not working on the highways declined shortly after the end of this period.

30 16 Car. 2. c. 4 (expired July 1667); 22 Car. 2 c. 1 (partially repealed 1688). After the first statute took effect on 1 July 1664, indictments were required only for defendants who were accused of attending conventicles after having been twice previously convicted of the offence.

31 See above, section 2.3. Isaacs discovered that after 1713 there were almost no indictments for unlicensed alehouses in Middlesex (Tina Beth Isaacs, "Moral crime, moral reform, and the state in early eighteenth-century England: a study of piety and politics" [Ph.D. diss. University of

indictments for keeping a bawdy house may have been due to the practice, advocated by an order of the Middlesex court for reasons of expedience, of summarily convicting madams of the related offence of selling ale or liquor without a licence.[32] With the reformation of manners campaign active throughout the second half of the period of this study, there was no lack of interest in prosecuting alehouse and sexual offences, but both legal and practical considerations led to the punishment of a growing number of offenders summarily. It is equally unlikely that the decline in the number of indictments for petty larceny at quarter sessions was due to a decrease in prosecutions for theft. Increasing numbers of defendants accused of petty theft were committed to houses of correction for immediate summary punishment; others may have been indicted at gaol delivery sessions at the Old Bailey.[33]

With the rise of summary conviction and changing regulatory practices, indictments in the early eighteenth century were increasingly limited to peace and property offences, particularly assault. While indictments for offences against the peace and property offences accounted for 51% of all indictments in 1663–64, by 1720–22 they accounted for 67%. Although indictments for these offences could be used to prosecute indirectly a wide variety of criminal and civil wrongs, they could only with difficulty be used for victimless offences, which were by 1720 rarely the subjects of formal indictments.

6.2 DROPPED PROSECUTIONS

The most surprising aspect of the results of prosecutions by indictment is the fact that the indictments of more than a third of all defendants never reached a final verdict (Table 6.3).[34] Why did plaintiffs allow so many prosecutions to be dropped before they reached a final verdict? Should dropped prosecutions be interpreted as signs that plaintiffs and defendants had reached an informal settlement? Or do they indicate that prosecutors had abandoned their cases out of frustration, apathy, or because defendants failed to cooperate? Although

Rochester, 1979], p. 233). These findings contradict Dowdell (*Quarter Sessions*, p. 35), who argues, apparently on the basis of three indictments in May 1718 and Sept. 1719, that prosecutors continued to prosecute this offence by indictment.

[32] MJ/OC/I, ff. 49–51d (Jan. 1719).

[33] I am grateful for the advice I have received on this subject from John Beattie, who is currently studying prosecutions of petty larceny in this period. For the punishment of theft in houses of correction, see below, section 7.1.

[34] Verdicts were searched for on the indictments in the sessions rolls (MJ/SR) and in the sessions process books (MJ/SBP). Random checks in the sessions books (MJ/SBB) revealed no additional evidence. The total number of dropped cases includes a small number (1.2%) in which indictments were formally discharged by the court for insufficient evidence or by the Attorney General. It does not include cases removed by writ of *certiorari*, which are discussed in the next section. In his discussions of prosecutions for regulatory offences, Dowdell notes several times that many cases never resulted in a final verdict (Dowdell, *Quarter Sessions*, chaps. 3, 4, and 6).

Table 6.3 *Dispositions of indictments by offence*[a]

	No verdict	Ignoramus	Found innocent	Found guilty	Pleaded guilty[b]	Other[c]	TOTAL (100%)
	%	%	%	%	%	%	N
Peace							
Assault	24	18	5	2	42	9	682
Aggravated assault	39	12	6	4	22	16	157
Riot	37	18	10	4	22	9	529
Common disturber/defamation	31	11	15	—	23	21	62
Vice							
Sexual offences	40	15	15	5	15	10	20
Alehouse offences	63	5	8	1	13	10	233
Gaming	36	34	3	3	12	12	59
Property							
Theft[d]							
Trespassing/damage	41	19	5	4	27	5	110
Fraud	36	12	14	8	14	16	137
Regulatory							
Neglect of office	49	4	8	3	33	4	156
Nuisance	56	7	5	—	27	5	222
Economic offences	41	9	21	1	13	14	90
Disaffection	25	6	6	49	13	—	63
Misc.	37	19	7	4	7	26	27
TOTAL	37	15	8	4	26	10	2759

[a] The unit of analysis is the defendant.

[b] Including cases in which the defendant initially pleaded innocent and subsequently changed the plea to guilty (6% of all cases).

[c] Including defendants who pleaded a general pardon (1% of all cases), indictments removed by *certiorari* (7%), and miscellaneous and unknown verdicts (1.5%).

[d] Cases of grand larceny are excluded because only *ignoramus* indictments for this offence are found in the sessions rolls.

evidence concerning dropped cases is quite limited, there is substance in both of these explanations.

A significant number of dropped prosecutions may be attributed to the failure of the defendant to appear in court. Assuming the defendant could be located (it is unknown how many prosecutions failed when defendants could not be found), he was required to enter into a recognizance to guarantee his appearance in court in order to enter a plea to the indictment. A small proportion of defendants who could not find sureties were committed to prison until sessions met.[35] Of those who entered into recognizances (about 70%), about a sixth chose to default on these rather than appear in court.[36] Warrants to arrest defaulters could be effective if the defendant remained in the same neighborhood, but more mobile defendants were difficult to apprehend. Thus, failure of the defendant to appear in court must account for a substantial proportion, perhaps a third, of the indictments which were dropped.

Many defendants who did appear appeared one or more sessions late. Even when defendants cooperated, it often took several months to arrive at a final verdict. Since many defendants were not present at the sessions at which they were indicted, they could not enter their pleas until the following sessions. If they pleaded innocent, their trials were further delayed to the subsequent sessions. In contrast to felonies, pleas and trials for misdemeanors could not be held on the same day, as "the party ought to have a convenient time to provide for the trial."[37] Thus, verdicts by confession were often entered one sessions, and verdicts reached by juries two sessions, after the sessions at which the indictment was preferred (Table 6.4). In fact, delays were even longer: 21% of the defendants who pleaded guilty did so two or more sessions (about three months in Middlesex) after the original sessions, and 19% of jury trials occurred three or more sessions (about half a year in Middlesex) after the indictment was approved by the grand jury. Nine percent of all verdicts were reached four or more sessions, or about eight months in Middlesex, after the indictment was filed. Because the Westminster court met half as frequently, delays were twice as long.

Such extended delays were usually caused by dilatory defendants. Because the responsibility for scheduling trials was left to defendants, who were required to notify their prosecutors and the court when they intended to stand

---

[35] See above, Table 5.2.

[36] It should be noted that this figure, while based on the same sample years, is not strictly compatible with the indictment figure since they are based on independant samples. It is thus unlikely that many of the indictments and recognizances sampled were for the same cases. The figure of 70% is based on a search for recognizances for all the defendants who were indicted in April 1723: MJ/SR/2399, 2402, 2404, 2407 (Feb.–July 1723). Similarly, Cynthia Herrup noted that in seventeenth-century East Sussex "eleven percent of the cases [indictments] in the quarter sessions where the appearance or absence of the defendant is noted lapsed because defendants defaulted on their promises to appear" (*The Common Peace*, p. 90).

[37] *Office of the Clerk of the Peace*, p. 163.

Table 6.4 *Time to final verdict*[a]

	Found innocent	Found guilty	Change plea to guilty	Pleaded guilty	TOTAL	TOTAL
	%	%	%	%	%	N
Immediate verdict	5	21	5	47	27	218
One session	39	48	60	32	40	316
Two sessions	35	18	14	11	18	143
Three sessions	12	2	8	3	6	48
Four or more sessions	9	11	14	7	9	69
TOTAL N (100%)	198	62	131	403	(100%)	794

[a] Middlesex sessions; conventicles excluded.

trial,[38] many defendants delayed contacting (or were unable to contact) their prosecutors and their trials were consequently postponed. In petitions to the court, defendants naturally blamed their prosecutors for these delays. Timothy Crome, indicted for assault, testified that he tried for six months to locate his prosecutor, and claimed that she had "run away into some remote parts" and could not be found.[39] The case of one prosecutor, however, demonstrates how defendants could manipulate this system to frustrate prosecutions. After John Lourey filed an indictment for riotous assault, the defendants forfeited their recognizances and failed to stand trial for almost a year. They then gave Lourey notice that they would appear for trial, "knowing that one of your petitioner's [Lourey's] material witnesses cannot this sessions appear ... without whose testimony your petitioner cannot go to trial."[40] Delays thus compounded the difficulties experienced by prosecutors in arranging for witnesses to testify in court.[41]

Postponements of trials did not always have such negative consequences. As with recognizances, the parties to indictments often used the time between the filing of an indictment and subsequent court appearances to reach a settlement of their differences. Such agreements ranged from informal understandings to formal releases from prosecution, sometimes arrived at by entering into bonds of arbitration.[42] Settlements were most likely to occur in cases involving property or peace offences, where the prosecutor was also the victim of the crime, and most involved the payment of monetary damages. In 1722, a surety negotiated a settlement in which in exchange for a formal release the defendant paid the prosecutor's legal costs. As the prosecutor was alleged to have said, by avoiding the cost of a trial such a settlement "would save them money and he [the prosecutor] might as well have it as counsel or attorneys."[43] This type of private settlement, which was endorsed by the Recorder of London in 1729,[44] appears to have occurred frequently. An order of the Middlesex court in 1722 complained that delays in the prosecution of defendants accused of receiving stolen goods and assault with intent to rape allowed "an opportunity to such offenders to agree and compound with the prosecutors for a sum of money, and thereby such prosecutions have been stifled, so that the offenders have escaped receiving condign punishment for their offences ... " While such settlements suited victims, the court complained that they did not result in sufficient punishment for the defendants considering the severity of the

---

[38] MJ/SBB/323, p. 42 (May 1675); MJ/SP/Dec. 1722, no. 7. For examples of such notices, see MJ/SP/Oct. 1719, no. 58; July 1720, no. 1a; Feb. 1723, no. 5.
[39] MJ/SP/Oct. 1692, no. 12.   [40] MJ/SP/Sept. 1719, no. 16.
[41] Edmund Bohun, *The Justice of the Peace; His Calling and Qualifications* (1693), preface.
[42] MJ/SP/Oct. 1707, no. 7; May 1720, no. 4; Sept. 1722, no. 55.
[43] GLRO, miscellaneous sessions papers, 3 Dec. 1722.
[44] PRO, SP 36/15, ff. 183–84, cited by Beattie, *Crime and the Courts*, pp. 457–58.

crimes.[45] Although the justices disapproved of extra-legal settlements of indictments for such "heinous and notorious" offences, it sanctioned them for defendants accused of lesser offences. Indictments for keeping an alehouse without a licence, failing to repair a highway, and recusancy were occasionally discharged by the court when the defendants took corrective action and obtained a licence, repaired the road, or appeared in church.[46] With the consent of the parties, the court occasionally referred indictments to formal arbitration by two justices, particularly when cross-indictments were filed.[47] Because arbitration was cheaper and more flexible than a trial, it appealed to both defendants and prosecutors.

It is impossible to determine how many dropped indictments resulted in informal settlements. Although evidence of only a few cases of informal settlements and arbitration survives, there was no regular means of recording such outcomes. As the Middlesex order just quoted suggests, the justices thought that out-of-court settlements often occurred. Nevertheless, the high proportion of indictments dropped by plaintiffs who were public officials suggests that there was another cause of dropped prosecutions. Both formal arbitration and informal settlements were generally unsuitable for offences prosecuted by public officials, where the plaintiffs could not reach private arrangements with defendants without being accused of corruption.[48] Yet, 85% of the indictments filed by constables and other public officials were dropped without a final verdict. The offences prosecuted by these officials were mostly victimless crimes, such as alehouse offences and nuisance offences. Constables were legally required to present these offences, but they were unwilling to spend the time and money necessary to bring such cases to trial, unless pressured to do so by the justices. In cases where such pressure was forthcoming, such as in the prosecution of conventiclers in 1664, the proportion of defendants whose cases did not reach a final verdict dropped to less than one third of the average for all other indictments. Such pressure was, however, rare. Since public officials were unpaid and generally unwilling to incur expenses in the execution of their office, it is likely that it is the trouble and expense of pursuing cases to a final verdict that explains why so many of their indictments were dropped without a final verdict.

---

[45] MJ/SP/Dec. 1722, no. 54. These offences were closely related to felonies, and compounding felonies was illegal.

[46] MJ/SPB, *passim.*

[47] For example, see MJ/SBB/575, p. 48 (Aug. 1700); 807, p. 58 (Dec. 1721). Arbitration was commonly used in the common law and church courts, and for petty crimes (Edward Powell, "Arbitration and the law in England in the late middle ages," *Transactions of the Royal Historical Society*, 5th series, 33 [1983], pp. 49–68; Sharpe, " 'Such disagreement betwyx neighbours'," pp. 167–87; *Arbitrium Redivium: Or, the Law of Arbitration* [1694]).

[48] See above, section 4.2. There is some evidence, however, that indictments for failing to repair roads were discharged without a verdict when justices certified to the court that the road had been repaired (Dowdell, *Quarter Sessions*, p. 94).

6.3 OBSTACLES TO PROSECUTION

The cost of obtaining a final verdict on an indictment was not trivial; indictments were the most expensive method of prosecuting misdemeanors. Like all legal proceedings in early-modern England, bringing an indictment to trial involved fees for each small step in the legal process. In addition to the cost of the warrant for the defendant's arrest (up to 2s.), prosecutors paid two shillings to the clerk of the peace to draw up the indictment, 4d. to the bailiff to carry the indictment to the grand jury, and 4d. to the cryer for swearing each witness.[49] Perhaps the greatest cost incurred by plaintiffs, however, was the time spent travelling to and attending sessions, which kept them away from their employment or business. Unlike prosecutors of recognizances, who rarely appeared in court, prosecutors of indictments were required to appear in court at least twice: first to prefer the indictment, and second for the trial (or to accept a guilty plea). Although trials were scheduled, other court business often necessitated long periods of attendance in court. An attorney in 1720, for example, spent two days in court when he preferred an indictment for damaging a turnpike (Table 6.5). As noted earlier, many defendants failed to appear in court as scheduled, thus necessitating further appearances in court. Costs were further increased by the custom of paying witnesses for their time and trouble in attending court. It is only possible to estimate the cost of travelling to and attending sessions after 1752, when a statute authorized the courts to reimburse prosecutors in certain circumstances for their expenses. In 1754, justice Dudley Ryder awarded 5s. per day per person for attendance at the home circuit assizes, in addition to what he allowed for court fees.[50] This figure should be multiplied by two or three to account for the fact that, in addition to themselves, most prosecutors arranged for one or two witnesses to testify in support of their case. Although residents of London spent less time travelling to the courts, geographical patterns of prosecutions suggest that even within the metropolis distance was an obstacle to filing prosecutions.[51]

With weekly wages running at about eight to twelve shillings a week for laborers and the lowest paid journeymen, the cost of prosecuting an indictment could easily add up to more than a week's wages. According to contemporary commentators, the costs of prosecution dissuaded many potential prosecutors from filing indictments for vice and theft.[52] Unfortunately, it is impossible to

---

[49] *Office of the Clerk of the Peace*, pp. 247–54; Thomas Powell, *The Attorney's Academy* (1647), pp. 400–05; MJ/OC/I, ff. 111–112d (Jan. 1721); P. S., *A Help to Magistrates* (1721), p. 19. For other estimates of the costs of prosecution, see Beattie, *Crime and the Courts*, p. 41; Sharpe, *Crime in Seventeenth-Century England*, p. 177.

[50] Beattie, *Crime and the Courts*, pp. 42–43.   [51] See below, section 10.1.

[52] See above, section 5.4; Henry Fielding, *An Enquiry into the Causes of the Late Increase of Robbers* (1751), pp. 106, 109–10; Roger North, *A Discourse of the Poor* (1753), pp. 26–27; [Edward Stephens], *A Plain Relation of the late Action at Sea ... and upon the present State of*

Table 6.5 *Attorney's fees incurred by the prosecutor of an indictment for damaging a turnpike, January 1720–October 1722*

	£	s	d
January sessions, 1720:			
Taking instructions in order to prefer indictment	0	3	4
For bill of indictment	0	3	4
Swearing witnesses thereon	0	1	0
Attendance and expenses at Hicks Hall [courthouse], two days with witnesses	0	2	10
Bench warrant [for arresting defendant]	0	1	0
Attending for same	0	3	4
October sessions, 1722:			
Attend court on defendant's notice to plead pardon, with witnesses and expenses	1	10	0
Counsel's fee	0	1	1
	£2	5	11

Source: WJ/SP/October 1722, nos. 21, 22.

verify these allegations since the social or economic status of prosecutors was very rarely identified on Middlesex indictments. Even more than with recognizances, however, the geographical distribution of misdemeanor indictments suggests that the poor were less likely to file indictments than their social superiors. Far fewer prosecutors per capita came from the poorest parishes of urban Middlesex, those lying north and east of the City of London, than from the affluent west end. Despite recent suggestions to the contrary, this evidence strongly suggests that the poor in early-modern England were significantly discouraged from prosecuting indictments by the costs of prosecution.[53]

Costs were considerably higher for prosecutors who chose to hire a solicitor to guide them through the often complex and mysterious procedures of the courts. Sessions were chaotic and the inexperienced participant could easily become disoriented. As Fielding complained in 1751, "the business of sessions is so complicated and various that it happens, as in all cases where men have too much to do, they do little or nothing effectually."[54] Attorneys could avoid costly pitfalls and instigate diversionary actions. James Annand, the prosecutor of an indictment for breaking and entering, "being ignorant in matters of law," failed to get the proper warrant issued and incurred as a consequence "charges

the Nation. Together with ... a Specimen of a Bill for a Reformation of Manners (1690), p. 8 of the Specimen of a Bill.
[53] This point is taken up in the conclusion. For the geographical evidence, see below, section 10.1.
[54] Fielding, *Enquiry into the Causes*, p. 421.

Table 6.6 Indictment dispositions by year[a]

	1663–64	1677	1693	1707	1720–22	TOTAL
	%	%	%	%	%	%
Ignoramus	6	11	18	19	22	14
No verdict	42	36	30	35	39	38
Found innocent	12	7	6	9	5	8
Found guilty	6	3	3	3	4	4
Changed plea to guilty	4	7	8	7	7	6
Pleaded guilty	22	28	22	15	13	20
Pardoned	—	—	—	—	3	1
Certiorari	7	7	12	11	3	7
Misc., unknown	1	1	1	2	4	2
TOTAL N (100%)	886	424	433	432	570	2745

[a] Not including cases of grand larceny, since only the *ignoramus* indictments were kept at sessions.

and damages to the value of ten pounds and upwards."[55] In this case, legal advice would have been cheaper: the cost of hiring a solicitor for prosecuting a misdemeanor varied depending on the individual circumstances of the case, but appears to have averaged four or five pounds for a case that went to trial.[56] Table 6.5 lists the charges for legal advice incurred by one prosecutor for an indictment for damaging a turnpike in 1722. Although the case was relatively simple (it was terminated before trial when the defendant pleaded a pardon), the solicitor charged over two pounds for his services. It is unknown how many prosecutors used solicitors at the Middlesex sessions.[57] Despite the widespread availability of solicitors in London, the high fees must have dissuaded most prosecutors from seeking legal advice.

Costs escalated further if the defendant obtained a writ of *certiorari* and removed the case to be tried at King's Bench. While writs of *certiorari* were rarely granted for defendants accused of felonies,[58] they were granted to 8% of

[55] MJ/SP/Oct. 1713, no. 35.
[56] One prosecutor, for example, demanded four or five pounds as the "costs of a suit of law" in return for dropping the prosecution of his indictment: MJ/SP/Dec. 1720, no. 14. See also nos. 21, 22, 25.
[57] For some comments on the use of attorneys for the prosecution of misdemeanors, see C. W. Brooks, *Pettyfoggers and Vipers of the Commonwealth: the 'Lower' Branch of the Legal Profession in Early Modern England* (Cambridge, 1986), p. 190.
[58] Hawkins, *Pleas of the Crown* (1716), vol. 2, p. 287; Herrup, *The Common Peace*, p. 43; Sharpe, *Crime in Seventeenth-Century England*, p. 25; Beattie, *Crime and the Courts*, p. 335.

the defendants indicted at the Middlesex sessions.[59] In theory, defendants could obtain writs of *certiorari* if they wished to question the legality of their indictment, they believed they would not get a fair trial at sessions, or they intended to plead a pardon from the king.[60] In practice, defendants also used writs as a vexatious tactic to obstruct prosecutors. Actions by the Middlesex court, King's Bench, and Parliament during the late seventeenth century attempted to stem this practice, and apparently as a result of these measures indictments removed by *certiorari* declined from a peak of 12% in the 1693 sample to 3% by the 1720–22 sample (Table 6.6).

Defendants who obtained writs of *certiorari* were often required to enter into a bond to pay the prosecutor's costs in the event that they were found guilty.[61] Initially, however, prosecutors had to pay legal costs out of their own pockets, and they were not reimbursed if the defendant was found innocent. Consequently, many plaintiffs whose indictments were removed to King's Bench chose to abandon their prosecutions. In 1661, the judges at King's Bench ruled that it would not hear cases of perjury, forgery, and other "grand misdemeanors" unless they had been tried at an inferior court, because their experience was that once cases were removed by *certiorari*, they were often not brought to trial.[62] This problem was clearly not restricted to "grand misdemeanors." In 1677, the Middlesex justices complained to the Lord Chief Justice that many of the indictments removed by *certiorari* were for

keeping bawdy houses and disorderly alehouses, and some for assaults, and others like offences, wherein there is no cause of difficulty; ... such writs of *certiorari* are brought chiefly to discourage and weary out the constables and other prosecutors, ... as the court is informed, the persons indicted seldom or never come to trial upon such indictments removed, but continue to do the same or like offences ...[63]

A statute passed in 1694 attempted to redress this problem by requiring defendants to enter into bonds of £20 to stand trial at King's Bench during the next term.[64] Having an indictment removed by *certiorari* was certainly sufficiently expensive to deter prosecutors, since contesting a case in King's Bench required the services of a barrister, who was likely to charge at least a pound

---

[59] Because of the absence of sessions process books for Westminster after 1679, it was not possible to include in the sample indictments removed by *certiorari* from Westminster during the last three sample periods. Consequently, the figures in this paragraph pertain to the Middlesex sessions only. The figures in Tables 6.3 and 6.6 do include Westminster sessions, however, and thus slightly underestimate the number of indictments actually removed.

[60] Blackstone, *Commentaries* (1769), vol. 4, p. 315.

[61] 21 Jac.1 c. 8, 13 and 14 Car. 2. c. 6. For examples of such "bonds of obligation", see MJ/SP/Sept 1691, nos. 10–14.

[62] Thomas Siderfin, *Les Reports des divers special cases argue et adjudge en le court del Bank le Roy* (2nd edn, 1714), p. 54.

[63] MJ/SBB/348, p. 35 (Oct. 1677). As the justices complained in 1675, indictments were often removed after the prosecutor had gone to the expense of bringing the case to the point of a trial at quarter sessions: MJ/SBB/329, p. 40. (Dec. 1675).

[64] 5 and 6 Wm. and M. c. 5.

for his services. Given this cost, the fees charged by King's Bench, the fee for removing an indictment from quarter sessions (6s. 8d.), and the necessity of entering into a bond, it is not surprising that *certiorari* was used disproportionately by wealthy defendants.[65] Although only 20 of the 135 men in the sample who obtained writs were gentlemen, indicted gentlemen were about 70% more likely to obtain writs than non-gentry males.[66]

Analysis of the offences listed on indictments removed by *certiorari* suggests that many were removed for vexatious reasons. Of the 203 defendants whose indictments were removed, 56% were accused of offences against the peace (assault, riot, barratry) and 11% were accused of vice offences (primarily keeping a disorderly alehouse). Although, as argued above, indictments for some of these offences (particularly assault) could result from disputes over complicated issues such as property rights, in general indictments for these offences did not pose difficult legal questions which would justify removing them to King's Bench. Contemporary complaints that *certiorari* was used as a tactic for frustrating prosecutions appear to have had some foundation. On the other hand, cases of fraud (10% of defendants) and violations of economic regulations (6% of defendants) may have involved genuine legal questions for which the expertise of the higher court was needed. In particular, the Middlesex justices may have been delighted to forward to the judges in Westminster an indictment of three women for committing fraud by incantation.[67] Similarly, indictments for perjury, counterfeiting, forgery, extortion, usury, and similar offences could present complicated legal issues. It is also likely that some defendants had their indictments removed on the (legitimate) grounds that they were so unpopular that they could not receive a fair trial at sessions. Thus, when two informers associated with the Societies for the Reformation of Manners were indicted for assault, they had the case removed to King's Bench.[68] Defendants indicted for regrating and engrossing victuals during a year of high bread prices, and clerks to the Commissioner for Regulating Hackney Coaches who were indicted for extortion in the execution of their office, could have also justified their writs of *certiorari* on the basis of their unpopularity.[69] Not all writs of *certiorari* were filed for vexatious reasons.

Defendants who sought to harass their prosecutors were able to cause even

---

[65] *Office of the Clerk of the Peace*, pp. 247–54; Geoffrey Holmes, *Augustan England: Professions, State and Society, 1680–1730* (1982), pp. 130–31. In 1720, Richard and Charity Hayward claimed they spent almost £200 defending themselves on an indictment in King's Bench for keeping a bawdy house: PRO, KB1/1; *London Journal, or, the Thursday's Journal*, 18 March 1720.

[66] The imprecise nature of the "additions" ascribed to male defendants, and the general lack of evidence concerning the socioeconomic status of indicted women, precludes more precise analysis of the socio-economic status of defendants.

[67] MJ/SR/1818, I. 93 (July 1693).   [68] MJ/SR/2351, I. 63 (Sept. 1720).

[69] MJ/SR/1523, I. 25, 28, 34 (Westminster sessions, April 1677); 1533, I. 40, 49 (Oct. 1677); 1272, I. 72, 75, 77 (Aug. 1663).

greater trouble by initiating vexatious prosecutions against them. Although vexatious counter indictments were relatively rare at quarter sessions,[70] they could substantially inconvenience prosecutors, particularly those who were unable to find bail. Martha Mitchell complained to the court in 1723 that after she indicted a headborough for keeping an unlawful gaming house, he "out of malice indicted your petitioner for a riot, of which she was no ways guilty." Because she was unable to find sureties to guarantee her appearance at sessions, she was imprisoned, first in New Prison and then in a house of correction, "where she was used after a very inhumane manner."[71] Another effective method of instigating a vexatious prosecution was to initiate a case in another court, particularly the Westminster common law courts or courts of debt such as the Marshalsea. As Martin Ingram noted in his study of vexatious prosecutions in early seventeenth-century Wiltshire, "the flexibility of trespass prosecutions probably made them useful instruments for vexatious exploitation ... merely to compare the record of the Court of Common Pleas for a single term, Michaelmas 1618, with the quarter sessions rolls reveals several very clear examples of the malicious prosecution of actions of trespass."[72] No attempt has been made to determine the number of plaintiffs from Middlesex who were subject to such prosecutions, but given the proximity of the Westminster courts it must have been significant.[73] The cost of defending a suit in the common law courts could be substantial. When a constable and four headboroughs indicted Frances Hinton alias West in the early 1690s for keeping or frequenting a bawdy house, she brought an action against them in the Court of Common Pleas. Although the suit was unsuccessful, the officers were unable, because of her poverty, to recover their costs, which they claimed amounted to over £24.[74] The mere threat of such a prosecution must have prevented some plaintiffs from bringing their indictments to trial.

It was also possible to get plaintiffs and witnesses arrested for small debts. It was notoriously easy to arrest people for debts of as little as a few pence, and the debts were often fictitious. Victims of these arrests suffered the miserable conditions of debtors' prisons, such as the Whitechapel and Marshalsea prisons in the metropolis, and had to pay the costs of their imprisonment and of getting themselves discharged.[75] When Elizabeth Martin indicted Elizabeth

---

[70] A survey of all the plaintiffs and defendants involved in indictments for riots at the Middlesex sessions in April and May 1713 revealed that only five out of seventy-six were involved in a reverse prosecution by September of that year: MJ/SR/2203, 2205, 2208, 2210, 2212, 2214.

[71] MJ/SP/May 1723, no. 15. See also MJ/SP/Aug. 1694, no. 7.

[72] Ingram, "Communities and Courts," pp. 120–21.

[73] Conversely, Douglas Hay has suggested that criminal prosecutions were often used to harass plaintiffs in civil cases ("Prosecution and power: malicious prosecution in the English courts, 1750–1850," in *Policing and Prosecution*, ed. Hay and Snyder, pp. 361–62).

[74] MJ/SBB/500, pp. 50–51 (Oct. 1692).

[75] George, *London Life*, pp. 297–302; [T. Baston, Esq.], *Thoughts on Trade, and a Public Spirit* (1716), pp. 96–97; Paul H. Haagen, "Eighteenth-century English society and the debt law," in

Power for assaulting and wounding her, Power and her husband "to discharge the matter ... arrested [Martin] and caused her to be put into the prison of the Marshalsea where she lieth on the bare boards."[76] Such arrests, or even the mere threat of such arrests, could hinder the defense as well as the prosecution. John Yerberry, indicted for a riotous assault in September 1719, complained that two material witnesses were unable to attend his trial because his prosecutor was a Marshalsea Court bailiff who "threatened to arrest the said parties in case they gave evidence" for the defense.[77]

In sum, even at the best of times prosecution by indictment required a considerable investment of time and money. Malicious defendants increased these costs by failing to appear in court, obtaining writs of *certiorari*, and initiating vexatious suits and prosecutions. The obstacles to prosecution outlined here constituted a major disincentive to bringing indictments to trial, or even to initiating them in the first place.[78] By bringing such pressure to bear on their prosecutors, indicted defendants hoped to get them to drop the prosecution, possibly in return for the payment of some money as damages and/or to reimburse legal costs. Thus, plaintiffs were often forced into accepting informal settlements, though not necessarily on favorable terms. Decisions concerning whether to drop prosecutions were also influenced by prosecutors' perceptions of the likelihood of obtaining a conviction, should the prosecution be continued, as well as by the nature of the punishments convicted defendants were likely to receive. Does the pattern of verdicts and punishments in Middlesex suggest that it was worthwhile for plaintiffs to follow through with their prosecutions?

6.4 VERDICTS

Prosecutors faced the considerable probability that they would obtain a conviction if they pursued their cases to a final verdict. Eighty-six percent of the indictments presented before the Middlesex grand jury were approved as true bills (Table 6.6). Petty juries presented more of a problem, as they found two-thirds of the defendants they tried innocent. Nevertheless, because so many defendants pleaded guilty, fully three-quarters of the final verdicts were

---

Social Control and the State, ed. S. Cohen and A. Scull (Oxford, 1983), pp. 222–47, esp. pp. 233–35. The condition of small debtors improved with the passing of the vexatious arrests act in 1726 (Joanna Innes, "Social problems: poverty and marginality in eighteenth-century England" [unpublished typescript, 1985], p. 110).

[76] MJ/SP/July 1690, no. 13. See also MJ/SP/Feb. 1709, nos. 23–24.

[77] MJ/SP/Oct. 1719, no. 59. See also MJ/SP/Dec. 1722, no. 11.

[78] Seven times during the period of this study, plaintiffs faced an additional obstacle when a general pardon terminated prosecution on many indictments. As a result of the pardon of 1721 (7 Geo. 1, c. 9), about a sixth of the defendants in the sample who were indicted between April and July 1721 successfully terminated their cases by pleading the pardon. Some were required to reimburse the prosecutors' costs before they were discharged.

convictions. Although final verdicts were generally favorable to plaintiffs, juries were less sympathetic to certain types of offences, offenders, and plaintiffs than to others.

Ultimately, without evidence about the *actual* guilt or innocence of defendants, it is impossible to reach any definite conclusions concerning the motivations behind jurors' decisions. Nevertheless, recent studies have suggested that juror decisions were likely to be affected by a number of identifiable factors. While jurors paid considerable attention to the quality of the evidence against the defendant, their decisions were also influenced by the nature of the offence, the social position of the complainant, the age, sex, social position and character of the defendant, and the apparent level of crime at the time.[79] Because depositions, judicial notebooks, and descriptions of trials do not survive for offences prosecuted at the Middlesex sessions, few of these conclusions can be tested in this study. Nonetheless, patterns of jury decisions suggest that Middlesex jurors were susceptible to certain prejudices. For example, while grand juries approved between 80 and 90% of the indictments brought before them for most offences, their judgements on four categories of offences were atypical. An unusually low proportion of indictments for gaming (66%) and very high proportions of indictments for disaffection (94%), neglect of office (96%), and alehouse offences (95%) were approved by grand juries.[80]

Many of the *ignoramus* indictments for gaming in the sample occurred at Westminster sessions in 1721 and 1722. These indictments were part of a campaign, organized by justices sympathetic to the reformation of manners campaign, which was undermined in Westminster by officials of the Westminster court of burgesses. Fearing the loss of lucrative fines imposed by the court of burgesses if keepers of gaming houses were punished instead at sessions, the high bailiff, who was responsible for summoning the sessions grand jury, allegedly selected jurors who would find indictments for gaming houses *ignoramus*.[81] The fact that eleven of the twenty defendants indicted for gaming in the 1720–22 sample were found *ignoramus* certainly suggests that the Westminster jury was corrupt. Similar accusations that juries had been improperly selected surfaced in the early 1680s, when grand juries refused to approve indictments against persons attending conventicles. Because of the overriding political importance of suppressing conventicles, the Middlesex

---

[79] Herrup, *The Common Peace*, pp. 110–30, 143–58; Beattie, *Crime and the Courts*, pp. 400–06, 410–19, 439–42; Peter King, "Decision-makers and decision-making in the English criminal law, 1750–1800," *Historical Journal* 27 (1984), pp. 34–42; John H. Langbein, "Albion's fatal flaws," *Past and Present* 98 (1982), pp. 105–08.

[80] Indictments for grand larceny have been excluded from this analysis. All approved indictments for grand larceny were forwarded to the Old Bailey for trial, while *ignoramus* indictments were left behind in the sessions rolls. Accordingly, all fourteen of the indictments for grand larceny in the sessions roll sample were found *ignoramus*.

[81] PRO, SP 35/27/56; *London Journal*, 13 Jan. 1721. See also below, section 9.2.

justices took the unusual step of dismissing one grand jury and, on another occasion, fining the sheriff £100 for returning a jury that was not geographically representative of the county.[82] In contrast, on the occasions when politically sensitive indictments were filed during the sample years, grand juries were zealously pro-government: only four of the sixty-three defendants indicted for conventicles, recusancy, and seditious words were exonerated. While grand juries routinely approved the vast majority of misdemeanor indictments, political or religious considerations could dramatically alter the normal pattern of juror decisions.[83]

Grand jury decisions were also influenced by the identity of the plaintiff and defendant. Indictments for victimless offences such as alehouse offences and failure to serve on the night watch were routinely approved because they were typically the result of constables' presentments. Not only did constables, as representatives of their communities, act in effect as grand juries in making such accusations, but since grand jurors had often served in such offices themselves, they were probably inclined to be supportive of constables' accusations.[84] None of the forty-one indictments prosecuted by constables in the 1664 and 1721 samples (including four indictments for assaults on constables in the execution of their office) was rejected by the grand jury. Turning to non-official plaintiffs, from limited evidence it appears that Middlesex grand juries did not discriminate according to the social status of the prosecutor.[85]

With regard to defendants, however, the evidence suggests that in some cases grand jurors may have succumbed to social prejudice. Although the legal qualifications for service on a grand jury were uncertain, sheriffs were advised to return "the most sufficient freeholders in the county."[86] According to jury lists, most grand jurors were gentlemen or high status tradesmen.[87] There was

[82] MJ/SBB/391, p. 56 (Oct. 1681); 396, p. 52 (April 1682); *A True List of the Names of the Good Men of the County of Middlesex, summoned to be of the Grand Jury in the Quarter Sessions, begun at Westminster 6 October 1681* (1681); CSPD, 1682, p. 82.

[83] See also Landau, *Justices of the Peace*, pp. 52–54.

[84] Joan R. Kent, *The English Village Constable 1580–1642* (Oxford, 1986); John Beattie, "London juries in the 1690s" in *Twelve Good Men and True: The Criminal Trial Jury in England 1200–1800* ed. J. S. Cockburn and Thomas A. Green (Princeton, 1988), pp. 248–50; Herrup, *The Common Peace*, pp. 104, 106.

[85] In contrast, see Herrup, *The Common Peace*, p. 118.

[86] *Office of the Clerk of the Peace*, p. 102; Nelson, *Office and Authority* (1715), p. 376; Hawkins, *Pleas of the Crown* (1716), vol. 2, p. 217; J. S. Cockburn, *Calendar of Assize Records: Introduction* (1985), pp. 46–47.

[87] Of the 195 grand jurors in 1664, 42% were listed as gentlemen: MJ/SR/1279–96 (Jan.–Dec. 1664, except gaol delivery rolls). Most of the remaining 58% were not identified by status or occupation, except that some practiced relatively high status trades, including a linendraper, bookseller, scrivener, and milliner: MJ/SR/1285 (Westminster sessions, April 1664). In the City of London, juries "included some men of modest means, but they were drawn preponderantly from among the City's more substantial and prosperous citizens" (Beattie, "London juries," p. 250). Because both the London and Middlesex sessions grand juries heard all criminal cases including the felonies that would be tried at gaol delivery, London grand jurymen were more

thus a social divide between members of the grand jury and many defendants. Because the evidence for the socioeconomic status of indicted defendants is somewhat limited,[88] it is impossible to break down verdicts according to the precise social position of the defendants. Nevertheless, the findings suggest that jurors were more willing to approve indictments against lower-class defendants: compared to yeomen, laborers were twice as likely to have their indictments rejected by the grand jury. While this suggests that grand juries were distrustful of laborers, they were equally willing to approve indictments against gentlemen.[89] It is possible that, because of the eminent social position of the accused, crimes allegedly committed by gentlemen were taken more seriously than those committed by others. Like grand juries in other parts of the country,[90] the Middlesex and Westminster grand juries were more sympathetic towards female defendants: only 80% of the indictments against single women and married women were approved, compared to 87% of men. (Widows, however, were treated like men: 89% of the indictments against them became true bills.) Because fewer women were accused of crime, grand juries were less likely to view them as potential criminals.[91]

Over the course of this period it became increasingly difficult to convince grand juries to approve indictments: the proportion of *ignoramus* indictments increased steadily across the five sample periods, from 6% in 1663–64 to 22% in 1720–22. There is little evidence to explain this dramatic change, except for the fact that the offences most likely to be found *ignoramus* were gaming (for reasons already explained), offences against the peace, theft, and cases of trespass and damage. With the exception of gaming, it is possible that the jury rejected many of these cases on the grounds that they were essentially civil disputes or vexatious prosecutions, or both; this is the explanation Douglas Hay uses to account for the fact that over half the assault indictments in Staffordshire in the second half of the eighteenth century were found *ignoramus*.[92]

socially elevated than their counterparts in the provinces (Beattie, *Crime and the Courts*, pp. 320, 323; Herrup, *The Common Peace*, pp. 99–100; J. S. Morrill, *The Cheshire Grand Jury 1625–1659* [University of Leicester, Department of English Local History, Occasional Papers, Third Series, no. 1, 1976], pp. 17–18).

[88] See section 8.1.

[89] Because, as noted above, they constitute a special case, the figures in this paragraph exclude indictments for grand larceny. While only 7% of the indictments against laborers and 8% of the indictments against gentlemen were found *ignoramus*, the indictments against 11% of tradesmen and craftsmen and 15% of yeomen were rejected. For similar findings, see Herrup, *The Common Peace*, p. 116. In the case of regulatory offences (Herrup's "offences against the communal peace"), however, Herrup's findings show that indictments against laborers were actually more likely to be rejected than indictments against gentlemen and yeomen.

[90] Beattie, *Crime and the Courts*, p. 403; Herrup, *The Common Peace*, p. 116.

[91] For a similar argument in the context of verdicts and pardons, see Beattie, *Crime and the Courts*, p. 439.

[92] Hay, "Prosecution and power," p. 362 and n. 68.

Once an indictment was approved by the grand jury, the next obstacle faced by prosecutors was the cost and trouble of pursuing the case to a final verdict. As we have seen, for a number of reasons a substantial proportion of indictments never reached a final verdict. For prosecutors who were able to secure a verdict, there was a good chance that the defendant would be convicted. Excluding persons attending conventicles (where thirty-six of thirty-seven defendants were convicted), 77% of final verdicts were convictions.[93] Only 10% of the convictions, however, were reached by juries; the vast majority resulted from confessions. The large number of confessions is surprising, especially since 74% of the defendants who pleaded innocent and went to trial were found innocent. Before discussing the circumstances which led to so many confessions, it is worth examining the decisions of trial jurors.

Why did trial jurors find so many defendants innocent? It is possible that this was the result of the use of solicitors at sessions. As noted below, it was the wealthier defendants who pleaded innocent and experienced a jury trial, and many of these defendants could have afforded to secure the services of one of the growing body of solicitors in London. In some cases, innocent verdicts may have been encouraged by bribery or manipulation of the composition of the jury.[94] More certainly, the high proportion of innocent verdicts partly resulted from the fact that trial jurors showed a remarkable sympathy to defendants indicted for regulatory offences. Eighty-seven percent of the defendants accused of alehouse offences, nuisances, and neglect of office were found innocent. Since most of these indictments were prosecuted by officers of the peace, it is clear that petty jurors were far less sympathetic than grand jurors to official prosecutions. Some of these cases, especially alehouse offences, were often prosecuted by informers, and it is possible that jurors had a decided antipathy to informers: only one of the twenty defendants tried for violations of economic regulations (which were frequently prosecuted by informers) was found guilty. While petty jurors exhibited a certain distrust of official prosecutors and informers and a sympathy for the ordinary citizen in the case of regulatory offences, however, they toed the government line when it came to political and religious disaffection: 89% of the defendants accused of these offences were found guilty.[95] Although there is no specific evidence on this point, it seems likely that the justices exerted considerable influence over jurors when such

---

[93] Because the pattern of verdicts is so unusual, conventicles have been excluded from the calculations of conviction and acquittal rates in this and the following paragraph.

[94] Henry Fielding, *The Coffee-House Politician; or the Justice Caught in his own Trap* (1730), p. 14; Peter Linebaugh, "(Marxist) social history and (conservative) legal history: a reply to Professor Langbein," *New York University Law Review* 60 (1985), pp. 232–33.

[95] In years other than the years sampled for this study, trial juries refused to convict persons indicted for attending conventicles (*The Proceedings of his Majesties Justices of Peace at the Sessions of Oyer and Terminer ... September the 6th, 1684, for the Tryal of the Constables ... of the Hamlets of Spittle-fields and Bethnal Green* [1684], p. 2).

sensitive issues came before the court.[96] The chances of obtaining a guilty verdict from a Middlesex jury, therefore, depended very much on the offence and the identity of the prosecutor.

It appears that trial jurors were also biased against their social inferiors. Although it is likely that the Middlesex trial jurors were less socially elevated than the grand jurors, they were still socially superior to laborers and other lower class defendants.[97] While the conviction rate for all other male defendants was 22%, 54% of the thirteen laborers tried were convicted.[98] If this finding is representative it may have been caused by the type of distrust advocated by the anonymous writer of a *Guide to Juries* in 1699. When listening to the testimony of a poor witness or defendant, the author suggested, "the jury may consider he may easier be biased or corrupted, [since] he has not so much to lose or forfeit for a crime, [and] he lies under several necessities and temptations a rich man does not ... "[99] Juror decisions frequently revolved around consideration of the defendant's character, and because of concern about criminality among the poor it was probably more difficult for lower-class defendants to convince jurors of their good character.[100] Despite the generally low conviction rates in Middlesex, jurors were apparently distrustful of low status defendants.

[96] For gentry influence over trial jurors at sessions, see Stephen K. Roberts, "Juries and the middling sort: recruitment and performance at Devon quarter sessions, 1649–1670," in *Twelve Good Men and True*, ed. Cockburn and Green, pp. 182–213. For the informal power of assizes judges over trial juries after Bushel's case outlawed judicial coercion in 1670, see Beattie, *Crime and the Courts*, pp. 406–10; Cockburn, *History of Assizes*, pp. 115, 122; Thomas A. Green, *Verdict According to Conscience. Perspectives on the English Criminal Trial Jury 1200–1800* (Chicago, 1985), pp. 249, 270–88; John H. Langbein, "The criminal trial before the lawyers," *The University of Chicago Law Review* 45 (1978), pp. 291–300.

[97] Jurors were to own lands or tenements providing forty shillings income per year (£20 between 1664 and 1677 and £10 after 1692) (Dalton, *Countrey Justice* [1677], p. 540; 16 and 17 Car. 2 c. 3; 4 and 5 Wm. and M. c. 24; WJ/SBB/784, p. 28 [July 1720]). Surviving returns of 101 potential jurors from nine Middlesex parishes in 1713 include twelve esquires, forty gentlemen, fifteen yeomen, and twenty-nine tradesmen and craftsmen. Because these returns were mostly from rural parishes, and include many gentlemen who were listed as also having a residence in the City of London or in other counties, they may not be typical. The one surviving return from urban Middlesex, for the relatively poor parish of Limehouse, included, in addition to three gentlemen and five respectable craftsmen, several people with low status occupations: six sailors, two cowkeepers, a soapboiler, a baker and a ropemaker: MJ/SP/Oct. 1713, nos. 103–08, 111. In the City of London, trial jurors were less wealthy than grand jurors, but there was a considerable degree of overlap (Beattie, "London juries," p. 243, Table 8.8). In the provinces, on the other hand, the social distance between grand jurors and trial jurors was larger (Beattie, *Crime and the Courts*, p. 389; Herrup, *The Common Peace*, p. 138; *Twelve Good Men and True*, ed. Cockburn and Green, chaps. 5–7 and 9–11).

[98] The limited evidence concerning the social status of defendants on indictments prevents more precise analysis of this issue.

[99] *A Guide to Juries: Setting Forth their Antiquity, Power, and Duty* (1699), p. 80.

[100] Beattie, *Crime and the Courts*, pp. 341, 623; Susan D. Amussen, *An Ordered Society. Gender and Class in Early Modern England* (Oxford, 1988), pp. 170–72.

The small proportion of guilty verdicts reached by Middlesex juries must, however, be understood in the context of the large number of defendants who pleaded guilty and thus forfeited their right to a trial. Compared to accused felons, defendants accused of misdemeanors relatively rarely defended themselves in front of a jury.[101] While 92% of the defendants in Beattie's sample of indictments for simple larceny tried at the Surrey quarter sessions and assizes courts between 1660 and 1715 pleaded innocent, only 36% of the defendants who entered pleas at the Middlesex sessions did the same.[102] As Beattie explains, because judges needed the information generated in felony trials for their sentencing decisions they encouraged virtually all defendants accused of felonies to plead innocent. With misdemeanors, where punishments were minor and more standardized, the court had no reason to encourage innocent pleas.

Regardless of their actual guilt or innocence, defendants had good reason to plead guilty to misdemeanor indictments: the prohibitive cost of a jury trial. At 12s., the minimum court fees for defending a plea of not guilty amounted to more than a week's wages for most lower-class defendants. These fees could be reduced by four-fifths, and the number of appearances in court cut in half, by pleading guilty.[103] Elizabeth Phillips, indicted in 1691 for being a common disturber, testified to the court that "by reason of her poverty [she] has not money to traverse and try the said indictment but is forced to confess the same."[104] While many poor defendants like Phillips had foreknowledge of the expenses involved in trying an indictment, others did not realize that a trial was beyond their means until they had already pleaded innocent. For every ten defendants who pleaded guilty initially, an additional three switched their plea to guilty at a subsequent sessions. Elizabeth Linsey, indicted for an assault in 1691, appeared in court accompanied by witnesses to try her traverse when, "being poor," she "chose rather to submit herself to the court than to trouble [the justices] with a trial" and so relinquished her plea of not guilty.[105] Even

---

[101] Beattie, *Crime and the Courts*, p. 336. Herrup's data also shows that relatively few defendants accused of misdemeanors experienced a jury trial (*The Common Peace*, p. 144).

[102] This figure includes seventy defendants (6% of all pleas) who pleaded innocent, but for whom no final verdict was recorded.

[103] Defendants who pleaded innocent had to pay fees to the clerk of the peace, the cryer, the bailiff, and the sheriff, including 2s. or 2s. 4d. for the recognizance for their first appearance in court, 2s. to enter a plea of not guilty, 2s. each time the case was continued to another sessions (which normally occurred at least once), 2s. 4d. for a recognizance to appear in court for the trial, 1s. for summoning the jury, 1s. 4d. for swearing the jury and witnesses, 1s. for keeping the jury during the trial, and 4d. for their discharge from court. Defendants pleading guilty avoided all but the fees for the first recognizance and the discharge from court (*Office of the Clerk of the Peace*, pp. 247–54; Thomas Powell, *The Attorney's Academy* [1647], pp. 400–05). In some cases, the court probably reduced fees for paupers. Weekly wage rates are discussed in section 5.4.

[104] MJ/SP/April 1691, no. 17. See also MJ/SP/April 1691, no. 27; Aug. 1706, no. 18; Oct. 1713, no. 96; Feb. 1722, no. 10.

[105] MJ/SP/Oct. 1691, no. 25.

after making most of the arrangements to stand trial, it was advantageous to change one's plea and confess to the indictment. Such testimony was clearly self-serving, since by putting themselves on the mercy of the court these defendants hoped to receive lenient punishments, but the link between poverty and pleading guilty was real, if not absolute. While only 65% of the forty-three gentlemen defendants who entered pleas in the sample pleaded guilty, 75% of the fifty-two laborers confessed.[106]

Defendants who were unable to find sureties to guarantee their appearance at a trial had the greatest incentive to plead guilty. As a commentator noted in the late eighteenth century,

if [the defendant] has neither money nor friends he must remain in jail untried, and is of course in a much worse situation than the more heinous offender [felons were tried at the same sessions they were indicted]. The editor has on such an occasion known the worshipful bench to persuade the defendant to retract his plea and confess himself guilty.[107]

Although the court made some effort to try poor defendants at the same sessions in which their indictments were found,[108] this practice occurred relatively rarely,[109] presumably because prosecutors, expecting that the case would be tried at a subsequent sessions, would have been unprepared for a trial. Given the manifold disadvantages of imprisonment, pleading guilty was the lesser of two evils for defendants who otherwise would have had to wait in prison until the next sessions for their trials. In 1722, when Edward and Francis Bird were indicted for an assault, they "being persons ignorant in matters of the law pleaded not guilty." They reversed their plea, however, after they found themselves committed to New Prison for want of sureties to guarantee their appearance at the next sessions. Even after pleading guilty, many defendants, including Edward and Francis Bird, remained in prison because they had not paid their court fees and prison fees, let alone their fines.[110]

The court encouraged guilty pleas by offering defendants the prospect of a lower fine. Defendants who pleaded guilty, as well as defendants who initially pleaded innocent and subsequently switched their plea to guilty, were far more likely to receive a low fine than those who were convicted by a jury (Table 6.7).

[106] Because virtually all the conventiclers pleaded innocent, they have been excluded from this calculation.

[107] *The Jurisdiction of the Court-Leet: Exemplified in the Articles which the Jury of Inquest for the King in that Court is Charged* (1791), p. xxii.

[108] Bond, *Complete Guide* (1707), p. 287; MJ/SP/April 1716, no. 67. Paradoxically, given the expense of hiring a solicitor, this practice was only permitted if the defendant obtained "an order of court granted upon the motion of counsel."

[109] Twelve percent of the defendants whose cases went to trial were tried the same day they pleaded, including five of the thirteen laborers. Defendants accused of attending conventicles are excluded from this calculation, since all but one were tried at the same sessions they were indicted.

[110] MJ/SP/Feb. 1722, no. 10; above, section 5.4.

Table 6.7 *Fines by defendant's plea*[a]

	Pleaded innocent, found guilty	Pleaded innocent, changed to guilty	Pleaded guilty	TOTAL
	%	%	%	%
Fine 1s.	6	13	16	14
Fine ≤ 3s. 4d.	19	54	49	47
Fine ≤ 13s. 4d.	22	18	24	22
Fine > 13s. 4d.	52	15	12	16
TOTAL N (100%)	63	165	500	728

[a] Not including conventicles.

While only 25% of defendants who were found guilty by a jury received a fine less than or equal to 3s. 4d., 65% of those who pleaded guilty received fines at or below 3s. 4d., including 15% who received the minimum fine of one shilling. While it appears that the court was willing to exchange guilty pleas for low fines as a form of plea bargaining, there is only one documented example of such bargaining: in 1728 several people indicted for assault, "being no longer able to bear the charges of prosecution ... and being softened by promises, and terrified by threats, submitted to plead guilty, on a solemn assurance, and agreement, made with [the plaintiff] before witnesses, of having but one shilling fine laid upon them."[111] The fact that many defendants switched their pleas from innocent to guilty during their second (or subsequent) appearance in court suggests, however, that such negotiations often took place. Defendants certainly expected to be rewarded for pleading guilty. Elizabeth Linsey, whose case was cited earlier, closed her petition to the court (in which she stated her intention to switch her plea to guilty) with a request for a small fine, and her hopes were fulfilled: she was given the minimum fine of one shilling.[112] Although legal opinion disapproved of the practice, this is not the first evidence of plea bargaining in the early-modern period to be discovered.[113]

As discussed below, justices possessed considerable flexibility in determining fines, and there are several reasons why they were willing to plea bargain with some defendants. First, as occurred at the Home Circuit assizes and the Old Bailey in the late sixteenth century,[114] plea bargaining gave the Middlesex justices a means of coping with the growing volume of judicial and administra-

[111] *Journals of the House of Commons* (1803), vol. 21, p. 279.   [112] MJ/SP/Oct. 1691, no. 25.
[113] Lambard, *Eirenarcha* (1619), pp. 577–78; *Memoirs of the Life and Times of Sir Thomas DeVeil* (1748), p. 55; Blackstone, *Commentaries* (5th edn, 1773), p. 379; Cockburn, *Introduction*, pp. 65–70, 105, 131; Herrup, *The Common Peace*, p. 149, n. 22.
[114] Cockburn, *Introduction*, p. 69.

tive business with which they were confronted. Only about forty defendants appeared at each sessions to answer indictments, but their cases competed for the justices' time with perhaps 200 defendants appearing on recognizances, as well as hearings of disputes between masters and their apprentices, appeals of bastardy, settlement, and poor relief decisions, and other county business. Second, following the conventional practice of adjusting fines to the defendant's ability to pay,[115] the justices were willing to reduce fines for poor defendants, and poverty appears to have been a major reason why so many defendants pleaded guilty. Third, as argued in the next section, the justices attempted to match punishments to the nature of the crime, and many confessed indictments concerned minor offences. Moreover, the justices could not take into account mitigating factors (such as that an assault was committed in self-defence) unless the defendant pleaded guilty.[116]

Finally, guilty pleas and reduced fines sometimes resulted from out of court settlements. Thomas Langford, indicted for a riot and assault in 1691, pleaded innocent and prepared to defend his case before a jury. By "the advice of friends," however, he changed his plea to guilty ("though he doubted not but to have proved himself innocent") and then negotiated an out of court settlement with his prosecutor. In response, the court reduced his fine, originally set at five marks (£3 6s. 8d.), to two.[117] As noted in the next section, in its sentencing decisions the court was inclined to be lenient to convicted defendants who had reached informal (or arbitrated) settlements with their prosecutors.

In sum, the most striking feature of the verdicts of defendants indicted for misdemeanors in Middlesex is the large number of guilty pleas, which account for two-thirds of all verdicts, and the high proportion of small fines meted out to defendants who pleaded guilty. Many defendants who confessed their indictments could not afford the costs of a trial. In return for a small fine, the justices sitting in court accepted such confessions as a means of expediting court business, particularly if the offence was minor or the offender was poor. While plaintiffs did not benefit directly from such judicial mercy, guilty pleas occasionally occurred as part of a negotiated settlement between the parties, with the defendant paying a lower fine in return for pleading guilty and paying damages to the plaintiff. Not all defendants who pleaded guilty, however, received minor punishments, nor were all negotiated settlements rewarded with lower fines. It is now necessary to examine the punishments sentenced by the Middlesex justices in greater detail.

[115] Blackstone, *Commentaries* (1769), vol. 4, pp. 372–73.
[116] William Salkeld, *Reports of Cases Adjudged in the Court of King's Bench*, 3 vols., 6th edn (1795), vol. 1, p. 55; Thomas Leach, *Modern Reports*, 12 vols., 5th edn (1793–96), vol. 7, p. 40 (Queen vs. Templeman). Thus, Elizabeth Linsey claimed that she had been assaulted first by the prosecutor's "pretended wife": MJ/SP/Oct. 1691, no. 25.
[117] MJ/SP/Jan. 1691, no. 1; MJ/SPB/8.

Table 6.8 *Fines for selected offences*

	1s.	3s. 4d.	3s. 5d. to 13s. 4d.	More than 13s. 4d.	TOTAL (100%)
	%	%	%	%	N
Peace					
Assault	19	58	18	6	288
(aggravated assault)	(5)	(49)	(15)	(32)	(41)
Riot	9	49	26	16	131
Common disturber	8	62	23	8	13
Vice					
Disorderly alehouse	—	21	53	26	19
Gaming	11	22	11	56	9
Property					
Trespass and damage	17	33	30	20	30
Fraud	9	9	36	46	11
Regulatory					
Not serving on watch	42	52	6	—	31
Other neglect of office	—	26	11	63	19
Not repairing highway	9	32	44	15	34
Keeping/slaughtering animals	—	54	31	15	13
Subdividing houses	7	67	27	—	15
Disaffection					
Attending conventicle	—	4	75	21	28
All Offences	14	46	24	16	756

6.5 PUNISHMENTS

The contrast between the judicial treatment of defendants indicted for mis-demeanors and those indicted for felonies was nowhere greater than with punishments. While defendants convicted of felonies faced a variety of pri-marily corporal punishments including whipping, branding, imprisonment at hard labor, transportation, and hanging, all but 4% of the defendants convic-ted at the Middlesex sessions were only fined. The justices possessed consider-able discretion in determining the size of the fines, however, which ranged from 1s. to £40. Except where prescribed by statute, the size of fines was left to the "wills and pleasures" of the justices, though William Lambard cautioned them "to take heed that the fines be reasonable and just, having regard to the quantity of the trespass, and to the causes for which they be made."[118] In

[118] Lambard, *Eirenarcha* (1619), p. 557; see also Hawkins, *Pleas of the Crown* (1716), vol. 1, pp. 134, 138; Blackstone, *Commentaries* (5th edn, 1773), p. 378.

practice, the justices' sentencing decisions took into account not only the gravity of the offence, but also the sex and social status of the offender and (as discussed above) whether the defendant pleaded guilty.

Although the limited descriptions of offences on indictments make it difficult to assess the gravity of many offences, the evidence in Table 6.8 points to the nature of the offence as a strong determinant of the size of fines. Whereas 47% of the defendants convicted of an aggravated assault (involving violence, the use of a weapon, false imprisonment, attempted rape, or an attack on an officer) received fines over 3s. 4d., only 24% of the defendants accused of simple assault received such high fines. On the other hand, defendants accused of a simple assault were almost four times as likely to receive the minumum fine of one shilling than those accused of an aggravated assault. As noted in chapter 3, some indictments for simple assault were in fact quite serious offences.[119] Nevertheless, as a grand jury complained in 1683, most assaults were rather minor offences which arose from "scolding, backbiting, and reproaching one another,"[120] and the justices adjusted the fines for simple assaults, and for defendants convicted of being a common disturber, accordingly. Two regulatory offences also resulted in low fines: subdividing tenements and failing to serve on the night watch. As prosecution for both these offences largely died out during this period, the justices' sentencing decisions reflect the fact that the laws governing subdividing and the night watch were impractical and unenforceable in a rapidly growing metropolis.[121]

Higher fines were allotted both to more serious offences, and were dictated by statute. The majority of the defendants convicted of attending conventicles, keeping disorderly houses, keeping gaming houses, and neglecting their offices were fined 6s. 8d. or more. On a first conviction, conventiclers were to be fined up to £5,[122] but only two were fined the maximum amount. Most were fined 6s. 8d., a sum considerably less than the statutory maximum but twice the median sessions fine of 3s. 4d. With such moderate fines, the justices expressed their disapproval of conventicles without causing undue controversy. Judging from the fines levied, the justices appear to have viewed alehouse offences equally seriously. While fines for keeping an unlicensed alehouse and permitting tippling were set by statute at 20s. and 10s. respectively,[123] keepers of disorderly houses were indictable as nuisances, for which the justices could set fines at their own discretion; fifteen of the nineteen discretionary fines were set at 6s. 8d. or above. One widow was fined £6 8s. 4d.; not only did she keep a disorderly coffee house but she was accused of living incontinently with a married man, "impudently walking together arm in arm in the day time to the

---

[119] Section 3.3.   [120] MJ/SBB/408, p. 47 (Oct. 1683).
[121] For subdividing, see Dowdell, *Quarter Sessions*, pp. 80–81. For the night watch, see Shoemaker, "Crime, Courts and Community," pp. 322–23.
[122] 16 Car. 2 c. 4.   [123] 5 Edw. 6 c. 25; 1 Jac. 1 c. 9; 21 Jac. 1 c. 7; 1 Car. 1 c. 4.

Table 6.9 *Fines by defendant's status and gender*

	1s.	3s. 4d.	3s. 5d. to 13s. 4d.	More than 13s. 4d.	TOTAL (100%)
	%	%	%	%	N
Gentleman	10	29	45	16	31
Tradesman/craftsman	8	45	30	17	111
Yeoman	13	47	22	18	333
Laborer	8	39	36	17	36
TOTAL MALE[a]	11	44	25	19	533
Unmarried female	16	49	25	10	51
Married female	22	54	16	8	120
Widow	26	37	24	13	46
TOTAL FEMALE[b]	21	50	20	10	218

[a] Includes twenty-two other men whose status is unknown.
[b] Includes one other woman whose marital status is unknown.

public view of his wife."[124] As the justices complained in several orders of the court, unlicensed and disorderly alehouses promoted vice, provided a shelter for rogues, thieves, and idle and disorderly persons, and increased poverty.[125] Similarly, gambling was thought to encourage vice, ruin servants, and cause quarrels and riots,[126] so it is not surprising that five of the nine defendants convicted of gaming or keeping a gaming house were fined more than a mark (13s. 4d.).[127] It is equally unsurprising that officers convicted of extortion and failing to execute their office received higher than average fines. Reflecting the importance of offences that undermined the rule of law, twelve of the nineteen fines were £1 or above. Crimes that were thought to encourage disorder, whether in the form of religious conflict, immoral behavior, idle and disorderly conduct, or disrespect for officers of the peace, were the most likely candidates for large fines.

Consideration was also given to the identity of the offender when fines were determined. As noted earlier, the defendant's ability to pay played a role in

[124] MJ/SR/1296, I. 9 and R. 7 (Dec. 1664).
[125] For example, see MJ/SBB/205c, p. 13 (April 1663); 802, p. 27 (Westminster sessions, June 1722); MJ/SP/May 1721, no. 2.
[126] MJ/OC/I, ff. 34–35 (July 1718); WJ/OC/I, ff. 4–4d (Oct. 1720).
[127] By 33 Henry 8 c. 9, keepers of unlawful gaming houses could be fined 40s. per day and those who frequented such houses could be fined 6s. 8d. per visit. Few of the nine fines in the sample, which range from 12d. to £10, appear to have been based on this statute.

determining the size of the fine: 61% of gentlemen, compared to only 44% of all other men, were fined more than 3s. 4d. (Table 6.9).[128] When the analysis is restricted to offences against the peace, the discrepancy is even greater: 65% of gentlemen were fined over 3s. 4d., compared to 34% of non-gentlemen. Nevertheless, many non-gentlemen, including six of thirty-six laborers, were given fines over one mark. Gender also had an effect on the size of fines, though once again the effect was not invariable. Just over 70% of women, compared with 55% of men, were fined 3s. 4d. or less. Married women received the lowest fines of all: 76% of their fines were 3s. 4d. or less, compared with 64% of unmarried women and widows. Much of this difference is explained by the fact that almost 90% of the women whose husbands were indicted with them received fines at or below 3s. 4d. It is possible that these low fines resulted from a peculiar interpretation of the legal principle that women could not be liable for certain crimes committed in the presence of their husbands.[129] The effect of gender was most marked in the case of the minimum fine of one shilling, which was given to women twice as often as it was given to men. Although most of the women who were fined only a shilling had pleaded guilty, when guilty pleas are excluded from the analysis women still received lower fines than men. Despite the growing number of women appearing before the court, the Middlesex justices treated women convicted of petty offences leniently. Like female felons, women convicted on misdemeanor indictments benefitted from the fact that women were not viewed as dangerous criminals in preindustrial England.[130]

In sum, the size of the fines meted to convicted petty offenders was influenced by three identifiable factors: the gravity of the offence and the social status and the sex of the offender. It is likely that justices' sentencing decisions were also affected by other, unrecorded, considerations, including the social status of the victim or plaintiff (an offence committed against a gentleman would be treated more seriously),[131] whether or not the defendant had reached any private accommodation with the plaintiff,[132] the defendant's age, character and demeanor in court, and the strength of the evidence against the defendant.[133]

---

[128] For a similar rough correlation between the social status of defendants and the size of fines, see Sharpe, *Crime in Seventeenth-Century England*, p. 119.

[129] Bond, *Complete Guide* (1707), p. 166; John Beattie, "The criminality of women in eighteenth-century England," *Journal of Social History* 8 (1975), pp. 95–96. Women whose husbands were also indicted were no more likely, however, to be found innocent.

[130] Beattie, *Crime and the Courts*, pp. 436–39.

[131] *Ibid.*, p. 458. In the sample used in this study five of the nine defendants (56%) prosecuted by gentlemen received a fine over 3s. 4d., compared to only 36% of the 137 defendants prosecuted by other men. Although this result is suggestive, the sample of gentlemen is obviously too small to be conclusive.

[132] *Ibid.*, pp. 457–58; Blackstone, *Commentaries* (1773), pp. 363–64.

[133] King, "Decision-makers," pp. 35–48; Langbein, "Fatal flaws," pp. 108–13; Herrup, *The Common Peace*, chap. 7.

Too often, sentences reveal discrepancies which cannot be explained with the existing evidence. For example, when four women pleaded guilty to an indictment for a riotous assault in 1707, two spinsters received a 1s. fine and a third was fined 6s. 8d. The fourth woman, who was married, was fined 20s.[134] Either these fines were graded according to the defendants' ability to pay, or, more probably, they were determined according to the extent of each defendant's participation in the riot. In any case, this example illustrates the considerable degree of flexibility the justices exercised in their sentencing decisions.

Judicial discretion in assessing fines is also clearly demonstrated by the small number of very large fines in the sample. Ten percent of the fines were £2 or above, including 1.5% at £10 or more. The highest fines in the sample were £50 against the inhabitants of a parish for not repairing a highway, £40 each for non-attendance at church and for attending a conventicle, £20 each for an assault and false imprisonment and for not repairing the highway, £13 6s. 8d. for assault with intent to rape, and £10 each for two riots, a wounding, two gaming house keepers, and a conventicler. While this list includes some of the most serious offences heard at sessions, not all offenders guilty of these offences received such high penalties.[135] The twelve defendants convicted of assault and wounding, for example, were fined 3s. 4d. (six times), 5s., 6s. 8d., 13s. 4d., £5 (twice), and £10. In only a few cases is it possible to determine why large fines were levied. When inhabitants of entire parishes were indicted for not repairing a highway, the court conditionally set a heavy fine (from 50s. to £300) to be levied if the road was not repaired before a certain date.[136] If the road was repaired, the fine was reduced considerably. Thus, the inhabitants of St Pancras were indicted in February 1677 for failing to repair the road from Tottenham Court to Kentish Town. The court's initial fine of £40 was reduced to 6s. 8d. in July 1681.[137] Because the court was more interested in getting roads repaired than in levying fines, it was willing to defer imposing such large fines for years while it waited for the roads to be repaired.

Following procedures used in King's Bench, the court also used large fines as

[134] MJ/SR/2086, I. 5 (Feb. 1707).
[135] The two defendants fined £40 appear to have been obstinate offenders. The sailor's wife convicted of attending a conventicle had been convicted twice previously and had refused to plead to the indictment. Because she was married and her husband was not indicted for the same offence, she was subject to a maximum £40 fine (or imprisonment) instead of transportation: MJ/SR/1294, I. 68 (Oct. 1664; see also *Middlesex Records*, ed. Jeaffreson, vol. 3, pp. xxv–xxvi). The yeoman convicted of non-attendance at church waited two years before pleading guilty to the indictment: MJ/SR/1286, I. 86 (April 1664). Recusants could be fined £20 for each month they failed to attend church (3 Jac. 1 c. 4).
[136] MJ/SR/1267, I. 55 (Westminster sessions, April 1663); 1823, I. 64 (Oct. 1693); MJ/SBB/296, p. 46 (Dec. 1672); Dowdell, *Quarter Sessions*, pp. 94–98; Sidney and Beatrice Webb, *English Local Government from the Revolution to the Municipal Corporations Act: The Story of the King's Highway* (1913), p. 52.
[137] MJ/SR/1521, I. 14 (Feb. 1677).

a means of encouraging convicted defendants to negotiate private settlements with their prosecutors, with the understanding that the fine would be mitigated if some sort of accommodation, usually including compensation for court costs and damages, was reached.[138] Thomas Charnock, for example, who was convicted in 1722 of an assault and battery and was fined £20, subsequently testified to the court "that your petitioner hath now satisfied and agreed with the prosecutor and ... releases are executed between them [which are] ready to be produced to the court." Consequently, his fine was reduced to £4.[139] Even if a defendant's efforts to contact his prosecutor and reach an agreement were unsuccessful, the court was willing to reduce the fine. When Alice Warner, fined £10 for an assault in 1715, testified to the court that her prosecutor "insists upon such unreasonable demands that your petitioner can in no ways comply with," the court reduced the fine to 6s. 8d.[140] Since the fines involved in this type of arbitration were initially quite large, it is not surprising that some prosecutors took the opportunity to try to extract considerable payments from their defendants. After John Hamilton was convicted of an assault in 1720 and fined £50, he offered £15 in damages to his prosecutor. The prosecutor, however, "taking advantage of [Hamilton] being so fined," demanded £22 4s.[141] Perhaps as the result of instances of such obstinacy, or more probably because few defendants were wealthy enough to pay such large sums for damages (defendants who incurred these prohibitive fines were disproportionately gentlemen and tradesmen), the court used this procedure infrequently. In fact, it is likely that this practice was reserved primarily for property disputes which were essentially civil in nature. Thus, an indictment for an assault in 1720 which resulted in a conditional fine of £100 concerned a dispute over a "right of the way."[142]

Only thirty-two (4%) of the 790 defendants in the sample whose punishments were recorded were punished by means other than a fine. According to William Hawkins, corporal punishments were reserved "for crimes of an infamous nature, such as petty larceny, perjury, or forgery at common law, gross cheats, conspiracy, keeping a bawdy house, bribing witnesses to stifle their evidence, and other offences of the like nature, against the first principles of natural justice, and common honesty ... "[143] The Middlesex justices followed this

---

138 For King's Bench, see Hawkins, *Pleas of the Crown* (1721), vol. 2, p. 210; *Original Weekly Journal*, 24 Feb. 1722. For other examples of this procedure, see CLRO, sessions papers, 1719/20 (undated, Thorold Mayor), petition of Elizabeth Jacobs; PRO, SP 36/15, ff. 183–84; Beattie, *Crime and the Courts*, p. 457.

139 MJ/SP/Sept. 1722, nos. 24, 25; MJ/SBB/804, p. 8 (Sept. 1722). See also MJ/SP/Dec. 1720, no. 14.

140 MJ/SP/Sept. 1715, no. 9.   141 MJ/SP/Dec. 1720, no. 19.

142 MJ/SP/Dec. 1720, nos. 31–33.

143 Hawkins, *Pleas of the Crown* (1721), vol. 2, p. 445. Hawkins goes on to recommend that defendants sentenced to corporal punishments should also be fined and bound over for their

advice selectively. All eight defendants convicted of petty larceny were whipped, usually at the cart's tail, and the only defendant convicted of forgery was sentenced to stand in the pillory. On the other hand, only eight of the eighteen defendants convicted of fraud suffered corporal punishment (two on the pillory, five by whipping, and one in the house of correction). The only defendant convicted of keeping a bawdy house, as well as the three women convicted as vagrants for prostitution, was only fined.[144]

Although a steady trickle of defendants continued to be punished on the pillory or with public whipping, the Middlesex and Westminster justices showed little interest in traditional shaming punishments.[145] In 1691, two men who were sentenced to the pillory for unlawfully pressing men into the army petitioned the court to have their punishment remitted. If forced to stand in the pillory, they complained, they would be "exposed to the mercy of the rabble and the scandal of their friends."[146] Although humiliation was precisely what the pillory was supposed to inflict, the court cancelled the punishment. A similar punishment, the stocks, was occasionally used for convicted defendants in the early seventeenth century,[147] but no defendants were sentenced to sit in the stocks during this period, and efforts by the court to ensure that stocks were properly maintained apparently ceased in the early eighteenth century.[148] The only reference to a ducking stool comes from a Middlesex grand jury presentment in 1683 which requested more frequent use of "the old legal way of a ducking stool" to punish assaults committed by the poor, since "shame may do that which we find other punishment will not."[149] This petition fell on deaf ears.

In the early eighteenth century, the justices adopted a new punishment for offences too serious to be punished simply by a fine: commitment to a house of correction, where punishments (whipping and/or hard labor) took place essentially in private. Of the nine defendants in the sample so punished, seven were punished in the 1707 and 1720–22 samples, for breaking and entering into a house and committing an assault, keeping a disorderly alehouse, participating in a riotous attack on a master's "house of call" during the tailors' strike in 1720 (two defendants),[150] fraudulently posing as a beggar for prisoners in the Gatehouse prison, and petty larceny (two defendants). Most if not all of these

good behavior for a specified time. This advice accords with the practice of the Middlesex court.
144 MJ/SR/1529, I. 26 (Westminster sessions, July 1677).
145 For a similar conclusion, see Sharpe, *Crime in Seventeenth-Century England*, p. 149.
146 MJ/SP/Feb. 1691, no. 8.
147 William Le Hardy, ed., *Middlesex Sessions Records (New Series) 1612–1618*, 4 vols. (1935–41), vols. 1–4, *passim*.
148 MJ/SBB, *passim*. It is possible, however, that justices continued to issue orders concerning the upkeep of stocks in their petty sessions.
149 MJ/SBB/408, p. 47 (Oct. 1683).
150 MJ/SR/2353, I. 18 (Westminster sessions, Oct. 1720); Dobson, *Masters and Journeymen*, p. 62.

crimes might have earlier been punished with one of the traditional corporal punishments. With the growing use of houses of correction as places to punish petty offenders committed by justices acting outside sessions, and, between 1706 and 1718, for punishing defendants convicted at sessions or gaol delivery of simple felonies,[151] it is not surprising that the Middlesex court adopted the house of correction as a punishment for "crimes of an infamous nature."[152] While it is possible that the justices had lost faith in the efficacy of traditional shaming punishments, it is more likely, given the continued sporadic use of the pillory and public whipping by sessions (and more frequently at the Old Bailey), that the justices' new sentencing practices simply reflected their growing familiarity with houses of correction.[153] Public whipping continued to be used at the end of the period for the punishment of defendants convicted of fraud and seditious words; the social position of these offenders was probably too high for them to be committed to an institution designed for the punishment and reformation of the poor. Nevertheless, the justices demonstrated their new interest in incarceration by giving three of these offenders an additional sentence of up to six months in prison.

Despite the wide range of punishments available, the Middlesex justices rarely sentenced offenders to more than a fine, and most fines were 3s. 4d. or less. Why were the sentences given by the Middlesex justices so lenient? In the absence of any explicit statements, it is only possible to speculate concerning the justices' motives. Many of the offences that led to indictments were clearly quite minor, and low fines may simply have resulted from a policy of making the punishment fit the crime. It is also possible that fines were difficult to collect, particularly from poor defendants, and that the justices sought to levy fines that defendants could afford. More importantly, the justices must have realized that convicted defendants had already been punished. Given the high cost of defending indictments, defendants incurred a significant penalty before they were even convicted.

During the period of this study fines decreased significantly. A growing

---

151 For summary convictions, see chap. 7. For the 1706 act, see 5 Anne c. 6; Beattie, *Crime and the Courts*, pp. 493, 499; Joanna Innes, "Prisons for the poor: English bridewells 1555–1800," in *Land, Labour and Crime*, ed. Francis Snyder and Douglas Hay, pp. 88–89.

152 Defendants committed to houses of correction after being convicted on an indictment were always given an additional punishment. Eight of the offenders were fined; the ninth was required to find sureties for his good behavior.

153 Public and judicial confidence in ritual and corporal punishments was not seriously eroded until the late eighteenth century (Michael Ignatieff, *A Just Measure of Pain: The Penitentiary in the Industrial Revolution* [1978], p. 90; Beattie, *Crime and the Courts*, pp. 614–16). For these punishments at the Old Bailey, see *The Proceedings on the King's Commission of the Peace, Oyer and Terminer, and Gaol Delivery of Newgate, held for the City of London, and County of Middlesex, at Justice Hall in the Old Bailey* (1715–1721), *passim*; Beattie, *Crime and the Courts*, pp. 461–68.

number of convicted defendants were fined only a shilling: whereas only 4% of the defendants convicted in the 1663–64 and 1677 samples were fined one shilling, this figure rose to 17% in 1693, 26% in 1707, and 36% in 1720–22. Concurrently, both the proportions, and the absolute numbers, of fines above 3s. 4d. fell dramatically. It is possible that the justices reduced fines in order to discourage prosecutions by indictment. Faced with a growing volume of other business, justices may have resented the considerable time taken up with hearing indictments, particularly since many indictments concerned rather petty offences. On the other hand, the volume of plea bargaining, another method used by the court to reduce business, did not increase during the period. Ultimately, many aspects of the justices' sentencing policies remain unexplained.

The flexibility of the definitions of peace and property offences allowed a wide range of both criminal and non-criminal behavior to be prosecuted by indictment. But given the high cost of prosecution, the large number of dropped prosecutions, and the minor punishments, why did plaintiffs bother to file indictments? Many prosecutors of indictments benefitted from private settlements. As we have seen, such settlements were negotiated both before and after final verdicts, and they could be quite lucrative. Some plaintiffs were no doubt motivated to prosecute solely by a desire for financial compensation for the injury they had received. The mother of a victim of an attempted rape in 1708 first used the services of a solicitor in seeking £50 damages; when negotiations with the two culprits failed she indicted them. In a subsequent meeting with the defendants, she was willing to accept £3 to drop the prosecution.[154] Only wealthy defendants, needless to say, had the resources to buy off prosecutors in this manner; cases involving gentlemen as defendants were 53% more likely to be dropped before prosecution than cases involving other defendants. Poor defendants, on the other hand, were likely to plead guilty and receive small fines, and prosecutors gained neither financial compensation nor vengeance from indicting them. For this reason, prosecutors of poor defendants often sought to have them committed to a house of correction, where at least it was certain that they would receive significant punishments.

Most prosecutors of victimless offences also gained little from prosecuting by indictment. For a few economic offences, informers could claim a portion of the fine.[155] Public officials, on the other hand, received nothing from fines for the offences they prosecuted and could not accept money from their defendants without being accused of corruption. Constables were required by law and by specific orders from justices to report ("present") certain types of victimless

---

[154] Camden Libraries, Swiss Cottage Branch, A/SF/30, William Woodehouse Journal, ff. 52–54.
[155] Sharpe, *Crime in Seventeenth-Century England*, pp. 43–47; Dowdell, *Quarter Sessions*, chap. 6.

offences to the grand jury, but there was no means of forcing these officers to follow through on the prosecutions once the indictments were drawn up and approved. The increasingly small punishments imposed on most convicted defendants certainly provided no incentive to seek a conviction. Consequently, the indictments of more than half of the defendants accused of alehouse offences and nuisance offences were dropped. Without an additional incentive (personal interest, moral outrage, pressure from other members of the parish), prosecutors of victimless crimes had little reason to devote the time and the money necessary to continue these prosecutions.

These disadvantages, combined with changing attitudes towards regulation, new methods of local government, and the increasing use of summary jurisdiction for certain offences, fuelled the decline in the number of victimless offences prosecuted by indictment during this period (Table 6.1). In 1663–64, 32% of indicted defendants were accused of regulatory offences; this proportion declined steadily over the next three sample years to 8% in 1707, before increasing to 17% in the 1720–22 sample period. Concurrently, the proportion of indictments for these offences which never reached a final verdict rose to 74%. Except for the unusually zealous efforts of the Societies for the Reformation of Manners during the last three sample periods, prosecutions of vice might also have declined. By the 1720–22 sample, two-thirds of indictments for vice also failed to reach a final verdict.

Indictments remained a popular method of prosecution at the end of this period, but they were used to address an increasingly narrow range of offences: crimes with identifiable victims such as assault, riot, and property offences. Similarly, the range of offenders narrowed as the number of indicted laborers declined. For those offences and offenders for which indictments were still thought to be appropriate, prosecutors faced a growing chance that the indictment would be rejected by the grand jury. Increasingly, potential plaintiffs turned to summary conviction for the prosecution of the offences and offenders that could not usefully be prosecuted by indictment.

7

Houses of correction

Starting with Bridewell Hospital in London, houses of correction were established in the late sixteenth century as places for punishing and setting to work poor people who committed petty offences such as vagrancy, begging, and other "idle and disorderly" conduct. The first houses of correction were established in urban areas, in part as a response to the social and economic problems occasioned by rapid population growth. After a national network of county houses of correction (including the Middlesex and Westminster houses) was established in the early seventeenth century, a new wave of foundations occurred in England between 1690 and 1720, partly in response to new economic difficulties. During times of social and economic dislocation, magistrates and urban élites found the combination of forced labor and whipping in houses of correction an attractive method of punishing the petty offences committed by the poor. Both in the late sixteenth and late seventeenth centuries, moreover, advocates of moral and religious reform were attracted to an institution that sought to reform offenders.[1] For the same reason, houses of correction were even adopted as a punishment for clergyable felonies in 1706.[2] As the population of London's surburbs surged, concern about social problems in the metropolis increased, and the reformation of manners campaign set to work, the 1690s and early 1700s were propitious times for houses of correction in London's suburbs. Commitments to both the Middlesex and Westminster houses increased dramatically between 1690 and 1717; over the period 1680–1725 commitments to the Westminster house increased by at least 86% and

---

[1] Innes, "Prisons for the poor," pp. 42–61, 79–84; A. L. Beier, Masterless Men. The Vagrancy Problem in England 1560–1640 (1987), pp. 164–69; Paul Slack, "Social policy and the constraints of government, 1547–58," in The Mid-Tudor Polity c.1540–1560, ed. J. Loach and R. Tittler (1980), pp. 107–11; E. M. Leonard, The Early History of English Poor Relief (1900), pp. 65–66, 110–15, 227–29, 293–95; and, in a European context, Pieter Spierenburg, "The sociogenesis of confinement and its development in early-modern Europe," in The Emergence of Carceral Institutions: Prisons, Galleys, and Lunatic Asylums, 1500–1900 (Centrum voor Maatschappijgechiedenis, vol. 12, 1984), pp. 9–77; Thorsten Sellin, Pioneering in Penology. The Amsterdam Houses of Correction in the Sixteenth and Seventeenth Centuries (Philadelphia, 1944), chap. 2.
[2] Beattie, Crime and the Courts, pp. 493–500.

between 1660 and 1725 the number of prisoners in the Middlesex house of correction in Clerkenwell at the time sessions met increased by 165%.[3]

For magistrates and potential prosecutors, commitment to a house of correction had a number of advantages over the alternative methods of prosecuting petty crime. Most importantly, if the justice agreed with the complaint, the punishment of the defendant was certain, immediate and corporal. Unlike recognizances or indictments, where defendants usually did not even have to appear in court for several weeks (if they chose to do so at all), defendants were committed to houses of correction for punishment immediately after their hearing before the justice. And, unlike the small fines meted to defendants convicted on indictments, punishments in houses of correction were substantial: many were whipped, and virtually all prisoners were put to hard labor beating hemp. Compared with indictments, moreover, summary conviction was significantly cheaper for the plaintiff. Plaintiffs seeking a summary punishment had to take the time to appear before a justice and pay a shilling for the warrant for the arrest of the defendant; but this was only a fraction of the trouble and expense of prosecuting an indictment.[4] In most cases, official plaintiffs arrested offenders in the course of their duties and did not even have to pay for an arrest warrant. The convenience and the low cost of committing defendants to houses of correction is a major reason why constables and night watchmen were responsible for so few prosecutions at sessions and so many commitments to houses of correction.[5]

From the point of view of a justice of the peace, houses of correction offered not only convenience but flexibility. A person committed to a house of correction could be discharged at any time by the committing justice. In contrast, a defendant bound over by recognizance could only be discharged after an appearance before the justices assembled at sessions, where other justices might interfere in the case. And while with summary jurisdiction the determination of guilt was entirely in the hands of an individual justice (or two justices for some offences), indicted defendants could only be convicted with the cooperation of two juries, the members of which may have had different attitudes towards controversial laws than the justice. For reasons of cost, convenience, and control, justices favored summary convictions whenever possible. When the Middlesex court recommended, in a petition to the Lord Chancellor in 1721, the creation of a new (and potentially controversial)

---

[3] Westminster house of correction calendars survive in a virtually unbroken series from 1680; this calculation is based on a comparison of the total number of commitments in the decade 1680–89 with those in the decade 1712–21. The Middlesex figure is based on the number of prisoners in the house of correction at the time sessions met (which is only a fraction of the total number of prisoners committed); figures for the decade 1662–73 (except the plague and fire years of 1665–66) were compared with 1716–25. See above, Figure 3.3.

[4] MJ/OC/I, ff. 111–112d (Jan. 1721); above, section 6.3.   [5] See below, section 8.3.

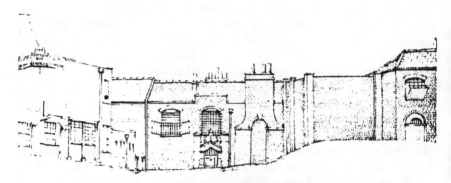

Plate 1 Westminster house of correction, Tothill Fields (early nineteenth-century sketch made shortly before it was demolished; Westminster City Archives)
A tablet over the gateway stated "Here are several sorts of work for the poor of this parish of St. Margaret's Westminster. As also this county according to law and for such as will beg and live idle in the said City and Liberty of Westminster. Anno 1655"

offence of refusing to open one's door to a constable upon demand, they requested the "penalties to be levied in a summary method."[6]

7.1 "LOOSE, IDLE AND DISORDERLY": OFFENCES PUNISHED IN HOUSES OF CORRECTION

Houses of correction were successful because they could be used to punish a wide range of petty offences. With the exception of defendants convicted of a few specific statutory offences, most prisoners were committed under the authority of the statute 7 Jac. 1 c. 4, which authorized the creation of houses of correction for the punishment of "rogues, vagabonds, sturdy beggars, and other idle and disorderly persons." Because there was little scope for judicial review of house of correction commitments, the phrase "idle and disorderly" came to be interpreted very broadly, both by the authors of manuals for justices of the peace and by the justices of the peace themselves.[7] Using the language of 7 Jac. 1 c. 4, more than one-fifth of the commitments state only that the defendant was accused of being "idle," "disorderly," or "loose, idle, and

---

[6] MJ/SP/May 1721, no. 2.   [7] Section 2.5.

Table 7.1 *Houses of correction: estimated annual numbers of commitments*[a]

	1670–80[b]	1693, 1697[b]	1712	1721	Total %
Loose, idle, disorderly; vagrant[c]	336	140	300	183	21.7
Lewd, nightwalker[c]	68	210	351	171	18.1
Prostitution	126	184	72	330	16.1
(Total prostitution, lewd, and nightwalker)	(194)	(394)	(423)	(501)	(34.2)
Other vice[d]	44	14	6	45	2.5
Theft and fraud	164	356	387	363	28.7
Servant, apprentice[e]	60	50	42	111	5.9
Poor law[f]	2	10	21	18	1.2
Peace	18	6	21	75	2.7
Unknown, misc.[g]	98	12	15	12	3.1
TOTAL	916	982	1215	1308	100.0
Sampling proportion	50%	50%	33%	33%	
Sample size	458	491	405	436	

[a] Method of calculation: sample counts multiplied by sampling proportion for each year (or composite year). As noted in the text, the following types of commitments were excluded from the sample: defendants committed for want of sureties to attend sessions and those who were subsequently bailed to attend sessions; defendants committed for "safekeeping"; and defendants committed by the bench at sessions. In total, these defendants account for 6.4% of the 1,913 commitments in the sample. Convicted felons whose punishment involved a sentence in a house of correction were also excluded from the sample (these commitments were recorded separately).

[b] Because comprehensive Middlesex calendars are rare before 1712, and Westminster calendars before 1680, the first two columns contain composite years assembled from available calendars.

The first column contains Middlesex calendars from May 1670, August 1670, September 1673, and February 1675 (MJ/SR/1387, 1392, 1442 [roll for January 1673], 1533 [roll for October 1677]). As each of these calendars was 100% sampled, and these four rolls constitute half the number of rolls in most years, this sample constitutes roughly 50% of a Middlesex year. The Westminster evidence in this column is from a 50% sample of all the rolls in 1680.

The second column contains Middlesex calendars from January through May 1697 (four rolls). As in the first column, these were 100% sampled and the resulting sample constitutes roughly 50% of an entire Middlesex year. The Westminster evidence in this column comes from a 50% sample of all the rolls in 1693.

[c] These are residual categories; where a more specific offence is mentioned the case is included in that category.

[d] Including adultery, gambling, defendants apprehended in a "disorderly house," and drunkenness.

[e] Complaints by master against their apprentices or servants. All other cases involving apprentices and servants are included under the appropriate offence.

[f] Bastardy, failure to support wife or children, miscellaneous settlement offences.

[g] Primarily cases where the offence was either not listed or illegible on the calendar.

disorderly" (Table 7.1).[8] Nevertheless, the majority of the commitments provide additional information about the offending behavior; although many persons were committed for offences related to vagrancy, a substantial number were accused of other offences including theft, prostitution, and offences against the peace.[9]

As defined by the Elizabethan statutes, rogues, vagrants, and sturdy beggars included unlicensed beggars, persons refusing to work and having no lawful means of maintaining themselves, men who deserted their families and refused to provide for them, and itinerant players and gamblers.[10] Justices of the peace possessed considerable discretion in the punishment of these offenders; they could be whipped, sent to a house of correction, and/or passed to their parish of legal settlement if not legally settled in the parish. In practice, many were probably passed without being committed to a house of correction, and many others were committed to a house of correction without being passed.[11] Only 1% of the prisoners sampled are recorded as having been passed to another parish upon their discharge from a house of correction. Of course, the records may not be complete, but given the cost of passing vagrants it is likely that many who were not legally settled were allowed to remain after their discharge from a house of correction. At a meeting of the Middlesex justices in May 1721, it was resolved that in their petty sessions justices were "to examine places of legal settlement of vagrant persons brought before them instead of sending them to the house of correction."[12]

Judging from the entries on house of correction calendars, however, it appears that persons accused of vagrancy offences were rarely sent to a house of correction unless their vagrancy was compounded with some other offence. Only 4% of the commitments were for vagrancy alone. Of the small number of beggars identified on the calendars, one was accused of cheating, another of committing an assault "in a cruel manner," and a third of pretending to be lame. Three were accused in 1697 of "making a disturbance at housekeepers' doors and threatening that if they would not relieve them to mark their doors

---

[8] The origin of the term "loose" is a mystery; it is not used in 7 Jac. I c. 4. Another phrase commonly used was "lewd, idle and disorderly." As explained below, it is likely that this term was frequently used to describe prostitutes.

[9] For the wide range of offences which occasioned commitments, see also Innes, "Prisons for the poor," pp. 68–71, 85; Sharpe, *Crime in Seventeenth-Century England*, pp. 151–52, 167–71; King, "Crime, law and society," p. 283; Ian Archer, "Governors and governed in late sixteenth-century London, c.1560–1603: studies in the achievement of stability" (Ph.D. diss., Oxford University, 1988), pp. 329–32; and, for the London Bridewell at this time, Bethlem Royal Hospital, minutes of the court of governors of Bridewell and Bethlem.

[10] 14 Eliz. c. 5; 39 Eliz. c. 4; both repealed and replaced by 12 Anne c. 23.

[11] Joanna Innes, "Social problems: poverty and marginality in eighteenth-century England" (unpublished typescript, 1985), p. 78.

[12] MJ/SP/April 1721, no. 10. It is not known whether this resolution had any effect.

for some ill designs."[13] Preventing disorder also appears to have been the motivation for committing two more exotic types of vagrants: a prize fighter who went "about the streets with a drawn sword in his hand and a drum beating thereby causing a great mob and a tumult" and two proprietors of puppet shows, "being this night taken beating a drum and playing a violin in order to entice and draw people together in a disorderly and tumultuous manner."[14] Vagrancy *per se* appears to have formed the basis of few commitments unless the offender committed, was suspected of committing, or threatened to commit other offences.

The related offence of not working and having no lawful means of supporting oneself resulted in a large number of commitments. Not only were such people potential charges on the poor rate, but their way of life was clearly suspicious. Many of the defendants committed simply for being "idle and disorderly" were probably accused of little more than being poor and able-bodied and not having a job. Like vagrancy offences, however, prisoners accused of being idle, not working, or not giving "a good account of their way of living" were often suspected of committing another offence. In many cases, the constables or night watchmen who arrested them appear to have suspected that they earned their living by prostitution or theft. Three women were committed in 1721, on the complaint of two constables and two informers associated with the reformation of manners campaign, after being "taken last night wandering the streets and misbehaving themselves," and in 1712 another woman was "taken strolling." All four failed to give an acceptable account of how they made their living, and the officers clearly had their suspicions.[15] People apprehended in these circumstances were frequently accused of nightwalking. Nightwalkers, according to John Bond, were people "suspected, or of ill fame, such as sleep in the day time, and in the night season haunt houses suspected for bawdry, or use suspicious company ... Nightwalkers suspected to be pilferers, or otherwise like to disturb the peace, or of evil fame, may be bound to their good behaviour."[16] In fact, nightwalkers were frequently committed to a house of correction. As noted below, women accused of nightwalking were frequently suspected of prostitution, while men accused of this offence were usually suspected of being thieves. One man had been apprehended by the watch at night "almost two miles from his house and [is] thought to be a nightwalker and a thief";[17] other male nightwalkers were suspected of picking locks or of being pickpockets.

With or without specific reference to vagrancy offences, theft and related

13 MJ/SR/1886, HC (Feb. 1697); 2369, HC (July 1721); 2374, HC (Oct. 1721); 1889, HC (April 1697).
14 MJ/SR/2363, HC (April 1721); 2376, HC (Dec. 1721).
15 MJ/SR/2192, HC (July 1712); 2374, HC (Oct. 1721).
16 Bond, *Complete Guide*, p. 186.   17 MJ/SR/1576, HC (Westminster sessions, April 1680).

property offences are the most frequent specific offences listed in house of correction calendars, accounting for 29% of all commitments. Pilfering was the most common type of theft, but defendants were also accused of picking pockets, embezzlement, receiving stolen goods, cheating, and extortion. Many of the goods stolen, such as clothes, food, and tools, were stated to be "of small value." In several cases, however, the stolen goods were of considerable value, including money (6s. out of a drawer, 10s. out of a pocket) and gold rings, and the offences clearly constituted grand larceny. Given the dissatisfaction with the available punishments for larceny in the early eighteenth century, it is likely that justices consciously punished accused thieves in a house of correction in lieu of formally indicting them. Hard labor and whipping in a house of correction was certainly a more substantial punishment than the branding or whipping typically meted to defendants convicted on indictments for petty larceny or simple grand larceny. Although this practice apparently disappeared later in the century, Henry Fielding thought it should be legalized for minor thefts in 1752.[18] In other cases, defendants accused of theft may have been committed to a house of correction because, while their behavior was suspicious, they had not actually committed indictable offences. Thus, a girl was committed after she was found at night inside a house "with a design to let in" her mother and others to commit a robbery.[19] Others were apprehended breaking or opening windows in order (it was supposed) to commit a theft. Since nothing was actually stolen, and it is difficult to prove the intention of theft, the simplest course of action was to commit such offenders to a house of correction.

Similar evidential problems must lie behind the large number of commitments for sexual offences, since it is difficult to apprehend couples in the act of intercourse. Although prostitution and adultery were ecclesiastical offences and not theoretically punishable by justices of the peace, constables did have the power to arrest would-be fornicators as a means of preserving the peace. Moreover, some authorities stated that adultery and prostitution were a form of "idle and disorderly" conduct and were thus punishable in houses of correction.[20] It is difficult to determine precisely how many commitments concerned sexual offences, but many women on house of correction calendars were charged with being "lewd women" and "nightwalkers" in circumstances

---

[18] Beattie, *Crime and the Courts*, pp. 269–70, 552; WJ/OC/I, f. 45 (28 June 1722); Henry Fielding, *Covent Garden Journal*, no. 16 (25 Feb. 1752). For an example of this practice, see *The Great Grievance of Traders and Shopkeepers, by the Notorious Practice of Stealing their Goods out of their Shops and Warehouses ... Humbly Represented to the Consideration of the Honourable House of Commons* [1700]. I am indebted to John Beattie for this reference.

[19] MJ/SR/1812, HC (Westminster sessions, April 1693).

[20] "A charge given by Hugh Hare, Esq., J.P., at the general quarter sessions for the county of Surrey, holden at Dorking, 5 April 1692," *Surrey Archaeological Collections* 12 (1895), pp. 127–28; *A Report of all the Cases Determined by Sir John Holt* (1738), p. 406.

which suggest that the offender was a prostitute. Although both terms were used more generally to describe evil and base behavior, they were frequently used to refer to prostitution. Three women committed to the Westminster house of correction, for example, were accused of being "loose, idle and disorderly" persons, nightwalkers, and "enticers of people to bawdry."[21] Since over 90% of the people accused of lewd behavior and nightwalking were women, prostitution must account for a substantial fraction of the commitments for these offences.[22]

In addition, 16% of the commitments in the house of correction sample make specific reference to sexual offences by describing the offending behavior as frequenting bawdy houses, picking up men in the street, soliciting, or being apprehended with a strange man (or woman). In addition, a small number (0.7% of all commitments) concerned adultery and unmarried couples who "lived incontinently." One couple were accused of "having lived in common debauchery together for many years."[23] In another case, a mother had a woman committed who had "cohabited" with her son and "almost ruined" him.[24] Needless to say, in dealing with sexual offences justices subscribed to the prevailing double standard of sexual conduct: prostitutes and female adulterers were typically committed to houses of correction while their male partners, if punished at all, were bound over by recognizance.[25] On the rare occasions when men were committed to houses of correction for sexual offences it often appears that they were also suspected of being involved in thefts. Thus, a man and woman who were accused of frequenting bawdy houses were "suspected to entertain thieves, whores and pickpockets."[26]

While offences such as prostitution and adultery could be interpreted as forms of "disorderly" conduct, they fit somewhat uneasily with the original purpose of houses of correction as places for the punishment of "rogues, vagabonds and sturdy beggars, and other idle and disorderly persons." Even further removed from the original purpose was the small but apparently growing number of men and women committed for offences against the peace, including assault, riot, and defamatory and seditious words, offences that account for 6.2% of the 1721 house of correction sample.[27] Defendants were committed for raising a riot in front of the house of a justice of the peace and for raising a tumult about the house of the envoy of Poland and charging him

---

[21] MJ/SR/1807, HC (Westminster sessions, Jan. 1693).
[22] This calculation excludes commitments (26 of 313) where the sex of the defendant was not known.
[23] MJ/SR/1823, HC (Westminster sessions, Oct. 1693).   [24] MJ/SP/Oct. 1713, no. 16.
[25] This practice was explicitly recognized by justice Samuel Ryder in his *Charge to the Grand Jury of the City and Liberty of Westminster, at the General Quarter Sessions of the Peace, held in Westminster Hall, October 6, 1725* [1726], p. 8.
[26] MJ/SR/2376, HC (Dec. 1721).
[27] As noted below, this discussion does *not* include commitments of defendants for want of sureties to attend sessions.

with fathering a bastard child.[28] One woman allegedly sent scandalous letters to a justice and his wife, and another was accused of "being an idle and abusive party amongst her neighbours and in particular for defaming one Mr. Clarke."[29] As the last example, which amounts to the indictable offence of being a common disturber, suggests, such offences were normally prosecuted by indictment or recognizance at sessions. Similarly, people who threatened physical harm to others or who threatened to burn down buildings were typically bound over for the peace, but a few nevertheless ended up in a house of correction.

Complaints by masters against their apprentices and servants merit separate discussion, although many of the offences have already been discussed. Several servants and apprentices were committed for pilfering or embezzling goods from their masters or mistresses and a few were accused of assaulting or abusing them (one servant even attempted to bite off his master's nose). Nevertheless, many complaints were unique to the master–servant relationship. Many apprentices and servants were committed for leaving their posts, either temporarily or permanently. Others were charged with failing to follow orders or with insulting their masters, though the calendars suggest that few were committed for these offences alone. Apprentices and servants were also committed to houses of correction for swearing, drinking, keeping bad company, and "disorderly" conduct, including one who was charged with "being rude with the serving maid and abusing his master and mistress."[30] It is unclear why masters committed their apprentices and servants to houses of correction when they possessed the power to administer physical punishments themselves. In most cases, commitment was probably a last resort after attempts to "correct" the recalcitrant offender at home had failed. Because of the ambiguous position of apprentices and servants in the household, masters and mistresses found themselves in an awkward position: although they were responsible for the good behavior of their charges, they lacked some of the disciplinary control possessed by parents.[31] In a small number of cases, however, parents committed their own children to houses of correction.

To a certain extent, houses of correction were viewed by parents and masters as a type of reform school where young offenders could be punished without incurring the social stigma of having been formally prosecuted. Although an apprentice to a periwigmaker was charged with being "so addicted to lying, thieving and cheating" that his master "lost above twenty pounds in value in hair, moneys, and other goods," the master committed him to a house of

---

[28] MJ/SR/2364, HC (April 1721); 2197, HC (Westminster sessions, Oct. 1712).
[29] MJ/SR/2358, HC (Westminster sessions, Jan. 1721); 1581, HC (Westminster sessions, July 1680).
[30] MJ/SR/2369, HC (July 1721).
[31] Ilana Krausman Ben-Amos, "Service and the coming of age of young men in seventeenth-century England," *Continuity and Change* 3 (1988), pp. 42–43.

correction: "considering the tenderness of his years [the master] hath not prosecuted him."[32] The professed leniency of this master is echoed by the sentences meted by justices of the peace; when committed to a house of correction by their masters, servants and apprentices tended to receive shorter sentences than other offenders, and were slightly less likely to be whipped.[33] It is possible that servants and apprentices were kept in a separate part of the house in order to prevent them from being corrupted by the other prisoners.[34]

In some respects, the Middlesex and Westminster houses of correction were treated as all-purpose places of confinement for people who it was thought should be kept off the streets. One man was described as being deaf and dumb, and a small number of prisoners were described as "mad."[35] More frequently, houses of correction were used as conventional prisons. Before 1720, a handful of prisoners (about 1% of commitments) either were explicitly committed for want of sureties to enter into a recognizance to attend sessions, or entered into recognizances upon their discharge.[36] In 1720, a statute authorized committing "vagrants and other criminals, offenders and persons charged with small offences" who were awaiting an appearance at sessions to houses of correction if they were unable to find sureties. Consequently, the number of prisoners committed for want of sureties rose to 7% of the commitments in the 1721 sample and gradually increased thereafter; by the 1760s and 1770s such prisoners accounted for over 75% of those committed to the Middlesex and Westminster houses of correction.[37]

Other prisoners were committed to a house of correction by the justices at quarter sessions after the prisoner had appeared to answer a recognizance or an indictment. As we have seen, a small but growing number of defendants convicted on indictments at the Middlesex and Westminster sessions were sentenced to periods of imprisonment in a house of correction.[38] In 1706, this

---

[32] WJ/SBB/728, p. 25 (Jan. 1715).   [33] See below, Tables 7.4 and 7.5.

[34] For evidence of this practice, see *Middlesex Records*, ed. Jeaffreson, vol. 2, p. 130; *A Foreign View of England in the Reigns of George I and George II. The Letters of Monsieur de Saussure to his Family*, ed. Mme. van Muyden (1902), p. 300. There is, however, no evidence of it in Middlesex during the period of this study.

[35] By the vagrancy act of 1713 (12 Anne c. 23), justices were authorized to order the incarceration of "furiously mad and dangerous" persons in any place of secure confinement. It does not appear that very many were committed to houses of correction (Roy Porter, *Mind Forg'd Manacles. A History of Madness in England from the Restoration to the Regency* [1987], pp. 117–19).

[36] This calculation is based on notations on house of correction calendars. It is of course possible that the calendars did not always record when prisoners entered into recognizances upon their discharge.

[37] 6 Geo. I c.19; Innes, "Prisons for the poor," pp. 57–58. In the entire sample, 20.9% of the prisoners were not discharged until sessions met. But most of these prisoners had coincidentally only recently been committed and had not yet served their sentence; few of these commitments appear to have been made with the intent of having the case heard by quarter sessions.

[38] See above, section 6.5.

Table 7.2   *Prosecutions of offences by different procedures: estimated annual averages*[a]

	Sample Years:				
Recognizances, indictments:	1663–64	1677	1693	1707	1720–22
Houses of correction:	—	1670–80	1693,1697	1712	1721
Prostitution					
Recognizance	67.5	85	55	160	69
House of correction[b]	—	194	394	423	501
Theft					
Recognizance	130	145	140	115	96
House of correction	—	160	344	375	351
Indictment	54	115	99	42	78
Offences Against the Peace					
Recognizance	937.5	990	1075	690	1209
House of correction	—	18	6	21	75
Indictment	494	561	597	783	640

[a]   The evidence in this table is subject to several possible distortions and is presented to establish general patterns only. The estimated numbers of prosecutions were calculated by multiplying sample results by the sampling proportions, which vary between 17% and 50%, depending on the sample years. As is evident in the table, the sample years for houses of correction do not correspond with those for recognizances and indictments. Finally, as noted in section 3.3, the language used to describe offences varies with each procedure and thus it is impossible to make precise comparisons between procedures. The unit of analysis is the defendant.
[b]   Includes nightwalkers and people accused of "lewd" behavior.

practice was extended to felons when a statute authorized incarceration in a house of correction as a form of punishment for defendants convicted on indictments of simple felonies. Between 1706 and 1718, when the introduction of transportation led to a decline in the use of houses of correction for this purpose, about a fifth of all defendants convicted of property crimes were committed to London's houses of correction.[39] Finally, a small number of people (7% of all commitments) were committed to houses of correction for "safekeeping." These include people suspected of serious crimes who were held pending the results of investigations, and victims and witnesses of serious crimes who were kept in a house of correction in order to ensure that they would appear to testify at trials (presumably they were unable to find sureties to enter into a recognizance).

Because defendants committed for want of sureties and for safekeeping were

[39]   Innes, "Prisons for the poor," pp. 50–52. Records of these prisoners were kept separate from the usual lists of commitments to houses of correction.

not committed specifically for punishment, and because convicted felons were committed after having been convicted on indictment, these categories of offenders have *not* been included in the quantitative analysis of house of correction commitments as a form of summary justice.[40] Nonetheless, the fact that such people were committed illustrates how far the Middlesex and Westminster justices were from believing that the sole purpose of houses of correction was for the punishment of "rogues, vagabonds, sturdy beggars, and other idle and disorderly persons."

To a degree, the growth in house of correction commitments during this period occurred at the expense of recognizances (Table 7.2). Although extrapolating long-term trends by comparing levels of prosecutions in the different sample periods is statistically unwarrantable, the evidence *suggests* that while the number of people bound over for theft decreased during this period the number of commitments for theft increased. Although indictments for theft at sessions show no clear trend, most indictments for theft were in any case prosecuted at the Old Bailey. Further research on prosecutions for theft at the Old Bailey, as well as more comprehensive sampling of recognizances and house of correction calendars, is clearly necessary. Nevertheless, there is a strong possibility that cases of petty theft in the early eighteenth century were increasingly prosecuted by commitment to houses of correction in lieu of prosecution by recognizance or indictment.[41] Similarly, with the exception of the 1707/1712 samples, house of correction commitments for prostitution increasingly outnumbered recognizances during this period. On the other hand, the increase in commitments for offences against the peace was dwarfed by much larger increases in the numbers of recognizances and indictments. Thus, only for certain offences did the growing importance of houses of correction occur at the expense of prosecutions by other procedures. In fact, some offences, particularly nightwalking and vagrancy, were rarely prosecuted by procedures other than summary jurisdiction throughout this period. The growth in commitments for these offences thus reflects a growth in the total number of people prosecuted for these offences, which was largely due to the adoption of less tolerant attitudes towards suspicious persons on London's streets. Nonetheless, just as summary convictions by fine replaced indictments for certain regulatory offences, commitment to a house of correction appears to have become, in lieu of binding over by recognizance, the preferred method of

---

[40] For similar reasons, the eight prisoners who were subsequently transferred to New Prison or Newgate were excluded from the analysis.

[41] It is possible that after the introduction of a new form of punishment for convicted felons in 1718, transportation, indictments regained some of their popularity as a method of prosecuting theft. Commitments to houses of correction for theft declined slightly between the sample periods 1712 and 1721, while indictments increased between the 1707 and 1721 samples (Table 7.2).

prosecuting minor offences such as petty theft and prostitution during this period.

7.2 SUMMARY JUSTICE?

The typical commitment to a house of correction was not so much the result of a single offence allegedly committed as it was of an assessment of the general character and reputation of the accused. Defendants were usually not accused of stealing a specific object but instead of being a "pilfering person," not of "loose, idle, and disorderly" conduct but of being a "loose, idle, and disorderly person," not of a specific act of prostitution but of being a "nightwalker" or a "lewd woman." This language raises important issues about the evidence used to justify commitments to houses of correction. On the one hand they suggest that persons had to commit several offences before it was deemed appropriate to commit them. One woman, for example, was accused of being an "idle pilfering wench" by her own confession, "having pilfered things of small value from John Blaker, George Silke, and others." Another was accused of stealing an apron and a napkin of small value, of committing an assault, and of "being a frequenter of strong water shops and drunk often."[42] On the more descriptive calendars, the examples of such combinations of offences are endless. But such long lists of offences, and the wide-ranging character offences described above, raise the question of the accuracy of the accusations. How was it known that defendants frequently committed thefts, or were frequent visitors to disorderly houses, or that they were prone to commit certain offences? How much evidence, and what types of evidence, did justices of the peace require as proof of these charges? How just, in other words, were the summary decisions of justices which resulted in commitments to houses of correction? Were legal authorities justified in their suspicions of statutes "which subject men to new and other trials, than those by which they ought to be tried by common law, being contrary to the rights and liberties of Englishmen"?[43]

Ultimately, it is impossible to provide definitive answers to these questions, largely because very little evidence survives of hearings that took place before individual justices.[44] Sufficient evidence exists, however, to raise doubts about

---

[42] MJ/SR/1817, HC (Westminster sessions, July 1693); 2369, HC (July 1721).

[43] Robert, Lord Raymond, *Reports of Cases Argued and Adjudged in the Courts of King's Bench*, 3 vols., 4th edn (1790–92), vol. 1, p. 581 (Chief Justice Holt). See also Dalton, *Countrey Justice* (1677), preface.

[44] Most of the evidence that has hitherto come to light concerns the game laws. In his article on "Poaching and the game laws in Cannock Chase," Douglas Hay argued that justices' decisions were often biased by class interests (*Albion's Fatal Tree*, ed. Hay *et al.*, pp. 240–44). To this argument P. B. Munsche has responded that "the evidence is, at best, ambiguous" (*Gentlemen and Poachers: The English Game Laws 1671–1831* [Cambridge, 1981], p. 161; see also pp. 94–96, 104, 161–63). See also Joanna Innes, "Statute law and summary justice in early modern England" (unpublished paper, 1986), pp. 28–36. Both Munsche and Innes argue that justices

the strength of the evidence that was used to justify commitments to houses of correction and to suggest that in many situations people were committed on the basis of weak or circumstantial evidence. Henry Fielding, a Westminster justice of the peace, describes a hearing in the novel *Amelia* in which several people apprehended by the night watch are brought before a justice of the peace, justice Thrasher. In a series of judgements Thrasher exhibits a weak knowledge of the law, draws stupid conclusions, and favors people who are well-dressed ("the magistrate had too great an honour for Truth to suspect that she ever appeared in sordid apparel"). In one case, a poor female servant who had been out on the streets after twelve o'clock at night in order to fetch a midwife for her mistress was declared to be "guilty within the statute of streetwalking, [and Thrasher] ordered her to Bridewell for a month."[45]

Although Fielding no doubt exaggerated the incompetence of "trading justices" in furtherance of his reforming agenda,[46] this fictional example highlights some of the potentially arbitrary aspects of the way prostitutes and other persons accused of victimless offences were arrested and convicted during the period of this study. These offenders were typically arrested by night watchmen or constables late at night, often on the authority of warrants from justices of the peace authorizing "private" searches for these types of offenders. They were typically charged with being nightwalkers or loose, idle, and disorderly people. As we have seen, most of these offences were vaguely defined in law and they could be used to charge defendants whose activities were merely suspicious. The arresting officers were unlikely to know personally many of the people they encountered during their searches, and they were forced to make hasty judgements concerning suspects' characters. On what criteria did the officers make these decisions, and on what basis did justices of the peace determine the guilt or innocence of those who were arrested?

In order for women to be arrested for prostitution, a correspondent of the Society for the Promotion of Christian Knowledge noted, either "matters of fact" needed to be proved against them or they could be charged with being "vagrant, disorderly persons having no visible way of living."[47] Judging by the number of women taken in bawdy houses, officers often had plenty of "matters of fact" against the women they arrested for prostitution. More women, however, were charged under the second justification, where the evidence against them was often much weaker. It appears that women on the streets or in alehouses were often arrested because they appeared to dress like prostitutes,

feared being the object of litigation for irregular convictions, but it should be noted that most of their evidence dates from the second half of the eighteenth century.

[45] Henry Fielding, *Amelia* (Dublin, 1752), vol. 1, pp. 3–9.
[46] Martin C. Battestin, "Introduction" to *Amelia*, by Henry Fielding (Oxford, 1983), pp. xxvi–xxx; Martin C. and Ruthe R. Battestin, *Henry Fielding, A Life* (1989), p. 477.
[47] Society for the Promotion of Christian Knowledge Archives, Papers of Moment, p. 97.

they were found in the streets where prostitutes were known to solicit, they were out late at night unaccompanied by men, or they had previously been arrested and committed to a house of correction. As the example of the hearing before justice Thrasher suggests, clothes could play a significant role in justices' decisions. The importance of dress in shaping opinions about who was a prostitute is suggested by the description in *The Tatler* of a justice Tearshift who imprisoned women "for being loose in [their] dress" if they "went only with one thin petticoat." The difficulty of making such judgements is high-lighted by a complaint that because even ordinary women had "gay dress and jaunty airs," it had become impossible to distinguish "the real strumpets."[48] Prostitutes, of course, typically wear revealing or outrageous clothes in order to attract business, but dress was an unreliable method of identifying prostitutes for arrest. In addition, in certain neighborhoods single women were immedi-ately suspected of prostitution; the streets around Drury Lane were searched particularly carefully for suspicious women. Thus, two women were arrested for being "lewd women and taken in brandy shops near the playhouse." As Fielding's story suggests, the chance of being arrested increased late at night: two women were committed simply for "walking in the streets at twelve o'clock at night."[49] The case of Jane Allridge, 13, illustrates the point that young women could be apprehended by the watch merely for being outside late at night, especially when they were not accompanied by men. Allridge testified to the court that between twelve and one o'clock one morning she was sitting outside on some stairs and "being afraid of the watch [it] being a late hour" she accepted the company of a strange man who subsequently raped her.[50]

The chance of being arrested also increased significantly if one had been arrested previously. Two women were "taken strolling in the streets and about the playhouse in Drury Lane and Bruges Street and [are] known to be old offenders."[51] The fact that constables were in the habit of making arrests on this basis was revealed in 1709 when John Dent, a constable active in the reformation of manners campaign, was killed by three soldiers after he had apprehended Ann Dickens in Covent Garden for being an "idle woman." During the trial of the soldiers, Chief Justice Holt used this case to highlight the questionable basis on which many such arrests were made. Holt asked one of the constables who had assisted Dent, "did you know she was a bad woman?" The constable replied "we brought her to justice before and we designed to do it again ... We knew her to be a very common woman of the town, and in a

---

[48] *The Tatler*, no. 14, 12 May 1709; [Daniel Defoe], *Some Considerations Upon Street-Walkers* [1726], p. 4. See also Henry Fielding, *The Coffee House Politician, or the Justice Caught in his own Trap* (1730), p. 70 and *passim*.

[49] MJ/SR/2192, HC (Westminster Sessions, July 1712, calendar for April 1712); 1864, HC (Jan. 1697).

[50] MJ/SP/July 1707, no. 81.   [51] MJ/SR/2192, HC (Westminster sessions, July 1712).

common plying place for such people, therefore we took her up."[52] Holt, complaining that "constables nowadays make a common practice of taking up people only for walking the streets," ruled that "the arrest of the woman was injurious and oppressive."[53]

Women arrested on this basis were, of course, often discharged without being committed to a house of correction after they were brought before a justice.[54] Nevertheless, the language of the house of correction calendars suggests that justices shared the same prejudices about who was and who was not a prostitute as the informers and constables who made the arrests. Most of the examples cited above are from the house of correction calendars and in all probability the language was the justices', having been copied from their warrants of commitment (*mittimuses*). In fact, because it was so easy to get justices to commit young single women who were not regularly employed to houses of correction for prostitution, there was considerable opportunity for vexatious prosecutions. Ann Morley, a lodger who was suspected by her landlord, Francis Lee, of stealing his possessions, complained in a petition to the Middlesex sessions that he had caused her to be committed to a house of correction by "swearing her to be a whore without any just cause."[55] One must, of course, view such self-serving testimony skeptically, but it is interesting that Morley thought that her complaint would appear plausible to the justices.

It is odd, however, that Lee felt it necessary to make a false complaint against Morley, since defendants were frequently committed to houses of correction on suspicion of theft. Twelve percent of the accusations for theft fall into this category, and in many cases the suspicion appears to have been grounded on very circumstantial evidence. People might be suspected of theft because they were taken in a suspicious location, such as the man who was not able to account for himself when found late at night in the watch house in Ship Yard; because they possessed suspected stolen goods, such as the man who was suspected of having stolen the silver tobacco box he offered for sale, or the man taken between one and two o'clock in the morning with "an old sail cloth of small value"; because they were seen in the company of known thieves; or because they were implicated by common fame, as the man "found in several stories."[56] In other cases, the evidence was even more circumstantial. Loitering

---

[52] *A Looking-Glass for Informing Constables: Represented in the Tryals . . . for the Murder of Mr. John Dent* (3rd edn, 1733), p. 6. See also below, section 9.2.

[53] BL, Add. MS 35,994, f. 96v and 35,979, f. 68.

[54] This is suggested by constables' reports to sessions concerning the results of their arrests of nightwalkers, beggars, wheelbarrow drivers, "shoe blacker boys," and related offenders: MJ/SP/July 1717, nos. 75–78, 83; Feb. 1718, no. 50.

[55] MJ/SP/1689 (undated).

[56] MJ/SR/1576, HC (Westminster sessions, April 1680); 2369, HC (July 1721); 2364, HC (April 1721).

on the wrong streets might be viewed suspiciously, as in the case of a man suspected of robbery and of being "a lewd pilfering fellow ... having been seen about the neighbourhood several times," and the man, referred to earlier, apprehended two miles from his house and "thought to be a nightwalker and a thief."[57] After a theft has been committed, Michael Dalton advised justices, "if a man liveth idly or vagrant, ... it is cause to arrest him upon suspicion ..."[58] Thus, two men and a woman apprehended in bed in a suspected bawdy house were "slightly accused of a robbery last night in St James" and a servant was committed for being idle and disorderly and "under slight suspicion of being accessory to a felony committed in the house of his master."[59] Whereas women apprehended in suspicious circumstances were suspected of being prostitutes, men were often suspected of being thieves: though men accounted for only 42% of the defendants committed for theft, they accounted for 59% of those committed for suspected theft.[60]

Why were justices of the peace so willing to commit people to houses of correction on such apparently weak evidence? In the first place, they faced little possibility that their actions would be reviewed. In theory it was, of course, possible to appeal commitments, either to sessions or to the higher courts with an action of false imprisonment or by obtaining a writ of *habeas corpus* or *certiorari*. In practice, however, very few appeals took place during this period. Most of the people committed to houses of correction were poor and unable to afford the time and money that an appeal would involve. In any case, judicial review was generally restricted to the written record: as long as the justice had cited legitimate grounds for commitment on the warrant ("idle and disorderly" behavior was sufficient), the commitment would be upheld.[61] As an observer noted in 1791, defendants without money or friends were "seldom known to complain, and much seldomer to obtain redress."[62]

More importantly, in a climate of public and official concern about immorality, vagrancy, and idleness, justices were encouraged to punish all suspicious characters. Because during the 1690s, 1710s and 1720s it was commonly thought that London was experiencing a "crime wave," and because all types of deviance, from irreligion and vice to theft and murder, were thought to be related, Londoners were particularly sensitive during this period

---

57 MJ/SR/2192, HC (Westminster sessions, July 1712); 1576, HC (Westminster sessions, April 1680).
58 *Countrey Justice* (1677), p. 413.
59 MJ/SR/1754, HC (Westminster sessions, April 1690); 1751, HC (Westminster sessions, Jan. 1690).
60 Table 7.3. These figures do not include 40 defendants committed for theft whose sex is unknown.
61 Above, section 2.5; Innes, "Prisons for the poor," pp. 85–86.
62 *The Jurisdiction of the Court-Leet: Exemplified in the Articles which the Jury of Inquest for the King in that Court is Charged* (1791), p. xxii.

to any form of suspicious and immoral activity. Grand jurors, members of the Societies for the Reformation of Manners, and others demanded not only that felons receive more effective punishments but also that vagrancy, begging, idleness, and immorality be suppressed.[63] In response to such complaints, the Middlesex justices issued numerous orders, in both petty sessions and quarter sessions, requiring constables to apprehend these offenders.[64] In this context, people who lived without a visible and lawful means of support, loiterers, and people apprehended in gaming houses, brothels, and disorderly alehouses were all viewed as potential criminals who should be summarily punished in the interest of preserving order in the metropolis. In determining who merited punishment in a house of correction at this time, it is not so much that standards of evidence were lowered but that definitions of crime expanded: suspicious and immoral activities were themselves treated as crimes.

Contemporary views about the causes of crime influenced not only the types of offences that were subject to intensive policing, but also the types of people who were most likely to be apprehended and committed to houses of correction. Concerns about vagrancy, begging, and idleness focused attention on the poor, especially those who were unemployed and/or were newcomers in the parish. House of correction calendars reveal little more than the sex of prisoners, but using other evidence it is possible to confirm that they were poor. Many of the offences punished in houses of correction, including petty theft and prostitution, were typically committed out of economic need. Moreover, many of the offences involving suspicious activities, such as begging and idleness, were by definition committed by the poor (there was no offence in living idly, as long as one had a lawful source of income). In any case, the poor were thought to be the only suitable inhabitants of houses of correction. Bridewells had been specifically created for the purpose of punishing poor delinquents and setting them to work, and subsequent parliaments confirmed that gentlemen and "men of quality" could not be punished there.[65]

Such strictures would not of course have prevented artisans or tradesmen from being committed to houses of correction, but in fact relatively few appear to have been committed. While skilled craftsmen (such as smiths) were found in

---

[63] See above, section 1.2.
[64] For example, see the printed orders of the Middlesex sessions, 10 July 1691 and 3 March 1701 (British Library shelfmark 816.m.3, nos. 72 and 100). For orders given out by groups of justices meeting in formal or informal petty sessions see MJ/SP/Feb. 1718, no. 49; Aug. 1721, no. 5; WJ/SP/Oct. 1725, no. 5; *An Account of the Endeavours that have been used to Suppress Gaming Houses* (1722).
[65] Joan R. Kent, "Attitudes of members of the House of Commons to the regulation of 'personal conduct' in late Elizabethan and early Stuart England," *Bulletin of the Institute of Historical Research* 46 (1973), p. 49; John Strange, *Reports of Adjudged Cases in the Courts of Chancery, King's Bench, Common Pleas, and Exchequer*, 2 vols., 3rd edn (1795), vol. 2, p. 1103; 16 Car. 2 c.4, quoted by Jeaffreson in *Middlesex County Records*, 3, p. xxvi.

the London Bridewell, contemporary accounts take notice of well-off prisoners in a manner which suggests that such people were rare sights in houses of correction.[66] Descriptions of the Middlesex house of correction emphasize the poverty of its inhabitants. In 1720, the Middlesex justices observed that the prisoners "are generally so very poor that not one in six is able to pay" the discharge fees. In 1741, the keeper observed that "the persons in his custody are even lower in life and poorer than those committed to the New Prison and often have not one friend come near them during the whole time they are confined …"[67] A prisoner who had completed his sentence in the house of correction in Clerkenwell in 1722 petitioned the court for his release, although he could not pay his fees: "I had not one body to come near me being a stranger not so much as to give me one bit of bread or a draught of drink so that I am almost starved to death with hunger. I have not one friend to do anything for me."[68] Not only were the prisoners poor, but they were without friends or family in London. This suggests that they had recently arrived in London and had not yet established any social ties. As suggested earlier, defendants in this situation were probably often committed to houses of correction for summary punishment and discharge because they were unable to find sureties in order to enter into a recognizance.[69] Recent migrants without connections or a job in London would have immediately attracted the attention of constables searching for vagrants; if suspected of any minor offence, they were likely to be passed back to their parish of settlement or committed to a house of correction.

Migrants to London were likely to be young, and in the early eighteenth century, as in most periods of concern about crime, the young attracted particular attention from social commentators and law enforcement officials. Juvenile delinquents were tomorrow's criminals, and in the early eighteenth century efforts were made to reform them by sending them to serve at sea, transporting them to North America, or committing them to a house of correction.[70] As we have seen, houses of correction were viewed as an appropriate place for sending delinquent servants and apprentices for moderate punishments. It is likely that many prisoners were servants who were temporarily out of work. The number of servants in London grew rapidly in the late

---

[66] Mr. *William Fuller's Trip to Bridewell* (1703), pp. 23–25; *A Foreign View of England*, ed. Mme. van Muyden, p. 301.

[67] MJ/SP/July 1720, no. 50; MJ/OC/IV, f.225 (Oct. 1741).   [68] MJ/SP/May 1722, no. 15.

[69] Section 5.4.

[70] Geoffrey Pearson, *Hooligan: A History of Respectable Fears* (1983), pp. 208, 221; Ivy Pinchbeck and Margaret Hewitt, *Children in English Society* (1969), vol. 1, pp. 104–23. Evidence on the age of defendants committed to houses of correction is unavailable. That many were young is suggested not only by the presence of significant numbers of servants, apprentices and newly-arrived migrants, but also by evidence that accused thieves in the assizes courts in the late eighteenth century tended to be in their late teens or early twenties (Beattie, *Crime and the Courts*, pp. 243–47; Peter King, "Decision-makers and decision-making in the English criminal law, 1750–1800," *Historical Journal* 27 [1984], pp. 34–36).

Table 7.3 *Gender of prisoners in houses of correction*[a]

	Male	Female	Total N[b]
	%	%	(100%)
Loose, idle, disorderly; vagrant	35.2	64.8	355
Lewd, nightwalker	8.0	92.0	287
Prostitution	6.3	93.7	268
Other vice	32.6	67.4	46
Suspected theft	59.3	40.7	59
Other theft/fraud	42.1	57.9	411
Servant, apprentice	74.8	25.2	103
Poor law	27.8	72.2	18
Peace	34.1	65.9	44
Unknown, misc.	38.2	61.8	55
TOTAL %	30.7	69.3	100
N	506	1140	1646

[a] For notes explaining the categories of offences, see Table 7.1.
[b] Excluded from this table are 144 cases where the defendant's sex is unknown because of the poor condition of the calendar.

seventeenth and early eighteenth centuries in response to growing demand from the middle classes as well as the increasing number of "new gentry" taking up residence in London.[71] Contemporaries complained that overpaid servants behaved insolently towards their masters and were prone to drunkenness, swearing, and other sins. Yet because they were hired on short-term contracts and demand for their services fluctuated, they were frequently unemployed. Both the antagonistic nature of master–servant relationships and the irregular character of their employment provided a context in which servants, particularly when they were out of work, were rarely trusted and quickly suspected of turning to crime or prostitution.[72] If prosecuted, because of their youth, poverty, and lack of employment it was more likely that they would be committed to a house of correction than bound over by recognizance.

Finally, women were more than twice as likely to be committed to houses of correction as men, and it is likely that the majority of these women were

[71] *London Journal*, 2 July 1720; Jean Hecht, *The Domestic Servant Class in Eighteenth-Century England* (1956), pp. 10–11. See also above, section 1.2.
[72] Daniel Defoe, *Everybody's Business is No-Body's Business* (1725), pp. 4–24, *The Great Law of Subordination Considered; or the Insolence and Unsufferable Behaviour of Servants in England Duly Enquired Into* (1724), and *Augusta Triumphans: or, the Way to Make London the Most Flourishing City in the Universe* (1728), p. 24; Bernard Mandeville, *Fable of the Bees* (3rd edn, 1724), pp. 348–51; Hecht, *Domestic Servant Class*, pp. 23–26, 77–87; Peter Earle, *The World of Defoe* (Newton Abbot, 1977), pp. 170–77.

unmarried (Table 7.3). Whether for reasons of economy or sexual prejudice, single women in the metropolis were carefully watched for any sign that they were "loose" or "lewd," particularly when they were out of work. Female servants who were out of work, for example, were easily suspected of prostitution. As Defoe complained, servants "don't save money: if they fall sick, or are out of place, they must prostitute their bodies, or starve ... and this is the reason why our streets swarm with strumpets. Thus many of 'em rove from place to place, from bawdy house to service, and service to bawdy house again."[73] Thus, commitments for prostitution peaked in the late spring and summer when the demand for servants in London was at its lowest. This concern with female sexual immorality was based, of course, on the traditional double standard: while the illicit sexual activities of men went largely unpunished, women were expected to remain chaste. While prostitution was an unavoidable consequence of the double standard, it was necessary to delineate prostitutes (by punishing them) as a separate "class of fallen women [that] was needed to keep the rest of the world pure."[74] Thus, women account for over 90% of the commitments for adultery, prostitution, nightwalking, and "lewd" behavior in the Middlesex and Westminster houses of correction. There was also, however, an economic reason for concern about the activities of single women: the fear that they, or their children, would be unable to support themselves and might become chargeable to the parish. Consequently, single women in London were disproportionately likely to be removed under the settlement laws.[75] For both moral and economic reasons, single women received unusual attention from parish officials. Perhaps it is a result of such close supervision that women were so frequently committed to houses of correction for a wide range of other offences as well; women outnumbered men in every category of offences except suspected theft and misbehavior by servants and apprentices.

Ultimately, it is impossible to evaluate the decisions taken by individual constables and justices of the peace three hundred years ago. Evidence from a variety of sources certainly suggests, however, that the decisions which resulted in commitments to houses of correction were frequently shaped by contemporary conceptions of what constituted suspicious behavior. Because idleness and

---

[73] Defoe, *Everybody's Business*, pp. 4–5. See also George, *London Life*, pp. 119–20. In a recent essay D. A. Kent paints a similar picture of the independent lifestyle of servants, but argues that they were economically better off than Defoe suggests: "Ubiquitous but invisible: female domestic servants in mid-eighteenth century London," *History Workshop Journal* 28 (Aug. 1989), pp. 118–21.

[74] Keith Thomas, "The double standard," *Journal of the History of Ideas* 20 (1959), pp. 197, 209.

[75] Dorothy Marshall, *The English Poor in the Eighteenth Century* (1926), pp. 165–66; Steven MacFarlane, "Studies in poverty and poor relief in London at the end of the seventeenth century" (Ph.D. diss., Oxford University, 1982), p. 186. For the extent of poverty among single women in London, see below, section 8.2.

immorality were thought to be the roots of serious crime, people found loitering late at night on the streets or in alehouses, particularly if they were unemployed, poor, young, and/or female, were easily suspected of being "idle," "disorderly," or "lewd." If punishment was thought to be desirable, their youth, poverty, and lack of social connections determined that they would be committed to a house of correction. In the early eighteenth-century war against crime in London, houses of correction were perceived to be a useful weapon.

7.3 PUNISHMENTS

Regardless of whether they were considered to have been formally convicted of a crime,[76] defendants committed to houses of correction received substantial punishments. Virtually all defendants were put to hard labor beating hemp, and half were whipped (Table 7.4). By ordering defendants to be whipped immediately instead of waiting for an order from sessions, the justices mitigated rather than increased the severity of sentences in houses of correction. If prisoners were required to remain in houses of correction until the court determined whether they should be whipped, the average length of stay would have been six weeks in Westminster, where sessions met only four times a year, and three weeks in the rest of Middlesex, where sessions met eight times a year. As it was, most prisoners who were whipped were discharged within two weeks and 83% were released before sessions met. For most prisoners, immediate "correction" followed shortly by release was no doubt preferable to a sentence lasting considerably longer at hard labor in miserable conditions while waiting for sessions to determine their fate. Most prisoners who were committed only for hard labor were also discharged before sessions met. Given the harsh conditions in houses of correction (discussed below) and the hard labor, these prisoners must also be considered as having been punished, even if technically it is questionable whether they had actually been convicted of an offence.

In sentencing prisoners, the committing justice determined both whether or not the prisoner should be whipped and the length of the sentence. Like punishments on indictments, house of correction punishments were probably tailored to the nature of the offence and the identity of the offender. Where the offence concerned only suspicious behavior, defendants were less likely to be whipped: defendants suspected of theft were whipped considerably less often than those more definitively accused of theft or fraud (Table 7.4). Nevertheless, 38% of suspected thieves were whipped. Other defendants commonly apprehended primarily on the basis of suspicions faced mixed punishments: although only 37% of those specifically accused of prostitution and 44% of those

---

[76] See above, section 2.5.

Table 7.4 *Punishments in houses of correction*[a]

	Hard labor only	Whipped[b]	Not punished[c]	Total
	%	%	%	N
Loose, idle, disorderly	50.0	44.2	5.8	138
Vagrant	28.6	57.1	14.3	42
Lewd, nightwalker	35.1	64.9	—	225
Prostitution	52.9	39.2	7.8	204
Other vice	44.4	55.6	—	18
Suspected theft	59.6	38.3	2.1	47
Other theft/fraud	25.2	67.4	7.4	258
Servant, apprentice	41.5	50.9	7.5	53
Peace	50.0	41.7	8.3	24
Other [d]	23.5	47.1	29.4	17
TOTAL %	39.7	54.4	5.9	(100%)
N	407	558	61	1026

[a] Because of the lack of punishment evidence on some calendars, this table includes only the Westminster sessions in the sample, with the following exceptions: the four Middlesex sessions for 1697 are included, and the Westminster sessions for October 1721 is not included.
[b] 85% of the prisoners who were whipped were also put to hard labor.
[c] Includes two cases where the punishment evidence was unreadable.
[d] Includes commitments for poor law offences, miscellaneous offences, and cases where the offence is not known.

accused of idle and disorderly conduct were whipped, the punishment was meted to 63% of those accused of "lewd" behavior and 69% of those accused of nightwalking. Women and men were equally likely to be whipped. Unfortunately, the house of correction calendars provide insufficient evidence to explain this pattern of punishments. In any case, it is likely that the intensity of the whipping varied depending upon such factors as bribes given to the man who carried out the punishment[77] and the social status and age of the prisoner. Ned Ward witnessed a woman of "modest mien" with "white skin" receive "gentle correction" in the London Bridewell.[78] Four women, charged in 1682 with being "lewd, idle, and disorderly" nightwalkers, were sentenced by the justice to hard labor with "respectively becoming correction, having respect to their condition and age."[79]

[77] William Fuller, sentenced by Queen's Bench for publishing a false libel, however, benefitted little from giving half a crown to the man who whipped him (*Mr. William Fuller's Trip to Bridewell*, p. 9). Bribes could also be used to lessen the intensity of the "hard labor" to which prisoners were put (François Colsoni, *Le Guide de Londres pour les Estrangers* [1693], p. 33).
[78] Edward Ward, *The London Spy Compleat* (5th edn, 1718), pp. 135–36.
[79] MJ/SR/1617, HC (Oct. 1682).

Table 7.5 *Length of imprisonments in houses of correction*[a]

	0–7 days	8–15 days	15 or more days	Not discharged[b]	Total
	%	%	%	%	N
Loose, idle, disorderly; vagrant	62.0	15.7	8.8	13.4	216
Lewd, nightwalker	45.7	20.7	9.0	24.5	188
Prostitution	67.0	12.0	7.3	13.6	191
Other vice	50.0	33.3	3.3	13.3	30
Suspected theft	45.5	27.3	6.8	20.5	44
Other theft/fraud	44.5	15.0	12.3	28.2	301
Servant, apprentice	64.6	7.6	8.9	19.0	79
Peace	51.3	20.5	10.3	17.9	39
Other[c]	30.3	21.2	15.2	33.3	33
TOTAL %	53.3	16.4	9.5	20.7	(100%)
N	598	184	107	232	1121

[a] Because of a lack of discharge evidence, this table does not include the following sessions in the sample: Westminster sessions, January 1680; Middlesex sessions, April 1697; and all the Middlesex sessions for 1712.
[b] Not discharged before sessions.
[c] Includes commitments for poor law offences, miscellaneous offences, and cases where the offence is not known.

Justices exercised similar discretion in determining the length of sentences. In most cases, defendants were committed for an indefinite time initially but were discharged within a few days, usually by the same justice.[80] A small number of prisoners were discharged the same day they were committed, but, of those discharged before sessions met, the median length of stay was four days (Table 7.5). The shortest stays were accorded to those specifically accused of prostitution and "loose, idle, and disorderly" conduct, and to servants and apprentices who were committed by their masters; over 60% of the prisoners in each of these categories were discharged within a week. Prisoners who remained in the house of correction the longest were accused of theft, nightwalking, and "lewd" behavior. When combined with the sentences of whipping tabulated in Table 7.4, this evidence suggests that justices viewed "loose, idle, and disorderly" behavior (when it was not combined with another offence) as the least serious of the offences punished in houses of correction and theft as the most serious. Prostitutes were treated differently depending on the specific offence

[80] There were occasional complaints, however, that justices discharged other justices' commitments without their consent: see below, section 8.4.

with which they were charged: those specifically accused of prostitution (picking up men) were treated leniently, while "lewd women" and nightwalkers received harsher sentences. It is difficult to explain this contrast, though it is possible that "lewd" women and nightwalkers were also suspected of other offences (such as vagrancy or theft). In January 1712, the lenient treatment of some prostitutes attracted the attention of the Westminster court, which complained that justices exhibited "too great tenderness" to prostitutes "in the undue and quick release of them." Consequently, justices were required to sentence such offenders to remain in the house of correction until sessions, unless discharged beforehand by three justices.[81] Although most prostitutes continued to be discharged by individual justices after short sentences, justices apparently did respond to the concerns expressed in this order by ordering virtually all prisoners in 1712 to be whipped. In 1721, however, only 17% were whipped. Outside sessions, the justices continued to possess a considerable degree of discretion in sentencing and discharging prisoners.

For this reason, the sentencing strategies of individual justices varied considerably. Of the justices responsible for fifteen or more commitments in the sample, the proportions of their defendants who received sentences of a week or less varied between 0 and 75%, and of those who were whipped between 7 and 100%, depending on the justice. A few justices can be characterized as consistently lenient or harsh in their sentencing decisions. Two justices were responsible for both a high proportion of short sentences and a low proportion of whippings (James Cutler and Thomas Boteler) and one justice was a consistently harsh sentencer (Charles Peter).[82] Since these patterns persist regardless of the nature of the offence, it can be concluded that they were shaped by the personal inclinations of each justice. Though there is no evidence on this point, it is possible that justices had varying opinions about the efficacy of corporal punishment and incarceration as methods of reforming offenders. Some justices may have been worried about the uncertain legal status of ordering whipping outside of sessions.[83] No doubt the age, social status, attitude, and previous criminal history of the accused also played a crucial role in shaping sentencing decisions, but these factors are also impossible to document.

An additional important factor in determining the length of sentences was the actions of the accused after they were committed. It is unlikely that justices kept close track of their prisoners and remembered to send warrants for their discharge after a predetermined sentence had expired. Rather, justices probably

---

[81] MJ/SBB/700, p. 24ff (Westminster sessions, January 1712).

[82] In the City, Sir William Turner was criticized for his "flogging spirit" in zealously ordering prostitutes to be whipped (*Good Sir W --- Knock. The Whore's Lamentation for the Death of Sir William Turner* [1693]).

[83] For more about the differing judicial philosophies of individual justices, see below, section 8.4.

had a general sense of how long prisoners should remain and issued release warrants at their own convenience or when pressured to do so. Prisoners could expedite their release, therefore, by procuring the intercession of friends to plead with the committing justice and arrange for their discharge fees to be paid. Prisoners who were still in the house of correction when sessions met were expected to arrange for friends to appear in court and testify on their behalf. A young woman committed just before sessions in 1716 told the court "that your petitioner being ignorant of the proceedings of the honourable bench did not prepare any person to come and give her character ... by means whereof she was remanded back to ... Clerkenwell Bridewell to continue a fortnight."[84]

Prisoners were discharged at the request of plaintiffs (including the masters of servants and apprentices), respectable friends of the prisoner, and parish officers.[85] Even disreputable friends could influence the time of discharge: keepers of bawdy houses allegedly secured the discharge of prostitutes, perhaps after having paid higher than normal discharge fees.[86] In a fictional example from 1725, "the Irish Society of Fortune Hunters" responds to the fact that a friend (a spinster from Drury Lane) has been committed to the house of correction by ordering that "the committee for characters do repair forthwith to the proper magistrate, and certify for the birth and good behaviour of the petitioner, and that if it be necessary Captain Shameless do swear himself to be her husband lawfully married in the County of Tyrone."[87] In deciding whether to discharge prisoners early, justices apparently responded favorably when they learned that the dispute with the plaintiff had been settled, or, in the case of victimless offences, that the defendant had a respectable place in the community. Descriptions of prisoners which note that they had "no friends" acquire new meaning when it appears that prisoners unable to secure favorable character references faced longer sentences.

In sum, even more than in the courts of gaol delivery and quarter sessions, justices possessed flexibility in sentencing offenders summarily. In their use of houses of correction, as well as with summary convictions punishable by whipping or fine,[88] justices acting outside sessions used considerable dis-

---

84 MJ/SP/July 1716, no. 13. See also MJ/SP/Dec. 1720, no. 41.
85 MJ/SP/June 1717, no. 5; GLRO, M79/X/I, 24 June 1737; P79/JN1/214, 29 Oct. 1731; [Jacob Ilive] *Reasons Offered for the Reformation of the House of Correction in Clerkenwell* (1757), p. 16; [Jacob Ilive], *A Scheme for the Employment of all Persons Sent as Disorderly to the House of Correction at Clerkenwell* (1759), p. 53; Hertfordshire Record Office, D/EP/F153 (*R vs Wood*); King, "Crime, law and society," p. 285.
86 [Ilive], *Reasons Offered*, p. 26; [Ilive], *Scheme for the Employment*, pp. 67–68.
87 *A View of London and Westminster: or, the Town Spy, etc. By a German Gentleman* (1725), p. 19.
88 For judicial discretion in the punishment of vagrants, see Joanna Innes, "Social problems," p. 78, and in determining fines on summary convictions, see *The Justicing Notebook of William Hunt 1744–49*, ed. Elizabeth Crittall, Wiltshire Record Society vol. 37 (Devizes, 1982), pp. 14–15

cretion in adapting punishments to suit the individual circumstances of each case.

7.4 LIMITATIONS

From the point of view of justices of the peace and plaintiffs, houses of correction were convenient places for punishing people accused of committing a wide range of minor offences. Not all offenders, however, could be punished there. Because houses of correction were intended, and publicly recognized, as places of punishment for the poor, middling and upper-class offenders were rarely committed there. Such offenders would typically have been able to provide sureties to guarantee their appearance at sessions, and it would have been difficult for justices to refuse to allow them to enter into a recognizance, even if the offence was typically summarily punished by commitment to a house of correction.[89] In addition, wealthier offenders could afford the legal costs of challenging a commitment. Perhaps it is fear of legal action that lies behind François Misson's comment about the London Bridewell in 1698 that "they send to Bridewell the scandalous people of both sexes, that is to say, such beggarly ones as they dare send thither."[90] As noted in chapter 10, offenders who lived more than a mile or two from a house of correction were also unlikely to be committed, because of the cost and trouble of conveying prisoners.

Even if the offender was poor and located close to a house of correction, plaintiffs and justices needed to think twice about the potential consequences of a commitment. While there is evidence that plaintiffs believed that the *threat* of a commitment was an effective means of reforming offenders,[91] there is little evidence, despite the high expectations of its founders, that a stint in a house of correction actually improved offenders' demeanor. In fact, the opposite was often the case. A woman committed by her husband in 1715 for debauchery had revenge by incurring debts of over £2 to the keeper during a six-day stay. By managing to get the sum charged to her husband, who was unable to pay, she procured his arrest.[92] Because sentences in houses of correction averaged less than a week, defendants were quickly back on the streets and free to harass their prosecutors. A midwife threatened with a vexatious charge of

(for thefts from orchards, gardens and woods, and for violations of the game laws); *Middlesex Records*, ed. Jeaffreson, vol. 3, pp. 346–49 (for conventicles); GLRO, P79/JN1/214, 18 Nov. 1732 (for not working on the highways).

[89] As illustrated in Table 7.2 above, the offences most commonly listed on house of correction calendars can also be found on recognizances.

[90] Henri Misson, *M. Misson's Memoirs and Observations in his Travels over England* (trans. J. Ozell, 1719), p. 21.

[91] GLRO, P79/JN1/214 (Hackney petty sessions minute book, 28 Feb. 1732, 11 Nov. 1734, 7 Oct. 1738); *Applebee's Original Weekly Journal*, 24 Feb. 1722.

[92] MJ/SP/Feb. 1715, no. 12.

having murdered a bastard child was able to get her accuser committed to a house of correction. When her accuser continued to threaten her, the midwife petitioned the court that upon release her accuser be required to find sureties by recognizance for her good behavior.[93] Other prosecutors petitioned the justices to extend the sentences of prisoners in houses of correction.[94] These examples suggest that, unlike recognizances, commitments to houses of correction often failed to bring about successful resolutions of disputes; further judicial action was often needed.

Defendants accused of victimless offences were no more likely to be reformed. Critics of the reformation of manners campaign argued that the reformers' prosecutions failed to reform offenders,[95] and these claims are supported by the degree of recidivism found in the lists of convictions published by the Societies. Of the 422 women convicted of prostitution (for which the punishment would have been a stint in a house of correction) in 1700, 35% were recidivists, including 8% who were convicted five or more times that year.[96] Even with such incorrigible offenders, the reformers nonetheless believed punishments were useful, both because they would deter others from committing similar offences and because offenders might be forced to practice their trade more discreetly.[97]

Even if plaintiffs were not discouraged (nor, probably, surprised) when houses of correction failed to reform offenders, justices of the peace had reason to worry, for commitments to houses of correction provoked hostility towards them. In 1681, Mary Paint allegedly said to justice Sir John Parsons, "young flirt do you send people to Bridewell, you do not do justice."[98] During the decades after 1690 when the reformation of manners campaign was largely responsible for the considerable increase in the number of commitments to houses of correction in the metropolis, informers, constables and justices of the peace were the target of frequent assaults and riots.[99] Justices interested in

---

[93] MJ/SP/1691 ND (undated), no. 10. See also MJ/SP/Feb. 1692, no. 19.
[94] MJ/SP/Oct. 1713, no. 16.
[95] Bernard Mandeville, *An Enquiry into the Causes of the Frequent Executions at Tyburn* (1725), pp. 1–2; [Defoe], *Some Considerations Upon Street-Walkers*, pp. 4–7, 18.
[96] *A Sixth Blacklist of Names or Reputed Names of 843 Lewd and Scandalous Persons … who … have been legally Prosecuted and Convicted in the Year 1700* (1700); A. G. Craig, "The movement for the reformation of manners, 1688–1715" (Ph.D. diss., University of Edinburgh, 1980), p. 117. These totals are somewhat inflated because some women appear to have used common aliases: the name Mary Smith appears 17 times in the 1700 list and 20 times in 1707 (Craig, p. 119). For evidence that summary convictions with punishment by fine also failed to reform offenders, see Shoemaker, "Crime, courts and community," pp. 116–17.
[97] Isaac Watts, *A Sermon Preach'd at Salter's-Hall, to the Societies for the Reformation of Manners, in the Cities of London and Westminster, October 6, 1707*, p. 42; John Disney, *A Second Essay upon the Execution of the Laws against Immorality and Profaneness* (1710), pp. 29, 47–49, 57, 107.
[98] MJ/SBB/387, p. 58 (July 1681). See also MJ/SBB/323, p. 47 (May 1675).
[99] See below, section 9.1.

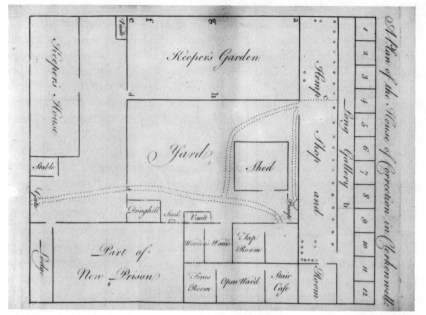

Plate 2 Floor plan of the Middlesex house of correction, Clerkenwell (from [Jacob Ilive], *Reasons Offered for the Reformation of the House of Correction in Clerkenwell* [1757]. By permission of the British Library)
This plan indicates the yard, hemp shop, close wards (nos. 1–12, where prisoners paid for extra beds), and open wards (where prisoners slept on the floor). By transforming the keeper's garden into the men's yard and by building strong partitions at (b) and (c), the author proposed to separate the male from the female prisoners.

maintaining informal authority in their neighborhoods needed to think twice before sending people to a house of correction.

It is not difficult to explain why prisoners and others were hostile to houses of correction. As already noted, many people appear to have been committed on the basis of weak and circumstantial evidence. Even if most commitments lasted less than a week, conditions inside the two houses of correction in urban Middlesex were unpleasant at best. Half of the prisoners were whipped, and in order to earn their food virtually all prisoners were supposed to be put to work beating hemp eleven hours a day using a beetle weighing about twelve pounds (the scene is depicted in plate IV of Hogarth's "Harlot's Progress").[100] Like prisons, houses of correction were run at a profit, and those without the money to pay for a bed and other special treatment suffered greatly. Three times during this period the Middlesex justices investigated complaints against the

---

[100] *Mr. William Fuller's Trip to Bridewell*, p. 10; see dust jacket.

governors for extorting fees, immoderate beating of the prisoners, and denying prisoners adequate food, water, and heat. In 1711, it was claimed that the prisoners were "forced to eat turnip tops ... off the dunghill," and one pregnant woman ate the "hard flesh off her shoulder for hunger." Several prisoners died that year. Prisoners were expected to pay a sizeable discharge fee (up to 6s. 2d.), and those who could not pay (in 1720, five-sixths of the prisoners) were held up to two weeks longer in the hope that they would produce the money.[101]

Under such conditions it was unlikely that prisoners would be reformed. It was reported that male and female prisoners were not separated, as intended, but intermingled freely in what was often a "scene of debauchery." Women prisoners were forced into prostitution in order to survive, and prostitutes were forced to continue their trade upon their discharge because their madams had paid their discharge fees.[102] Moreover, discharged prisoners had acquired a label of untrustworthiness which made it difficult to return to normal life. Ned Ward observed that committing young women to Bridewell exposed them to "shame and scandal, never to be washed off by the most reformed life imaginable; which unhappy stain makes them always shunned by virtuous and good people."[103] It was argued in 1696 that during times of war people that have "already been in a gaol or house of correction" should be some of the first chosen to serve in the army.[104] As we have seen, moreover, previously convicted offenders were liable to rearrest on the slightest suspicion. It is no wonder that reporting that someone had been "whipped in bridewell" was considered to be defamatory.[105] In a society where assessments of character and respectability were very important, people who had been in houses of correction faced an uphill struggle to reestablish a good reputation.

Inevitably, as increasing numbers of prisoners were committed to houses of correction, public confidence in their ability to reform prisoners waned. Considerable faith in their potential for reform is still evident in the 1706 statute that allowed persons convicted of clergyable felonies to be sentenced to up to two years in a house of correction in lieu of being branded, whipped, or transported.[106] Complaints that houses of correction only corrupted prisoners (they turned half-rogues into complete rogues, according to Roger North) had

---

[101] MJ/SP/Oct. 1711, nos. 66, 67, 70, 71; Dec. 1710, no. 2; July 1720, no. 50; [Ilive], *Reasons Offered*, pp. 11–37; *Mr. William Fuller's Trip to Bridewell*. Although 6s. 2d. was the discharge fee set by an order of the court, in practice prisoners were charged only between 1s. and 2s.: MJ/SP/Dec. 1711, no. 29; Feb. 1721, no. 47. For evidence that prisoners were kept when they failed to pay their fees, see Ward, *London Spy Compleat*, p. 138; *A Foreign View of England*, ed. van Muyden, p. 303; MJ/SBB/557, p. 35 (Dec. 1698); 710, p. 46 (Dec. 1712).
[102] [Ilive], *Reasons Offered*, pp. 13–26.
[103] Ward, *London Spy Compleat*, p. 142. See also BL, Add. MS 35,601, f. 263.
[104] *A Discourse about raising men* (1696), p. 7.
[105] MJ/SR/1531, R. 311 (Sept. 1677).
[106] Beattie, *Crime and the Courts*, pp. 492–500.

already been voiced, however, and such complaints appear to have increased in intensity in the first half of the eighteenth century, culminating in Henry Fielding's description of houses of correction in 1751 as "schools of vice" and "seminaries of idleness."[107]

In fact, in terms of the summary punishment of petty offenders, it is likely that the early eighteenth century was the heyday of houses of correction in London. In addition to growing disillusion about the effects of incarceration, summary judgments were more closely questioned in the "increasingly scrupulous legal climate of the later eighteenth century."[108] Already in 1722 the Westminster sessions, uncomfortable about the large number of commitments for pilfering, urged justices not to order such offenders to be punished. Where sufficient evidence was available, justices were requested to order the offenders to be kept until sessions so that they could be tried by indictment.[109] The number of commitments appealed to higher courts increased during the century, to the point where Sir John Fielding complained in 1770 that it was not possible to punish common prostitutes without justices and officers being prosecuted by "low attorneys."[110] Consequently, absolute numbers of commitments for both "idle and disorderly" conduct and pilfering in the metropolis appear to have decreased during the century, despite continuing population growth and public concern about crime.[111] It is possible that people liable to be committed as "idle and disorderly" persons were siphoned off into the numerous parochial workhouses which were established in Middlesex and Westminster after the passage of the Workhouse Test Act in 1723.[112] In some

---

[107] Roger North, *A Discourse of the Poor* (1753 [written *c.* 1688]), p. 18; Charles Hitchen, *A True Discovery of the Conduct of Receivers and Thief-Takers in and about the City of London* (1718), pp. 7–9; *The Form of a Petition ... for Relieving, Reforming and Employing the Poor* (1722), p. 5; Mandeville, *An Enquiry into the Causes of the Frequent Executions*, pp. 1–2; Henry Fielding, *An Enquiry into the Causes of the Late Increase of Robbers* (1751), p. 63; Thomas Alcock, *Observations on the Defects of the Poor Laws, and on the Causes and Consequences of the Great Increase and Burden of the Poor* (1752), p. 67. The convicted felons, in fact, were held responsible for corrupting the other prisoners ([Ilive], *Reasons Offered*, p. 31).

[108] The phrase is John Styles': see "Embezzlement, industry, and the law in England, 1500–1800," in *Manufacture in Town and Country Before the Factory*, ed. M. Berg, P. Hudson, and M. Sonenscher (Cambridge, 1983), p. 195. See also Innes, "Statute law and summary justice," pp. 21–22, 26.

[109] WJ/OC/I, f. 45 (28 June 1722). See also PRO, SP 35/67/8.

[110] *The Parliamentary History of England* (1813), vol. 16, p. 940 (10 April 1770), cited by Sydney and Beatrice Webb in *English Local Government. English Poor Law History, vol. 1: the Old Poor Law* (1927), p. 353. See also Alcock, *Observations*, p. 67; Innes, "Statute law and summary justice," p. 32; *Jonathan Wild's Advice to his Successor* (1758; reprinted in Frederick J. Lyons, *Jonathan Wild. Prince of Robbers* [1936]), p. 294. The reduction in judicial flexibility concerning the use of houses of correction is exemplified by Henry Fielding's comment in 1751 that "the justices in very few instances (in none of idleness) hath any power of ordering" whipping in houses of correction (Fielding, *An Enquiry*, p. 63).

[111] Innes, "Prisons for the poor," p. 95; Beattie, *Crime and the Courts*, p. 18.

[112] This suggestion merits further research on the powers and practices of the governors of London's parochial workhouses. The threat of a commitment to a house of correction could

respects, houses of correction became more like prisons during the eighteenth century as greater numbers of prisoners were committed to await an appearance at sessions, and, at certain points, convicted felons were committed for long terms of imprisonment.[113] By the second half of the century, people committed for summary punishments no longer dominated the lists of prisoners committed to the Middlesex and Westminster houses of correction.

It appears that a number of factors converged to reduce the role of the metropolitan houses of correction in the punishment of petty crime by mid century. With more stringent legal requirements, reduced faith in the efficacy of house of correction punishments, and the use of these houses for more serious offenders, the range of petty offences leading to summary commitments appears to have narrowed. The considerable freedom exercised by justices of the peace, in conjunction with both private and official plaintiffs, in committing a wide variety of petty offenders and suspected petty offenders, to houses of correction in the early eighteenth century did not last. Even at the peak of their popularity, however, few middle- or upper-class offenders were committed, and it was impractical to commit offenders living more than one or two miles from the house. Moreover, there is little evidence that prisoners emerged from their confinement in a mood to reform their behavior or to resolve their differences with their plaintiffs. Despite their considerable advantages, in many contexts houses of correction were no substitute for prosecution by recognizance or indictment.

easily be used as a means of forcing people into workhouses: GLRO, P79/JN1/214 (11 Nov. 1734). See also Innes, "Prisons for the poor," p. 93. Between 1723 and 1730, twenty parochial workhouses were founded in Westminster and urban Middlesex (T. V. Hitchcock, "The English workhouse: a study in institutional poor relief in selected counties, 1696–1750" [D. Phil., Oxford University, 1985], pp. 272–75).

[113] Sydney and Beatrice Webb, *English Prisons Under Local Government* (1922), pp. 15–17 ; Innes, "Prisons for the poor," pp. 94–99; Beattie, *Crime and the Courts*, pp. 492–500, 560–63, 576–82, 604–08.

Part III

THE CONTEXTS OF
MISDEMEANOR PROSECUTIONS

8

The participants: plaintiffs, defendants, and justices of the peace

With such contrasting social consequences, the choice of a procedure for prosecution was an important one. In making this choice, the most important consideration was what the plaintiff wanted to achieve from the prosecution. Did he (or she) want the defendant to be formally convicted and punished for the crime, or did he hope to receive compensation for his injuries by negotiating an informal settlement? While each procedure could be manipulated in various ways, clearly plaintiffs seeking private settlements made different choices from those seeking formal punishments. While this decision was no doubt influenced by personal considerations that are inaccessible to the historian, it was also shaped by the socioeconomic status and gender of the parties involved, as well as by the wishes of the justice of the peace handling the case. This chapter assesses the extent to which the identities of the participants in prosecutions – plaintiffs, defendants and justices – influenced the choice of a procedure. By comparing the social profiles of the participants involved in each type of prosecution it becomes possible to identify some of the distinctive social contexts in which misdemeanor prosecutions most frequently occurred.

8.1 SOCIAL STATUS

Although evidence of the social status of plaintiffs and defendants in misdemeanor prosecutions is patchy, it is clear that wealth and social position shaped people's experiences of the criminal justice system. Few prosecutors were listed on house of correction calendars,[1] and it is not possible to identify the status or occupation of the prosecutors of most recognizances and indictments. Indirect evidence, however, suggests that wealth was one of the factors that shaped plaintiffs' choices of procedures for prosecution. As we have seen, the cost of a warrant or a summons, which was necessary in order to

---

[1] In any case, because summary cases were largely initiated by official plaintiffs, decisions to prosecute by summary jurisdiction were shaped by different constraints than those affecting private plaintiffs: see below, section 8.3.

bring the defendant before a justice, could be beyond the means of the poor.[2] As suggested by the geographical distribution of prosecutions within urban Middlesex (discussed in chapter 10), far fewer prosecutions of recognizances and indictments per capita were initiated from the poorer parishes north and east of the City of London than from the relatively prosperous parishes in the west end. And because prosecution by indictment was the more expensive of the two procedures, indictments were concentrated in the wealthy western districts of the metropolis to a greater extent than recognizances.[3] This is not to say that paupers and laborers never prosecuted by indictment. Per capita, however, they were considerably less likely to do so than their wealthier neighbors.

To a greater extent than their social superiors, the poor must have used informal mediation for their disputes. Evidence of the social status of complainants in cases resolved by informal mediation is hard to come by, but almost half of the complainants in agreed cases in William Hunt's notebook whose status could be identified were laborers, servants, or other employees.[4] Peter King has argued that the poor frequently and successfully used petty sessions in Essex in the second half of the eighteenth century as a "court of appeal" for disputes over poor relief, unpaid wages, and conditions of work. Such cases were frequently settled informally and the plaintiffs' costs (which were in any case low) were sometimes reimbursed by the defendant.[5] With the exception of poor relief cases (which were not criminal), relatively few such cases are recorded in Henry Norris' notebook and the surviving petty sessions minutes in Middlesex. In fourteen years, the justices at the Brentford petty sessions heard an average of only 1.5 cases per year.[6] Few records of informal mediation survive, however, and those that do may not be comprehensive. Ultimately, it is impossible to determine the social composition of the complainants whose cases were resolved by informal mediation.

The choice of a procedure for prosecution was also influenced by the social status of the defendant. While people of all social classes were prosecuted by informal mediation, the poor were largely sent to houses of correction and not bound over by recognizance or indicted. House of correction calendars provide no evidence of the status or occupations of the prisoners, but as we have seen indirect evidence (the offences that prisoners were charged with, and their inability to pay their fees) strongly suggests that houses of correction

---

[2] See above, section 5.4.　　　[3] See above, section 6.3, and below, section 10.1.

[4] See also Dietrich Oberwittler "Crime and authority in eighteenth-century England: law and enforcement on the local level," *Historical Social Research/Historische Sozialforschung* 15 (1990), pp. 3–34.

[5] King, "Crime, law and society," pp. 277–79.

[6] GLRO, Accession 890 (Brentford petty sessions), the years sampled were 1661–69 and 1689–93. See also P79/JN1/214 (Hackney petty sessions); M79/X/I (Notebook of Henry Norris).

fulfilled their original purpose as places for setting to work and punishing *poor petty offenders*, many of whom were young.[7] As argued in chapter 5, many defendants were committed to houses of correction because they were unable to find sureties in order to be bound over by recognizance. These prisoners either had just immigrated to London, or they lacked socially and economically respectable contacts who were willing and qualified to serve as sureties, or both.[8] Thus, few poor defendants were prosecuted by recognizance or indictment. In any case, prosecuting the poor by indictment was rarely rewarding since they could not agree to informal settlements involving the payment of damages and if convicted they generally received low fines.[9] This is not to say that all poor offenders were committed to houses of correction; judging by the large number of petty thefts informally mediated by the Wiltshire justice William Hunt, some poor defendants who were perceived to be trustworthy reached informal settlements with their prosecutors.[10] Nonetheless, the poor were largely unsuitable for prosecution by recognizance or indictment and consequently large numbers of them were committed to the two houses of correction in urban Middlesex.

In contrast, defendants prosecuted by recognizance or indictment were considerably more socially respectable: between 6 and 12% were gentlemen, and 42 to 58% were tradesmen or craftsmen (Table 8.1).[11] In fact, the social profiles of defendants bound over by recognizance and indictment appear to have been remarkably similar, both to each other and to the population of Middlesex. Though no estimates of the social composition of the county's population exist, Peter Lindert's rough estimates of the composition of the population of the City of London in 1670 and of England in 1688, based on a sample of lists of inhabitants and burials recorded in parish registers, provide useful benchmarks for comparing urban and rural patterns of prosecutions. Several aspects of the Middlesex population make it unique, however, and should be considered when interpreting Table 8.1. Because Westminster was the seat of Parliament and the law courts, the number of gentlemen residing in both the urban and rural parts of the county was higher than anywhere else in the country. Like any urban area, London also had high concentrations of tradesmen and craftsmen. Yet the social status of artisans and shopkeepers in urban Middlesex, especially in the east end, was certainly lower than that of their counterparts in the City of London. When these adjustments are taken

[7] See above, section 7.2.   [8] See above, section 5.4.   [9] See above, sections 6.4 and 6.5.
[10] See above, Table 3.2. As is evident in Table 3.1, however, the Middlesex justice Henry Norris settled few petty thefts informally.
[11] Evidence on the social status of indicted defendants was derived from those who were also bound over by recognizance, since the social and occupational labels on indictments have been found to be unreliable (J. S. Cockburn, "Early modern assize records as historical evidence," *Journal of the Society of Archivists* 5 [Oct. 1975], pp. 224–25; Shoemaker, "Crime, courts, and community," pp. 279–81).

Table 8.1 Social or occupational status of male defendants bound over by recognizance compared with the adult male population[a]

Urban	Middlesex Recognizance sample		"Rough estimates" of adult male population[b]
	Indicted	Not indicted	City of London, 1670
	%	%	%
Gentlemen	12	11	2
High social status trades/crafts[c]	9	9	18
Other trades/crafts	32	31	26
Yeomen, agricultural[d]	5	6	—
Low social status trades/crafts[e]	17	16	6
Laborers	3	5	8
No bail risked[f]	20	21	[Not applicable]
Apprentices and servants[g]	1	1	39
Poor, pensioners	[Not applicable]	1	1
Total N	337 (100%)	1143 (100%)	40,875 (100%)

Rural	Indicted	Not indicted	England, 1688
	%	%	%
Gentlemen	8	6	2
High social status trades/crafts	4	5	4
Other trades/crafts	26	20	18
Farmer	14	15	17

Low social status trades/crafts	13	17	14
Laborers	10	14	18
No bail risked	26	21	[Not applicable]
Apprentices and servants	—	2	15
Poor, pensioners	[Not applicable]	[Not applicable]	7
Unknown/other	—	—	5
Total N	85 (100%)	145 (100%)	1,406,036 (100%)

a Officers are excluded from the table, since defendants described as officers were not given a social or occupational label on their recognizances.

b From Peter H. Lindert, "English occupations, 1670–1811," *Journal of Economic History* 40 (1980), pp. 702–04.

c The social status categories are based on findings from V. B. Elliott's study of apprenticeship indentures and marriage licences in late seventeenth-century London, in which she was able to group many trades according to similar marital and apprenticeship choices ("Mobility and marriage in preindustrial England: a demographic and social structural analysis of geographic and social mobility and aspects of marriage, 1570–1690, with particular reference to Middlesex, Kent, Essex and Hertfordshire" [Ph.D. diss., Cambridge University, 1978], pp. 81, 132). Unfortunately, a large residual category of unplaced trades remained, here labelled as "Other trades/crafts." Because of the small number of defendants from Elliott's high and middle status groups, the two groups are combined and labelled as the "high" status group. Included within the "high" social status group are apothecaries, barber surgeons, blacksmiths, bricklayers, brewers, chandlers, clothiers, clothworkers, doctors, goldsmiths, grocers, haberdashers, innkeepers, jewellers, joiners, mercers, merchants, surgeons, and vintners.

d In the court records, these were primarily yeomen; in Lindert's estimates this category includes farmers, husbandmen, and other agricultural occupations (except laborers).

e Includes bakers, butchers, carpenters, coopers, cordwainers, gardeners, glovers, masons, painters, porters, sailors, shoemakers, tailors, and weavers.

f See text.

g Apprentices and servants were not consistently identified as such in the court records.

into account, with the exception of the lowest social classes (discussed below) the social composition of defendants prosecuted in urban and rural Middlesex by both procedures appears roughly similar to the probable composition of the county's urban and rural populations. Apart from the poor, the residents of urban Middlesex were equally likely to be prosecuted at sessions regardless of their social class. In contrast, those accused of felonies disproportionately came from a narrower range of social backgrounds. Most felonies involved some type of theft, and, unsurprisingly, the majority of the accused were from the lower classes. Whereas gentlemen make up 11% of the indicted defendants at the Middlesex sessions (where few felonies were tried), they accounted for only 1 or 2% of felony indictments. On the other hand, defendants from the lowest status groups account for over half of all felony accusations but only 41% of the Middlesex sessions indictments.[12]

A substantial proportion of the male defendants bound over by recognizance were given no occupational or status label because they were not a party to the financial bond which guaranteed that the recognizance would be obeyed. Since bailiffs did not need to know how to locate them if the recognizance was forfeited, their occupations and residences were not recorded. These defendants were almost certainly poorer than those defendants who did risk bail; many were probably the laborers, apprentices and servants, and paupers who otherwise appear to be underrepresented as defendants in Table 8.1. Unfortunately, this sizeable category of defendants without social or occupational labels prevents more specific analysis of defendants prosecuted from the lower end of the social spectrum. It is, in any case, impossible to determine the proportion of poor people actually living in urban Middlesex at this time.

There were few significant differences in the social profiles of the defendants accused of the most common misdemeanor offences. Defendants prosecuted at sessions for offences against the peace, the largest category of offences, came from each social status category in proportions roughly similar to the social composition of the Middlesex population. Members of some social groups, however, were disproportionately likely to be charged with certain other petty offences. Gentlemen, for example, were disproportionately accused of gambling (but not of running gaming houses). Laborers and men who did not risk bail, on the other hand, were more likely to be accused of theft and less likely to be accused of regulatory offences, such as failure to fulfill obligations to keep the streets repaired or serve on the night watch, which were by definition committed by householders. Certain occupations were vulnerable to occu-

---

[12] For evidence of the social status of defendants accused of felonies, see Herrup, *The Common Peace*, p. 116; Sharpe, *Crime in Seventeenth-Century England*, pp. 95, 109; Beattie, *Crime and the Courts*, pp. 250–51; King, "Crime, law and society," chap. 3. Because social status and occupational labels can be misleading, especially when evidence from different sources is compared, and because historians do not group them into uniform categories, precise comparisons between different studies are impossible.

pationally related prosecutions: victuallers were accused of selling ale without a licence and permitting disorder in their houses, and artisans and shopkeepers were charged with a variety of regulatory offences from using false weights and measures to obstructing the highway with their refuse. As employers who could easily fall on hard times, low status tradesmen and craftsmen were particularly likely to be the subjects of complaints for failing to pay wages. It should be emphasized, however, that these differences are ones of proportion; although within every status category there were at least a few defendants in virtually every category of offence, offences against the peace were the most commonly prosecuted offences in each social group.

With the significant exception of the fact that poorer defendants were typically dealt with informally or committed to houses of correction, the social status of the accused does not appear to have been a major factor determining the choice of a procedure for prosecution: the social compositions of defendants bound over by recognizance and indictment were virtually identical. Thus, the same offences committed by people with similar social backgrounds were often prosecuted using different procedures. As we have seen, one factor which shaped the choice of a procedure was the wealth of the prosecutor. Another factor was gender. Because of the lack of evidence concerning the social status of female prosecutors and defendants, this discussion has so far been restricted to male defendants. How did the gender of the parties shape prosecutorial decisions?

8.2 GENDER

Experiences of the legal system differed considerably according to the sex of the parties involved. As revealed in Table 8.2, gender differences were greatest among plaintiffs. While women and men were equally likely to prosecute by recognizance (if recognizances issued at the behest of official plaintiffs – who were all men – are excluded), more than two and a half times as many men filed indictments as women, and, on the basis of limited evidence, it appears that twice as many men were responsible for commitments to houses of correction as women (again excluding official plaintiffs). Given the limited role accorded to women in public life in preindustrial England, what is surprising about these statistics is not the small number of female prosecutors who used indictments or houses of correction but the large number of women who prosecuted by recognizance – it is probable that women used recognizances more frequently than any other type of legal procedure in the secular courts.[13]

[13] Only widows were likely to file civil suits; single women could not afford to litigate and married women were disabled from filing civil suits on their own. For the small number of indictments filed by women in other counties, see Herrup, *The Common Peace*, pp. 116–17; Sharpe, *Crime in*

Table 8.2 Gender of plaintiffs and defendants

| | Plaintiffs[a] | | | | |
	Male	Female	Officer	Unknown	TOTAL N
	%	%	%	%	(100%)
Recognizances					
(non-indicted)	36.1	34.9	11.7	17.3	2039
Indictments[b]	42.4	18.2	9.0	30.4	467
Houses of correction[c]	10.1	4.2	21.1	64.6	792

| | Defendants | | | |
	Male	Female	Unknown	TOTAL N
	%	%	%	(100%)
Recognizances				
(non-indicted)	63.4	35.8	0.8	2353
Indictments	71.6	27.2	1.2	2759
Houses of correction	28.3	63.7	8.0	1790

[a] The unit of analysis is the crime (except house of correction commitments, where the unit of analysis is the defendant).
[b] Based only on the sample years 1664 and 1721. Official plaintiffs were not consistently identified on the 1664 indictments.
[c] Based only on the sample years 1680, 1693, and 1721.

A key aspect of this phenomenon is the fact that female prosecutors of recognizances lived overwhelmingly in urban areas: while female plaintiffs outnumbered men in urban Middlesex, men outnumbered women in rural Middlesex. In fact, female plaintiffs rarely appeared before justices of the peace in rural areas, except in cases that were settled informally.[14] Similarly, urban women served proportionally more frequently as witnesses in the church courts.[15] As John Beattie has suggested in a different context (explaining the larger number of women prosecuted for felonies in urban Surrey), women in urban areas were more frequently involved with the law because they were

Seventeenth-Century England, pp. 95, 109; Beattie, Crime and the Courts, pp. 193, 239–40. In the church courts, on the other hand, women initiated large numbers of suits concerning sexual slander (Ingram, Church Courts, p. 302).
[14] For the gender distribution of prosecutors of recognizances and indictments in urban and rural Middlesex, see below, Table 10.2. Women account for less than 15% of the plaintiffs who appeared before justices Norris and Hunt, but one-third of the informal settlements they presided over involved female plaintiffs.
[15] David Souden, "Preindustrial English local migration fields," (Ph.D. diss., Cambridge University, 1981), pp. 46, 59.

Table 8.3 *Marital status of female plaintiffs and defendants*

	Unmarried	Married	Widow	No label	TOTAL N
	%	%	%	%	(100%)
Plaintiffs[a]					
Recognizances					
(non-indicted)	4.2	25.1	1.0	69.7	712
Indictments[b]	13.7	56.6	10.9	18.9	175
Defendants					
Recognizances					
(not indicted)	9.8	39.4	8.7	42.2	808
Indictments	27.1	50.5	21.1	1.3	750
City of London adult					
women 1695[c]	55.4	36.8	7.7	—	11,999

[a] The unit of analysis is the crime.
[b] Based on the 1663–64 and 1720–22 samples only.
[c] Based on the Marriage Tax assessment lists from 1695 for a sample of forty parishes, compiled by D. V. Glass: "Notes on the demography of London at the end of the seventeenth century," *Daedalus* 97 (1968), pp. 583–84. Those labelled as "children" have been excluded from this table; it was assumed that 50% of the children were female.

more independent than their rural counterparts. Urban women were more likely to work outside the home, and when involved in disputes they were less likely to have access to informal mediators such as local landowners and the clergy.[16] Unmarried women and widows, especially if they were lower-class, were particularly likely to work outside the home,[17] and it appears that it is precisely these women who were most likely to initiate recognizances, if women who were not described as married can be interpreted to be single or widows (Table 8.3).[18] Because of their more public lifestyles, and the insecurity of their employments, single women and widows in urban areas were more likely to enter into disputes and less likely to settle their disputes out of court.

[16] Beattie, *Crime and the Courts*, pp. 241–43. See also below, section 10.2. For the occupations of urban women, see also Boulton, *Neighbourhood and Society*, p. 82; Peter Earle, "The female labour market in London in the late seventeenth and early eighteenth centuries," *Economic History Review*, second series, 42 (Aug. 1989), pp. 328–47; George, *London Life*, chap. 4, *passim*.
[17] Earle, "The female labour market," pp. 337–38.
[18] It appears that the marital status of female plaintiffs on recognizances was only systematically recorded for married women. It is thus likely that the women whose marital status was not described (71% of all women) were predominantly unmarried or widows. That many female plaintiffs needed to work for a living is suggested by Table 10.4, which demonstrates that in urban Middlesex female plaintiffs were most likely to come from relatively poor parishes east and north of the City of London rather than from the west end.

Why did these women choose to prosecute their disputes by recognizance? Typically the crimes were not serious: 81.5% of the recognizances issued at the behest of women were for offences against the peace (the equivalent figure for men was 61%), and relatively few of these were for violent assaults or riots. Most were recognizances to keep the peace, or involved minor assaults or cases of defamatory words. Many of the disputes, particularly those involving scandalous words, were between women. Moreover, recognizances worked for female plaintiffs. Recognizances prosecuted by women were more likely than those prosecuted by men to be resolved without further legal action: 69% of the defendants appeared and were discharged at the first opportunity (compared to 58% of those prosecuted by men), and only 19% were indicted (compared to 23% of those prosecuted by men).[19] Potential female prosecutors must have been encouraged by the fact that recognizances were apparently successful in reducing tensions and resolving disputes involving women.

Women prosecuted far fewer people by sending them to houses of correction or indicting them. Women account for about one third of the private plaintiffs who were identified on house of correction calendars. It is possible that justices of the peace were less willing to commit defendants solely on the basis of a complaint by a female plaintiff, but there is no evidence to support this hypothesis. More probably, this pattern results from the fact that women rarely prosecuted the types of offences typically prosecuted at houses of correction: property offences and victimless offences. The offences women did prosecute, offences against the peace, typically arose out of disputes between people who knew each other, and it is likely that female plaintiffs did not want to commit their antagonists to an institution, an action that was likely to exacerbate rather than diminish tensions between the parties.

Women were responsible for less than a fifth of the indictments prosecuted in Middlesex. Like the recognizances women prosecuted, the vast majority of these prosecutions were for offences against the peace. Unlike the prosecutors of recognizances, however, married women account for almost three-fifths of the female plaintiffs, and widows were apparently overrepresented in comparison with their share of the population.[20] One of the causes of the relative dearth of female plaintiffs on indictments, therefore, is the absence of single women as prosecutors. Single women were no doubt discouraged by the considerable expense of indictments, at a time of life – between leaving home and marriage – that could be the most economically insecure part of a woman's life, especially if

---

[19] Whereas the preceding discussion has been based only on recognizances that did not lead to indictments, these figures include recognizances that led to indictments if the indictment was filed *after* the recognizance was issued. This pattern persists regardless of the nature of the offence.

[20] In the absence of any suitable data for urban Middlesex, this conclusion is based on the proportion of widows in the population of the City of London, as calculated by D. V. Glass. See Table 8.3.

she lived in London.[21] More generally, women may have been discouraged from prosecuting indictments because they were intimidated by formal legal procedures. The law was predominantly a male domain, and there is some evidence that women believed that the courts would not take them seriously. When a Manchester woman heard a "spirit" tell her of a murder, she was told that she should report it to a justice of the peace. She replied that "she was but a woman and the justice would take no notice of it because she wanted evidence."[22] In fact, cases prosecuted by women were initially less likely to be taken seriously by the courts: female-initiated indictments were 37% more likely to be found *ignoramus* by the grand jury than cases prosecuted by men. (On the other hand, petty juries were more likely to find defendants prosecuted by women guilty.)[23] It is also possible that women thought that they were morally above engaging in conflict and litigation. Proposing to take advantage of the "deference and respect" usually paid to women, John Disney suggested that it would be advantageous to use women as informers during the reformation of manners campaign. Few women, however, heeded his call.[24]

Whatever the causes of women's reluctance to prosecute by indictment, it decreased significantly during this period in urban Middlesex. The proportion of indictments prosecuted by women more than doubled between the two sample periods for which this evidence was collected, from 11.8% in 1663–64 to 25.3% in 1720–22. More detailed sampling of recognizances to answer indictments confirms this increase, though it suggests that the growth in indictments prosecuted by women was less dramatic. By the end of this period, women were responsible for only 38% fewer indictments than men, and they prosecuted 9% *more* recognizances (excluding prosecutions initiated by parish officers). It is a mark of how comfortable London women had become with prosecuting misdemeanors in the early eighteenth century that one Sarah Winslow, the prosecutor of an indictment against five people for an assault in 1722, was accused by her defendants of being "a litigious person continually afflicting poor people[,] nay people of the better sort fear her base tongue [because she is] always threatening to swear the peace against them."[25]

---

[21] For young female migrants to London, this period averaged seven years. Many of the poorer migrants worked as servants while they tried to accumulate a dowry (V. B. Elliott, "Single women in the London marriage market: age, status and mobility, 1598–1619," in *Marriage and Society. Studies in the Social History of Marriage*, ed. R. B. Outhwaite [New York, 1982], pp. 86–95).

[22] Manchester Central Library, Archives MS F347.96, Diary of justice Nathaniel Mosely, 11 Dec. 1662.

[23] Similarly, Herrup identified circumstances in which petty juries counteracted the apparent biases of grand juries, but she found that female prosecutors were *more* likely to have their indictments approved by the grand jury and *less* likely to be found guilty by the petty jury (*Common Peace*, pp. 153–55).

[24] John Disney, *A Second Essay upon the Execution of the Laws Against Immorality and Profaneness* (1710), p. 213. For sources on the identity of informers, see below, section 9.1.

[25] MJ/SP/October 1722, no. 45.

Too little is known about women's lives in preindustrial London to explain this increased willingness to prosecute petty crimes, especially by indictment. Two factors, however, are likely to have contributed. First, the substantial growth in female literacy during this period may have given women increased self-confidence and led them to be less intimidated by the law.[26] Second, the growth of domestic service and other employment opportunities may have exposed more women, especially single women, to the perils of public life while giving them the independence and economic means to prosecute those who wronged them.[27] These changes in urban women's lives may explain why an observer complained in 1725 that London women had once been subservient to their husbands, but now had become vain, impudent, and spendthrift.[28] Although female prosecutors still disproportionately favored prosecution by recognizance over indictments and houses of correction at the end of this period, the gender gap in patterns of prosecutions had narrowed considerably.

Just as female prosecutors tended to avoid formal prosecutions in court, the plaintiffs, both male and female, who prosecuted female defendants favored methods of prosecution that did not require court appearances. The notebooks of justices Hunt and Norris show that, although both justices arranged informal settlements equally frequently for male and female defendants, they were more likely to issue "orders" or summarily convict women and somewhat more likely to refer cases involving men for further legal action. Similarly, prosecutors of women in Middlesex favored summary jurisdiction over more formal legal action. Although female defendants account for 64% of the commitments to the Middlesex houses of correction, they account for only 36% of the recognizances and 27% of the indictments (Table 8.2). The house of correction statistic is strongly influenced by the large number of prostitutes committed, but even if prostitution and related offences are excluded women still account for over half of the commitments.[29]

Women were prosecuted differently from men both because they committed less serious crimes than men and because prosecutors and the courts viewed

---

[26] David Cressy, *Literacy and the Social Order: Reading and Writing in Tudor and Stuart England* (Cambridge, 1980), pp. 128–29, 144; Earle, "Female labour market," pp. 333–36.

[27] Michael Roberts, "'Words they are women, and deeds they are men': images of work and gender in early-modern England," in *Women and Work in Preindustrial England*, ed. Lindsey Charles and Lorna Duffin (1985), pp. 156–58; D. A. Kent, "Ubiquitous but invisible: female domestic servants in mid-eighteenth century London," *History Workshop Journal* 28 (Aug. 1989), pp. 118–24. See also above, section 7.2. The growth in the number of women employed as domestic servants had the effect of increasing the number of women in London, but this increase was probably not large enough to account for the increase in the number of female prosecutors.

[28] *A View of London and Westminster: or, the Town Spy, etc. By a German Gentleman.* (1725), pp. 54–58.

[29] The gender of prisoners in houses of correction according to the offences they were charged with is set out above, in Table 7.3.

female criminality as less of a threat than male criminality. Women were disproportionately likely to be prosecuted for two types of crime: sexual offences and offences against the peace. As a result of the "double standard" governing sexual conduct, women were the participants in illicit sex more likely to be prosecuted, accounting for 85% of the commitments to houses of correction, and 64% of the recognizances, for prostitution and adultery.[30] Women were also frequently charged with the less serious forms of offences against the peace: recognizances to keep the peace and cases of barratry and defamation. On the other hand, women were (and still are today) accused of committing far fewer violent crimes than men;[31] women were responsible for less than a fifth of the assaults involving violence or the use of a weapon. Women were also rarely accused of regulatory offences (few were householders), gambling, and political and religious disaffection.[32] The differences in types of prosecuted female criminality and male criminality thus largely mirror the contrasting social roles ascribed to the sexes.[33]

Differences in the types of offences men and women were accused of committing do not entirely explain the differences in the proportions of men and women prosecuted by the several procedures. This pattern persists even after these differences are taken into account (so far as this is possible). Thus, of those accused of offences against the peace, female defendants account for 66% of the commitments to houses of correction, 37% of the recognizances, and 30% of the indictments. Similarly, 51% of the defendants accused of theft in houses of correction were women, compared to 39% of recognizance defendants, and 35% of indictment defendants.

Why were so many women committed to houses of correction and so few women indicted? Like female plaintiffs, the vast majority of female defendants lived in urban areas.[34] Peter King has suggested that urban women were most likely to be prosecuted when the courts were accessible and lenient punishments were available; in Essex, both conditions were met by the borough

---

[30] Mothers were rarely prosecuted for bearing bastard children, however, as long as they were willing to name the father.

[31] John Beattie, "The criminality of women in eighteenth-century England," *Journal of Social History* 8 (1975), pp. 82–89; Carol Z. Wiener, "Sex roles and crime in Elizabethan England," *Journal of Social History* 8 (1975), p. 49; Shoemaker, "London 'mob'," p. 285.

[32] Women did, however, account for one-third of the conventiclers convicted by summary jurisdiction (T. J. G. [Tim] Harris, "Politics of the London crowd in the reign of Charles II" [Ph.D., Cambridge University, 1985], p. 279).

[33] Wiener, "Sex roles," pp. 38–60; André LaChance, "Women and crime in Canada in the early eighteenth century," in *Crime and Criminal Justice in Europe and Canada*, ed. Louis A. Knafla (Waterloo, Ontario, 1981), pp. 157–78.

[34] Less than one-fifth of the defendants who appear in the notebooks of justices Norris and Hunt were women. See also Landau, *Justices of the Peace*, p. 197; Beattie, "Criminality of women," pp. 96–99; Sharpe, *Crime in Seventeenth-Century England*, pp. 95, 117, 118, 129; below, section 10.2.

courts.[35] In Middlesex, houses of correction met the first condition of accessibility: both houses were located in the metropolis, and it was the defendants who lived closest to them, both male and female, who were most likely to be committed to them.[36] But it is difficult to characterize commitment to a house of correction, with hard labor often accompanied by whipping, as a lenient punishment. The fact that so many women were committed to houses of correction in urban Middlesex probably has more to do with their poverty. There was a large number of poor young women in the metropolis who depended upon uncertain income derived from casual labor or domestic service, and who were very carefully watched during this period for any sign that they engaged in prostitution or petty theft or were likely to become dependant on poor relief.[37] Because such women were usually unable to find bail, it was easiest to prosecute them by commitment to a house of correction.

A tendency to favor lenient, accessible punishments for women does explain, however, the tendency of prosecutors to prosecute women more often by recognizance than by indictment. Recognizances could be issued by the local justice and they were lenient. Moreover, they were well suited to the type of minor offences, such as assaults and defamatory words, that women were frequently accused of committing. Recognizances involving female defendants, just as those involving female prosecutors (over half of the former were also prosecuted by women), were somewhat more likely than those involving men to reach satisfactory settlements without further legal action. In contrast, prosecuting women by indictment often did not yield satisfactory results. Although women were equally likely to be found guilty as men, they were given smaller fines: convicted women were twice as likely to receive the minimum fine of one shilling, and half as likely as men to be given fines over 13s. 4d.[38] This difference is probably due both to the fact that female criminality was perceived to be less serious than male criminality,[39] and to plea bargaining: some of the women had pleaded guilty because they could not afford the cost of a trial.[40] Such women were also unable to conclude an informal settlement by paying damages to the prosecutor. Consequently, prosecutors of poorer women, such

[35] King, "Crime, law and society," p. 141–43.   [36] See below, section 9.1.
[37] Beattie, *Crime and the Courts*, pp. 241–43; George, *London Life*, p. 174; Nicholas Rogers, "Carnal knowledge: illegitimacy in eighteenth-century Westminster," *Journal of Social History* 23 (1989), p. 366; above, section 7.2; and, concerning women in Bristol, Mary E. Fissell, "'The sick and drooping poor' in eighteenth-century Bristol and its region," *Journal of the Social History of Medicine* 2 (April 1989), p. 47. King shows that women were most frequently prosecuted for theft when they were in their early 20s, when they were usually unmarried and in domestic service ("Crime, law and society," p. 145).
[38] Table 6.9.
[39] Beattie, *Crime and the Courts*, p. 439. Susan Amussen, however, has suggested that "disorderly women" were viewed as a more serious threat to the social order in the period before 1640 (Susan D. Amussen, *An Ordered Society: Gender and Class in Early Modern England* [Oxford, 1988], p. 123).
[40] See above, section 6.5.

as those who were unmarried, shunned prosecution by indictment: relative to their position in the urban population, single women were least likely to be indicted. Instead, Table 8.3 suggests that such women were frequently bound over by recognizance (if the absence of any indication of marital status can be interpreted to mean that defendants were unmarried) or committed to a house of correction. Women were prosecuted more often by recognizance than indictment not only because recognizances were lenient and convenient, but also because so many women were poor and women were typically charged with minor offences.

In certain circumstances, however, indictments were considered to be useful for prosecuting married women and widows. Many married women were indicted along with their spouses, primarily for riots, assaults, and alehouse offences; the principle that women were not legally responsible for certain crimes committed in the presence of their husbands does not appear to have been followed.[41] Widows, who account for one-fifth of all indicted women, were indicted primarily for offences that other women could not commit on their own because they were not householders or did not own property in their own right: alehouse offences (running an unlicensed alehouse, keeping a disorderly alehouse), running bawdy houses, failing to serve (or hire a substitute) on the night watch, failure to repair the highway, and offences arising from property disputes. Even if these offences are excluded, however, widows still account for 13% of the women indicted, more than their share of the female population in the City of London (Table 8.3). It is possible that plaintiffs favored prosecuting widows by indictment because wealthy widows could be forced to pay substantial damages out of court: 41% of the indictments against widows were dropped before they were brought to trial, suggesting that the parties had reached some kind of informal accommodation.

In sum, whenever a woman was involved in the prosecution of a misdemeanor, the case was more likely to be prosecuted by summary jurisdiction or with a recognizance. Compared with men, women were less likely to prosecute, or be prosecuted by, indictments. The sources of these gender differences are complex; this discussion has pointed to the fact that women committed (or at least were accused of committing) less serious crimes, female crime was not believed to be as serious a problem as male crime, poverty was a greater problem in London among single women than single men, and female prosecutors may have been intimidated by the male-dominated legal system. Gender differences were far smaller in urban areas than in the country, however, and they decreased during the period of this study as growing

---

[41] Such women did, however, receive lower fines: see above, section 6.5. Many married couples jointly ran alehouses (Peter Clark, *The English Alehouse: a social history 1200–1830* [1983], pp. 82–84).

Table 8.4 *Plaintiffs: private prosecutors vs. parish officers*[a]

	Private prosecutors	Parish officers[b]	Unknown	TOTAL
	%	%	%	N
Recognizances	71	12	17	2039
Indictments[c]	65	20	15	198
Houses of correction[d]	14	21	65	792

[a] The unit of analysis is the crime.
[b] Including justices of the peace, high constables, constables, headboroughs, beadles, watchmen, churchwardens, overseers of the poor.
[c] 1721 sample only.
[d] Does not include the samples for 1670–73, 1675, 1697, 1712.

numbers of women both initiated prosecutions and were prosecuted. Clearly, women's use of law in the metropolis is one facet of the significant contrast between women's lives in the city and in the country in the preindustrial period. Nevertheless, at the end of this period prosecutors continued to take advantage of the choice of procedures offered by the legal system to prosecute crimes differently according to the gender of the parties involved.

8.3 OFFICIAL PLAINTIFFS

In identifying the prosecutors of petty crime, this discussion has so far been restricted to private individuals, in most cases the victims of the offences prosecuted. Indeed, the private prosecutor was the mainstay of the judicial system in preindustrial England, a situation markedly different from that of the present day.[42] Nonetheless, a small but significant proportion of offences were prosecuted by public officials acting in their official capacities. As Table 8.4 demonstrates, although private prosecutors formed the vast majority of the prosecutors of recognizances and indictments, justices of the peace and parish officers (constables, night watchmen, churchwardens, and overseers of the poor) were responsible for 20% of the indictments and 12% of the recognizances.[43] These officers were responsible for a much higher proportion, probably even the majority, of commitments to houses of correction, but the

[42] Douglas Hay, "Controlling the English prosecutor," *Osgoode Hall Law Journal* 21 (1983), pp. 167–68.
[43] This discussion ignores prosecutions initiated by officers whose duties did not include the prosecution of petty offences, including officers of courts of debt such as the Palace Court of Westminster and collectors of taxes. For these, see Shoemaker, "Crime, courts and community," pp. 320–21.

large number of commitments in which the complainant was not identified makes it impossible to estimate the proportion of house of correction commitments initiated by officers. As their choice of legal procedures suggests, public officials who prosecuted crime used the law very differently from private citizens.

One of the duties assumed by constables and other parish officers involved apprehending, or reporting the names of, people who committed misdemeanors. Thus, constables were traditionally responsible for apprehending breakers of the peace, suspicious persons such as nightwalkers, and "lewd men and women that are together, and about to be incontinent and lewd." In the course of the sixteenth and seventeenth centuries, constables' duties were increased when they were required to apprehend, and in some cases punish on their own authority, vagrants, "disorderly" persons, gamblers, and the keepers of gaming houses, and to report to justices of the peace the names of people who committed various offences such as tippling or permitting tippling in alehouses and several religious offences. In addition, constables were increasingly required by justices and others to "present" people who violated social and economic regulations to courts leet or sessions.[44] Thus, in his charge to the Middlesex grand jury in 1682, Sir William Smith told high and petty constables to present, in addition to the offences mentioned above, unrepaired highways and bridges, cottages built on less than four acres of land, profane cursers and swearers, and forestallers, regrators, and engrossers.[45] In addition, constables were occasionally given specific instructions to present or apprehend such diverse offenders as conventiclers, profaners of the Sabbath, keepers of unlicensed or disorderly alehouses, prostitutes, players of "drolls and interludes," singers of seditious ballads, people who sold oranges from wheelbarrows, and landlords who divided tenements or kept inmates.[46]

Constables were to be aided in these tasks by night watchmen, overseers of the poor, and churchwardens. Watchmen under the supervision of constables patrolled the streets between sunset and sunrise during the summer months. They were responsible for apprehending "all rogues and vagabonds, nightwalkers, evesdroppers, scouts, and the like, and such as go armed," as well as examining all strangers in the streets and, if they were suspicious, keeping them until morning, when they were to be brought before a justice of the peace. Churchwardens and overseers of the poor were required to work with

---

[44] Joan R. Kent, *The English Village Constable 1580–1642* (Oxford, 1986), pp. 25–39; *The Complete Constable. Directing Constables, Headboroughs, Tithingmen, Churchwardens, Overseers of the Poor . . . in the Duty of their Offices* (1724), pp. 9–49; George Meriton, *A Guide for Constables, Churchwardens, Overseers of the Poor* (1669), pp. 10–11.

[45] William Smith, *The Charge Given by Sir William Smith, Baronet, at the Quarter Sessions of the Peace held for the County of Middlesex* (1682), pp. 10–11.

[46] For example, see MJ/SBB/487, p. 78 (July 1691); 575, p. 46 (Aug. 1700); 802, p. 27 (Westminster sessions, June 1722); MJ/OC/I, ff. 34–35 (10 July 1718); MJ/SP/Feb. 1718, no. 49.

constables in presenting alehouse offenders at sessions and ensuring that the fathers of bastard children provided for their maintenance.[47] With the exception that constables had the power to punish vagrants on their own authority, these officers were only responsible for reporting offenders to justices of the peace or sessions, not for punishing them. If the offence was a victimless one (as were most of the offences officers were under obligation to report) and further legal action took place, the officer was normally listed as the plaintiff.[48] The records of misdemeanor prosecutions, therefore, provide some evidence (though it is far from comprehensive) of the activities of parish officers in reporting offences and acting as plaintiffs in prosecutions, and it is instructive to consider the methods they chose, in consultation with justices of the peace, of carrying out those prosecutions.

Summary conviction was clearly the preferred method of prosecution by official plaintiffs. Not only did official plaintiffs (primarily constables) account for two-thirds of the known plaintiffs on house of correction calendars, but they were also frequently involved in prosecutions using summary conviction by fine. Records of convictions for profaning the sabbath reveal the names of several active constables.[49] The Middlesex court recognized that wherever possible summary conviction was preferable to prosecution at sessions for victimless offences. A court order in 1719 stated that the best way of prosecuting the keepers of bawdy and gaming houses was to convict them summarily of selling ale without a licence, since prosecution by indictment was too costly to be used for all but the most obstinate offenders.[50] Consequently, the only offences official plaintiffs prosecuted by indictment in significant numbers in 1721 were keeping disorderly alehouses (where the keeper probably did have a licence) and highway offences (failure to perform statutory labor and failure to repair the highway in front of one's house). However, over 90% of these indictments, which were apparently the result of constables' presentments to the grand jury, never reached a final verdict, and in the other cases the defendant pleaded guilty. None of the cases went to trial. Given the high cost of prosecuting by indictment, it is not surprising that constables, who would have been forced to pay the costs out of their own pockets (except in unusual circumstances),[51] were unwilling to pursue such cases to final ver-

---

[47] *Complete Constable*, pp. 26, 122; Meriton, *Guide for Constables*, p. 144; [John Disney], *An Address to Grand-Juries, Constables, and Churchwardens, Representing their Power in the Suppression of Vice and Profaneness* (1710), p. 39.

[48] Anyone who was willing to pay the necessary fees could of course prosecute victimless offences, but in practice private citizens rarely did so (except when they acted as informers, which are discussed in section 9.1).

[49] Bodleian Library, Rawlinson MS D1396, 1398, 1399, 1402, 1404.

[50] MJ/OC/I, ff. 49–51d (Jan. 1719).

[51] In a few cases, costs were paid by the parish or the county: MJ/SBB/551, p. 62 (Feb. 1698); MJ/OC/I, ff. 49–51d (Jan. 1719).

dicts. In any event, justices acting out of sessions could handle both types of cases.[52]

As a result of the increased use of summary jurisdiction for a number of offences, the number of victimless offences prosecuted by indictment decreased over the course of this period as constables' presentments were largely abandoned as a means of prosecuting vice and nuisances.[53] Presentments delivered to the grand jury could result in only one type of prosecution: an indictment. Instead, constables were increasingly required to submit the names of offenders to justices meeting at petty sessions, where the justices handled cases informally or by summary conviction, referring only the most serious cases, and those that could not legally be handled summarily, to sessions. The report of a committee of justices appointed to consider measures for preventing an outbreak of the plague in October 1721, for example, recommended that people whose activities posed a threat to public health should be dealt with as follows: vagrants and beggars were to be carried by constables before justices meeting at petty sessions, who were to order summary punishments (whipping, commitment to a house of correction) according to the recent vagrancy statute, 12 Anne c. 23; the keepers of brandy and gin shops who did not possess an alehouse licence were to be suppressed (and possibly summarily convicted) by justices acting out of sessions; and only persons who kept too many lodgers were to be indicted at sessions for "harboring inmates." Similarly, a court order in 1716 concerning a wide range of offences including people who left open their cellar doors and thereby endangered passersby, the keepers of gaming houses, and beggars, directed constables to apprehend the offenders and bring them before justices of the peace, who were to commit them to a house of correction or bind them over by recognizance "as to the said justices shall seem meet or agreeable to law." The only offenders who were to be

---

[52] Two justices could suppress the licence of a keeper of a disorderly alehouse (though they could not formally convict him) and levy fines for refusing to perform statutory labor on the highway. In 1729, the judges at King's Bench ruled that prosecuting the latter offence by indictment was illegal, since the statute specified prosecution by summary jurisdiction (Dowdell, *Quarter Sessions*, pp. 99–100).

[53] For the decline in indictments for victimless offences, see above, section 6.5. The "juries of constables" referred to in justices' charges to the Middlesex grand jury in the 1720s (Webbs, *The Parish and the County*, p. 462), appear to have been little more than an assembly of the constables who appeared at the April and October sessions in order to turn in their presentments. Between one-third and one-half of the constables actually appeared at any one sessions, but their presentments have not survived. Unless a very large number were rejected by the grand jury, these presentments included few accusations in the 1720s. In contrast, presentments in the early 1670s accounted for more than half of the indictments in the April and October sessions: MJ/SBP/6. Although, in their campaign to usurp the jurisdiction of the Westminster court of burgesses, the Westminster justices appear to have aggressively encouraged constables' presentments in the early eighteenth century (WJ/SBB/728, p. 29 [Jan. 1715]; WJ/SP/Oct. 1719, no. 7), they had little success (Samuel Ryder, *The Charge to the Grand Jury of the City and Liberty of Westminster, at the General Quarter Sessions of the Peace* [1726], p. 26). For the conflict between the justices and the burgesses, see below, section 9.2.

presented to the grand jury at sessions were constables who neglected to carry out the order.[54] As we shall see, this strategy of using summary convictions wherever possible for the prosecution of victimless misdemeanors was adopted by the Societies for the Reformation of Manners in their campaign against vice in the 1690s and the early eighteenth century.[55]

As Table 8.4 suggests, the recognizance played a decidedly minor role in prosecutions initiated by parish officers. Many of the offences they did prosecute by recognizance, moreover, were peace offences in which they were the victims. Forty-five percent of the recognizances issued at the request of constables and night watchmen were for assaults committed against them while they were making arrests or carrying out other duties of their office. Constables did prosecute some vice cases by recognizance (particularly alehouse and sexual offences), but the number of prosecutions is quite low in comparison with the number of offenders prosecuted by officers who were summarily convicted and punished by fine or commitment to a house of correction. That officers prosecuted some people accused of vice by recognizance is nonetheless significant, for they were treated far more leniently than the majority of offenders, who were summarily convicted and punished. The choice of recognizances in these cases is probably explained by the identity of the defendants. Many of the sexual offenders bound over by recognizance were the male clients of prostitutes, and these men clearly benefitted from the "double standard" that governed responses to sexual misconduct. The few women who were bound over by recognizance for prostitution were probably well enough connected to find sureties in order to avoid being committed to a house of correction. The reason more people were not prosecuted by recognizance for these offences is clear from the unsatisfactory outcomes of many of the recognizances that were issued: defendants accused of gambling, alehouse, and sexual offences were disproportionately likely to fail to appear in court or to have their cases continued to a subsequent sessions at the request of dissatisfied plaintiffs.[56] Recognizances had little effect on vice offenders unless plaintiffs closely monitored the subsequent actions of the defendant and complained to the justices when he or she failed to appear in court or further misbehaved; few officers could take the time to observe defendants so closely.

It is impossible to evaluate directly how diligent officers of the peace were in fulfilling their legal responsibilities of apprehending and reporting offenders. Not only is it impossible to know how many offences went unprosecuted, but records of summary convictions with punishment by fine for offences other than vice and attending conventicles are rare. It is of course prima facie unlikely that constables and their parish colleagues systematically fulfilled the manifold

---

[54] MJ/OC/I, ff. 126–28 (Oct. 1721); f. 8 (July 1716).   [55] See below, section 9.1.
[56] See above, section 5.3 and Table 5.1.

duties with which they were burdened. Justices of the peace were certainly quick to point out deficiencies in the Middlesex and Westminster constabulary. At times, they alleged, constables even failed to fulfill their most basic duties. Six times during this period the justices issued orders reminding constables that they were required to nail staffs to their doors so that persons seeking assistance or desiring to report offenders would be able to find a constable quickly. In 1663 and 1671, the court even complained that constables hid themselves so as to avoid being summoned, and that their wives and servants lied about their whereabouts.[57]

Given the failure of some constables to fulfill their most basic duties, justices' orders to apprehend or report the names of all persons guilty of specific misdemeanors were bound to be often ignored. Constables were repeatedly condemned for failing to carry out orders concerning vagrancy, begging, vice, nuisances, conventicles, and other offences.[58] When ordered to report incidents of improper behavior on the Sabbath to the Middlesex sessions, for example, nineteen returns by constables and other officers from the east end in 1702 unanimously reported that "all is well" in their districts.[59] Other returns in response to similar orders reveal small numbers of persons accused of begging, vagrancy, playing dice in wheelbarrows, shining shoes in the street, night-walking, not repairing the highway, keeping disorderly alehouses and bawdy houses, and related offences; the average number of offenders reported by each constable was only about three.[60] Night watchmen, who were under the supervision of constables, could be equally inefficient. There were frequent complaints that the nightly watches were set too late at night and relieved too early in the morning, and that watchmen failed to apprehend offenders.[61]

There are several reasons why constables and other parish officials failed to execute their offices efficiently.[62] The office was unpaid and carried out in addition to the officer's regular employment, so even the best intentioned constable faced practical difficulties in carrying out his duties. But there were more serious disincentives to act. Since constables only served in the office for a year, they were typically more interested in preserving good relations with their neighbors than with impressing the justices with their zealous behavior.[63]

---

[57] MJ/SBB/210, p. 34 (Dec. 1663); 283, p. 21 (Oct. 1721); MJ/SBR/9, p. 59 (Dec. 1663).

[58] Dowdell, *Quarter Sessions, passim.* Kent (*English Village Constable*, pp. 190–200) suggests that constables were somewhat more diligent in presenting offenders before 1642.

[59] MJ/SP/May 1702, nos. 8–26. See also MJ/SBB/728, p. 29 (Westminster sessions, Jan. 1715).

[60] MJ/SP/July 1717, nos. 75–78, 83; Feb. 1718, nos. 48, 50; Dec. 1720, nos. 64–66; Jan. 1721, nos. 70–76.

[61] MJ/SBB/575, p. 49 (Aug. 1700); MJ/SBB/766, p. 45 (Oct. 1718); 769, pp. 62–64 (Jan. 1719); [Daniel Defoe], *Parochial Tyranny: or, the House-keeper's Complaint Against the Insupportable Exactions, and Partial Assessments of Select Vestries, etc.* [1727], p. 20.

[62] Kent, *English Village Constable*, chaps. 6 and 7.

[63] Keith Wrightson, "Two concepts of order: justices, constables and jurymen in seventeenth-century England," in *An Ungovernable People*, ed. Brewer and Styles, pp. 29–32, and "Ale-

Where popular support for laws was absent or divided, as was the case with the laws against vice and conventicles, constables were particularly reluctant to act. In 1684, constables in the Tower Hamlets obstinately refused, despite intense pressure from justices meeting in petty sessions, to present their neighbors for attending conventicles.[64] Even when constables were willing to try to suppress offences, it is likely that in many cases they preferred to deal with their neighbors informally rather than report them to the justices.[65]

Some constables, of course, were corrupt. The intense pressure to report offenders for vice, together with the fact that only a small proportion of offenders were actually prosecuted, provided a perfect opportunity to extort money from offenders in return for "screening" them from prosecution.[66] A major cause of such practices, according to the justices, was that alehouse keepers, who were themselves guilty of permitting immoral conduct in their houses, were often appointed as constables and headboroughs.[67] In fact, over a third of the constables in Holborn division in 1720 were victuallers.[68] Another cause, according to the justices, was the practice of hiring deputy constables when substantial householders were chosen to serve. Despite efforts by the justices to prevent this, the practice continued, though it was not widespread.[69] Because deputy constables were often poor, it was alleged that they treated the office as a business by extorting bribes from keepers of disorderly houses in return for not prosecuting them and by fomenting riots in order to make arrests.[70]

houses, order and reformation in rural England, 1590–1660," in *Popular Culture and Class Conflict 1590–1914*, ed. Eileen and Stephen Yeo (Brighton, 1981), p. 15.

[64] MJ/SBB/417, p. 56 (Sept. 1684); *The Proceedings of his Majesties Justices of Peace at the Sessions of Oyer and Terminer... September the 6th, 1684, for the Tryal of the Constables... of the Hamlets of Spittle-fields and Bethnal Green* (1684). For the reluctance of constables to prosecute vice, see below, section 9.1.

[65] For example, in 1720 several people in Holborn who had failed to repair the pavements outside their houses amended them "upon notice given," and their names were not reported to sessions: MJ/SP/May 1720, no. 27. See also Kent, *English Village Constable*, pp. 273ff; and Sharpe, *Crime in Seventeenth-Century England*, p. 218.

[66] Daniel Dolins, *The Charge of Sir Daniel Dolins, Kt. to the Grand Jury and Other Juries of the County of Middlesex* (1725), p. 24; *An Account of the Endeavours that have been used to Suppress Gaming Houses* (1722), pp. 8–9.

[67] MJ/SBB/704, p. 55 (April 1712); 769, pp. 62–64 (Jan. 1719); Dowdell, *Quarter Sessions*, pp. 19–20.

[68] MJ/SP/May 1720, no. 28. According to Peter Clark, the fact that constables kept alehouses was one sign of the growing social respectability of the alehouse (*The English Alehouse*, p. 236).

[69] MJ/SBB/395, p. 30 (Feb. 1682); 704, p. 55 (April 1712); Westminster City Archives, WCB 7, 1 Oct. 1724. Dowdell, *Quarter Sessions*, pp. 19–20. See also Sydney and Beatrice Webb, *English Local Government from the Revolution to the Municipal Corporations Act: The Manor and the Borough* (1908), p. 221; Kent, *English Village Constable*, p. 74. Between 1701 and 1707, three out of seventeen Middlesex constables who served in a sample of urban parishes did so continuously over several years, which suggests that they were hired: MJ/SR/1965–2099 (April 1701–Oct. 1707).

[70] MJ/SBB/704, p. 55 (April 1712); [Jacob Ilive], *A Scheme for the Employment of all Persons Sent as Disorderly to the House of Correction at Clerkenwell* (1759), pp. 53–54.

Constables had many reasons not to act, so perhaps the more interesting question is why they prosecuted victimless offences at all. Most obviously, at times they were under direct pressure from justices to return lists of offenders or face prosecution for neglect of office.[71] It was easy enough to avoid making thorough presentments to sessions, but when given a specific order or warrant to execute against a specific type of offender, there was less room for manoeuvre. The occasional long series of indictments in the Middlesex records for offences such as obstructing the highway, keeping gaming houses, and keeping alehouses without a licence were clearly the result of constables' presentments returned in response to specific orders. In response to the King's proclamation against vice in 1698, for example, the Middlesex justices "unanimously resolved" to "order and strictly require" high constables, constables, and other officers to make "frequent searches" for people guilty of all types of immorality, particularly people who profaned the Sabbath by working or tippling. At the next sessions, constables made presentments that led to the indictments of 114 defendants for keeping alehouses without a licence.[72] Similarly, justices' warrants to make general searches for vagrants and related offenders could generate a substantial number of commitments to houses of correction. In the early 1690s, several justices met periodically in petty sessions in the parish of St. Martin's in the Fields and issued warrants to parish officers to search for prostitutes and other "loose, idle, and disorderly" people. Arrests made in response to these warrants account for almost a fifth of all the commitments to the Westminster house of correction in 1693.[73]

In fact, officers were rarely prosecuted for neglect of office, which suggests that other factors besides fear of prosecution motivated them to prosecute victimless offences. Pressure to prosecute came not only from justices, but also from irritated neighbors. Five women apprehended in a bawdy house were committed to a house of correction by the constable in St. Martin's in the Fields, for example, not only for idle and disorderly conduct but also for being "common disturbers of the neighborhood." Tim Curtis demonstrated that people in Cheshire occasionally petitioned constables or justices about the immoral behavior of their neighbors.[74] In early seventeenth-century Essex, such demands came from parish notables motivated by Puritan ideals and "a growing concern to discipline the parish poor"; in the late seventeenth and

---

71 Kent, *English Village Constable*, pp. 225–33; Wrightson, "Two concepts of order," pp. 37–39.
72 MJ/SBB/551, p. 38 (Feb. 1698); MJ/SR/1909 (May 1698).
73 For example, see MJ/SR/1754 (Westminster sessions, April 1690); 1817 (Westminster sessions, July 1693).
74 MJ/SR/1751 (Westminster sessions, Jan. 1690); Tim Curtis, "Quarter sessions appearances and their background: a seventeenth-century regional study," in *Crime in England*, ed. Cockburn, p. 139. For petitions from the neighbors of bawdy houses to the Middlesex justices, see, for example, MJ/SP/May 1702, no. 5; Oct. 1706, no. 24. See also, Kent, *English Village Constable*, pp. 270ff.

early eighteenth centuries constables were pressured by supporters of the Societies for the Reformation of Manners.[75] In addition, officers were probably more inclined to prosecute offenders, instead of warning them or ignoring them, if the offender insulted or assaulted the officer. One-third of the official prosecutions by recognizance for frequenting or keeping bawdy houses and loose, idle and disorderly conduct include accusations that the defendant had abused or assaulted the officer. A baker taken late at night in 1664 "straggling in the streets," had, according to his recognizance, abused the headborough with evil language and, upon further examination, "confessed he sat up all the night before in an alehouse known by the sign of the Rose in Hell at East Smithfield."[76] Had the defendant not insulted the officer, it seems likely that he would have escaped with a warning. Parish officers could thus be motivated to prosecute victimless offences by complaints from neighbors and because they were personally attacked by offenders. What has been less stressed in this discussion, because they are difficult to document, are the officers' own impulses to prosecute, whether through a sense of duty to the law or religious zeal. Constables who joined the Societies for the Reformation of Manners, for example, were motivated in part by a desire to save the country from Divine punishment for its sins.

Most prosecutions for which constables and other officials are listed as the plaintiffs, however, were probably in fact stimulated either by orders from justices of the peace or requests from private citizens. As concern about crime and vice grew in late seventeenth-century London, so did complaints that night watchmen and constables failed to carry out the duties of their offices. In response to the perceived deficiencies of officers of the peace, two innovations in law enforcement practices were introduced. One involved reforming the night watch by hiring salaried watchmen and placing them under the control of prominent local inhabitants instead of constables.[77] The other tactic, adopted by the reformation of manners campaign was to use informers to stimulate prosecutions by reporting offenders to justices.[78]

In sum, official plaintiffs adopted different prosecutorial strategies from those pursued by private citizens. For reasons of cost and convenience, officers favored summary convictions in lieu of prosecutions at quarter sessions. And because officers responded primarily to pressures from others, the offences they were primarily responsible for prosecuting, victimless offences, were prosecuted even less frequently and even more erratically than other offences.

---

[75] Wrightson, "Two concepts," pp. 43–44, and "Alehouses, order and reformation," p. 19; below, section 9.1.

[76] MJ/SR/1287, R. 104 (May 1664).

[77] Dowdell, *Quarter Sessions*, pp. 26–27; Shoemaker, "Crime, courts and community," pp. 322–25.

[78] See below, section 9.1.

8.4 JUSTICES OF THE PEACE

Justices of the peace rarely acted as plaintiffs in misdemeanor prosecutions, except when they were the victims of assaults or scandalous words or when they personally witnessed victimless offences such as failure to repair the highway. In their capacity as judges and legal advisers, however, individual justices of the peace played a central role in influencing the shape and results of prosecutions. Although it is likely that justices took the wishes of plaintiffs into account, it was up to the justice to decide whether to try to mediate the dispute informally, to bind the defendant over by recognizance, to commit the defendant to a house of correction, or to advise the plaintiff to file an indictment. Since justices typically had the advantage not only of legal authority, but also of social superiority over plaintiffs, justices strongly influenced the choice of a method of prosecution. This is significant because different justices adopted strikingly different approaches to prosecuting crime. Not only did levels of activity of individual justices on the bench vary considerably,[79] but there were also important contrasts in the patterns of decisions taken by active justices.

The types of business heard by seventy-one active justices are mapped out in appendix II. The statistics demonstrate clearly that justices adopted, or advised their plaintiffs to adopt, a variety of different prosecutorial strategies. While some justices committed large numbers of defendants to houses of correction, for example, others clearly favored binding their defendants over by recognizance.[80] The ratio of recognizances to house of correction commitments varied considerably among active justices, from 0.4 recognizances for each commitment (justice Isaac Tillard in 1721) to twenty-eight recognizances for each commitment (justice William Moore in 1721). These patterns of behavior were obviously determined in part by the nature of the cases that were brought before each justice, but the evidence strongly suggests that, faced with the same types of business, some justices favored houses of correction while others favored recognizances. Commitments to houses of correction, as we have seen, frequently involved victimless offences prosecuted by parish officers. Consequently, justices who often committed defendants to houses of correction, such as Isaac Tillard, issued no recognizances at the request of official plaintiffs – all the cases brought before them by official plaintiffs that resulted in further

---

[79] See above, section 3.3.
[80] It should be noted that the number of recognizances actually issued by individual justices does not precisely reflect the number of cases in which they ordered defendants to enter into a recognizance. This is because defendants arrested on such warrants may have been brought by the constable before another justice in order to enter into the recognizance; others who were unable to find sureties were committed to prison or a house of correction instead of entering into a recognizance.

Table 8.5 *"Mediating" justices*[a]

Sample years	Name of justice	Indictment rate[b] %	Low status defendants[c] %	Female plaintiffs[d] %	Peace offences %	Area of activity[e]
Business involving primarily low status defendants						
1663–64	Thomas Byde	None	70	67	70	East urban
	Thomas Lucy	10.5	75	42	53	North urban
1693	Theophilus Eyton	12.5	60	67	59	Whole area
	William Withers	12	60	58	72	North urban
1707	John Chamberlayne	8	62.5	20	22	Westminster
1720–22	John Fuller	10	71	60	73	North urban
	Matthew Hewitt	11	71	67	78	North urban
	Alexander Ward	12	67	48	69	West urban
AVERAGE		9.5	67	54	62	
Business involving primarily higher status defendants						
1663–64	Nathaniel Snape	12.5	22	50	53	West urban
1677	James Dewy	None	18	71	74	Westminster
	Edmund Godfrey	9	15	27	54	Westminster
1720–22	D'Oyley Michel	10	12.5	47	72	East urban
AVERAGE		8	17	49	63	
Others						
1663–64	Richard Abell	11	47	58	68	East urban
	Francis Blomer	7	41	45	70	North urban
	Charles Pitfield	10	50	43	48	North urban
	Richard Powell	5	37	63	58	North urban
	John Smith	4	50	25	39	North urban

1677	Reginald Forster	5	38.5	27	54.5	North urban
1693	Launcelot Johnson	6	36	33	42	North urban
1707	Thomas Ellis	6	Unknown	75	81	West urban
1720–22	Robert Kyrby	12	50	46	90	East urban
AVERAGE		7	44	46	61	
All mediating justices		8	48	49	62	
All other justices[f]		26	43	49	57	

[a] Defined as those justices whose defendants were least likely to be indicted: 12.5% or less of their defendants were subsequently indicted. This calculation does not include recognizances issued concerning existing indictments.

[b] See note a.

[c] Defendants in low status occupations and those who were unable to risk bail. Because their status is difficult to identify, this calculation excludes apprentices, servants, officers, and women. Also excluded are defendants prosecuted by officers of the peace.

[d] This calculation excludes official plaintiffs and unknowns.

[e] The areas are defined in Table 10.1.

[f] See below, appendix II.

legal action resulted in commitments to houses of correction. In contrast, some justices, including William Moore, who made few commitments to houses of correction, issued many recognizances at the request of official plaintiffs – in Moore's case, one quarter of the recognizances he issued. Similarly, justices who committed many defendants to houses of correction tended to bind over few defendants for property offences (which were frequently punished in houses of correction), while justices who tended to use recognizances instead of the house of correction bound over more defendants for property offences. Although they had less direct influence over the decision, justices appear to have also adopted contrasting approaches to the question of whether defendants who were bound over should subsequently be indicted. Patterns of business heard by individual justices varied considerably on this question, ranging from justices Thomas Byde and James Dewy, whose recognizances in the sample never led to indictments, to justice William Rosewell, half of whose defendants were subsequently indicted.

Since these distinctive patterns of judicial preferences cannot simply be explained by the different types of offences heard by each justice, it is clear that the personal preferences of individual justices played a major role in shaping strategies for prosecution. Some justices instinctually favored mediation, while others were more interested in convictions and punishments. As the types of action they favored became known, it seems probable that individual justices attracted different types of business: some justices attracted plaintiffs seeking informal settlements, while those who favored formal methods of prosecution attracted plaintiffs more interested in punishment than in negotiation. To examine the different patterns of judicial business that resulted from these contrasting approaches, it is useful to construct three ideal types of justices: the "mediating" justice, the "law and order" justice, and the "social control" justice.

Mediating justices, as described in Table 8.5, tended to encourage the parties to reach informal settlements and to discourage prosecution by indictment. (They have been defined as those justices whose indictment rate on their recognizances was 12.5% or less.) Unsurprisingly, these justices tended to attract business involving less serious offences, particularly offences that typically occurred between people who knew each other. Thus, offences against the peace dominate the business of mediating justices to a greater extent than the sample average: on average, 62% of the cases heard by mediating justices involved offences against the peace, compared with 57% of the business heard by the other justices listed in appendix II. In addition, mediating justices attracted different types of defendants than other justices. Many tended to attract cases involving low status defendants: eight of the justices in Table 8.5 had 60% or more of their defendants from the lower classes (either the defendants were described as having low-status occupations or they were unable to risk bail). This phenomenon is no doubt a result of the difficulty of prosecuting poor defendants by indictment. Mediating justices whose defendants tended to be lower class also tended to attract high proportions of female plaintiffs: on average, 54% of the private plaintiffs who appeared before them were women, compared with 48% of the plaintiffs appearing before all other justices.

Norma Landau has shown that urban justices who catered to the demands of women and the poor were often labelled as "trading justices." Like the justices in Table 8.5, justices so labelled tended to issue large numbers of recognizances and few of their cases resulted in further legal action. Thus, John Poulson, an alleged Middlesex trading justice who "industriously employed himself as a justice" in the east end, issued hundreds of recognizances in 1716, mostly for minor peace offences that did not lead to indictments.[81] Because they were typically socially inferior to their colleagues on the bench and because they depended upon the income from their fees, trading justices acquired a bad reputation. They were accused of fomenting business by encouraging false charges and of accepting (or demanding) bribes in return for not prosecuting vice.[82] Poulson was accused of binding over several people unjustly, and one of the mediating justices in Table 8.5, Thomas Ellis, was accused by an enemy of making "it his business as he hath reason to believe to encourage pretended assaults to the great prejudice of your majesty's good subjects."[83] Similarly, a play performed in London in 1717 centered around the activities of a justice Bind-over, who is quick to grant warrants and issue recognizances and encourages night watchmen to knock gentlemen down in the streets and swear riots against them the next morning. When some actors are arrested under the vagrancy laws, for example, he states "I only desire to bind 'em over; I shall be satisfied with my fees, and five pieces afterwards to stifle the indictment."[84]

It is difficult to believe that justices actually encouraged the offences that led them to issue recognizances. Landau's evidence that trading justices issued recognizances as a means of charging fees to the participants in disputes that they resolved informally suggests, however, that while the recognizances these justices issued may have been technically unnecessary, they resulted from real

---

[81] Hertfordshire Record Office, D/EP/F157, Wm. Ashurst to Lord Cowper, 23 Oct. 1717; MJ/SR/2273, R. 20–52, 77–100, 168–90.

[82] Landau, *Justices of the Peace*, pp. 184–203; Webbs, *The Parish and the County*, pp. 326–37; [Samuel Butler] *Hudibras. The Third and Last Part* (1684), Part III, canto iii, pp. 204–06; [Edward Stephens], *The Beginning and Progress of a Needful and Hopeful Reformation* (1691), p. 13; [T. Baston], *Thoughts on Trade and a Public Spirit* (1716), pp. 129–33; Henry Fielding, *The Coffee-House Politician; or, Justice Caught in his own Trap* (1730).

[83] PRO, SP44/239, p. 187, petition of Simon Fanshaw (cited by Landau, *Justices of the Peace*, p. 185, n. 26).

[84] [C. Bullock], *The Per-Juror. As it is Acted at the Theatre in Lincoln's Inn Fields* (1717), p. 14 and *passim*.

disputes.[85] Whether the justices used the office for profit is another question, which even if true would not necessarily imply that the mediation they performed was not genuine. Mediating justice John Chamberlayne, who was accused of profiting from his office, denied the charge, adding that he never "wronged or oppressed the meanest person that ever came before me."[86] In any case, not all justices who encouraged mediation can have needed the money. Although contemporaries complained that trading justices were socially inferior and practiced in "the poorest parts of town,"[87] some of the mediating justices listed in Table 8.5 worked in London's west end and often handled cases involving relatively wealthy defendants. Four of the justices specialized in hearing cases involving defendants from the middle or upper classes, and it is unlikely that these justices were socially inferior to the people who demanded mediation from them. One of these justices was Edmund Godfrey, a timber and coal merchant who was a "court justice," and who died in mysterious circumstances in the Popish Plot. Godfrey was very active in local government and was in frequent contact with government ministers.[88] Mediating justices were neither inevitably corrupt nor consistently socially inferior. As Landau concluded, the stereotype of the "trading justice" fits uneasily with the reality of mediating justices as revealed in the recognizance evidence.

It is not surprising that wealthier Londoners, like their poorer neighbors, sought informal mediation from justices who specialized in informal settlements. What is significant is that so many justices appear to have specialized in hearing disputes involving people from similar social backgrounds. Table 8.5 includes eight justices who specialized in lower class defendants and four who worked primarily with higher status defendants. These caseloads did not always reflect the social composition of their neighborhoods: justices John Chamberlayne and Alexander Ward specialized in cases involving poor defendants in Westminster and the west end while D'Oyley Michel heard cases involving higher status defendants in the east end. Justices must have acquired reputations, based in part on their own status and background, concerning the types of cases they normally mediated, and it appears that some litigants sought out justices accustomed to dealing with people like themselves.

Not all justices adopted such an informal approach to the law. Some "law and order" justices frequently encouraged plaintiffs to file indictments or committed many defendants to houses of correction for immediate punishment. While the average indictment rate for offences against the peace for all other justices (for whom sufficient information was available) was 13%, five justices had indictment rates of between 33 and 55.5%. Faced with similar offences, some

---

[85] Landau, *Justices of the Peace*, pp. 185–86.
[86] Hertfordshire Record Office, D/EP/F153, letter to William Cowper.
[87] Baston, *Thoughts on Trade*, pp. 129–30.   [88] Webbs, *The Parish and the County*, p. 338.

justices clearly counselled formal prosecution instead of (or in addition to) mediation. Similarly, as we have seen, several justices advocated commitment to houses of correction over other procedures. Seven justices in the sample committed as many or more people to houses of correction as they bound over by recognizance,[89] while the median number of people bound over by the other justices in the sample for each person they committed was 2.5. Given the wide range of offences punished in houses of correction, it is likely that many of the same offences which mediating justices handled by recognizance were punished in houses of correction by law and order justices. The caseloads of some law and order justices, however, were quite different from those of other justices. Judging by the large number of property cases they heard (up to 35% of the recognizances and 60% of the house of correction cases), a few of these justices appear to have concentrated on more serious crimes, which may explain why they adopted such a formal approach to prosecution. On average, however, law and order justices were no more likely to hear misdemeanor property offences than other justices.[90]

Four of the house of correction law and order justices specialized in the punishment of prostitutes, who accounted for between 61 and 87% of their commitments. These justices, along with four others, may be characterized as "social control" justices, who used the judicial system to attempt to reform the morals of the lower classes (Table 8.6). Social control justices may be defined as those who heard large numbers of cases of vice and whose defendants were frequently poor. Justices Chamberlayne and Negus in 1707, for example, issued disproportionately large numbers of recognizances for vice and over 60% of their defendants were from the lower class. Six other justices targeted the same types of cases, but committed their defendants to houses of correction. Between 64 and 100% of the house of correction business heard by these justices involved victimless offences. (Because they tended to use houses of correction for victimless offences, these justices issued fewer recognizances for vice.) Given their tendency to use houses of correction and their willingness to facilitate prosecutions of victimless offences, social control justices tended to favor the punishment of defendants rather than negotiation. It is thus not surprising that they issued proportionally fewer recognizances for female plaintiffs than other justices (43% vs 49.5%).[91] As we have seen, women tended to avoid formal prosecutions and punishments and instead sought mediation, exactly what social control justices were unlikely to provide. Only a fifth of the private plaintiffs on the recognizances issued by justice John Chamberlayne in

---

[89] Hugh Chamberlaine, Thomas Colthurst, William Conne, Joseph Haynes, D'Oyley Michel, Richard Newton, and Isaac Tillard.

[90] A thorough analysis of this problem, however, would require analysis of the felony cases that these justices heard.

[91] Unfortunately, too few private plaintiffs were identified on house of correction calendars to compile similar statistics for commitments to houses of correction.

Table 8.6 "Social control" justices[a]

Name of justice	Vice offences % of recogs.	Low status defendants % of recogs.[b]	Ratio: recogs. to house of correction commitments	Victimless offences % of house of correction commitments	Official plaintiffs % of recogs.	Female plaintiffs % of recogs.	Region of activity
Using recognizances (1707)							
John Chamberlayne	72	62.5	N/A	N/A	29	20%	Westminster
Francis Negus	31	75	N/A	N/A	25	47	Westminster
Using houses of correction (1720–22)							
Thomas Boteler	9	85	1.1	95	None	50	Westminster
Thomas Colthurst	N/A	N/A	0.5	74	N/A	N/A	Westminster
William Conne	18	70	1.0	73	4	41	Westminster
Joseph Haynes	N/A	N/A	0.2	89.5	N/A	N/A	West urban
Richard Newton	N/A	N/A	0.9	100	N/A	N/A	West urban
Jeffery Saunders	22	32	2.0	64	11	55	Westminster
AVERAGE	16	62	0.95	83	5	43	
All other justices[c]	9	42	4.0	43[d]	13	49.5	

[a] Defined as justices who frequently heard cases of vice *and* whose defendants were primarily lower class (as indicated by the status or occupational labels on their recognizances or by the fact that they made frequent commitments to houses of correction). See text.

[b] Defendants in low status occupations and those who were unable to risk bail. Because their status is difficult to identify, this calculation excludes apprentices, servants, officers, and women. Also excluded are defendants prosecuted by officers of the peace.

[c] Average of all other justices for whom sufficient information is available. These are listed in appendix II.

[d] Calculation based on justices from the 1693 and 1720–22 samples only, since these were the only samples in which both recognizance and house of correction evidence were collected.

N/A: insufficient information available.

1707 were female; this may well be related to the fact that almost three-quarters of his recognizances were for vice.

Some justices who tended to encourage negotiation by recognizance, however, also committed large numbers of defendants to houses of correction for punishment. Justices William Conne and James Dewy, for example, encouraged mediation when they issued recognizances (few of their recognizances led to indictments) *and* they punished large numbers of defendants in houses of correction. The two groups of prosecutions, however, took place in very different contexts. Dewey issued recognizances primarily against middle- and upper-class defendants, while the defendants he committed to houses of correction were probably poor. Similarly, justice D'Oyley Michel issued many recognizances but encouraged few indictments against the high status defendants who appeared before him for peace offences, but he was responsible for a relatively large number of commitments to houses of correction, primarily for theft. Some justices acted as mediating justices for the rich and social control justices for the poor. As one observer explained, many justices were unsympathetic to the poor, especially when their prosecutors were "great men": "if a controversy happens between a poor servant, labourer, or tenant, and the lord of the manor, or other rich person, all the arts in the world ... [are] mustered [by justices] to prove the poor party in the wrong ..."[92] In situations like that, the accused was likely to be committed to a house of correction.

Of course, the actions taken by most justices do not neatly conform to one of the three types of justices outlined above. Each justice had his own unique judicial personality. Nevertheless, the categories of mediating, law and order, and social control justices do, between them, characterize the behavior of just under half of the seventy-one active justices whose business is detailed in appendix II. Justices did not all mechanically respond to similar cases in similar ways, but neither were their decisions inevitably shaped by extrajudicial considerations such as patronage networks specific to each case. The dramatic differences in judicial behavior revealed in this discussion document fundamentally different conceptions of the nature of justice and the purpose of prosecutions and punishments. Consequently, people's experiences of the criminal justice system varied considerably depending on the identity of the justice who handled the case.

Differences in judicial styles among active Middlesex and Westminster justices were inevitable, given the fact the justices rarely acted as a single body, and when they did their collective decisions carefully protected their freedom to act individually as they saw fit. Those justices who attended sessions constituted,

---

[92] [Edmund Bohun], *Justice of Peace: His Calling and Qualifications* (1684), pp. 111–12. The author later observes that justices sometimes favored men because they were poor, but this "doth not happen so frequently" (p. 114).

for the few days during which the sessions continued, the courts of quarter sessions for the county of Middlesex or the City of Westminster. Although the justices meeting at sessions had no power to change the law, they could issue orders that altered specific aspects of legal procedures or required stricter enforcement of certain laws. For several reasons, the regulations adopted were often ignored. Most importantly, those who attended court rarely constituted more than about one-quarter of the justices on the Middlesex commission.[93] (Although the cellar of the Middlesex sessions house, Hicks Hall, had to be enlarged in 1672 to hold a "sufficient quantity of beer to entertain the justices during the time of their meetings," this action is apparently more indicative of the justices' drinking habits than of their habitual attendance at sessions.[94]) Even many of the justices who were active in issuing recognizances and making commitments to houses of correction did not regularly attend sessions. Richard Powell and Thomas Byde failed to attend any sessions in the first half of 1664, for example, despite the fact that between them they accounted for 8% of the recognizances issued to attend those sessions. Since recognizances were typically discharged at sessions unless the plaintiff appeared to make a complaint (which occurred rarely), justices must have felt that it was unnecessary to attend the sessions at which their defendants were bound over to appear. Even fewer of the justices active in making commitments to houses of correction appeared in court, since sessions did not hear the cases of these defendants unless they were still incarcerated at the time sessions met. Because justices who were actively involved in prosecutions often did not attend the sessions where judicial policies were made, it was virtually impossible to standardize judicial practices.

In any case, many of the orders made by the justices who did attend sessions tended to preserve the flexibility of individual justices to conduct their business without interference. The only substantive efforts made by the courts to regulate judicial behavior were designed to preserve that independence by prohibiting two practices by which justices interfered in each other's business: acting outside their local area, and bailing or discharging each other's commitments from prisons or houses of correction. With a large number of justices living in the metropolitan area, conflicts between justices over political and legal issues were not uncommon and on occasion these conflicts involved disputes over the handling of criminal cases.[95] Five orders of the court during

---

[93] In 1691, there were 167 justices on the Middlesex commission, and eighty-five on the Westminster commission, not including those who were honorarily appointed because they held important government offices (GLRO, MJP/CP/14, WJP/CP/15). The largest number of justices attending sessions that year was forty-three in Middlesex and nineteen in Westminster (MJ/SBB/480–491). Many of the other justices on the commission probably did not even bother to take out their *dedimus*, which gave them the legal authority to act (Landau, *Justices of the Peace*, pp. 320–21).

[94] MJ/SBB/288, p. 23 (Feb. 1672).

[95] For example, see above, section 4.3 and below, section 9.2.

this period addressed the problem of justices hearing criminal cases outside their local areas. In such cases, the court complained, the justice could not know the character of the parties involved and the individual circumstances of the case. What is more, although the court did not state this explicitly, such actions threatened to harm relations between justices who lived nearby and local residents.[96] Four orders of the court addressed the problem of justices bailing each other's prisoners or discharging prisoners from houses of correction without consulting the committing justice. Not only did these justices interfere in their colleagues' relations with their local communities, but, the court complained, they acted without knowing "the circumstances and aggravations" of the prisoners' offences. The language of these orders, however, reveals how hesitant the justices were to regulate even these practices. In 1675, justices who bailed other justices' prisoners from the house of correction were simply to be notified of the contents of the order forbidding the practice, and in Westminster in 1712 the court simply resolved that it would "take notice of" and "discountenance" such practices, and that the resolution would be entered into the sessions records.[97]

The courts' weak language was a product of both impotence and realism. The justices had no means of enforcing these regulations except by petitioning the government to eject egregiously disobedient justices from the commission. Moreover, justices occasionally had good reason to release each other's prisoners, such as when the committing justice did not have time or neglected to issue a warrant to release the prisoner himself. Justices who rarely made commitments to the house of correction, especially if they lived far away, were likely to delegate this task to another justice. To allow justices some flexibility to deal with situations like these, the 1694 order included a clause that "at least" two justices could discharge other justices' prisoners, and in 1716 the court restricted the ban on discharging each other's commitments to the urban area within the Bills of Mortality.[98]

Attempts to remove justices who did not comply with the regulations of the court occurred only in exceptional circumstances. Nine Middlesex justices were the subject of petitions to the Lord Chancellor between 1685 and 1728, and at least four more were threatened with this procedure. Of these thirteen justices, one was charged with having libelled the Middlesex commission, three with extortion or accepting bribes, three with issuing irregular warrants, and six with improperly bailing prisoners. The charges against nine of these justices, those related to issuing warrants and bailing prisoners, were directly related to the attempts by the Middlesex justices to prevent judicial interference

---

[96] MJ/SBB/288, p. 22 (Feb. 1672); 407, p. 49 (Aug. 1683); 490, p. 52 (Oct. 1691); MJ/OC/I, f. 14 (Oct. 1716); MJ/SP/Dec. 1716, nos. 44, 45, 47; WJ/OC/II, ff. 24–27 (Oct. 1725).
[97] MJ/SBB/323, p. 43 (May 1675); 700, p. 23 (Westminster sessions, Jan. 1712).
[98] MJ/SBB/510, p. 58 (Westminster sessions, Jan. 1694); MJ/OC/I, f. 14 (Oct. 1716).

in each other's activities. The circumstances surrounding these accusations suggest that they were products of special circumstances and not of systematic attempts by the justices to enforce court orders. The three justices accused of issuing irregular warrants, for example, were active in the reformation of manners campaign, and although the circumstances surrounding these cases are complicated, they appear to have been initiated by justices who were hostile to the campaign.[99]

The behavior of the justices who were presented to the higher authorities for improperly bailing prisoners was particularly egregious. William Moore was charged with a series of misdemeanors, including issuing warrants without any just cause, in addition to the accusation that he discharged several prisoners committed by other justices without consulting them, and he refused to appear in court to answer the accusations.[100] Sir Harry Dutton Colt bailed a principal participant in riots at the New Mint in 1724 without consulting the justice who committed him, and Francis Jennison bailed his brother without taking security in 1728 after he had been imprisoned by another justice for obstructing the high constable in the execution of his office. Colt had been put in and out of the commission several times since 1689, apparently for political reasons, and both justices refused to justify their behavior to the court.[101] In contrast, three other justices who were accused of improperly bailing prisoners in the 1720s were apparently exonerated after two explained their actions in court and the other apparently agreed to fire the clerk who had convinced him to bail the prisoner.[102] Clearly, petitioning to dismiss errant justices from the commission was a last resort reserved for the most serious offences and the most uncooperative and unpopular justices. Despite attempts by the court to regulate judicial practices, to a considerable extent the justices maintained their independence to perform their duties in any manner they wished, even when their actions interfered in each other's business.

The independence possessed by individual justices in the execution of their office had varied consequences. Most justices, of course, for the most part declined to act; business was concentrated in the hands of a few very active justices. Judging from the business they conducted, some active justices appear to have discouraged prosecutions of certain types of offences (such as vice) or cases initiated by certain types of plaintiffs (such as officers or women). Other justices, however, took advantage of the flexibility of the judicial system and used their offices aggressively to encourage certain types of prosecutions. We have seen that mediating justices, who were actually accused of creating

---

[99] The justices were Ralph Hartley, Nathaniel Blackerby, and Thomas Boteler. See below, section 9.2.

[100] MJ/OC/I, ff. 114–15 (Jan. 1721).

[101] MJ/OC/II, f. 139 (Jan 1725); III, ff. 160–64 (Dec. 1728). On Colt, see Lionel K. J. Glassey, *Politics and the Appointment of Justices of the Peace* (Oxford, 1979), pp. 125, 149, 151.

[102] MJ/OC/I, f. 106d (Sept. 1720); III, f. 136–36d (June 1728); MJ/SP/Feb. 1727, nos. 51, 53.

offences, facilitated large numbers of prosecutions for offences against the peace. Other justices appear to have encouraged prosecutions for victimless offences by pressuring parish officers to perform their duties more efficiently. Clearly, some justices did not sit passively in their parlors waiting for business to appear before them. By their actions on previous cases, by pressuring parish officers, and by cultivating relationships with informers and neighbors, justices encouraged plaintiffs to bring specific types of business before them. Thus, the judicial system allowed justices of the peace, like private plaintiffs and parish officers, considerable flexibility to respond to petty crimes according to their personal inclinations and circumstances. Only in cases of serious misconduct were efforts made to control their activities. As we shall see, however, the limits of judicial flexibility were dramatically revealed during the reformation of manners campaign, when zealous justices and officers who attempted to prosecute vice systematically encountered substantial opposition.

The different sides of the law in preindustrial England are revealed in the contrasting social profiles of the participants in each type of prosecution. Recognizances were used disproportionately by women, who tended to avoid the more formal procedures for prosecution, and by others who could not afford to prosecute by indictment. These plaintiffs, as well as the "mediating" justices who frequently issued recognizances, favored this procedure because it was inexpensive, it rarely required plaintiffs to appear in court, and it often facilitated informal settlements. As a more formal and costly procedure, the indictment was suited for plaintiffs who demanded formal convictions and punishments (or lucrative out-of-court settlements). Plaintiffs were wealthy enough to pay the legal fees, and most plaintiffs and defendants were men; justices who favored this procedure can be characterized as "law and order" justices who often heard serious offences. Houses of correction, on the other hand, were used primarily by official plaintiffs for the punishment of prostitution and other victimless offences; the defendants were typically poor, female, and without social connections. Many of the justices who frequently used houses of correction can be characterized as "social control" justices who used summary jurisdiction to punish "disorderly" behavior among the poor. Depending on the wealth and gender of the participants, and the predilections of individual justices and parish officers, the law of misdemeanors could be used for very different purposes in preindustrial England. In chapter 10, a geographical dimension will be added to this analysis of the contrasting social contexts of misdemeanor prosecutions, but first we will focus special attention on a group of plaintiffs whose activities constitute the most distinctive approach to prosecuting misdemeanors in preindustrial London: the Societies for the Reformation of Manners.

9

The reformation of manners campaign

Soon after his accession to the throne in 1689, members of the court of William III began to push for a campaign to end debauchery and promote virtue in London and the nation. As William wrote in a letter to the Bishop of London and the two archbishops,

We most earnestly desire and shall desire a general reformation of manners of all our subjects as being that which must establish our throne and secure to our people their religion, happiness, and peace, all which seem to be in great danger at this time by reason of that overflowing of vice which is too notorious in this as well as other neighbouring nations.

Consequently, ministers and churchwardens were ordered to do everything in their powers to suppress vice.[1] Although the church can take some of the credit for getting the ball rolling, it was in fact voluntary societies and justices of the peace who organized a campaign against vice that was to last for almost half a century.

The first evidence of activity comes from a petition to the Middlesex sessions from the churchwardens and overseers of the poor of the parish of St. Martin in the Fields, encouraged no doubt by their minister and future archbishop, John Tillotson, requesting the suppression of bawdy houses.[2] In response, a small group of justices of the peace in Westminster started to act, committing over 200 prostitutes and other "loose [or lewd], idle and disorderly persons" to the Westminster house of correction between October 1689 and April 1690. The number of these commitments, which account for over half of all house of correction commitments during that period, was so high that the total number of people committed to the Westminster house of correction in the year ending October 1690 was far higher than any previous year for which records survive.[3]

---

[1] *His Majesties Letter to the Lord Bishop of London* (1690), p. 4; Tony Claydon, "Debauchery and the Revolution: the idea of luxury in late Stuart London," seminar given at the Institute of Historical Research, 14 March 1990.

[2] WJ/SP/Aug. 1689, no. 10; MJ/SBB/468, p. 6 (Westminster sessions, Aug. 1689).

[3] See above, Figure 3. The justices responsible for these commitments were Robert Fielding and John Ward (both appointed to the commission in 1689) and the justices who met at the St. Martin's Vestry, whom I have been unable to identify.

This prosecution wave, however, was short-lived, and commitments fell dramatically in 1692, by which time the impetus for a campaign against vice had switched to voluntary societies. The first such society was founded in the autumn of 1690, when in response to a royal proclamation for the apprehending of highway robbers a group of parish officers and inhabitants in Tower Hamlets in the east end of London met and resolved to take steps to suppress bawdy houses and punish prostitutes. Shortly thereafter, a group of more prominent men convinced Queen Mary to write a letter to the Middlesex justices of the peace, requiring them to enforce the laws against a broad range of vice offences: profaning the Sabbath, drunkenness, profane cursing and swearing, and "all other lewd, enormous and disorderly practices." The Middlesex justices and the Lord Mayor of London dutifully responded with orders requiring inferior officers to enforce these laws, and subsequently several "societies" of private citizens interested in suppressing vice formed in different parts of London. Thus, the Societies for the Reformation of Manners were born.[4]

What came to be called the "reformation of manners campaign" was not, of course, the first organized campaign of prosecutions against vice in England, nor was it to be the last.[5] With a legal system which depended upon unpaid, part-time officials for the prosecution of vice and other victimless offences, the scope for more efficient and more systematic prosecutions of victimless offences was, as we have seen in the previous chapter, considerable. What distinguishes the 1690s campaign is first of all its duration – the societies issued annual reports of their activities up to 1738 – and secondly the fact that its supporters were for the first time organized into independent societies which not only lobbied for better enforcement of the laws but also assumed (to a certain extent) the duties of parish officers, systematically informing against and prosecuting large numbers of offenders themselves. In doing so, the societies threatened to undermine the judicial and prosecutorial flexibility which was the hallmark of the criminal justice system before the introduction of the police. This chapter examines this attempt to transform the judicial process

---

[4] *Antimoixeia: or, the Honest and Joynt-Design of the Tower-Hamblets for the General Suppression of Bawdy-Houses, as Incouraged by the Publick Magistrates* (1691); MJ/SBB/487, p. 78 (July 1691); A. G. Craig, "The movement for the reformation of manners, 1688–1715," (Ph.D. diss., University of Edinburgh, 1980), chap. 1; T. C. Curtis and W. A. Speck, "The Societies for the Reformation of Manners: a case study in the theory and practice of moral reform," *Literature and History* 3 (1976), pp. 45–47; Garnet V. Portus, *Caritas Anglicana* (1912), pp. 35–37; D. W. R. Bahlman, *The Moral Revolution of 1688* (New Haven, 1957), pp. 15–18.

[5] Keith Wrightson, "Alehouses, order and reformation in rural England, 1590–1660," in *Popular Culture and Class Conflict 1590–1914*, ed. Eileen and Stephen Yeo (Brighton, 1981), pp. 1–27, and *English Society 1580–1680* (1982), pp. 168–70, 210–15; Anthony Fletcher, *Reform in the Provinces* (1986); Joanna Innes, "Politics and morals: the reformation of manners movement in later eighteenth-century England," in *The Transformation of Political Culture: England and Germany in the late Eighteenth Century*, ed. Eckhart Hellmuth (Oxford, 1990), pp. 57–118.

from one largely characterized by negotiation and flexibility to one characterized by systematic prosecutions and punishments.

Much has been written about the reformation of manners campaign, but the best work in recent years has been in two unpublished dissertations, by A. G. Craig and Tina Beth Isaacs.[6] These dissertations tell the story of the campaign and the difficulties the reformers encountered in greater detail than in previous published works, and they begin to set the societies in their wider ideological and political contexts. Both works fail, however, to analyze very carefully how the reformers actually prosecuted vice, and as a consequence they perpetuate two misconceptions about the campaign. First, because they do not recognize the extent to which the reformers' prosecutorial tactics conflicted with traditional judicial practices, they misunderstand the judicial opposition to the campaign, falsely characterizing the opponents' motives as corrupt and immoral. Second, by focusing solely on the religious motivations of the reformers, they fail to recognize the extent to which prosecutors of vice in London were motivated by concerns about the perceived growth of crime and disorder in the metropolis, especially among the poor. An examination of the reformers' activities as prosecutors of vice sheds light not only on the extent to which the judicial system could be manipulated by a powerful interest group, but also on the goals and motivations of the reformers themselves.

9.1 STRATEGIES FOR PROSECUTION

Initially, the reformers adopted traditional law enforcement methods and relied on the people legally responsible for apprehending or reporting vice offenders, parish officers. Despite the enthusiasm of some officers (many constables and churchwardens were members of the early societies[7]), the reformers soon discovered that parish officials more often hindered than helped the campaign. They complained that officers frequently failed to apprehend and report offenders, or even execute warrants against the offenders the justices convicted. It was alleged in 1694 that "maybe one-half, if not two-thirds" of the parish officers "instead of being suppressors, are rather supporters and encouragers of [vice] either by neglect of duty, or by giving bad examples."[8] Other constables leaked information that searches were about to be conducted, and some

---

[6] Craig, "Movement for the reformation of manners"; Tina Beth Isaacs, "Moral crime, moral reform, and the state in early eighteenth-century England: a study of piety and politics" (Ph.D. diss., University of Rochester, 1979). See also Isaacs, "The Anglican hierarchy and the reformation of manners 1688–1738," *Journal of Ecclesiastical History* 33 (1982), pp. 391–411.

[7] *Antimoixeia*; MJ/SBB/500, pp. 50–51 (Oct. 1692); Edinburgh University Library, Laing MS III, 394, pp. 473–80.

[8] *Proposals for a National Reformation of Manners* (1694), p. 29. See also Laing MS III, 394, p. 385; John Disney, *A Second Essay upon the Execution of the Laws against Immorality and Profaneness* (1710), pp. xvii, 37; Samuel Ryder, *The Charge to the Grand Jury of the City and Liberty of Westminster, at the General Quarter Sessions of the Peace* (1726), p. 26.

allegedly engaged in bribery and extortion in order to "screen" offenders from prosecution.[9] All of these complaints seem quite plausible: as we have seen in chapter 8, there were many reasons why constables did not execute their duties efficiently. Certainly the considerable popular hostility to the reformation of manners campaign provided a compelling disincentive to cooperating with the reformers. Referring to supporters of the campaign, one Londoner staying in Dublin boasted that "he wondered at the people of Ireland to suffer such rogues for that in London they used them like dogs."[10] Officers attempting to make arrests were often assaulted by angry mobs, and two reforming constables were killed while apprehending offenders.[11] At the funeral of one of the officers, John Dent, it was claimed that he had "often been much abused, beaten, mobbed, and wounded; and in a very great danger of his life in detecting, and bringing to justice, the lewd and disorderly persons."[12]

Regardless of the possibility of violence, officers who wished to remain on good terms with their neighbors were forced to think twice before enforcing the laws too rigorously. Popular attitudes are of course difficult to assess, but it seems clear that the reformers' enthusiasm for prosecuting vice attracted little popular support in many neighborhoods. It is significant that John Disney noted that the stocks, a form of punishment which attempted to embarrass a criminal in front of his friends and neighbors, was "of little or no effect" in punishing persons who were guilty of vice. Consequently, constables and churchwardens, conscious that they only held office for a year, were "afraid of being strict upon the faults of the neighbourhood, lest they should lose the good will of their neighbours, and expose themselves to the revenge of those that are to succeed them."[13]

From the start, the reformers were aware that innovative strategies were needed to surmount the apathy or hostility of both the general public and public officials. Although, as discussed below, several justices of the peace were active supporters of the campaign, it was impossible to make use of the magistrates' support if offenders were not reported to them. Consequently, the societies made considerable use of volunteer or paid informers to report offenders to justices (in the case of crimes which could be prosecuted by recognizance or summary conviction) or to prosecute them by indictment. The

[9] *An Account of the Endeavours that have been used to Suppress Gaming Houses* (1722); PRO, KB 10/17, Part 3, I. 42 (Hilary 7 Geo. I); Edward Ward, *The London Spy Compleat* (1703), pp. 351–56; [John Dunton], *The Nightwalker: or, Evening Rambles in Search after Lewd Women* (Oct. 1696), p. 19; *Post Man, and the Historical Account*, 3–5 June 1701.
[10] MJ/SP/July 1703, no. 21.   [11] Shoemaker, "London 'mob'," p. 300.
[12] Thomas Bray, *The Good Fight of Faith ... Exemplified in a Sermon Preached the 24th of March 1708–9 at the Funeral of Mr. John Dent* (1709), p. 15.
[13] Disney, *Second Essay*, pp. xviii, 154–55. Officers were also dissuaded from apprehending or reporting offenders by the fact that defendants occasionally brought vexatious suits against them (Charles Hitchin, *A True Discovery of the Conduct of Receivers and Thief-Takers in and about the City of London* [1718], p. 17).

original Tower Hamlets society employed two persons "to search out houses of lewdness and bawdry and persons that haunt them in order to their legal prosecution, conviction, and punishment."[14] Queen Mary's letter to the Middlesex justices of the peace prompted the justices not only to require officers of the peace to report offenders, but also to recommend "to all good Christians ... [to] give due information against the offenders beforementioned."[15] The second society of reformers, which was formed in the Strand, developed a system of using informers to initiate large numbers of prosecutions. Dozens of informers were responsible for reporting offences punishable by summary conviction to clerks, who recorded the information in registers and filled in the appropriate blanks in printed warrants. The warrants were then brought before a justice to be signed and, if the defendant was convicted, distributed to the appropriate parish officers, who were required to collect the penalties. To keep the officers honest, the reformers compiled abstracts of the warrants of convictions and brought them to the justices' petty sessions, where constables were required to "give a public account of the execution of the said warrants." And to keep the informers active, they were required to report their accomplishments at weekly meetings of the societies.[16]

The reformers claimed early on that they had enlisted 150–200 informers, most of whom were skilled craftsmen.[17] The bulk of the informations, however, were performed by a few dedicated individuals. Although some three dozen informers are listed in the registers of over 9,000 accusations and convictions kept by the societies, two were by far the most active: John Wright (a member of the Tower Hamlets Society), and John Beggarly.[18] Of the thirty-five persons who served either as witnesses on indictments or as plaintiffs on recognizances in cases of vice at the Middlesex and Westminster quarter sessions in the second half of 1693, only four were responsible for five or more prosecutions: William Gonson (high constable of Finsbury division), James Jenkins, Bodenham Rewse (an embroiderer living in the Strand), and Jonathan Easden (a joiner living in Tower Liberty). Both Jenkins and Rewse were clerks to the Tower Hamlets Society in 1694, and Easden was listed as a member of that Society in 1691. In the early 1720s, the most active informers in the sessions records were Phillip Cholmondley, a stationer, and Edward Vaughan, a basketmaker, both of St. Martin in the Fields.[19]

---

[14] Laing MS III, 394, p. 465.   [15] MJ/SBB/487, p. 78 (July 1691).
[16] Laing MS III, 394, pp. 49–54, 233–40, 421–36; [Edward Fowler], A *Vindication of a Late Undertaking of Certain Gentlemen in Order to the Suppressing of Debauchery and Profaneness* (1692), pp. 8–10; Bodleian Library, Rawlinson MS D129, f. 11.
[17] Laing MS III, 394, p. 49; Curtis and Speck, "The Societies," p. 48; Craig, "Reformation of manners," pp. 92–94.
[18] Rawlinson MS D1396–1404.
[19] Rawlinson MS D1312, f. 16; Laing MS III, 394, pp. 507–10; *Antimoixeia*; PRO, KB 1/1, Trinity 5 Geo. I, depositions vs. Mary Evans als Carey and Elizabeth Whaley.

Although a few other misdemeanors (primarily violations of economic regulations) were occasionally prosecuted by informers,[20] no other offences were prosecuted systematically by informers during this period. Unsurprisingly, the use of informers for the prosecution of vice was the source of much of the popular opposition to the reformation of manners campaign. Informers were so unpopular that "the base name of informer among persons unconcerned" tended to "raise the mobile upon" them.[21] In addition to the fact that many people did not agree with the goal of systematically eradicating vice, popular hostility to informing had several causes. In the 1670s informers had acquired a bad reputation when they were used to suppress conventicles.[22] Allegations were frequently made that, like officers of the peace, informers were corrupt, often extorting money from people in return for not reporting their offences. At other times informations were "slight, trivial, or unwarrantable, or the persons themselves of greedy, mercenary tempers, or of vile, dissolute lives."[23] Although the reformers repeatedly denied that any of their informers were guilty of such practices, Jonathan Easden was accused of extortion in 1693–94 and was the subject of an (apparently inconclusive) investigation by quarter sessions.[24]

Many people objected to the intervention into their lives of what amounted to voluntary policemen. Speaking to members of the societies, Isaac Watts noted in 1707 that it was commonly stated that "ye are busy-bodies, 'tis the magistrate's place to punish vice, 'tis his work to put the laws in execution, and not yours."[25] According to Henry Sacheverell and other Tory high churchmen, the practice of informing undermined the natural hierarchy of authority and gave ordinary people power to act "as privy counsellors" over their fellow citizens.[26] In fact, since informers occasionally got themselves appointed as constables or deputy constables, and members of the societies occasionally

[20] Dowdell, *Quarter Sessions*, chap. 6. For the early history of informing, see M. W. Beresford, "The common informer, the penal statutes, and economic regulation," *Economic History Review*, 2nd series, vol. 10 (1957), pp. 221–38; M. G. Davies, *The Enforcement of English Apprenticeship* (Cambridge, 1956), chaps. 2 and 3.

[21] Laing MS III, 394, p. 265; MJ/SR/2343, R. 81 (Westminster sessions, April 1720).

[22] Gerald R. Cragg, *Puritanism in the Period of the Great Persecution 1660–1688* (Cambridge, 1957), pp. 60–63; *The Character of an Informer. Wherein his Mischievous Nature, and Lewd Practices are Detected* (1675). For the connection between the two types of informers in the popular mind, see *Athenian Mercury* 3:7 (18 Aug. 1691).

[23] Daniel Dolins, *The Second Charge of Sir Daniel Dolins, Kt., to the Grand Jury, and Other Juries of the County of Middlesex* (1726), p. 12. See also [Jonathan Swift], *A Project for the Advancement of Religion, and the Reformation of Manners* (1709), p. 18.

[24] MJ/SBB/509, p. 49 (Dec. 1693). Easden was subsequently indicted for barratry, extortion and riotous assault, but all of the indictments were apparently dropped before reaching a final verdict: MJ/SR/1827, I. 20, 45 (Jan. 1694); 1829, I. 4 (Feb. 1694).

[25] Isaac Watts, *A Sermon Preach'd at Salters-Hall, to the Societies for the Reformation of Manners* (1707), p. 36.

[26] Henry Sacheverell, *The Communication of Sin: A Sermon Preached at the Assizes held at Darby* (1709), p. 20; Isaacs, "Anglican hierarchy," pp. 401–02.

supervised the activities of constables, these charges contained more than a grain of truth.[27] In 1715–16, this opposition to the methods used by the reformation of manners campaign was combined with several other currents of popular opposition to what was perceived as the Whig government's attack on popular liberties.[28] Given the many sources of popular hostility, it is not surprising that the reformers recommended that informers prosecute people living outside their neighborhood, "who if [the informer] were to come face to face would not know him and consequently do him no harm ... "[29] Faced with such opposition, few people who volunteered to act as informers actually informed against more than a handful of offenders.

It took some time for the reformers to determine which legal procedure was most appropriate for prosecuting vice offenders. In their first report, the societies claimed that in the year ending January 1694 they had prosecuted 155 keepers of bawdy houses and 157 prostitutes in London.[30] It is likely that the bawdy house keepers were prosecuted primarily by indictment and that most of the prostitutes were committed to houses of correction. Many of the indictments prosecuted by the societies were filed not at sessions but at King's Bench, where cases of first instance from London and Middlesex could also be prosecuted. There were several possible advantages of prosecuting indictments at King's Bench: convicted defendants received more severe punishments (bawdy house keepers were fined 10s. or more, sentenced to be whipped along the Strand from Charing Cross to Somerset House and ordered to stand in the pillory), the cases received more publicity (some were reported in the newspapers), and it is possible that convicted defendants were required to pay costs and damages to their prosecutors.[31] In addition, the considerable expense of defending an indictment at King's Bench (one bawdy house keeper claimed she spent almost £200 on her defence[32]) may have forced keepers to agree to close down their houses in order to convince the reformers to drop the prosecution.[33]

---

[27] Laing MS III, 394, f. 460. It was said at the funeral of John Dent, the constable who was murdered while in the process of arresting an "idle woman" in 1709, that he had supported the reformation of manners campaign for 17 or 18 years. His funeral was attended by thirty constables and beadles (Bray, *Good Fight of Faith*, pp. 2, 15). Dent and several other constables gave informations which were recorded in the Societies' registers: Bodleian Library, Rawlinson MS, D1396–1404.

[28] Nicholas Rogers, "Popular protest in early Hanoverian London," *Past and Present* 79 (1978), pp. 91–94.

[29] Laing MS III, 394, pp. 352–53.

[30] *Proposals for a National Reformation of Manners*, pp. 34–35.

[31] *Original Weekly Journal*, 27 June 1719; *Weekly Journal; or Saturday's Post*, 27 June 1719; Hawkins, *Pleas of the Crown*, vol. 2, p. 210. I am grateful for the advice I have received on this issue from Ruth Paley.

[32] PRO, KB 1/1, Trinity 5 George I, petition of Richard and Charity Hayward.

[33] Many of the indictments for keeping disorderly houses or gaming houses at King's Bench apparently never reached a final verdict, which may signify that they resulted in such informal settlements.

Table 9.1 *Prosecutions initiated by the Societies for the Reformation of Manners by probable procedure of prosecution*

Year ending December	By indictment[a]	Summary conviction: by fine[b]	Summary conviction: by house of correction[c]	Total prosecutions
1693[d]	155	N/A	157	
1700	102	N/A	1063	
1701	69	N/A	1136	
1702	80	N/A	1077	
1704	15	N/A	1175	
1707	57	N/A	844	
1708[e]	81	1963	1255	3299
1709	42	2140	794	2976
1715	44	1375	1152	2571
1716	17	737	1066	1820
1717	33	949	1927	2909
1718	39	714	1253	2006
1720	30	740	1189	1959
1721	19	883	1197	2099
1722	139	862	1223	2224
1723	78	749	1622	2449
1724	52	720	1951	2723
1725				2506
1726				1060
1727				1363
1728				778
1729				1226
1730	57	446	251	754
1731				895
1732	9	289	230	528
1733	3	395	89	487
1734	20	220	170	410
1735	28	240	318	586
1736	20	437	212	669
1737	91	302	95	488
1738	104	389	52	545

Source: Portus, *Caritas Anglicana*, Appendix V; Isaacs, "Moral crime," pp. 252, 259; supplemented by the societies' annual accounts where necessary. The figures for 1693 are from *Proposals for a National Reformation of Manners*, pp. 34–35. The unit of analysis is the defendant.

[a] Keeping bawdy houses, gaming houses, and disorderly houses; picking pockets; assaulting constables in the execution of their office; butchers working on the Sabbath (1734–38 only, the accounts explicitly state that they were indicted). An unknown number of these offenders were prosecuted by recognizance only.
[b] Profaning the Sabbath; profane swearing and cursing; drunkenness.
[c] "Lewd and disorderly" persons; prostitutes. An unknown number of these offenders were prosecuted by recognizance only.
[d] Year ending January 1694.
[e] In 1708 the societies began to report the number of defendants prosecuted, regardless of whether or not they were convicted. The figures up to 1708 are for convictions only.

The reformers soon realized, however, that prosecution by indictment was so expensive and time consuming that it would quickly bankrupt the campaign. A vexatious suit filed by a bawdy house keeper they had indicted cost the reformers over £24 to defend in 1692.[34] In 1694, the Tower Hamlets society alone spent £80 prosecuting indictments. Not surprisingly, it advised its members "not to direct any prosecutions against bawdy houses unless they know there is money sufficient in some of the treasurers' hands to go through with the prosecution."[35] By 1700, the year of the next surviving report of the societies' prosecutions, the number of offenders prosecuted for indictable offences had decreased by almost a third to 102 and the number of people accused of offences punishable in houses of correction, 1,063, was seven times higher than in 1693–94 (Table 9.1). The pattern of prosecutions reported in 1700 continued for over two decades – only twice during the remaining history of the societies were more than one hundred people indicted in one year: during the justices' campaign against gaming houses in 1722 and in the last year of the societies, when 138 butchers were indicted for offering meat for sale on the Sabbath. Only twice between 1700 and 1724, on the other hand, were less than 1,000 prostitutes and lewd and disorderly persons committed (or threatened with commitment) to a house of correction.

In their prosecution of sexual offences, the societies thus shifted their activities from the keepers of bawdy houses, whom they prosecuted by indictment, to prostitutes, most of whom were punished in houses of correction. With the exception of the short-lived activities of a small group of Westminster justices in the early 1690s, the early reformers had a relatively modest impact on the levels of commitments to the Middlesex and Westminster houses of correction. From the late 1690s, however, the total number of commitments at both houses increased, and it appears that the reformers were partly responsible for this growth. Whereas vice-related offences accounted for between 46 and 62.5% of the commitments to the Westminster house of correction in the sample years 1680, 1690 and 1693, in 1702 and 1712 such offences accounted for 70% and 68% respectively of all commitments. Indeed, the reformers' activities accounted for such a large proportion of the commitments at the Middlesex and Westminster houses of correction that fluctuations in the total number of commitments in the early eighteenth century were often caused by changes in the intensity of the reformers' efforts.[36]

The growing use of houses of correction by the reformers was undoubtedly due to the fact that summary conviction was far cheaper and easier than prosecuting offenders by indictment. From the start, the reformers had also prosecuted many people for profaning the Sabbath and profane swearing or cursing by summary conviction with punishment by fine, and, as suggested by

---

[34] MJ/SBB/500, pp. 50–51 (Oct. 1692).   [35] Laing MS III, 394, pp. 453, 507–10.
[36] See above, section 3.3.

their system of collecting and distributing warrants, they quickly realized that large numbers of offenders could be prosecuted summarily with a minimum of effort. As John Disney noted, "if prosecutions against swearing, etc. be confined to the method of indictment, you will have too few offenders punished; perhaps three or four at a session; but if you form convictions nearer to home, you may bring a very considerable number to punishment."[37] As we shall see, in only two months in 1691 justice Ralph Hartley issued over 500 warrants of summary conviction. Although the controversy over Hartley's activities and his ejection from the commission of the peace temporarily discouraged summary prosecutions of offences punishable by fine, the reformers did not abandon this method of prosecution. The societies' accounts did not report the number of people prosecuted in this manner until 1708, but from 1704 large numbers of such convictions are recorded in registers kept by the societies.[38] The number of such convictions reported in 1708, almost 2,000, certainly suggests that the system had been working efficiently for some time. When the figures in Table 9.1 for summary convictions with punishment by fine are combined with the commitments to houses of correction, the societies' overwhelming preference for summary conviction over indictments becomes obvious. As will become clear in section 9.2, this reliance on summary conviction was an important source of the judicial opposition to the campaign.

The number of recognizances issued as a result of the societies' efforts is difficult to determine from their annual accounts, but evidence from the sessions rolls suggests that, although a significant number of vice offenders were bound over, recognizances were considerably less popular than summary conviction for the prosecution of vice. While an estimated 188 prostitutes and "loose, idle and disorderly" people were committed to the Westminster house of correction in 1693, only about 30 people were bound over in Westminster for these offences.[39] Nonetheless, the impact of the reformers' activities on the number of recognizances issued for vice was significant and long lasting. According to a sample of August or September sessions of the Middlesex court, in the twenty years prior to the start of the reformation of manners campaign an average of 7.9 defendants accused of prostitution, keeping bawdy houses, and loose, idle and disorderly conduct were bound over by recognizance at each sessions; in the subsequent twenty years this number tripled. Prosecutions for gaming also increased significantly after 1690.[40] In 1707, sample evidence

---

[37] John Disney, *An Essay upon the Execution of the Laws against Profaneness and Immorality* (1708), p. 19. Disney also noted that summary conviction was a "milder" method of prosecution, which was more suitable for "reforming" offenders.
[38] Rawlinson MS D1396–1404.
[39] These estimates are based on a 50% sample of the house of correction calendars and a 20% sample of the recognizances.
[40] Shoemaker, "Crime, courts and community," Table 35, p. 337.

suggests that about 250 defendants were bound over for vice, primarily for sexual offences.

In general, however, reforming justices appear to have avoided recognizances when dealing with vice cases. In two other recognizance samples, 1693 and 1720–22, reforming justices issued fewer recognizances for vice as a proportion of their total recognizance business than all other justices, including those justices who can be identified as hostile to the campaign. As we shall see in the next section, justices who opposed the campaign strongly favored recognizances over houses of correction for the prosecution of vice. Opposing justices may have favored recognizances because they were lenient and encouraged informal mediation; reforming justices probably avoided them because they were not an effective procedure for punishing or preventing vice without the threat of a possible indictment, a threat which diminished along with the reformers' financial resources. By themselves, as we have noted, recognizances in vice cases were frequently unsuccessful.[41]

The choice of offences prosecuted by the societies is revealing of the diverse motives of the campaign's supporters. The three offences prosecuted most frequently were Sabbath breaking, profane cursing and swearing, and lewd and disorderly conduct. The first two offences reflect the reformers' attempts to encourage religiosity by defending important Christian symbols. The third offence, lewd and disorderly conduct, reflects rather different concerns. This was the offence first prosecuted by the Westminster justices in 1690, and it became the largest category of offences prosecuted by the societies. It was also the most vaguely defined; as we have seen, people committed to houses of correction for this offence were accused of a variety of offences, including prostitution, idleness, vagrancy, and theft.[42] With the exception of prostitution, these offences were rarely discussed in the societies' voluminous printed propaganda. The leaders of the societies may not have been preoccupied with these offences, but the informers, constables and justices of the peace who conducted prosecutions clearly were, to the extent that they prosecuted more people for these offences than any others.

In the late seventeenth century, concerns were voiced about the growth of poverty, crime, and disorder in the metropolis,[43] and the foundation of the societies and subsequent conduct of the reformers constitute one of the responses to these perceived problems. This aspect of the reformation of manners campaign has been largely ignored by historians, despite the fact that the petition from the parish officers of St. Martin in the Fields which initiated

---

[41] See above, section 5.3.   [42] See above, section 7.1.   [43] See above, section 1.2.

Plate 3 "Harlot's progress," plate III, by William Hogarth [1732] (Guildhall Library, City of London)
The reforming justice Sir John Gonson and three constables enter the harlot's room (in the vicinity of Drury Lane) and are about to arrest her and commit her to the house of correction (where she appears in plate IV: see the dust jacket).

the campaign demanded the suppression of brothels because they contributed to the "daily increase of poor in the said parish" and caused "several great disorders and misdemeanors ... against the peace."[44] Moreover, the first society devoted to a reformation of manners (in Tower Hamlets) was formed in response to a royal proclamation for the apprehending of highway robbers. For the members of the first society, the suppression of bawdy houses was necessary, "as they are not only the nurseries of the most horrid vices, and sinks of the most filthy debaucheries, but also (as we suppose them) the common receptacles, or rather, dens, of notorious thieves, robbers, traitors and other criminals, that fly from public justice ... "[45] This reasoning reflects the

---

[44] WJ/SP/August 1689, no. 10.   [45] *Antimoixeia.*

common belief of the time that serious crime was the inevitable result of irreligion, immorality, and idleness, especially among the poor.[46]

Although by this logic all forms of irreligion and immorality should be eliminated, particular attention was focused on "lewd and disorderly" conduct because it was easily punished (in houses of correction), it was thought to contribute to poverty (as argued by the parish officers of St. Martin in the Fields), and the offences which were punished under this rubric were more directly linked with serious crime than other sins. Prostitution was associated in the public mind with the crime of picking pockets, and prostitutes were thought to associate with thieves generally. Begging, vagrancy, and unemployment ("idleness") were also thought to lead to theft.[47] Consequently, prosecutions for prostitution and "lewd and disorderly conduct" rose and fell to a certain extent with concerns about more serious crimes, concerns which were highest in the periods immediately following wars when soldiers were demobilized.[48] Thus, it may be the peace of 1697 which explains the high level of commitments to houses of correction by the reformers in the surviving accounts of 1700–02 (in comparison to the only previous surviving report, for 1693) and fears about crime following the Treaty of Utrecht in 1713 which caused the high levels of commitments in the ensuing decade (Table 9.1). In the same years, prosecutions for Sabbath offences declined.

As argued in chapter 7, people committed to houses of correction for offences like "lewd and disorderly" conduct were commonly committed on the basis of little evidence of wrongdoing; besides the fact that they were poor, lacked a proper job, and were found in suspicious circumstances such as loitering in the streets or in disorderly houses, especially late at night.[49] Such people were clearly viewed as potential criminals, and they were committed to houses of correction because it was believed that they posed a threat to public order. Contemporaries frequently complained that the societies punished the vices of the poor while leaving wealthy offenders undisturbed. As Daniel Defoe wrote in his *Review*, "the punishing vices in the poor, which are daily practised by the rich, seems to me to be setting our constitution with the wrong men upward, and making men criminals because they want money."[50] The reformers advanced numerous justifications for not punishing the rich, but few denied Defoe's charge. In his sermon to the societies in 1698, for example, John Shower "hope[d] that the punishment of meaner persons will so far influence

---

[46] Beattie, *Crime and the Courts*, pp. 421–22, 494–96, 624–25; MJ/OC/I, ff. 34–35 (July 10, 1718); MJ/SBB/408, p. 47 (Oct. 1683); 575, p. 46 (Aug. 1700).

[47] [John Dunton], *The Nightwalker* (Feb. 1697), preface; Timothy Nourse, *Compania Foelix; or, a Discourse of the Benefits and Improvements of Husbandry* (1700), p. 226; Roger North, *A Discourse Of the Poor* (1753 [written *c.* 1688]), p. 22.

[48] Beattie, *Crime and the Courts*, pp. 213–35.   [49] See above, section 7.2.

[50] [Daniel Defoe], *A Review of the Affairs of France*, I, no. 85 (26 Dec. 1704).

the greater sort, as to bring them to be more private, and less scandalous in their crimes."[51]

Not all people prosecuted by the reformers, however, were poor. While those committed to houses of correction were undoubtedly from the lower classes, many of those summarily fined were better off. Those convicted of profane swearing and cursing practiced a wide variety of occupations, while those accused of working on the Sabbath were typically victuallers and keepers of shops who sold food. Nevertheless, the accused tended to be of lower social status than the informers who prosecuted them. Although the known occupations of informers include a carpenter, two porters, and several tailors, most informers were more socially prestigious skilled craftsmen, such as a jeweller, a goldsmith, a master bookbinder, a locksmith, a perfumer, a brass turner, a cane chair maker, an engraver, an embroiderer, and a pewterer. Among the informers there were no victuallers, bakers, and fruiterers, trades which account for over half of the people accused of working on the Sabbath, and no servants, laborers, chairmen, watermen and related occupations, occupations which, along with victuallers and bakers, account for a third of those accused of profane swearing and cursing. Several higher status shopkeepers (chandlers, vintners, and grocers) were accused of working on the Sabbath, and some gentlemen and high status tradesmen and craftsmen were convicted of profane swearing and cursing, but the majority of the people prosecuted for these offences were engaged in relatively low status trades and crafts, occupations which were typically less socially prestigious than those practiced by their prosecutors.[52] In the case of working on the Sabbath, this pattern may well result from the fact that, like today, it was the keepers of food shops, whose jobs are typically low in status, who were most likely to open on Sunday. On the other hand, it seems unlikely that people engaged in lower status occupations were more inclined to swear and curse; it is more likely that artisans were unwilling to inform against swearers and cursers in occupations of

---

[51] John Shower, *A Sermon Preached to the Societies for the Reformation of Manners* (1698), p. 45. It was claimed that "greater people are punished in the afterlife," they were more susceptible to private admonishment, punishing them would "do more hurt than good," and in any case it was more desirable to punish *public* vices, which offended public decency and openly showed contempt for the laws (Laing MS, III, 394, p. 131; Disney, *An Essay*, p. 106; Isaacs, "Moral crime," pp. 167, 328, 349).

[52] For the occupations of the prosecuted, see Rawlinson MS D1396–1404; GLRO, WC/R1, pp. 167ff. There is little evidence on the identities and occupations of informers. These conclusions are based on a list of forty-seven informers compiled by A. G. Craig ("Movement for the reformation of manners," pp. 92–93), though for only a few of these informers is there evidence that they actually prosecuted Sabbath offences or swearing and cursing. Assessing the social status of occupations is notoriously difficult; I have been guided by the findings of V. B. Elliott, "Mobility and marriage in preindustrial England: a demographic and social structural analysis of geographic and social mobility and aspects of marriage, 1570–1690, with special reference to Middlesex, Kent, Essex, and Hertfordshire" (Ph.D. diss., Cambridge University, 1978), pp. 81, 132.

equivalent or higher status than themselves. In any case, whether the offence was prostitution, swearing or cursing, or working on the Sabbath, the evidence supports contemporary complaints that the reformers showed a marked inclination towards prosecuting their social inferiors.

9.2 JUDICIAL ATTITUDES TO THE CAMPAIGN

Despite their reluctance to prosecute the socially respectable, the reformers encountered opposition from many quarters, and one of the most important sources of criticism and obstruction was justices of the peace. Upon receipt of Queen Mary's letter of the 9th of July 1691, the Middlesex justices "unanimously" declared their willingness to execute the laws against vice.[53] The reformers quickly discovered, however, that many justices paid only lip service to their cause. Some justices, they complained, "put off, checked, and discouraged" people who attempted to inform against offenders.[54] Indeed, though they often misunderstood the motives of their opponents on the Middlesex bench, the reformers' complaints of judicial indifference and hostility to the campaign were well founded.

Evidence of judicial opposition to the campaign can be located first in patterns of judicial business and second in attempts by groups of justices to remove some of the most active supporters of the campaign from the commission of the peace. Judging from the number of cases of vice heard by each justice, many justices failed to encourage, and may even have discouraged, prosecutions. Even more than with other offences, prosecutions for vice were concentrated among a few active justices: in 1712, for example, six justices accounted for about half of the estimated 750 house of correction commitments for victimless offences (prostitution, nightwalking, loose, idle and disorderly conduct), and in 1707 only four justices issued 55% of the estimated 240 recognizances for vice. The societies' own records of summary prosecutions of Sabbath offences reveal even greater concentrations of judicial activity: two-thirds of the 1,548 cases prosecuted in 1707 were heard by only four justices. These figures suggest that the reformers' frequent complaints that many justices refused to cooperate with informers had some justification. (One reformer complained that informers were often forced to spend more than half a day traveling around town trying to find a justice who was willing to hear their accusations.)[55] In fact, the large number of magistrates who failed to act led Daniel Defoe to place the principal blame for the failure of the reformation of

[53] MJ/SBB/487, p. 78 (July 1691).
[54] [Edward Stephens], *The Beginning and Progress of a Needful and Hopeful Reformation* (1691), p. 14.
[55] Josiah Woodward, *An Account of the Rise and Progress of the Religious Societies in the City of London, etc. And of their Endeavours for a Reformation of Manners* (4th edn, 1712), p. 63. See also Laing MS III, 394, p. 256.

manners campaign on the justices' shoulders: "the greatest encouragement to vice, and obstruction to our reformation, lies in the negligence and evil example of our magistrates."[56]

Judicial opposition to the reformation of manners campaign was not confined to justices who stubbornly refused (or who could not be bothered) to accept informations and prosecute offenders. Some justices actively obstructed the reformers. Three times during the campaign, reforming justices in Middlesex were the subject of attempts by some of their fellow justices to have them dropped from the commission of the peace. An examination of the most influential of these cases, that involving justice Ralph Hartley, demonstrates not only the extent of judicial opposition to the campaign but also some of the motives of the justices who opposed the reformers.

Shortly after Queen Mary's letter was sent to the Middlesex justices in the summer of 1691, Ralph Hartley began to convict large numbers of alehouse keepers and shopkeepers for practicing their trades on Sunday. Over a period of two months in the autumn, he issued over 500 warrants of summary conviction for these offences.[57] In December, the Middlesex Bench petitioned the Lords Commissioners for his removal from the commission of the peace. According to the reformers,[58] Hartley was accused of convicting people without first summoning them to appear and defend themselves, and consequently there had been irregularities in at least two of the convictions. Moreover, he had heard cases in conjunction with Sir Richard Bulkeley, who was not a justice, in an office in Lincoln's Inn belonging to another non-justice, William Yates. It was alleged that Bulkeley had impersonated a justice and had directed the proceedings, and that informers who brought cases to other justices threatened those justices that if they refused to sign their warrants they would be reported to Bulkeley's office. Bulkeley had also printed, at his own expense, thousands of blank warrants for making convictions, as well as numerous copies of the July Middlesex sessions order against vice and he had distributed these throughout England. After meeting with some of the Middlesex justices, the Lords Commissioners approved their request to have Hartley removed from the commission. It took the reformers almost a year to recover from the loss of morale caused by Hartley's removal.[59]

Hartley's practices clearly had been sloppy, but did they merit his ejection from the Middlesex commission of the peace? In defence of Hartley and

---

[56] [Defoe], *Review of the Affairs of France*, no. 29 (10 May 1705).

[57] MJ/SBB/490, pp. 57–58 (Oct. 1691); Laing MS III, 394, pp. 315–22.

[58] It is impossible to identify the precise reasons the justices gave to the Lords Commissioners, since apparently no copy of the justices' petition to them survives.

[59] Craig, "Reformation of manners," pp. 41–47, 85–89; Laing MS III, 394, pp. 315–22 (reprinted in full in Craig, pp. 46–47); BL, Portland Loan, 29/185, f. 254; MJ/SBB/490, pp. 52, 57–58 (Oct. 1691), 491, pp. 50–51, 58 (Dec. 1691); [Fowler], *Vindication of a Late Undertaking*, pp. 15–18.

Bulkeley, the reformers argued that Hartley made so many convictions because other justices refused to accept accusations from informers, that the irregularities in the warrants were trivial (which they were), that he had only occasionally used the office in Lincoln's Inn, and that Bulkeley had not acted as if he were a justice.[60] A. G. Craig, who has analyzed this case most closely, suggests that Edward Stephens was right to conclude that the report of the Middlesex justices against Hartley was largely fabricated, and he implies that the justices who attacked Hartley were motivated by a desire to protect immoral behavior, possibly for financial gain.[61]

Some of the motivations for attacking Hartley were indeed improper: one of Hartley's fellow justices reacted vindictively when Hartley convicted and fined him for profane swearing at a justice's dinner![62] Hartley had a habit of convicting people of swearing or cursing in awkward circumstances: he convicted several persons during his appearance before the Lords Commissioners. One can easily imagine how such impolitic acts contributed to his downfall.[63] Another dubious motivation for removing Hartley, expressed by both the Middlesex justices and the Lords Commissioners, was the fear that if alehouse keepers were prosecuted too rigorously for permitting tippling on Sunday, the crown's excise revenues would suffer, and this would be a serious problem at a time when the nation was at war and the crown had recently lost so many other sources of income.[64] It is also possible that the Hartley affair had a party political dimension, in the sense that Hartley's enemies were Tories whose hostility to the societies was motivated by the participation of so many Whigs in the campaign.[65]

Despite these possible ulterior motives, Hartley's opponents were motivated primarily by substantial legal and philosophical objections to his behavior. Legally, the most important objection was that Hartley had convicted and sentenced offenders without first summoning them to appear before him to answer the accusations. This is the objection that was most frequently stated in the orders of the Middlesex court.[66] When an informer presented him with an information, Hartley simply examined the informer and if he felt a conviction was justified he issued a warrant to a constable to levy the fine by making a distress on one of the offender's possessions. Thus, the first the offender knew

---

[60] [Stephens], *Beginning and Progress*, pp. 16–17, 19, 27.

[61] *Ibid.*, p. 20; Craig, "Reformation of manners," pp. 44–45, 60–61.

[62] Craig, "Reformation of manners," pp. 54–55; Laing MS III, 394, pp. 197–203.

[63] Laing MS III, 394, p. 281.

[64] Craig, "Reformation of manners," p. 51; Portland Loan, 29/185, f. 254d; S. B. Baxter, *The Development of the Treasury 1660–1702* (1957), pp. 107–08. It was argued, implausibly, that the statute creating the excise had removed the power of justices to regulate alehouses, and therefore that Hartley had no powers to make convictions.

[65] I have been unable to find enough evidence about the political sympathies of the Middlesex justices to be able to substantiate this possibility.

[66] See, for example, MJ/SBB/491, pp. 60–61 (Dec.1691).

about the whole affair was when a constable showed up at his door to demand the payment of a fine, threatening to confiscate a silver spoon or some other household possession if the money was not forthcoming. Even then he may not have known the offence he was convicted of, since offences were not listed on Hartley's warrants of conviction.[67] It is hardly surprising that the Middlesex justices received several complaints about Hartley's behavior.

The Middlesex justices who investigated the case argued that making summary convictions for practicing one's trade on the Sabbath without summoning the offender was illegal. Since the relevant statute, 29 Car.2 c. 7, stated that working on the Sabbath was illegal, *except in cases of necessity or charity*, they argued that justices could not possibly make convictions without first ascertaining from the defendant whether the work was for necessity or charity. However, the legal situation concerning summoning defendants before making summary convictions was far more ambiguous than the Middlesex justices were willing to admit. The statutes which authorized summary convictions for vice did *not* state that the defendant had to be summoned. One of the posthumous editions of Dalton's Countrey Justice, citing a King's Bench ruling from the 1620s, stated that the defendant should be summoned and examined before justices made summary convictions for tippling or violating the assize of beer, because the defendant might have a good excuse or defence.[68] However, this ruling does not appear to have been very influential. Neither William Sheppard's manual for justices' clerks in 1660 nor Hugh Hare's charge to the Surrey sessions in 1692 states that offenders should be summoned in summary cases.[69] The King's Bench judges did not issue another ruling on this subject until 1703, when it was ruled that the defendant must be summoned. According to Chief Justice Holt, "where an act of parliament orders the offender should be convicted, that must be intended after summons, that he may have an opportunity of making his defence ... it is abominable to convict a man behind his back."[70] Subsequent decisions reinforced this ruling, and in 1745 it was embodied in a statute against swearing.[71] Although Hartley's opponents had a strong case, the issue does not appear to have been settled at that time.

Subsequent to the Hartley affair the reformers changed their practices and began to insure that defendants accused of working on the Sabbath were given

---

[67] MJ/SBB/491, p. 50 (Dec. 1691).
[68] Dalton, Countrey Justice (1677), pp. 27, 492, citing case determined by Sir Nicholas Hide, CJ.
[69] William Sheppard, The Justice of the Peace, His Clerk's Cabinet (1660), pp. 86–88; "A charge given by Hugh Hare, Esq., J. P., at the general quarter sessions for the county of Surrey, holden at Dorking, 5 April 1692," Surrey Archaeological Collections 12 (1895), p. 117.
[70] R. vs. Dyer, in Thomas Leach, Modern Reports, 12 vols., 5th edn (1793–96), vol. 6, p. 41; A Report of all the Cases Determined by Sir John Holt (1738), p. 157; William Salkeld, Reports of Cases Adjudged in the Court of King's Bench, 3 vols., 6th edn (1795), vol. 1, p. 181.
[71] 19 Geo. 2 c. 21.

a chance to defend themselves before they were convicted. Gradually, they appear to have extended this practice to other offences.[72] However, another thorny issue remained unsettled: should the identity of the informer be revealed to the accused, and should the defendant be allowed to confront and cross-examine him? Despite a sessions ruling that informers should be identified to their defendants,[73] after the Hartley affair died down a group of Middlesex justices sympathetic to the campaign privately resolved that they would not call in the informer to face the accused "unless it shall be necessary," and even then they would not reveal his name or habitation "unless that also be necessary."[74] This was another area of legal ambiguity; the earliest relevant King's Bench case appears to be a conviction for keeping a lottery office in 1745, when it was held that the defendant should be confronted with the full evidence against him, even if the witness was not present.[75]

Justices sympathetic to the reformers wanted to protect the identities of informers so as to prevent them from being attacked. Informers were certainly often subject to public ridicule and violent assaults. In the course of the investigation of Hartley's convictions the names of his informers and the place where they met was revealed. Apparently, some opponents of the campaign directed press masters to the meetings of these informers in the hope that they would be carried off to sea.[76] From the point of view of the informers, the requirement that defendants should be allowed to confront them was simply a means of discouraging informations. But from a legal standpoint, the Middlesex justices were ahead of their time in attempting to introduce some procedural safeguards into summary jurisdiction by requiring the appearance of both the defendant and the informer before the justice at the same time. The frequent complaints during the campaign about corrupt and extortionate informers and constables certainly suggest that such safeguards were necessary.

Another objection to Hartley's practices, stated by both the Middlesex justices and the Lords Commissioners, was that he convicted offenders who lived out of his own division.[77] In fact, Hartley did not live in the county at all – he lived in the City of London – but he convicted people who lived all over the metropolis.[78] To this accusation the reformers replied that by law a justice's

---

[72] Laing MS III, 394, pp. 307, 415–20. SPCK, Papers of Moment, p. 96, suggests that this practice was only gradually adopted, especially for other offences.
[73] MJ/SBB/490, p. 52 (Oct. 1691).　　[74] Laing MS III, 394, pp. 415–20.
[75] John Strange, Reports of Adjudged Cases in the Courts of Chancery, King's Bench, Common Pleas and Exchequer, 2 vols., 3rd edn (1795), vol. 2, p. 1240. Subsequently, it was ruled that the witness or informer must be present when the defendant was confronted with the evidence, so that the defendant could have the opportunity of cross-examining the witness (James Burrow, Reports of Cases Argued and Adjudged in the Courts of King's Bench, 5 vols., 5th edn [1812], vol. 2, p. 1163).
[76] BL, Portland Loan, 29/186, f. 11.
[77] MJ/SBB/490, p. 52 (Oct. 1691); [Fowler], Vindication of a Late Undertaking, p. 18.
[78] Laing MS III, 394, pp. 315–22.

commission applied to the entire county, and of course they were right.[79] Once again, however, Hartley was unwittingly caught up in changing legal requirements. With the growing administrative and judicial powers of justices acting outside sessions, and with the growing number of petty sessions handling that business,[80] the Middlesex court at this time began restricting the justices' powers of acting outside their local area.

There were precedents for such restrictions, but they were not directly relevant. Justices were already accustomed to restricting some of their administrative activities, such as licensing alehouses, to their own division.[81] Moreover, in 1672 an order of the Middlesex bench required that persons apprehended by the night watch could only be bailed or discharged by justices from the division in which they were apprehended.[82] Nevertheless, administrative duties and hearing the cases of persons apprehended by the watch were not equivalent to hearing and determining summary convictions. Significantly, although the Middlesex justices berated Hartley for making summary convictions outside his division, the Bench issued no formal order against this specific practice until 1716. According to this order, which was ordered to be printed in the *London Gazette* and which was repeated by the Westminster sessions in 1725, justices were not to convict persons living out of their division for selling drink on Sundays or in short or unsealed measures, or for similar offences because the justices often did not know "the true character and credit" of the informers or the persons they accused. (Consequently, it was alleged that "several undue convictions had been made."[83]) This order attacked not only Hartley's practice of hearing cases from outside his division, but also the reformer's strategy of using informers who lived at a distance from the persons they accused as a means of preventing reprisals.[84] While the reformers were trying to depersonalize the process of summary conviction, the court attempted to keep convictions a local affair, in which the justices knew the parties involved.

It is doubtful whether the justices' orders restricting the activities of justices outside their divisions had the force of law.[85] In 1720, three justices were summoned to explain to the Middlesex Bench why they had issued warrants against several persons who lived outside their division, requiring those persons to appear before them at their local vestries. We do not know what offences these warrants were for, but it is possible that they concerned vice since all three of the justices, Nathaniel Blackerby, Thomas Boteler, and Thomas Railton, were active supporters of the reformation of manners

---

[79] [Stephens], *Beginning and Progress*, p. 22.
[80] Shoemaker, "Crime, courts and community," pp. 50–58, 561–63.
[81] Dowdell, *Quarter Sessions*, pp. 8–10, 34, 90–92.   [82] MJ/SBB/288, p. 22 (Feb. 1672).
[83] MJ/OC/I, f. 14 (Oct. 1716); MJ/SP/Dec. 1716, nos. 44, 45, 47; WJ/OC/II, ff. 24–27 (Oct. 1725).
[84] Craig, "Reformation of manners," pp. 85–86, citing Laing MS III, 394, pp. 329–58.
[85] Webbs, *The Parish and the County*, pp. 393–95; Landau, *Justices of the Peace*, pp. 28–29.

campaign. Although an order of the court threatened these justices with a complaint to the Lord Chancellor,[86] it is not surprising that no further action was taken against them. Blackerby was the future author of manuals for justices of the peace[87] and he no doubt pointed out to his colleagues that the requirement that justices limit their activities to their own division had no legal authority. In 1725, the societies still allowed informers to work outside their own local areas.[88] On legal grounds, this objection to Hartley's behavior had less merit than the objection that he failed to summon defendants before convicting them.

Regardless of the legal issues, one can see in the justices' reactions to Hartley's practices a desire to protect the flexibility and independence of justices to administer the law as they saw fit in their own neighborhoods. Justices were often more concerned with maintaining their reputations in their local community than with enforcing laws rigorously, and in any case many justices preferred to enforce the law through negotiation and mediation than through systematic punishments.[89] In 1696, Middlesex justice Edward Chamberlayne claimed that the poor frequently brought their complaints to him because "I never treated any roughly and insultingly but endeavoured reconciliation and saving charges."[90] Chamberlayne appears to have made no commitments to the house of correction in 1697, the first year of complete calendars in Middlesex.[91] The contrast between Chamberlayne's approach to his office as a mediator and the reformers' attempt to punish offenders systematically could not have been greater. From the point of view of justices like Chamberlayne, the informers used by the Societies for the Reformation of Manners constituted an unwanted intrusion into their local affairs. Informers were usually only interested in punishment, not negotiation, and when one justice refused to convict they took their prosecutions to a more sympathetic one.[92]

Such concerns provide the context for an incident in 1721, when justice John Ellis angrily confronted two active reformation of manners informers near Drury Lane after they had helped some officers apprehend several "lewd" and "disorderly" women, at the instigation of three other justices. With a large mob of people in attendance, Ellis threatened to nail one of the informers to the

---

[86] MJ/SP/Sept. 1720, no. 35; MJ/OC/I, f. 107 (9 Sept. 1720). Railton's name was not included in the final order of the court.

[87] Nathaniel Blackerby, *The Justice of the Peace his Companion, or a Summary of all the Acts of Parliament, whereby ... Justices of the Peace ... are Authorized to Act ... Begun by Samuel Blackerby ... and Continued ... by Nathaniel Blackerby* (1723); Nathaniel Blackerby, *The Second Part of the Justice of Peace his Companion; or, Cases in Law (Wherein Justices of Peace have a Jurisdiction)* (1734).

[88] SPCK, Papers of Moment, p. 96.   [89] See above, sections 4.1 and 8.4.

[90] MJ/SP/Sept 1696, no. 29.

[91] This finding is based on a 50% sample of the 1697 Middlesex house of correction commitments.

[92] Laing MS, III, 394, p. 256.

pillory by his ears, claiming that he and justice Milner "had always strived to keep these fellows out of the parish." He then told some constables to carry the two informers to prison if they ever saw either of them in the parish again.[93] It is unlikely that Ellis' motives in this incident were simply to undermine the prosecution of vice, since both he and Milner were active at other times in encouraging vice prosecutions.[94] Rather, Ellis appears to have been concerned to protect his authority and reputation with the inhabitants of his parish, as represented by the mob that harassed these informers. It must have been sentiments like Ellis and Chamberlayne's concerns to protect their positions in their local neighborhoods which led Hartley's opponents to assert that his zealous practices had rendered "magistracy itself uneasy to the people."[95] Given the substantial popular hostility to the reformers in some neighborhoods, it was in the interest of justices who wished to maintain their local credibility to distance themselves from the reformation of manners campaign. (It is significant that both Ellis and Chamberlayne appear to have been competing with other justices for authority in their neighborhoods.) Since Hartley lived in the City, he did not have a local community to which he felt responsible. In fact he had little other experience dealing with people as a justice: he participated in no other sessions business and he issued only one recognizance in 1690 and 1691.[96]

The conflict with Hartley may thus have been not so much over whether to prosecute vice as over *how* to prosecute vice. Hartley's opponents on the Middlesex bench did not object to the prosecution of vice *per se*, but they clearly favored mediation rather than punishment: while they issued about a hundred recognizances for vice offences in 1693, they failed to commit a single defendant to the house of correction for a victimless offence. In contrast, Hartley's supporters issued fewer recognizances for vice, but they committed over a hundred defendants to the Westminster house of correction for victimless offences.[97] Clearly, Hartley's opponents were inclined to give offenders a chance to mend their ways instead of punishing them. Similarly, some of the justices who supported the campaign in later years adopted a more lenient line than Hartley. In the register books of accusations kept by the

---

93 MJ/SP/Aug. 1721, no. 5.
94 Milner was active on four justices' committees concerned with encouraging the prosecution of vice between 1718 and 1725. Ellis was involved on at least one such committee, and he signed several recognizances and commitments to houses of correction for vice offences in 1721. Because there was also a Westminster justice of the same name it is difficult to determine the precise number of prosecutions the Middlesex Ellis presided over, as well as whether the Middlesex Ellis should be credited with membership of one other committee.
95 MJ/SBB/491, pp. 60–61 (Dec. 1691).
96 He did, however, attend most meetings of sessions during those years: MJ/SBB/471–491 (Jan. 1690–Dec. 1691).
97 The Middlesex house of correction calendars do not survive for 1693. The 1693 estimates are based on samples: 20% of the recognizances, 50% of the house of correction commitments.

societies, some justices often released persons who were accused of profaning the Sabbath on the promise that they would reform their ways.[98] It is unlikely that Hartley ever discharged offenders on promise of reformation since he never summoned them to appear before him in the first place. In any case, the sheer number of convictions recorded by Hartley prevented him from judging the character of many of the informers, let alone the alleged offenders, he dealt with.

It is likely that some of the people Hartley convicted had first been brought before another justice who had refused to convict the accused. If that justice had not merely refused to hear the case, but had determined that the evidence was insufficient, or that it was better to warn the offender rather than convict him, then Hartley could not hear the case without interfering in another justice's affairs. If Hartley did act in this manner, the hostility towards him becomes even more understandable. Clearly summary jurisdiction could not work if prosecutors could take cases to as many justices as was necessary until they obtained a conviction. As we have seen, the Middlesex justices were quite sensitive on this issue of interference in each other's affairs, an issue which cropped up most frequently when justices bailed prisoners who had been committed to prison or the house of correction by another justice.[99] Because such practices threatened to undermine the justices' authority outside sessions, justices who interfered in each other's business were very unpopular on the Middlesex bench.

Whatever the real motives of the judicial opponents of the reformation of manners campaign, the Hartley affair suggests that one of the most effective methods of attacking the reformers was to raise legal objections to their tactics. In addition to the questions raised by Hartley's behavior, three other important legal issues played central roles in conflicts involving the reformers: the extent of constables' powers to arrest people for "loose, idle and disorderly" conduct, the validity of search warrants, and the conflicting jurisdictions of quarter sessions and the court of burgesses in Westminster.

In the early eighteenth century the reformers punished more than a thousand people per year in houses of correction in London for prostitution and "lewd and disorderly" conduct. By using houses of correction so extensively, the reformers entered another legal quagmire, since, as noted in chapter 2, the statutes that authorized the building of houses of correction failed to specify with any precision the range of offences punishable there, beyond stating that houses of correction were to be used for the punishment of rogues, vagabonds, and "idle and disorderly persons."[100] At least four of the reformers' commitments for idle and disorderly conduct were reviewed by King's Bench. The first

[98] Bodleian Library, Rawlinson MS D1399–1404.   [99] See above, section 8.4.
[100] See above, section 2.5.

two cases were decided against the reformers and the second two in their favor. In 1701, a commitment to New Prison by the reforming justice John Perry was quashed because merely being apprehended in a bawdy house at a "seasonable" (i.e., not late) hour was deemed insufficient grounds for commitment to either New Prison or a house of correction as an idle and disorderly person.[101] In 1709, the reformers were dealt a more serious setback during the trial of three men for the murder of an active supporter of the campaign, John Dent. Dent was killed in a scuffle with three soldiers after a constable, Samuel Bray, had apprehended Anne Dickens in Covent Garden for being an "idle woman" (or a "disorderly woman," or a "nightwalker" – reports differ). It was questioned whether the soldiers should be convicted of murder or manslaughter. Led by Chief Justice Holt, the court ruled that it was manslaughter because there was no legitimate reason for arresting Dickens. The constables had justified the arrest by stating that she had previously been convicted and was found in a street that prostitutes were known to frequent, but the judges ruled that these were insufficient grounds for a constable to commit a woman to prison on suspicion of prostitution – "there must be some fact done." In a lengthy peroration, Holt invoked the Magna Carta in arguing that the soldiers had been provoked to murder Dent: "If a man is oppressed by an officer of justice, under a mere pretence of an authority, that is a provocation to all the people in England."[102]

Needless to say, this case was very demoralizing for the reformers, both because Dent had been a long-time active supporter of the campaign, as a constable and as an informer, and because Holt appeared to set new standards of evidence for punishing prostitutes and loose, idle, and disorderly people. But if this case is examined more closely, it becomes clear that this ruling did not in fact reduce the powers of *justices* in punishing people for these offences. Holt simply ruled that people like Dickens who were suspected of being "lewd and disorderly" could only be apprehended by constables who had a warrant for their arrest, and they could only be committed to houses of correction after they had been brought before a justice. The only restrictions imposed by Holt's ruling were that constables could not make arrests and commitments for suspicion of lewd and disorderly conduct on their own initiative, and constables could not act outside their own parishes.[103] These decisions do not

---

101 Robert, Lord Raymond, *Reports of Cases Argued and Adjudged in the Courts of King's Bench*, 3 vols., 4th edn (1790–92), p. 699; *Report of all the Cases Determined by Sir John Holt*, p. 406.

102 *A Looking-Glass for Informing Constables: Represented in the Tryals ... for the Murder of Mr. John Dent* (3rd. edn, 1733), p. 6; *Report of all the Cases Determined by Sir John Holt*, pp. 485–92. See also above, section 7.2.

103 *Report of all the Cases Determined by Sir John Holt*, pp. 489–90; BL, Add. MS 35,979, ff. 68–69; 35,994, ff. 95d, 96d; Leach, *Modern Reports*, vol. 11, pp. 246, 249. It had become accepted practice for constables to make arrests outside their parishes – a practice that clearly benefitted the reformers, who could not count on the presence of a sympathetic constable in every parish.

appear to have adversely affected the reformation of manners campaign: with the exception of the Westminster house of correction in 1709, commitments to both the Middlesex and Westminster houses of correction increased significantly over the next decade, and the number of prosecutions for "lewd and disorderly" conduct in the societies' reports remained high.[104] Although Middlesex and Westminster constables lost some of their powers, constables in the City of London continued to have greater powers due to the "customs of London": City constables could act throughout the City, and they could make commitments for suspicious behavior on their own initiative. These customs were upheld by a King's Bench decision favorable to the reformers in 1717.[105] The reformers received further encouragement in 1731, when, in the midst of a campaign against vice in St. Martin in the Fields, a King's Bench ruling further upheld the powers of justices of the peace to commit idle and disorderly persons to houses of correction.[106]

From these rulings, it does not appear that the King's Bench judges were particularly hostile to the reformation of manners campaign. It is often said that Chief Justice Holt was a bitter enemy of the reformers,[107] but his decisions suggest that he was more even-handed. In the case of the murder of the reforming constable John Cooper, Holt interpreted the law favorably for the reformers. Although there was no evidence to prove who had actually committed the murder, Holt argued that all of the participants in the riotous assault on the constable should be convicted of murder, not manslaughter.[108] On the whole, it appears that Holt's objections to the reformers arose primarily from the legal issues raised by their innovative practices. In the ruling on the case of Dent's killers he said,

I like a religious zeal for reformation very well, but let this zeal be according to knowledge and consistent with the laws of our country, not furious and mistaken. No man ought to think himself so far more righteous than his neighbours as to enter into such voluntary societies for reformation of manners, as contradict our laws and endanger our rights and liberties.[109]

The Dent case established that outside the City of London constables could not make arrests for suspicious behavior without a warrant. But how specific

---

[104] See above, section 3.3 and Table 9.1. The societies' accounts for their activities do not survive for the years 1710–14.

[105] John Strype, *A Survey of the Cities of London and Westminster ... by John Stow*, 2 vols. (1720), vol. 2, bk 5, chap. 3, p. 32, citing a case from February 1717 between some reformation constables and Ingram on an action of imprisonment.

[106] Leach, *Modern Reports*, vol. 11, p. 415; MJ/OC/II, ff. 101d–105d (April 1731).

[107] Craig, "Reformation of manners," p. 124. [Richard Steele *et al.*], *The Tatler*, 14 (1709), cited by Sir John Campbell in *The Lives of the Chief Justices of England* (1849–57), vol. 2, p. 172; Speaker Onslow's comments in Gilbert Burnet, *History of His Own Time* (1724–34; Hildesheim, 1969), vol. 5, p. 18.

[108] *Report of all the Cases Determined by Sir John Holt*, p. 484.

[109] BL, Add. MS 35,994, f. 99.

did such warrants need to be? This question was raised when a single warrant was used to arrest hundreds of people over a period of several months in 1725. On April 28th, two Westminster justices, Henry Harpur and John Troughton, issued a warrant to the constables of Westminster to search the coffee house of Mary Ealey alias Shase in Charing Cross (where, it was alleged, loose, idle, and disorderly persons were entertained), and "all other houses ... that you shall suspect such disorderly persons as well men as women to be harbour'd or entertained in." The constables were also directed to apprehend all "persons strolling in the streets at an unseasonable hour and giving no good account of themselves" and bring everyone they apprehended before a justice of the peace to be examined. In the subsequent five months, Sampson Cooke and other constables used this warrant to search several houses and taverns and make numerous arrests. According to a report by a committee of justices appointed to investigate the case, on the authority of this warrant between July and October Henry Harpur committed 169 people to the Westminster house of correction and 10 people to the Gatehouse prison, and he caused 45 people to be bound over by recognizance. Upon hearing the report at their October sessions, the Westminster justices resolved that "the granting the warrant mentioned in the report in the general manner it appears to be framed and the not making it returnable or calling for a return thereof in due time, but suffering the same to be so many months in the hands of the constable was irregular and illegal."[110]

Like Hartley's case, this dispute arose because supporters of the reformation of manners used conventional legal procedures to prosecute an unconventionally large number of offenders in a short period of time. When prosecutions for vice by other reforming constables and justices are added to those initiated by Cooke and Harpur, the reformers' prosecutions constituted a large proportion of Westminster's criminal business in 1725: 17% of all the recognizances to appear at the October sessions, and 55% of the commitments to the house of correction in the month of July.[111] And like Hartley's case, while this report can be interpreted as an attack on the reformation of manners campaign, there was also an important legal issue at stake – the validity of "general warrants." These warrants, which did not specify the identity of the person to be arrested but instead authorized constables to arrest all persons who were suspected of a particular type of offence, were, needless to say, very useful to the reformers. But were they legal? Based on a case from the reign of Charles I, Matthew Hale declared that general warrants for searching for felons or stolen goods were illegal, on the grounds that such a warrant gave too much discretion to "a

---

[110] WJ/SP/Oct. 1725, nos. 5–7; WJ/OC/II, ff. 21–23 (Oct. 1725).
[111] MJ/SR/2450 (Oct. 1725). The house of correction calendar survives only for the period from 26 June to 1 August.

common officer" in choosing which houses to search and whom to arrest.[112] A sample warrant of this kind was, however, included in a late seventeenth-century edition of Dalton's *Countrey Justice*.[113] General warrants issued by secretaries of state to search for the authors and publishers of seditious papers were also technically illegal after the expiration of the licensing act in 1695, but they continued to be used until they were definitively ruled illegal in the John Wilkes affair in the 1760s.[114] Despite these doubts about their validity for felons and the publishers of seditious words, general warrants to arrest certain types of petty offenders were apparently still legal in the early eighteenth century: warrants to search for rogues, vagabonds, and sturdy beggars were authorized by the vagrancy statute of 12 Anne, and constables did not even need warrants to arrest nightwalkers and men and women found together in bawdy houses.[115]

The Westminster justices skirted these legal issues when they ruled simply that general warrants had to be issued with a specific return date. Nevertheless, the legality of general search warrants was hotly contested at this time: as early as 1719 William Cowper complained in his charge to the Westminster sessions that officers frequently refused to execute such warrants, "believing them to be illegal."[116] In 1728 and again in 1730 the Westminster justices petitioned the secretary of state for financial help for constables who were subjected to vexatious suits "for executing warrants to search night cellars and other disorderly houses ... where felons and other disorderly persons frequently resort, and in apprehending such persons; whereby the said constables have been put to great expense and charges, which has discouraged and deterred them from doing their duty."[117] It was presumably the fact that suspected felons were arrested in such searches which provided grounds for challenging their legal validity; the fact that justices continued to issue search warrants to apprehend unidentified rogues, beggars, idle and disorderly persons, and the keepers of disorderly houses suggests that the justices' powers to issue general warrants for the arrest of petty offenders remained intact.[118] Even with the promise of royal help, however, the tremendous cost and inconvenience of

---

[112] Matthew Hale, *Historia Placitorum Coronae* ([1676] 1736), vol. 1, p. 580 and vol. 2, pp. 114 and 150, citing a case from 1648 where a warrant of justice Swalowe was reviewed by justice Roll. See also Hawkins, *Pleas of the Crown*, vol. 2, c. 13, s.10, 17–19.

[113] Dalton, *Countrey Justice* (1677), c. 169, p. 482.

[114] William Holdsworth, *A History of English Law*, 12 vols. (1923–1972), vol. 10, pp. 659–71; S. J. Lewis, "An instrument of the new constitution: the origins of the general warrant," *Journal of Legal History* 7 (1986), pp. 269–72.

[115] Joseph Shaw, *The Practical Justice of Peace: or a Treatise Showing the Power and Authority of all its Branches*, 2 vols. (1728), vol. 1, pp. 322, 326, 351 and vol. 2, p. 54.

[116] William Cowper, *The Charge of William Cowper, Esq., to the Grand Jury of the City and Liberty of Westminster ... October the 7th, 1719* (1719), pp. 29–31.

[117] WJ/OC/II, ff. 69d–70 (26 Oct. 1728), 87–87d (July 1730), and 89–89d (Aug. 1730); MJ/OC/III, f. 157d (Nov. 1729).

[118] MJ/OC/III, f. 266 (Dec. 1730); WJ/OC/II, ff. 101d–105d (April 1731).

fighting such lawsuits must have discouraged many constables and supporters of the reformation of manners campaign, and it appears that the Westminster justices' investigation of general warrants in 1725 crystallized their discontent. The number of prosecutions initiated by the reformers of prostitutes and other "lewd and disorderly" persons dropped by more than half in 1726 and never again approached the 1725 level.[119] A staple tool of the reformers, the warrant to search the streets and disorderly houses for vice offenders had been seriously damaged by legal uncertainties.

The final legal issue raised during the reformation of manners campaign concerned the overlapping jurisdictions in Westminster of the court of burgesses and justices of the peace. This issue came to a head in the early 1720s when a group of justices began a concerted campaign against gaming houses in Covent Garden. The campaign rapidly ran into opposition, and some of the opponents were once again justices of the peace themselves. Although an important legal issue was at stake, this time the motives of the opposing justices also appear to have been blatantly improper: it was alleged that some of the justices actually owned the houses in which gambling parlors were located, which they let at rents three times the market rate. Justices were also accused of being gamblers themselves. These justices (four were named) allegedly obstructed their colleagues by persuading constables not to execute warrants issued by other justices, warning the gaming houses when they were about to be raided, and even advising persons who wished to bring vexatious suits against the constables who did act.[120]

The justices who undermined the campaign against gaming houses, however, may also have been motivated by a legitimate concern: to protect the business heard by the Westminster court of burgesses from interference by quarter sessions. Both courts had jurisdiction over cases of nuisance and regulatory offences, and in the early eighteenth century the burgesses' court heard many more such cases, including cases involving gaming houses and bawdy houses, than the Westminster sessions.[121] Because of the notorious corruption of some of the burgesses' court officers, in the early 1720s the Westminster sessions attempted to usurp some of the court's powers, and the gaming house campaign was one of their first efforts towards that end. No doubt the considerable opposition the justices encountered, not only from their fellow justices but also from the officers of the burgesses' court, encouraged the reforming justices to probe further, and in December 1722 the Middlesex court appointed a committee (full of reforming justices) to investigate "by what

---

[119] Unfortunately, the societies' reports do not list the number of prosecutions for each offence between 1725 and 1729 (Table 9.1). Given that the societies' work by this point was dominated by prosecutions of prostitutes and other "lewd and disorderly" persons, however, the decline of the total number of prosecutions after 1725 must have been largely the result of a significant decrease in this category of offences.

[120] PRO, SP 35/27/56 (July 1721); *An Account of the Endeavours.*   [121] See above, chap. 2.

authority or pretence" the court of burgesses levied fines, appointed scavengers, and collected money "on pretence of cleaning the streets."[122]

Justices sympathetic to the burgesses' case, therefore, may have believed that, because the burgesses' court was under threat, it was necessary to undermine the campaign against gaming houses orchestrated by sessions. Considerations of personal gain and their own local reputation, however, cannot have been far from these justices' minds. Presentments of gaming houses at the burgesses' court were quite profitable, and the high bailiff had worked out a cosy relationship with the keepers in which the keepers were fined for keeping annoyances, but significant portions of the fines were remitted and the keepers were able to keep their houses open.[123] In addition to their rental income, some justices may well have received a portion of the profits from these fines. These justices may also have tolerated gaming houses as a means of protecting their reputation in their local neighborhoods – many of the residents of places like Drury Lane and Covent Garden depended on these houses for their livelihoods, and a justice hostile to gaming houses would have been unpopular in these neighborhoods.[124]

Unlike the laws concerning felonies, the laws surrounding the prosecution of misdemeanors, especially summary conviction, were still in many respects ill-defined during this period and the reformers were victims of a long trend in which the powers of justices of the peace were becoming more precisely delineated in the seventeenth and eighteenth centuries. The sheer scale of the reformers' activities meant that the questions of legal procedure which were raised could no longer be avoided, especially in London, where numerous "Old Bailey solicitors" encouraged malicious lawsuits against officers and justices whenever permitted by ambiguities in the law.[125] The justices who opposed the reformers may not always have been preoccupied with the finer points of the law, but as we have seen such legal questions often provided useful tools for attacking the reformers. Probably of more concern to the opposing justices, however, was the reformers' strategy of systematically prosecuting offenders without regard to the individual circumstances of each case, a strategy which threatened to undermine individual justices' powers of discretion and flexi-

---

122 PRO, SP 35/27/56; *London Journal*, 13 January 1721; Cowper, *Charge*, p. 36; Ryder, *Charge*, p. 26; MJ/SP/Dec. 1722, no. 52; WJ/SP/Oct. 1722, no. 1; PRO, KB1/1 (Hilary, 1721); *The Case of the Inhabitants of the Liberty of Westminster against the Clauses proposed by the Justices of the Peace, to a Bill now Passing, to Require Quarantine* [1721]; Westminster City Archives, WCB 7 (30 June 1724); Sydney and Beatrice Webb, *English Local Government from the Revolution to the Municipal Corporations Act: The Manor and the Borough* (1908), pp. 224–27.
123 BL, Add. MS 35,601, ff. 260–62; Westminster City Archives, WCB3. At a meeting in 1721 the presentments resulted in £900 of fines, most of which were from gaming houses (*London Journal*, 13 January 1721/2).
124 See below, section 10.3.
125 Thomas DeVeil, *Observations on the Practice of a Justice of the Peace* (1747).

bility in enforcing the law. As was particularly evident from the riot led by justice John Ellis near Drury Lane, justices sought to protect their powers to govern their local neighborhoods on their own terms. These justices also sought to protect the reputation of the commission of the peace as a whole, both from the general unpopularity of the reformation of manners campaign and from the allegations of corruption which were so frequently levelled at reforming justices.[126] Thus, the Westminster justices who investigated the general warrants case claimed that the reformers' use of such warrants led "to the great reproach and dishonour of the commission of the peace,"[127] a concern which was also expressed by justice Hartley's opponents.

This concern was most evident in the case of another reforming justice who was the subject of a letter to the Lord Chancellor requesting his removal from the commission of the peace. Justice John Fuller, an active supporter of the campaign, was justifiably outraged when the Lord Chancellor's secretary and several Westminster justices interfered with his attempts to prevent "interludes" from being performed in Moorfields during Easter week in 1717. (Like many of the reformers, Fuller believed that the theater directly promoted vice.) After the Westminster justices ordered constables not to execute Fuller's orders and then discharged two players whom Fuller had committed to the house of correction, Fuller lost his temper and published an angry account of the incident in the *Flying Post*. At the subsequent sessions, the Middlesex justices closed ranks and unanimously passed a resolution declaring Fuller's article "a false, scandalous and malicious libel ... highly reflecting upon several justices therein named and the whole commission of the peace ... " and decided to try to get Fuller removed from the commission (the attempt was unsuccessful).[128] The justices were generally concerned to prevent interference in each other's affairs, and Fuller's grievances may well have received a more sympathetic hearing from his colleagues had he not publicized the dispute. Like many of the reforming justices, Fuller's principles were stronger than his political instincts, and his refusal to discuss the case in private must have alienated his colleagues. The justices had enough of an image problem without having their dirty linen washed in public.

In response to the considerable opposition they encountered, reforming justices developed strategies of prosecution which minimized the possibility of conflict with their colleagues. By using summary convictions instead of recognizances and indictments, reforming justices were able to hear cases individually without being exposed to the scrutiny of their opponents at quarter sessions.

---

126 Webb and Webb, *The Parish and the County*, p. 335.   127 WJ/SP/Oct. 1725, no. 6.
128 MJ/SP/April 1717, nos. 73–83; Hertfordshire Record Office, Panshanger MS, D/EP/F57, F157; *The Flying Post or the Post Master* 3948 (23–25 April 1717); Lionel K. J. Glassey, *Politics and the Appointment of Justices of the Peace 1675–1720* (Oxford, 1979), p. 255.

Opposing justices could also be excluded from petty sessions, where reforming justices frequently met to hear cases, issue warrants, and formulate strategies. Technically, any meeting of two or more justices (if one was a member of the quorum) to handle criminal or administrative matters was a sessions; aside from formal meetings of quarter sessions these meetings could occur whenever "it shall please the justices themselves or any two of them."[129] During this period petty sessions (also known as "private" or "special" sessions) occurred with increasing frequency, especially in the metropolitan parts of Middlesex, as a result of the justices' need to conduct some of their growing burden of local administrative and judicial business outside quarter sessions.[130] Most areas of the county had regularly scheduled petty sessions during this period, but other meetings of local justices occurred irregularly. In fact, petty sessions were held so frequently and so irregularly that the Middlesex court complained twice that parish officers were "often required to appear at several places at one and the same time."[131]

Since petty sessions were so unorganized, reforming justices had no trouble establishing their own sessions for promoting the prosecution of vice. Shortly after the start of the campaign, the *Athenian Mercury* reported that "a petty sessions is held weekly in Bloomsbury court house and Hicks Hall, by a number of worthy justices, for the conviction of [vice] offenders; and the like is beginning to be set up in the Liberty of Westminster."[132] Evidence of the results of such meetings comes from house of correction calendars: in Westminster in 1693 one-quarter of all the commitments in the house of correction sample were made from petty sessions; 85% for victimless offences such as prostitution and loose, idle, and disorderly conduct. The most active of these groups, justices meeting at the St. Martin's vestry, started committing prostitutes to the house of correction in 1690, before any of the societies was founded, and continued to commit prostitutes and related offenders for more than twenty years. Other places from which justices acting in petty sessions committed large numbers of prostitutes and related offenders include the parishes of St. James and St. Anne in Westminster (also meeting at the vestries), Holborn, and the east end.[133] Such commitments could of course be made by a single justice, but given the unpopularity of the reformation of manners campaign the added authority of a group of justices was no doubt useful when

---

[129] Bond, *Complete Guide*, p. 250; Joseph Keble, *Assistance to Justices of Peace for the Easier Performance of their Duty* (1683), p. 370, citing Lambard's *Eirenarcha*.

[130] Shoemaker, "Crime, courts and community," p. 244 and Appendix One; Webb and Webb, *The Parish and the County*, pp. 396–411; Fletcher, *Reform in the Provinces*, pp. 122–35.

[131] MJ/SBB/628, p. 60 (April 1705); MJ/SP/Feb. 1716, no. 6.

[132] *Athenian Mercury* 3:3 (4 August 1691).

[133] For examples, see the house of correction calendars on the following sessions rolls: MJ/SR/ 2268, 2371, 2376 (April, July and Oct. 1716), and, for St. Martin's in the Fields, MJ/SR/1754 (April 1690); 1883 (Jan. 1697); 2037 (Oct. 1704); 2187 (July 1712).

ordering constables to apprehend offenders and carry them to a house of correction.[134]

In the 1720s, justices used petty sessions to organize their campaigns against the keepers and frequenters of gaming houses and other "disorderly houses." In 1720–22, in response to stiff resistance to their attempts to close gaming houses, a group of reforming justices in Westminster met secretly in order to prevent their plans for arresting gamblers from being revealed. In 1723, twenty-six justices "entered into a society to suppress gaming houses in the Liberty of Westminster and the County of Middlesex," which they called "a convention." Subsequent campaigns against disorderly houses in 1728 and 1730–31 also involved petty sessions. As the Middlesex court resolved in 1728, the "most effective means of suppressing" gaming houses and other disorderly houses was for the court to appoint "a committee of justices" who were expected to report back to sessions. Indeed, groups of justices meeting privately could achieve impressive short-term successes, at least in terms of the number of vice offenders arrested.[135]

Using summary jurisdiction and petty sessions, sympathetic justices were able to keep the reformation of manners campaign going despite both active and passive opposition from many of their colleagues. Reforming justices did not, however, all adopt the same strategies for prosecuting vice. As suggested by the fact that there was not one Society, but several societies, the reformation of manners campaign was a loose-knit organization in which the supporters contributed in different ways and with varying degrees of enthusiasm. Some justices who were known supporters of the campaign and who heard large numbers of cases involving other types of crime heard few cases of vice. Differences in judicial strategies for suppressing vice are also evident in the types of vice offences justices heard and the procedures they chose for prosecuting them. Some justices concentrated on Sabbath offences to the exclusion of other types of vice. Justice Thomas Frampton, for example, heard 177 cases involving summary punishment by fine in 1712, of which virtually all were Sabbath offences, but he committed only about six people to the house of correction for prostitution and related offences during the same period. On the other hand, justices Ireton, Negus, and Railton issued a total of about 95 recognizances for vice offences in 1707 (prostitution, adultery, gaming, and keeping disorderly alehouses), while hearing only 72 cases involving punishment by fine (mostly Sabbath offences) between them. Although justices active in the prosecution of vice typically favored houses of correction over recogni-

---

[134] One other function of these petty sessions was to audit constables' accounts of the execution of warrants for the punishment of offenders by fine, in order to ensure that the money was properly collected and given to churchwardens for the use of the poor: Laing MS III, 394, pp. 269–72.

[135] *An Account of the Endeavours*, pp. 12–14; WJ/OC/I, f. 127d (April 1728); MJ/OC/III, f. 167d (Dec. 1728); WJ/OC/II, ff. 101d–105d (April 1731).

zances, some reforming justices, such as John Mercer and Isaac Tillard, prosecuted equal numbers of vice cases using each procedure. Even when hearing the same offences by the same procedure, reforming justices responded differently: John Bond, John Perry, and Roger Smith all heard more than one hundred and fifty accusations of working on the Sabbath in 1707, but whereas Bond convicted almost one-half the defendants who appeared before him, Perry and Smith convicted only 27%.[136]

Despite such differences in tactics, on average justices who were active in prosecuting vice adopted different strategies for prosecuting crime than their colleagues. For reasons already discussed, reforming justices favored prosecution by summary jurisdiction over recognizances and indictments, thereby placing themselves in the categories of the "law and order" or "social control" justices identified in chapter 8.[137] Of the twelve justices who were most active in prosecuting vice in the samples, eight were identified as social control or law and order justices and only one, John Chamberlayne, was a mediating justice. Chamberlayne, who was first secretary of the S.P.C.K., was also, however, identified as a social control justice. Supporters of the reformation of manners campaign did not invariably adopt an uncompromising attitude towards the offenders who appeared before them, but they were far more likely to do so than other justices.

After 1725, the numbers of prosecutions reported in the societies' annual accounts dropped sharply. The immediate cause of this decline was undoubtedly legal obstacles that interfered with the reformers' strategies for apprehending or reporting offenders, notably the Westminster general warrants case discussed earlier, and new legal requirements concerning convictions for profane swearing and cursing.[138] The reformers continued to produce annual reports, chronicling an ever-decreasing number of prosecutions initiated, until 1738 (Table 9.1). Circumstantial evidence strongly suggests that hostility to informers aroused by the enforcement of the Gin Act in 1737 and 1738 provided the final blow to the societies.[139] Given the long period of

---

[136] Bodleian Library, Rawlinson MS D1396–1404. While cases were sometimes dismissed because the plaintiff failed to appear, lenient justices discharged many defendants without punishment because it was a first offence, or on promise of "amendment."

[137] Section 8.4.

[138] SPCK, Papers of Moment, p. 96 (Nov. 1725); Francis Hare, *A Sermon Preached to the Societies for the Reformation of Manners* (1731), p. 58; *R vs Sparling*, Hilary 8 Geo. I, reported in Strange, *Reports of Adjudged Cases*, vol. 1, pp. 497–98; PRO KB33/13/10.

[139] Portus, *Caritas Anglicana*, p. 182; Peter Clark, "The 'mother gin' controversy in the early eighteenth century," *Transactions of the Royal Historical Society* 5th series, vol. 38 (1988), pp. 80–82; Lee Davison, "Experiments in the social regulation of industry: gin legislation 1729–51," in *Reform and Regulation: The Response to Social and Economic Problems in England 1689–1750*, ed. Lee Davison, Tim Hitchcock, Tim Keirn, and Robert Shoemaker (forthcoming).

decline, however, it is more important to consider the long-term causes of the campaign's collapse. Although a comprehensive explanation would include changes in the political and intellectual climate that weakened support for a reformation of manners campaign,[140] perhaps the most important long-term cause of the failure of the campaign was opposition to the reformers' innovative methods of prosecuting offenders.

Regardless of the extent of public support for their actions, the reformers could never succeed in the long term without overcoming the serious obstacles raised by their strategies for prosecuting offenders systematically. Most obviously, the reliance on voluntary informers created several problems. The donations of time and money from private citizens that were necessary to sustain the flow of informations could not be counted on indefinitely. In addition, the use of informers gave considerable ammunition to the societies' critics. Not only were informers generally unpopular, but their use inevitably encouraged corrupt practices: even if the reformers were truthful in their claims that none of their informers had ever acted improperly, their very use allowed other people to pose as informers and extort money from offenders in return for not prosecuting them. Informers must also bear some of the responsibility for another charge commonly levelled at the societies, that they ignored the vices of the rich: informers were typically skilled craftsmen, and they were rarely willing to inform against their social superiors.

More fundamentally, the societies' goal of systematically prosecuting offenders directly contradicted traditional judicial practices, in which constables and justices of the peace possessed considerable independence to execute the law flexibly, according to the specific circumstances of each case. While sympathetic constables and justices could always be located, reforming justices were never able to control the activities of their more numerous unsympathetic colleagues, who viewed their local neighborhoods as their own territories and resented any outside interference. Ultimately, the failure of the reformation of manners campaign suggests how much power individual justices and constables possessed over the enforcement of the law in their own neighborhoods, and how difficult it was for a single interest group to manipulate the preindustrial criminal justice system for its own ends.

Instead of identifying the reasons for the collapse of the campaign, it is perhaps more important to ask why it lasted so long – for almost a half a century. Pride of place in such an explanation would clearly go to the outburst of evangelical religious enthusiasm in the late seventeenth century which led first to the foundation of religious societies in the 1670s and subsequently in the 1690s and

---

[140] Portus, *Caritas Anglicana*, pp. 188–89; Isaacs, "Anglican hierarchy," pp. 400–11; Curtis and Speck, "The Societies for the Reformation of Manners," pp. 59–61. On the decline of the societies more generally, see also Isaacs, "Moral crime," pp. 310–39.

early 1700s to the formation of the S.P.C.K. and the Society for the Propagation of the Gospel, as well as the Societies for the Reformation of Manners. The reformers' desires to prosecute vice systematically would not have been so successful, however, were it not for the fact that the judicial system offered tremendous opportunities (as well as obstacles) to their designs: cheap and expeditious summary procedures, the possibility of bypassing inactive parish officials by using informers, and the ability to hold petty sessions as a means of organizing justices and constables who supported the campaign. Indeed, the very independence of individual justices which led so many to oppose the campaign allowed others to work very hard in its support.

In explaining the long-term success of the reformation of manners movement specifically in London, however, it is also necessary to consider social conditions in the London suburbs around the turn of the eighteenth century, where rapid demographic growth and social change had resulted in growing public fears about the increase of crime and social instability.[141] As we have seen, the first and subsequently the most common offences prosecuted by the reformers in London were prostitution and "lewd and disorderly conduct", offences which were punished in houses of correction and which were the type of vice most closely associated with more serious crime. What have been labelled as "social control" justices were most active in making such commitments to houses of correction, and despite the theoretical imprecision of such a term in essence such prosecutions *can* be characterized as an attempt at social control: the informers and justices responsible for these commitments were attempting to discipline people whose behavior, whether it was prostitution or simple loitering, was perceived as a threat to urban social stability. Not for the first time, the concern for a religious or moral reformation became intertwined with a desire for a social reformation.[142] The reformation of manners campaign in London was more than a movement which sought to reform shopkeepers and others who worked on the Sabbath and used the Lord's name in vain. Through its extensive use of houses of correction, it also constituted a major assault by middle- and upper-class Londoners on the capital's underclass of prostitutes, vagrants, and unemployed.

[141] See above, section 1.2.
[142] Keith Wrightson and David Levine, *Poverty and Piety in an English Village: Terling 1525–1700* (New York, 1979); William Hunt, *The Puritan Moment: The Coming of Revolution in an English County* (Cambridge, Mass., 1983), pp. 79–84, 228–29, 250–52; David Underdown, *Revel, Riot and Rebellion: Popular Politics and Culture in England 1603–1660* (Oxford, 1987), chap. 3; Margaret Spufford, "Puritanism and social control?" in *Order and Disorder in Early Modern England*, ed. Anthony Fletcher and John Stevenson (Cambridge, 1987), pp. 41–57.

10

Geographical contexts

Decisions about prosecuting crime were strongly influenced by social conditions in the neighborhoods in which the parties lived. Not only was the nature of the relationship between the plaintiff and the accused important, but relationships between the two parties to the dispute and other people who knew about or were affected by the crime were significant, since the latter might serve as mediators or supervisors of informal settlements. More generally, attitudes towards crime and the law were shaped by perceptions of the extent of social stability or instability in the neighborhood: in conditions of social instability, plaintiffs were less likely to trust informal mediation, and more likely to seek formal convictions and punishments. By examining plaintiffs' choices in the contrasting geographical contexts of rural Middlesex and several London suburbs, it is possible to identify the specific social conditions in which each procedure for prosecution was most likely to be chosen. Conversely, by comparing what we know about the types of social relations for which each procedure was most suited with geographical patterns of prosecutions, it is possible to learn more about the relative social stability of different parts of London. By analyzing the geographical distribution of prosecutions, this chapter sheds light not only on the social contexts most suited to each of the procedures used to prosecute petty offences, but also on social conditions in the rapidly growing metropolis in the late seventeenth and early eighteenth centuries.

In theory, each criminal accusation involves three significant locations: the residences of the defendant and the plaintiff and the place where the crime allegedly occurred. In practice, of course, the evidence is much more limited: the house of correction calendars include no direct information on any of these locations, recognizances normally only provide the parish of residence of the defendant, and indictments only supply the location of the crime.[1] The

[1] Although indictments ascribe a parish of residence to the defendant, in practice it is nearly always the same parish which is given as the location of the crime. That this parish is the true location of the crime is suggested by the facts that when several defendants are indicted for the same crime,

273

evidence forces one to compare, therefore, data generated by one legal procedure on the locations of crimes with data produced by another on the residences of defendants. In practice, these two locations were often in the same parish. A comparison of the indictment and recognizance evidence for forty defendants indicted at the April 1723 Middlesex sessions discovered that twenty-three (57.5%) allegedly committed the crime in the parish in which they lived. A further ten defendants (25%) lived in a parish contiguous to the parish in which the crime took place.[2] That defendants normally lived close to the sites of their alleged offences is also suggested by the parishes of residence of defendants who committed offences in Westminster and were bound over to appear at the Westminster sessions: excluding cases where the defendant's parish was unknown or he lived outside the county, 92% of the 479 defendants lived in Westminster, and two-thirds of the remaining defendants lived nearby in the parishes of St. Giles in the Fields and St. Andrew Holborn. While accusations of theft and other felonies were frequently levelled against outsiders,[3] the majority of defendants accused of misdemeanors on recognizances and indictments appear to have been local residents. Given this congruity, it would be surprising if plaintiffs did not also live near where the crime was committed. Unlike thefts, the most common misdemeanor, an offence against the peace, was typically the result of tensions generated by personal acquaintance. In the absence of additional evidence, it has been assumed for the purpose of this study that the location of the crime and the residences of the defendant and the plaintiff were in the same or neighboring parishes.

Although the house of correction calendars do not include any geographical evidence, the region of the county in which incidents occurred can be inferred from the name of the justice of the peace who made the commitment. Since most justices issued the majority of their recognizances against defendants living in a cluster of only two or three parishes, it was assumed that the defendants those justices committed to the house of correction had been apprehended in the same area of the county. (Since many of the prisoners were unemployed, or had been unable to find sureties, it would be unwise to draw any conclusions about their places of residence.) Using this method, and assuming that all the defendants in the Westminster houses of correction came from Westminster, it was possible to assign a location to 85% of the defendants

they are almost inevitably all listed as residing in the same parish, and when defendants are indicted more than once they are often noted on each indictment as coming from a different parish. When indictments are compared with recognizances for the same defendant the parishes of residence frequently differ, and since the evidence on recognizances was needed to locate the defendant in order to collect the bail if the recognizance was forfeited, it is more likely to be accurate. See J. S. Cockburn, "Early-modern assize records as historical evidence," *Journal of the Society of Archivists* 5 (Oct. 1975), p. 225.

2 MJ/SR/2399, 2402, 2404, 2407 (Feb.–July, 1723).
3 Martin J. Ingram, "Communities and courts: law and disorder in early seventeenth-century Wiltshire," in *Crime in England*, ed. Cockburn, pp. 129, 133.

in the 1721 house of correction sample. The same method was used for defendants bound over by recognizance whose parishes of residence were not listed because they did not risk bail.[4] All such cases in which the location of the offence was inferred from the justice who handled the case were included only in analyses of the general regional distribution of prosecutions, and not where the unit of analysis is the parish.

Statistics of the geographical distribution of prosecutions are meaningless without adjusting the figures according to the population size of each region or parish. Fortunately, population estimates exist for most parishes in Middlesex for most of the years in which the sessions records were sampled. These estimates, which are listed in appendix III, are derived from the hearth tax of 1664, the Compton Census of 1676, the four shillings in the pound tax of 1694, and estimates of the number of houses in the metropolis in 1708, 1732, and 1737. Although all these estimates, especially those derived from the Compton Census and the estimates of the numbers of houses in the early eighteenth century, are subject to a considerable degree of uncertainty, the rough congruence between the population figures calculated from the different sources suggests that they are reliable as rough approximations of the relative size of the Middlesex parishes. After converting numbers of households to population figures and correcting for the sampling proportions, it is thus possible to calculate per capita prosecution rates for many urban parishes. Despite the fact that these rates are subject to several possible sources of error, the general patterns which emerge from the five sample periods are remarkably similar. The results, expressed in terms of the number of prosecutions per year per thousand inhabitants, are summarized in Table 10.1 by region of the county.

10.1 EXPLAINING THE GEOGRAPHICAL DISTRIBUTION OF PROSECUTIONS

Table 10.1 demonstrates significant regional differences in the geographical distribution of prosecutions in Middlesex: Westminster and the "west urban" parishes had prosecution rates around three times as high as those in the "east urban" parishes, and more than four times higher than rural Middlesex, with the "north urban" parishes having rates closer to those of the eastern than to those of the western suburbs. Even greater discrepancies are found with the house of correction evidence, where per capita rates were eight or nine times higher in the western urban parishes than in the east end. (Even if all the

---

[4] One-quarter of the defendants did not have a parish of residence listed on their recognizances. Using this method a region of residence was ascribed to 60% of these defendants. In addition, for the small number of recognizances where the victim was given a parish of residence and the defendant was not, the victim's parish was used in the analysis.

Table 10.1 Per capita rates of prosecution by geographical region: recognizance/indictment rates per 1,000 inhabitants per year[a]

	1663–64	1677	1693	1707	1720–22	Average	House of correction 1721
Westminster[b]	9.0/6.9	10.8/9.5	10.8/6.3	6.1/3.9	6.5/4.1	8.6/6.1	9.2
West urban[c]	17.4/8.7		7.0/5.1	7.4/4.4	10.9/5.7	10.7/6.0	7.5
North urban[d]			11.3/3.8	3.4/3.5	6.2/2.4	7.0/3.2	4.1
East urban[e]	7.0/2.2		3.5/2.5	2.2/2.0	2.1/1.2	3.7/2.0	0.8
Urban periphery[f]							g
Rural Middlesex	1.7/2.2	1.3/1.5	4.3/4.5			1.5/1.85	g

[a] Method of calculation: The numbers of prosecutions in each of the samples were multiplied by the sampling proportion and divided by the number of years sampled to yield estimates of the annual number of prosecutions. Recognizances in cases where an indictment was filed were not included. For the population estimates used in these calculations, see Appendix III.

[b] Excluding St. Mary-le-Strand and St. Clement Danes.

[c] St. Giles in the Fields, St. Andrew Holborn, St. Clement Danes, and St. Mary-le-Strand (despite the fact that the latter two were legally in Westminster).

[d] St. James Clerkenwell, St. Leonard Shoreditch, St. Sepulchre, and the Middlesex portion of St. Giles Cripplegate.

[e] St. Katharine by the Tower, St. John Wapping, St. Botolph Aldgate (Middlesex portion), and Stepney.

[f] Islington, Hackney, St. Pancras, St. Marylebone, Hampstead, Chelsea, Kensington, Paddington. The Stepney hamlets on the urban periphery (Poplar and Blackwall, Bethnal Green, Mile End, and Bow) are included in the "east urban" category because the hamlets were not consistently identified in the records, especially on indictments.

[g] No identifiable commitments from these regions.

defendants whose region of residence could not be ascribed came from the east urban parishes, the per capita rate for this region would still be less than half that of the western parishes.)

Why were people so much more likely to prosecute offences in the western parts of the metropolis than in the urban parishes east of the City of London or in rural Middlesex? Needless to say, prosecution rates were determined by many factors, including the number of offences which actually occurred, the trouble and costs potential plaintiffs faced in filing prosecutions, and the nature of social relations in the neighborhood in which the alleged crime took place. In assessing the relative importance of these factors, the first, although unmeasurable, is probably the least important, since the most common misdemeanors (assault, riot, loose, idle, and disorderly conduct, prostitution) were so widespread and so vaguely defined that only a very small proportion of these offences was ever prosecuted. In these circumstances, variations in the inclination to prosecute played a far more important role in determining the level of prosecution rates than changes in the number of offences which actually occurred. With few exceptions, peace offences were the most common offences prosecuted in each parish, and only occasionally can high prosecution rates in a parish be explained by an outbreak of prosecutions against other offences (such as vice or regulatory offences). Similarly, victimless offences such as prostitution and "loose, idle, and disorderly" conduct formed the largest category of commitments to houses of correction from every region of the county, and differences in the types of offences prosecuted do not explain the tremendous regional variations in per capita commitments. In general, high prosecution rates must be assumed to have been the result of a greater tendency to prosecute all types of offences, especially offences against the peace (for recognizances and indictments) or victimless offences (for houses of correction).

Of the other factors which may explain differences in prosecution rates, the first, the ease or difficulty of making prosecutions, will be discussed in this section, while the second, concerning the nature of social relations in the neighborhood in which the alleged offence took place, is discussed in the following two sections.

Decisions about whether (and how) to prosecute offences were influenced by the costs, both financial and otherwise, involved in conducting prosecutions, and these varied geographically. The two most important costs were the time spent traveling to and from the courthouse (or house of correction) and the court fees required for initiating recognizances and indictments. The time spent traveling to and from sessions, as well as the time spent waiting for cases to be heard in court, kept plaintiffs away from their jobs. (Although recognizances only required the defendant to appear in court, both the justice and the plaintiff may have been unwilling, when the offence was minor and the parties lived far

away from the courthouse, to impose the burden of travel on the defendant.)
Consequently, prosecutors who lived nearest the courts were most likely to
file prosecutions. The highest regional prosecution rates in the county were
found in Westminster, which had its own quarter sessions meeting conveniently in Westminster Hall, and in the parishes in urban Middlesex west of
the City of London, which were conveniently located near the Middlesex
courthouse, Hicks Hall, in Clerkenwell. In contrast, urban parishes east of the
City of London, which were located one or two miles (of busy roads through
the City) away from Clerkenwell, had considerably lower prosecution rates.
Prosecution rates for some parishes, however, varied independently of the
distance between the parish and the courthouse: Clerkenwell, home of the
Middlesex courthouse, had prosecution rates considerably lower than the
neighboring west end parishes.

Distance also influenced rural prosecution rates. Although there are not
enough cases in the sample to calculate separate per capita rates for individual
parishes in rural Middlesex, it is possible to separate the rural parishes into
three categories: parishes just outside London and within three miles of
Clerkenwell (the "urban periphery"); parishes three to ten miles away from the
courthouse in Clerkenwell; and parishes ten or more miles away from
Clerkenwell. Unfortunately, because of sparse population evidence, it was only
possible to calculate prosecution rates for the urban periphery for the 1693
sample and rates for the other rural parishes for the 1663–64 sample. Nonetheless, the resulting prosecution rates clearly suggest that distance had a significant influence on the inclination of rural inhabitants to prosecute. Prosecution rates for parishes on the urban periphery (4.3 recognizances and 4.5
indictments per 1,000 inhabitants) were higher than the rates for parishes three
to ten miles away (2.8 recognizances and 3.3 indictments) and rates in the two
regions nearest the metropolis were considerably higher than those for parishes
more than ten miles away (0.8 recognizances and 1.3 indictments).

The importance of the accessibility of a court for encouraging prosecutions
is further illustrated by the difference between prosecution rates in urban
Middlesex (including Westminster) and in nearby urban Surrey (Southwark).
Since the City of London sessions in Southwark appear not to have been active
in the early eighteenth century, prosecutions from urban Surrey had to be
directed to the Surrey quarter sessions, which were held four times a year in
different parts of rural Surrey, the closest of which was Croydon, nine miles
from Southwark. The highest per capita rates of indictments for assault in
urban Surrey between 1660 and 1800 were in 1723 and the 1730s, when up to
1.25 indictments per thousand people were filed annually.[5] In contrast, rates of

---

[5] John Beattie, "Pattern of crime," pp. 52–53 (n. 16) and 68–69. For the places where the Surrey
quarter sessions were held, see *Surrey Quarter Sessions Records 1663–1666* (Surrey Record
Society, no. 39, vol. 16, 1938), *passim.*

indictment for assault in urban Middlesex in the 1720–22 sample varied from 0.6 along the riverside parishes east of London to 2.4 in the west end, or twice the highest figure attained in Surrey. In the early 1660s, prosecution rates for assault in urban Middlesex varied between 0.8 in the east end and 2.25 in the west end, while the rate in urban Surrey in the 1660s and 1670s fluctuated between only 0.1 and 0.4. The only plausible explanation of such dramatic differences in rates of prosecution between the Surrey and Middlesex portions of the London metropolis is the ease of access to the Middlesex and Westminster courts; not only were they located within the urban area, but the Middlesex court met eight times a year, twice as often as the Surrey court.[6] In rural areas, rates of prosecution north and south of the Thames were similar: 0.7 indictments for assault per thousand people in the 1663–64 Middlesex sample compared with between 0.15 and 0.5 in Surrey and Sussex in the 1660s. While a significant difference between rates of prosecution in urban and rural areas can be found in both counties, the placement of the Middlesex courts in the metropolis greatly increased the difference in Middlesex. As historians are beginning to realize, the location of the courts exercised an important influence over the geographical distribution of prosecutions in preindustrial England.[7]

Distance played an even more important role in determining the geographical distribution of commitments to houses of correction. While Westminster had its own house of correction (in Tothill Fields in St. Margaret's parish), the Middlesex house of correction in Clerkenwell received commitments from the rest of the county. In fact, as is evident in Table 10.1, commitments came predominantly from the western and northern urban parishes which were closest to Clerkenwell; few commitments can be identified as coming from the east end of the metropolis, and none from rural parishes. Since house of correction calendars do not include any geographical evidence, these findings are based on the region of activity (according to the recognizances they issued) of the justices who made the commitments. Although 15% of the defendants could not be assigned a region on this basis, the discrepancy between the west end of urban Middlesex and other parts of the county is too large to be explained by missing evidence.[8]

Parish officers in the east end frequently complained about the burden of

---

[6] Although the Westminster courts met only four times a year, impatient prosecutors from Westminster could (and frequently did) bring their cases to the Middlesex court when it met in Westminster.

[7] Peter King, "Newspaper reporting, prosecution practice and perceptions of urban crime: the Colchester crime wave of 1765," *Continuity and Change* 2 (1987), p. 425; Herrup, *The Common Peace*, p. 58.

[8] This finding is confirmed by the fact that the justices who attended the Brentford petty sessions committed only two or three prisoners a year to the Middlesex house of correction, according to the 1697 and 1712 house of correction samples. For the Brentford petty sessions, see GLRO, Accession 890. For similar findings, see the authorities cited by Innes, "Prisons for the poor," p. 92.

carrying prisoners to the house of correction in Clerkenwell and petitioned for a house of correction or other place of confinement in the east end. In July 1681, they apparently succeeded when the Middlesex court ordered the erection of a house of correction on Mile End Green, at the charge of the parishes of the Tower Hamlets. The court noted that "the present house of correction is so remote from a great part of those hamlets that [parish officers] cannot with safety to themselves convey malefactors [there]."[9] This new house of correction apparently had a very short life, for only one other reference to it is recorded, and it is not listed on Joel Gascoyne's *Survey of Stepney* of 1703.[10] Faced with the burden of conveying petty offenders to Clerkenwell, parish officers in the east end simply failed to arrest many offenders: in 1707 it was noted that "there are several lewd and vicious persons residing in [Tower Division] who with impunity commit divers disorders and irregularities, occasioned chiefly by the great distance and remoteness of the prisons of Bridewell and New Prison from the said division and the great trouble and charge which her Majesty's peace officers sustain by carrying them so far."[11] While many offenders went unpunished, others were imprisoned (illegally) in debtors' or other private prisons, or even in watchhouses, despite several attempts by the Middlesex justices to stop such practices.[12] Consequently, only one-sixth the number of prisoners per capita were committed to the Middlesex house of correction from the east end as from the northern parishes where it was located. For petty thefts, however, where plaintiffs were private individuals who did not face this problem regularly, plaintiffs may have been willing to pay the cost of having the offender taken to Clerkenwell.[13] Whereas 40% of the prisoners from the east end were accused of theft, theft accounted for only a quarter of the prisoners in the west end, where most of the commitments were for victimless offences such as prostitution. For east end plaintiffs and justices, only the most serious offences justified the trouble of carrying offenders to the house of correction in Clerkenwell.

Potential prosecutors considered not only the inconvenience of travel when deciding whether to initiate a prosecution, but also the financial costs of prosecution, and the geographical evidence shows that people living in the

---

[9] MJ/SBB/387, p. 51 (July 1681).

[10] For what appears to be a list of prisoners in this house of correction at the time sessions met, see MJ/SBB/420, p. 52 (Dec. 1684).

[11] MJ/SP/Oct. 1707, no. 31. See also Thomas Alcock, *Observations on the Defects of the Poor Laws, and on the Causes and Consequences of the Great Increase and Burden of the Poor* (1752), p. 67; Walter J. King, "Vagrancy and local law enforcement: why be a constable in Stuart Lancashire?" *The Historian* 42 (1980), pp. 278–83.

[12] MJ/SP/Oct. 1677, no. 1; Jan. 1691, no. 17a; July 1691, no. 21; MJ/SBB/280, p. 50 (July 1671); 328, pp. 47–49 (Oct. 1675); 362, p. 35 (June 1679); 471, p. 52 (Jan. 1690).

[13] In principle the accused were responsible for this charge, but in most cases they would have been unable to pay.

poorest parts of the metropolis were significantly less likely to initiate prosecutions than those living in wealthier neighborhoods. The relative wealth of different parishes can be measured using the 1664 hearth tax returns, which report the number of hearths in each household (a rough proxy for the wealth of the inhabitants), and the 1694 four shillings in the pound tax returns, which report the rents paid by each household and the income derived from business wealth and investments (stocks).[14] The per capita rates of indictments for the urban parishes were statistically correlated with every indicator of wealth calculated from these returns. Indictment rates were positively correlated with the average number of hearths per household and the proportion of households with five or more hearths, and negatively correlated with the proportion of households who were excused from paying the hearth tax (primarily on the grounds of poverty).[15] Similarly, positive correlations occurred between the indictment rate and average rents paid per household and the average income derived from stocks per household. Reflecting the fact that recognizances were far less expensive to prosecute, per capita rates of prosecution by recognizance were only weakly correlated with indicators of wealth and poverty.[16]

Because most of the poorest parishes in the metropolis, in the east end, were also those located furthest from the courthouses, potential prosecutors in those parishes faced a double disincentive to prosecuting petty offenders. Over half of the households on the hearth tax returns in the east end were listed as poor and/or not chargeable for the tax,[17] and prosecutors needed to travel up to two miles through the crowded streets of the City in order to get to Clerkenwell. Of

---

[14] For permitting me to make use of their work on these taxes, I am indebted to Beatrice Shearer (hearth tax) and James Alexander (four shillings in the pound tax). For the latter, see James Alexander, "The economic and social structure of the City of London, c.1700" (Ph.D. diss., University of London, 1989), p. 17. For the hearth tax, I have also used figures from M. J. Power, "The east and west in early-modern London," in *Wealth and Power in Tudor England: Essays Presented to S. T. Bindoff*, ed. E. Ives *et al.* (1978), p. 181.

[15] For a discussion of the significance of exemption from payment of the hearth tax, see Tom Arkell, "The incidence of poverty in England in the later seventeenth century," *Social History* 12 (1987), pp. 32–38.

[16] The Pearson correlation coefficients for seventeen urban parishes are as follows (a value of 1.0 would represent a perfect positive correlation, a value of − 1.0 would indicate a perfect negative correlation, and a value of 0 would indicate no correlation between the two variables):

	Indictment Rate	Recognizance Rate
Average number of hearths per household	0.66	0.37
Households with five or more hearths	0.68	0.44
Proportion of households not chargeable	− 0.63	− 0.29
Average rent paid per household	0.87	0.59
Average stocks per household	0.81	0.56

In order to avoid the distortion caused by the presence of a few very wealthy households in a parish, in the calculation of the average number of hearths per household all households with over five hearths were calculated as having just five.

[17] M. J. Power, "The social topography of Restoration London," in *London 1500–1700*, ed. A. L. Beier and Roger Finlay (1986), p. 205.

the two factors, it appears that wealth was the more important in shaping the geographical distribution of indictments. Within the metropolis, parochial wealth was more strongly statistically correlated with indictment rates than with distance to the courthouse.[18] Thus, the relatively poor parishes of St. Margaret Westminster and Shoreditch both had comparatively low prosecution rates despite the fact they were both located close to the courthouses (Table 10.3).

In contrast to the misdemeanor evidence, parochial rates for felonies were not significantly correlated with indicators of wealth or distance from the courthouse in the metropolis.[19] This contrast between patterns of misdemeanor and felony prosecutions illustrates the greater role of prosecutorial discretion in the prosecution of misdemeanors. Because in general the impulse to prosecute misdemeanors was weaker than with more serious offences, practical considerations played a greater role in shaping the decision to prosecute.

Statistically, however, distance and wealth can explain only part of the variation in misdemeanor prosecution rates between parishes. By squaring the correlation coefficients listed in the notes it is possible to estimate what proportion of the variation is explained by the two variables. By this calculation, distance accounts for 27% of the variation in indictment rates and 20% of that in recognizance rates, and the strongest indicator of wealth, average rents, accounts for 76% of the variation in indictments and 35% of that in recognizances.[20] With over three-fifths of its households with five or more hearths and a location close to the Middlesex courthouse in Clerkenwell, the parish of St. Andrew Holborn, for example, should have had much higher prosecution rates than 4.7 recognizances and 4.6 indictments per thousand inhabitants. At the other extreme, despite the fact the east end parish of St. Katharine by the Tower was located a mile and a half from Clerkenwell and only 9% of its households had five or more hearths, more than thirty recognizances per thousand inhabitants were initiated in the 1663–64 sample. Clearly, other factors contributed to shape parochial prosecution rates.

One such factor was the presence of active justices of the peace. Particularly in the early part of the period when judicial activity was most highly concentrated among a small number of justices,[21] some of the highest parochial recognizance rates were largely the result of the activities of one or two very active justices. Thus, the unusually high rate in St. Katharine by the Tower in 1663–64 can be

---

[18] The Pearson correlation coefficients for the per capita prosecution rates of the urban parishes with distance from the courthouse were 0.52 for indictments and 0.45 for recognizances.

[19] This statement is based on a 25% sample of the gaol delivery indictments for Middlesex between May 1720 and April 1722.

[20] Of course, the existence of a strong statistical correlation does not by itself indicate a causal relationship between the two variables.

[21] See above, Table 3.6.

partially attributed to the activities of two justices, Richard Abell and Thomas Swalowe, who between them issued three-quarters of the recognizances from that parish. Abell was also responsible for unusually high (for the east end) recognizance rates in Shadwell and Whitechapel, where he accounted for two-thirds of the recognizances. Similarly, in the west end Robert Jegon, the most active justice in the sample, was responsible for two-thirds of the unusually high recognizance rates in the parishes of St. Clement Danes and St. Giles in the Fields in 1663–64. As suggested in chapter 8, it is likely that the presence of such active justices in a parish encouraged prosecutions which otherwise would never have taken place. Nonetheless, the presence of active justices does not consistently explain variations in parish prosecution rates; in Westminster in 1677 and St. Giles in the Fields in 1720–22, for example, several justices combined to make the recognizance rates some of the highest in the county. Moreover, the persistence of regional variations in prosecution rates over five sample periods and sixty years suggests that prosecution rates were shaped more by the enduring social and geographical characteristics of each parish than by the actions of individual justices.

Just as high prosecution rates were occasionally facilitated by the activities of one or two active justices, it is possible that low rates were caused by an absence of justices willing to act. As we have seen, at times during this period purges of active justices from the Middlesex and Westminster commissions led to a reduction in the number of recognizances issued.[22] Norma Landau has assembled some evidence that justices of the peace were unwilling to serve in poor urban parishes during this period because the poor troubled them so frequently with what were perceived to be petty disputes and allegations. Thus, the low prosecution rates in London's east end may have resulted from a dearth of justices willing to hear accusations.[23] As is evident from appendix II, there were far more active justices working in the western suburbs than in the eastern suburbs, despite the fact that the population of the west end was only slightly larger. Nonetheless, given the large number of justices who issued recognizances in the east end (fifteen in the 1663–64 sample, fourteen in the 1720–22 sample), it is likely that east Londoners could have found a justice if they wanted to. To the extent that east enders were discouraged from prosecuting

---

[22] See above, section 3.3.

[23] Landau, *Justices of the Peace*, pp. 202–03. Landau shows that in urban Kent so-called "trading justices" stepped in to fill this gap by hearing disputes informally. If such justices were active in London's east end, they left little evidence of their activities. It is possible that these justices issued recognizances but failed to return them to sessions if the cases were resolved informally, but, as explained in section 5.2, this practice does not appear to have occurred in Middlesex. If it did, the disposition of those recognizances that were returned from the east end would differ markedly from that of those returned from other parts of the metropolis (more would result in further legal action), but this was not the case. One east end justice who was accused of being a trading justice, John Poulson, returned his recognizances to sessions: Hertfordshire Record Office, D/EP/F157, Wm. Ashurst to Lord Cowper, 23 October 1717.

cases by practical considerations, it is more likely that this was due to the costs and travel involved rather than to the difficulty of finding a justice willing to hear the case. It is also possible, however, that the low prosecution rates in the east end and in rural areas resulted from the fact that social conditions in these areas left inhabitants feeling less need to use the law to deal with petty offenders. It is to this possibility that we now turn.

10.2 URBAN–RURAL DIFFERENCES

With the exception of the east end, per capita prosecution rates in the urban Middlesex parishes were considerably higher than in rural Middlesex.[24] It is possible that, as John Beattie concluded from his study of felonies in urban and rural Surrey, crime was less of a problem in rural areas because there was both less poverty and fewer temptations to steal.[25] Poverty played less of a role in causing people to commit misdemeanors (especially offences against the peace), however, and it is unlikely that significantly fewer petty crimes were actually committed in rural areas. It is more likely that rural victims had better reasons not to prosecute than their urban counterparts: not only were they discouraged from prosecuting by the trouble of travelling to the Middlesex courthouse, but they felt less need to prosecute offenders as a result of the greater availability of informal mediation in rural areas.

As we have seen, informal mediation was most likely to succeed both when the parties to a dispute were well acquainted with one another and when their neighbors were able and willing to help supervise the settlement.[26] Although we should not exaggerate the social stability of rural parishes (especially parishes located so close to a big city), their small size and relative isolation must have encouraged stronger social ties between parishioners than occurred in London. Certainly justices of the peace were more likely to mediate disputes informally in rural areas. When compared with their urban counterparts, justices in rural Kent in the early eighteenth century settled a higher proportion of the disputes which came before them without issuing recognizances.[27] We have seen that justice William Hunt, who practiced in rural Wiltshire in the 1740s, settled at least half of the cases he heard informally, while Henry Norris, who lived on the periphery of the metropolis, settled only 38% of his cases.[28] Criminal accusations in rural areas were often settled informally by justices meeting at petty sessions, which occurred in Middlesex in Brentford, Hayes,

---

[24] Rural parishes located on the immediate periphery of the metropolis are included under the category of "urban periphery" in Table 10.1 and are discussed separately at the end of this section.

[25] Beattie, *Crime and the Courts*, p. 14.   [26] See above, section 4.3.

[27] Landau, *Justices of the Peace*, pp. 191–94.

[28] See above, Tables 3.1 and 3.2.

Isleworth, South Mimms, and Staines during this period.[29] Rural disputes were also mediated by other figures of authority such as employers, landlords, ministers, and resident gentry.[30] That rural inhabitants preferred to settle disputes among themselves is suggested by the nature of the petitions they sent to the Middlesex court, which assured the justices that a defendant's character was honest and industrious or requested the court to dismiss a case or deliver a light sentence.[31]

The pattern of prosecutions that were initiated from rural areas suggests that informal mediation may have been common. Perhaps because only the most serious cases were referred to sessions, indictments outnumbered recognizances. In contrast, in urban Middlesex 1.7 recognizances were issued for every indictment filed. Minor offences that in the city might have resulted in a recognizance were settled informally or simply went unresolved in rural parishes; only the most serious offences were prosecuted, and these were often prosecuted by indictment. Thus, disputes involving women, which typically involved minor offences, were less likely to be prosecuted in rural Middlesex than in London. Whereas 37% of the defendants on recognizances and 29% of the defendants on indictments in the metropolis were female, women account for only 11% of the defendants on rural recognizances and 19% on rural indictments (Table 10.2). In addition, rural women were less likely to prosecute recognizances, but not indictments.

Similarly, Beattie found that women accounted for a higher proportion of the defendants indicted for crimes against the person and property crimes in Southwark than in rural Surrey during the eighteenth century. Beattie attributed this difference to the fact that rural women were subject to a greater degree of control by their families and communities; in urban areas, on the other hand, women lived more independent lives, in part because they were more frequently employed outside the home. Both because women were "less protected, sheltered, and restricted," and because they frequently faced economic hardship resulting from unemployment or poorly paid jobs, women committed more crimes in the city.[32] It is also likely, however, that women suspected of crimes were more likely to be prosecuted in urban areas. Many accusations against rural women were probably settled informally through the intervention of family members and neighbors; in the city this process was less

[29] King, "Crime, law and society," pp. 275–81; GLRO, Accession 890 (Brentford petty sessions minutes); Shoemaker, "Crime, courts and community," pp. 50–58 and Appendix One.
[30] Sharpe, "'Such disagreement betwyx neighbors'," pp. 184–85; Keith Wrightson, *English Society 1580–1680* (1982), pp. 57–58; Ingram, *Church Courts*, p. 111.
[31] MJ/SP/Oct. 1707, no. 56; Jan. 1718, no. 24 a and b; Oct. 1718, no. 3; Dec. 1720, no. 41.
[32] John Beattie, "The criminality of women in eighteenth-century England," *Journal of Social History* 8 (1974–75), pp. 97, 109; and *Crime and the Courts*, pp. 241–43. For a similar argument, see Nicole Castan, *Justice et Répression en Languedoc à l'Epoque des Lumières* (Paris, 1980), pp. 233–37.

Table 10.2 *Gender of defendants and plaintiffs: urban vs rural parishes[a]*

	Urban	Rural	Urban periphery
Recognizances:[b]			
% Female defendants	37	11	15
% Female plaintiffs	50	38	40
Indictments:[b]			
% Female defendants	29	19	13
% Female plaintiffs	34	30	17

[a] Non-indicted recognizances only.
[b] Excluding unknowns, and, in the case of plaintiffs, official plaintiffs.

successful because women had fewer close acquaintances and were less likely to be trusted with an informal settlement. As we have seen, single women in London were viewed with particular suspicion because of concern that they might become prostitutes and/or have bastard children. Recognizances and houses of correction provided convenient methods of prosecuting such women without filing a formal indictment. Twice as many women as men were committed to houses of correction, and virtually all of these were from urban parishes. Proportionally over three times as many women were bound over by recognizance in London as in rural areas. Similarly, Peter King has shown that the easy accessibility of borough courts with minor punishments appears to have encouraged prosecutions against women in eighteenth-century Essex towns.[33]

It is likely that the frequency of informal settlements varied considerably within rural areas, depending upon the nature of social relations in each village and the availability of respected mediators.[34] Within rural Middlesex, prosecutorial strategies no doubt differed depending on whether one lived in the rapidly growing parishes on the edge of the metropolis, the market gardening villages full of Londoners' country houses along the Thames, or arable farming parishes inland.[35] There was insufficient evidence in the sample, however, to calculate per capita prosecution rates for specific rural parishes or groups of parishes. It was possible, however, to calculate a separate prosecution rate for the rural part of the county closest to London, the "urban periphery." These parishes, defined as those located within five miles of the center of London,

[33] See above, section 8.2 and Table 8.2; Peter King, "Crime, law and society," pp. 141–43.
[34] David Underdown, *Revel, Riot and Rebellion* (Oxford, 1987), pp. 11–18.
[35] L. Martindale, "Demography and land use in the late seventeenth and eighteenth centuries in Middlesex," (Ph.D. diss., University of London, 1968); Daniel Defoe, *A Tour Through the Whole Island of Great Britain* (1724–26; Harmondsworth, 1971), pp. 174–80, 344–47.

have been excluded from the previous discussion. They include, Bow, Bethnal Green, Poplar and Blackwall, and Mile End to the east; Hackney, Islington, Hampstead, and St. Pancras to the north; and Marylebone, Paddington, Kensington, and Chelsea to the west. In 1694, they were inhabited by a total of about 20,000 people.[36]

These parishes were strongly influenced by their proximity to the metropolis. As Defoe noted, "the villages round London partake of the influence of London so much, that it is observed as London is increased, so they are all increased also, and from the same causes."[37] In addition to population growth, these villages suffered from the disruptions caused by several important London roads which passed through them and the growing business of entertaining visitors from London. The roads brought trouble from highway robbers, while the entertainment business attracted other disreputable characters.[38] Defoe described how Hampstead's popularity as a place for fashionable society to gather and take the waters eventually caused it to lose its "good name." "You see more gallantry than modesty," he wrote, "so that the ladies who value their reputation, have of late more avoided the wells and walks at Hampstead, than they had formerly done." At nearby Belsize, a "house of pleasure" was so successful that "the wicked part at length broke in" and turned it into a gambling house.[39] Complaints reached the court during this period of fairs held in Tottenham Court, Bow, Bromley, and Hampstead which were patronized by residents of the metropolis. The court and many of the inhabitants repeatedly objected to the disreputable people these fairs attracted and the numerous vices, especially gambling, that they encouraged.[40] Other inhabitants, however, no doubt profited from fairs or "houses of pleasure" or were sympathetic to them. It is likely that the entertainment business in these parishes was a divisive issue.

Because social conditions in these parishes differed from those in the rest of rural Middlesex, patterns of prosecutions also differed. Per capita, almost three times as many recognizances, and over twice as many indictments, were filed in the urban periphery as in the other rural parishes. The proximity of the courthouse is no doubt largely responsible for the higher prosecution rates, but the high indictment rate was also caused by a higher than usual number of regulatory offences, especially highway offences and, in Islington, erecting

---

[36] Appendix III. The villages east of London were part of Stepney parish during this period, and recognizances and indictments from these villages often give Stepney as the residence of the defendant or location of the crime. Since Stepney was primarily an urban parish, these villages could not figure in the calculation of the prosecution rates for the urban periphery.

[37] Defoe, *Tour*, p. 337.

[38] N. G. Brett-James, *The Growth of Stuart London* (1935), pp. 264–65.

[39] Defoe, *Tour*, pp. 143, 339–40, 703.

[40] MJ/SP/June 1709, no. 41; April 1719, no. 40; MJ/SBB/671, p. 49 (July 1709); MJ/OC/I, ff. 34–35 (July 1718).

cottages without the statutory four acres of land. The relatively large number of indictments for these offences suggests that population growth in the urban periphery overwhelmed the primitive arrangements for road repair and caused pressure to build on small pieces of land. Even if nuisance and regulatory offences are ignored, however, the indictment rate in the urban periphery was higher than the indictment rate not only of the rest of rural Middlesex, but also of the east urban parishes.

The high indictment rate in the urban periphery, together with the fact that there were more prosecutions by indictment than by recognizance, suggests that a high level of social tension in these parishes led plaintiffs to be unwilling to treat defendants leniently. It is also possible to argue, however, that the relatively small number of recognizances in these parishes (in comparison with the metropolitan parishes) was due to the fact that, as in the rest of rural Middlesex, informal mediation was so common that recognizances were unnecessary. Certainly many cases were settled by informal mediation in the urban periphery; justice Henry Norris, who lived in Hackney in the 1730s, settled informally almost two-fifths of the disputes which were brought before him.[41] Ultimately, both hypotheses are probably true, but for different parishes. Social and economic conditions varied considerably among the parishes on London's periphery; conditions in the industrial and market gardening parishes of Poplar and Blackwall and Bethnal Green no doubt differed from life in resort parishes like Hampstead or more prosperous outposts like Hackney and Chelsea, where City merchants built their country retreats.[42] Such contrasts were more than likely accompanied by differences in attitudes towards prosecuting crime, but the evidence does not permit analysis of patterns of prosecutions at this level of detail.

Given the fact that rates of prosecution in the rural and urban periphery parishes were greater than the rates for some of the eastern and northern metropolitan parishes, it would be wrong to overstate the differences between urban and rural approaches to prosecuting misdemeanors. It is quite possible that informal mediation was more common in some urban parishes than in some rural parishes. Nonetheless, on average far more disputes per capita resulted in prosecutions in urban Middlesex than in the rural parts of the county. The story of the prosecution of misdemeanor crime in Middlesex is primarily an urban one.

---

[41] See above, Table 3.1.

[42] C. Kerrigan, *A History of the Tower Hamlets* (1982), pp. 16–19; M. J. Power, "The urban development of east London, 1550–1700," (Ph.D. diss., University of London, 1971), p. 210; George, *London Life*, pp. 76, 179; Defoe, *Tour*, pp. 177, 337–38, 345–46.

10.3 LONDON: "AN AGGREGATE OF VARIOUS NATIONS"

"When I consider this great city in its several quarters and divisions," Addison wrote in *The Spectator* in 1712, "I look upon it as an aggregate of various nations distinguished from each other by their respective customs, manners and interests."[43] The ability to view the metropolis in such terms was largely a result of the increased social segregation which accompanied London's rapid population growth in the sixteenth and seventeenth centuries. With the growth of the suburban parishes around the City, for the first time significant portions of London acquired distinct social characters. While the east end developed primarily as an artisans' district, the west end was inhabited by the upper classes and the servants and tradesmen they employed. This bifurcation was encouraged by the locations of the docks (east of London Bridge, in order to accommodate ocean-going vessels) and the seat of national government (in Westminster). It may also have been related to the prevailing winds, which blew the noxious fumes of the City eastwards.[44] A recent study by M. J. Power of the 1664 hearth tax returns and parliamentary surveys from the 1650s describes the emerging social and economic differences between east and west in detail: houses in the east had fewer rooms, fireplaces, and gardens, and were far less likely to be built out of brick, than houses in the west end. Houses in the east end were more likely to be put to an industrial use, to be empty, or to be inhabited by the poor. A much higher proportion of titled people lived in the west end. In sum, although the west end included some poorer districts, it was a wealthier and socially more respectable place to live than the portions of urban Middlesex east of the City of London:

The type of persons attracted to each area obviously differed greatly. In the west – by the late sixteenth century – parliament and the Inns of Court were drawing great numbers of gentry, lawyers, government servants, and men of affairs, and a large service population of shopkeepers and the like to support them. In the east we find a more homogeneous society of mariners, craftsmen, sailors, victuallers, almost all moderately humble working people.[45]

As is evident in Table 10.1, these socioeconomic contrasts were reflected in prosecution rates: almost three times as many recognizances and indictments were filed in Westminster and the western suburbs as in parishes east of the City of London.[46] As we have seen, this difference can partly be explained by the fact that east enders found it less convenient to file prosecutions – the courts were less accessible, and fewer people could easily afford the costs of prosecution. Yet pragmatic considerations do not provide a complete explanation:

---

43 *The Spectator* 403 (12 June 1712).   44 George, *London Life*, p. 74.
45 Power, "East and west," pp. 167–85, esp. pp. 182–83.
46 I use the term "west end" to refer to all the urban parishes west of City, both Westminster and the western urban Middlesex parishes (which are labelled "west urban" in Table 10.1).

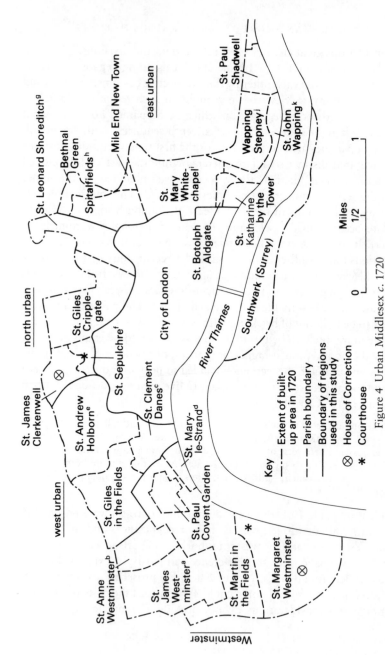

Figure 4 Urban Middlesex *c.* 1720

[a] Formed from St. Martin in the Fields in 1685. [b] Formed from St. Martin in the Fields in 1678. [c] Includes the Liberty of the Rolls and the Middlesex portion of the Temple. [d] Includes the Precinct of the Savoy and the detached portion of St. Clement Danes. [e] Includes Gray's Inn and Lincoln's Inn and the Liberties of Ely Rents, Saffron Hill, and Hatton Garden. [f] Includes the Charterhouse. [g] Includes Norton Folgate Liberty. [h] Formed from Stepney in 1729. Includes the Old Artillery Ground. [i] Includes Holy Trinity Minories. [j] Formed from Stepney in 1729. [k] Formed from Whitechapel in 1694. [l] Formed from Stepney in 1670.

Table 10.3 *Socioeconomic characteristics and prosecution rates of urban parishes*[a]

	% Exempt from hearth tax[b]	% Households with five or more hearths[c]	Prosecution rates: recogs./indicts.[d]
Westminster			
St. Margaret Westminster	48	34	6.0/3.1
St. Martin in the Fields	19	42	9.5/7.4
St. Paul Covent Garden	10	70	12.2/10.3
West urban			
St. Giles in the Fields	27	39	13.0/8.6
St. Andrew Holborn	24	61	4.7/4.6
St. Clement Danes[e]	4	58	8.1/5.0
North urban			
St. Leonard Shoreditch	59	17	2.5/2.3
St. James Clerkenwell	51	18	5.7/5.7
East urban			
St. Mary Whitechapel	70	9	3.6/2.6
St. John Wapping	53	15	1.6/1.4
Stepney	47	18	2.4/1.8
Shadwell	44	13	2.4/1.9[f]
Spitalfields	45	18	1.5/NA[g]

[a]   Small parishes like St. Sepulchre and St. Katharine by the Tower are not included in this table because statistically significant prosecution rates could not be calculated for them.

[b]   Power, "East and west," p. 181; L. Martindale, "Demography and land use in the late seventeenth and early eighteenth centuries in Middlesex" (Ph.D. diss., London, 1968), App. XVI.

[c]   From figures generously provided to me by Beatrice Shearer.

[d]   The average of the prosecution rates per 1000 inhabitants from each of the samples where population estimates were available.

[e]   Including St. Mary-le-Strand.

[f]   It was not possible to calculate the indictment prosecution rate for the individual hamlets of Stepney because all indictments from the hamlets listed the defendant's parish of residence as Stepney. Since Shadwell was formed from Stepney in 1670 it was possible to calculate an indictment rate for the subsequent sample periods.

[g]   See previous note.

statistically, wealth and distance do not fully account for the geographical variations in prosecution rates. In order to make full sense of these contrasting rates, it is necessary to examine social conditions in east and west London in greater detail.

Like most of the suburban parishes, the population of Westminster and the western Middlesex suburbs rose dramatically during this period, from about 50,000 people in 1664 to over 100,000 in the early 1720s.[47] Yet it is not the experience of population growth *per se* that lies behind the high prosecution rates in these parishes (the eastern suburbs experienced a similar population increase) but the fact that the west end came increasingly to contain a large number of poor as well as wealthy inhabitants, causing the social character of some inner west end parishes to decline markedly during this period. The two parishes with the highest prosecution rates in the metropolis, St. Paul Covent Garden and St. Giles in the Fields, experienced this transition most intensely as what were once socially prestigious neighborhoods became social battle-grounds (Table 10.3).

At the time of the hearth tax surveys in 1664, Covent Garden had the lowest proportion of residents excused from payment in urban Middlesex, only 4%. Since the parish was largely built up before the Restoration, its population increased little between 1660 and 1725. Its social character, however, changed significantly. As more fashionable streets and squares were erected to the west in St. Martin's and St. James' parishes, Covent Garden lost its position as London's most socially prestigious parish. The area's decline was hastened by the introduction of shops into the Piazza and market stalls into the square, as well as by the growing number of theaters, brothels, and gaming houses that opened in nearby Drury Lane.[48] In 1712, a group of inhabitants complained to the court that "loose, lewd, disorderly, and vagrant women have and do frequently, in the evenings and in the night time, in great numbers, stop up the passages to the houses of the petitioners and others ... by means whereof many quarrels, riots, and bloodsheds and affrays have been committed."[49] By 1720, the gaming houses had moved in:

... when any house in or near either of the playhouses happens to be vacant ... these vermin [gaming house keepers] take them over honest tradesmen's heads, which they turn over to thieving shops ... in so much that the parts of the town that are frequented by these creatures are dangerously infected with robbers and knaves, and the streets as dangerous in the night as they are in Padua ...[50]

---

[47] See below, Appendix III.
[48] R. Webber, *Covent Garden: Mud-Salad Market* (1969), pp. 34–85.
[49] MJ/SBB/700, p. 24 (Westminster sessions, Jan. 1712).
[50] *An Account of the Endeavours that have been used to Suppress Gaming Houses* (1722), pp. 20–21.

HE AND HIS DRUNKEN COMPANIONS RAISE A RIOT IN COVENT GARDEN.

Plate 4 "He and his drunken companions raise a riot in Covent Garden" 1735 (Westminster City Archives).

The changing character of Covent Garden is evident in this print depicting a group of drunken rakes who "swagger and swear and riots make / And windows, lamps & lanthorns break." Rudely attacking "all that in petticoats they meet," the men treat the women as if they were prostitutes. The watch, "alarmed by the outrageous noise," attempt to suppress the riot.

By 1720, Covent Garden had started its long slide towards becoming one of the worst slums in the metropolis.[51]

Although the nearby parish of St. Giles in the Fields started with a higher proportion of those excused from the hearth tax in 1664 (27%), at the same time it was still the home of many prosperous households: 39% had five or more hearths. Like Covent Garden, St. Giles experienced social decline over the next sixty years. In 1720, Strype described it as "of a very large extent, and as populous, with a mixture of rich inhabitants, to wit of the nobility, gentry, and

---

[51] George, *London Life*, pp. 91–92 describes the inner west-end slums in the eighteenth century.

commonality; but withal, filled with abundance of poor."[52] In 1675, the vestry expressed concern about the "daily" increase of the poor, and complaints about the increasing number of poor people living in the parish recur frequently over the next fifty years. In 1711, it was estimated that there were ten times as many "tradesmen and poor inhabitants" in the parish as "nobility and gentry."[53] By the mid-eighteenth century, there were "great numbers of houses set apart for the reception of idle persons and vagabonds, who have their lodgings there for two-pence a night."[54] As in Covent Garden, this process of social decline was accompanied by some of the highest prosecution rates in the county, not only for misdemeanors but also for felonies.[55]

Like the inhabitants from Covent Garden who petitioned the Westminster sessions in 1712, many residents fought to preserve the social character of these two parishes. During Queen Anne's reign, the inhabitants of Monmouth Street near Seven Dials petitioned for the suppression of the sale of rags in the street, claiming that several of the vendors "by reason of their poverty are likely to be chargeable to the said parish."[56] In 1664, the residents of Lincoln's Inn Fields petitioned the king for permission to pull down several sheds erected for puppet shows in the fields, because they attracted "multitudes of loose disorderly people." The crown was certainly sympathetic to attempts to maintain the social respectability of the west end; in 1671, the king himself issued a proclamation designed to forbid the building of "small and mean habitations" in the area west of St. Giles and Covent Garden.[57] Given the gentry's demand for servants and shopkeepers, the west end was always going to need houses for the less well off, but gentlemen in these parishes nonetheless attempted to isolate themselves from their social inferiors by inhabiting exclusive streets or squares, such as the Piazza at Covent Garden or Lincoln's Inn Fields, where few non-gentlemen could be found.[58] In some cases, the residents of these enclaves paid for their own police protection in the form of a separate nightly watch.[59] In St. Giles, the wealthy residents living in the northern part of the parish, who disliked travelling through disreputable streets on the way to the church, successfully petitioned that they be allowed to form a

[52] John Strype, A Survey of the Cities of London and Westminster ... by John Stow, 2 vols. (1720) vol. 2, p. 75. In the same year, the Middlesex grand jury presented five keepers of brothels from the parish: MJ/SP/Feb. 1720, no. 2.

[53] John Parton, Some Account of the Hospital and Parish of St. Giles in the Fields (1822), pp. 302–05; Reasons, Humbly Offered for a Bill to Rebuild the Parish-Church of St. Giles's in the Fields [1717?]; The Case of the Parish of St. Giles's in the Fields, as to their Poor and a Workhouse Designed to be Built for Employing Them [1722?].

[54] Henry Fielding, An Enquiry into the Causes of the Late Increase of Robbers (1751), p. 91

[55] The prosecution rate for felonies was 2.5 per 1,000 inhabitants, compared with 1.3 in Westminster and 0.8 in the east end.

[56] MJ/SP/With 1713 ("Temp Anne"), no. 1.

[57] Brett-James, Growth of Stuart London, pp. 158, 304; CSPD, 1671, p. 172.

[58] Power, "East and west", p. 180.   [59] MJ/SBB/481, pp. 71–72 (Jan. 1691).

separate parish. The new parish, St. George Bloomsbury, "almost wholly" consisted of nobility and gentry.[60]

Wealthy inhabitants attempted to preserve the social character of these inner west end parishes because they wished to avoid paying high poor rates and they feared an increase in crime. Both eventualities were likely to result from the increase in brothels and other disorderly houses which inevitably seemed to accompany the declining social respectability of a parish. Not only did these "notorious evil houses" cause neighboring inhabitants "disturbance, danger, and disquiet," but they drove respectable people away. Several "reputable inhabitants" of an alley off Chancery Lane where one brothel was located complained that they were ashamed to tell their friends where they lived, "it being reputed an ill place." On another brothel-infested street, the inhabitants felt compelled to move out, and five out of twenty-two houses were empty.[61]

It is thus not surprising that the west end parishes were a major focus of the reformation of manners campaign. Three-fifths of the justices who supported the campaign and whose region of judicial activity could be identified were active in the west end. The streets around Drury Lane were a major target of the reformers. As a "German Gentleman" wrote in 1725,

there are reckoned to be one hundred and seven pleasure-houses, within and about this settlement, the Ladies whereof ply the passengers at noon-day, as publicly as the solicitors do their clients at Westminster ... the Societies for the Reformation of Manners have taken more pains, and expended as large sums to reclaim this new sodom, and would have fitted out a force sufficient to have conquered the Spanish West Indies.[62]

The metaphor of a battle is an appropriate one in this context; the reformers encountered considerable opposition from residents who profited from the brothels and gaming houses or who resented the intrusive activities of informers. When the Westminster justices launched a campaign against gaming houses in Covent Garden in 1720, they encountered considerable opposition from gamblers, local residents, and even constables and fellow justices.[63] In 1721, a justice of the peace, supported by a mob of over one hundred people in Drury Lane, threatened to arrest two informers and forced them to leave the parish. Only 400 feet away on Little Wilde Street, on the other hand, eighteen "landlords and inhabitants" submitted a petition to the Middlesex court requesting the removal of several brothels.[64] Attitudes towards vice in these

[60] MJ/SBB/481, p. 71 (Jan. 1691); *The Case of the New Parish in Bloomsbury, Intended to be Taken out of St. Giles's in the Fields* [1716?]; Ben Weinreb and Christopher Hibbert, eds. *The London Encyclopedia* (1983), p. 707.
[61] MJ/SP/May 1702, no. 5; Oct. 1706, no. 24; Dec. 1716, no. 29.
[62] *A View of London and Westminster: or, the Town Spy, etc. By a German Gentleman* (1725), p. 12.
[63] *An Account of the Endeavours*; above, section 9.2.
[64] MJ/SP/Aug. 1721, no. 5; Dec. 1716, no. 29.

parishes were clearly sharply divided. In this volatile situation riots could be raised both to attack disorderly houses and to defend them from constables and informers who were attempting to suppress them.[65]

The battle to maintain the social respectability of the inner west end thus appears to have resulted in considerable social tensions. In St. Giles in the Fields, it was reported that justices of the peace were "worn out in determining and healing the breaches as continually happen among these various species of people."[66] Such tensions are reflected not only in the frequency, but also the character, of the misdemeanor prosecutions initiated in these parishes. Formal methods of prosecution were favored: almost as many indictments as recognizances were filed in Covent Garden. Throughout the west end, justices and prosecutors were quick to send offenders to houses of correction; per capita commitment rates in Westminster and the west urban parishes were considerably higher than in the northern or eastern suburban parishes (Table 10.1). Reflecting the concerns about vice and the large number of offenders sent to houses of correction, all of the "social control" justices identified in chapter 8 lived in the west end. On the other hand, proportionate to the number of justices active in the region, fewer "mediating justices" worked in the west end than in other parts of the metropolis.[67]

Although, as reported above, the justices of St. Giles frequently "determined and healed" disputes, informal mediation of disputes was less likely to succeed in the inner west end parishes than in other parts of the metropolis. The natural mediators of preindustrial England, the gentry, faced difficulties in settling disputes in areas where significant social tensions existed, particularly conflicts between rich and poor. Moreover, since both rich and poor residents of the west end parishes moved so frequently, they had little chance of developing the kinds of social relationships which facilitate mediation. Defoe noted that the poor "at the court end of town ... shift from place to place" in order to evade high parish taxes.[68] Similarly, Lawrence Stone has noted that the nobility "seemed incapable of settling down, and the big houses [in the west end] changed hands with remarkable frequency in the late seventeenth and early eighteenth centuries."[69] Instead of acting as mediators, gentlemen were themselves frequently involved in prosecutions: gentlemen accounted for 26% of the male defendants bound over in Covent Garden and 40% of those indicted.

---

[65] Shoemaker, "London 'mob'," pp. 299–300; PRO, SP 35/34/152; *Jonathan Wild's Advice to his Successors*, reprinted in Frederick J. Lyons, *Jonathan Wild, Prince of Robbers* (1936), pp. 294–95.

[66] *A View of London and Westminster*, p. 12.   [67] See above, Tables 8.5 and 8.6.

[68] Andrew Moreton [Daniel Defoe], *Parochial Tyranny: or the House-keeper's Complaint Against the Insupportable Exactions, and Partial Assessments of Select Vestries, etc.* (1727), p. 22.

[69] Lawrence Stone, "The residential development of the west end of London in the seventeenth century," in *After the Reformation. Essays in honour of J. H. Hexter*, ed. Barbara C. Malament (Manchester, 1980), pp. 195–96.

From a more limited sample, gentlemen filed 8% of the indictments prosecuted by male private plaintiffs in the west end.

Another reason informal mediation was less likely to succeed in these parishes is that a significant proportion of the prosecutions were for vice offences, which were typically not successfully resolved informally. The efforts of the Societies for the Reformation of Manners and their allies are reflected in the large number of house of correction commitments from the west end for prostitution and loose, idle, and disorderly behavior, as well as in the disproportionately large number of indictments for vice offences from the inner west end parishes. Alehouse offences alone accounted for 20% of the indictments in St. Giles in the Fields and 21% of the indictments in the neighboring parish of St. Andrew Holborn, while 13.5% of the indictments in Covent Garden were for gaming offences. Although fewer recognizances were issued for vice, at 9% St. Giles had the highest proportion of recognizances for sexual offences of any parish in the metropolis.

Both concern about vice and the apparent distrust of the poor help to explain the large number of prosecutions involving women in the west end. Over 70% of the defendants committed to houses of correction from Westminster and the western urban Middlesex parishes were women, compared with only 54% of those committed from elsewhere in the county. Most such women, needless to say, were suspected of prostitution; most were poor and unmarried, and without respectable social connections. Many may have been, or have once been, the domestic servants who were in such demand in these parishes. Reflecting the heavy use of houses of correction for the punishment of women, women in the west end were generally underrepresented on recognizances and indictments. Women in St. Giles, however, were, compared with other parishes, overrepresented, both as prosecutors and defendants on recognizances and as defendants on indictments. A large proportion of the female defendants on indictments were unmarried (35%). Together with the house of correction evidence, this suggests that unmarried women in St. Giles were particularly likely to become involved in misdemeanor prosecutions. These women probably worked for a living, and thus were more likely to become involved in conflicts, and they were easily suspected of prostitution.[70] Perhaps because of a lack of close relationships with the more established residents of the parish, they were unable to benefit from informal mediation.

The conditions that encouraged high prosecution rates in London's western suburbs were most prominent in the inner west end parishes of Covent Garden and St. Giles, but to a certain extent these conditions were also present in other west end parishes. Social conditions in the neighboring parish of St. Martin in

[70] Above, section 7.2.

the Fields (which surrounded Covent Garden) were similar: a large and growing contingent of the poor threatened the exclusivity of its aristocratic streets and squares. While 42% of the households had five or more hearths in 1664, a fifth of its households were not chargeable for the hearth tax. This social divide persisted and probably increased over the next sixty years: in 1720, John Strype described the streets of St. Martin's as alternately "well inhabited," "ordinary," and "ill inhabited and nastily kept."[71] Due to their "miserable appearances and clamourous begging," in 1722 the poor of the metropolis were described as "most of all troublesome within the parishes of St. Martin's in the Fields, St. James' and St. Anne's Westminster: in which three parishes, most of your nobility, and many of the principal gentry, and others of distinction, in the winter reside."[72] Given the fact that in 1664 the proportion of non-chargeable households in east end parishes was two to three times higher than in St. Martin's, the idea that London's worst poverty was to be found in St. Martin's is implausible; such complaints reveal more about attitudes towards the poor than the actual extent of poverty. A heightened sensitivity to the presence of the poor was also evident in fashionable St. Anne's parish (formerly part of St. Martin's), where an observer reported that "pauper dress [was] esteemed a dreadful impiety."[73] As in St. Giles and Covent Garden, the wealthier inhabitants of St. Martin's distanced themselves from their neighbors by living in socially exclusive courts, which could be fenced off, or in streets and squares where the system of building leases ensured that only wealthy inhabitants could find accommodation.[74] The ultimate method of social segregation was the formation of new parishes; as in St. Giles, some of the wealthiest parts of St. Martin's were formed into the separate parishes of St. James and St. Anne's in the 1680s. As Strype noted in 1720, "the parish of St. James's is large [and] well replenished with fine open streets, which are graced with good buildings, and generally well inhabited, especially St. James Square, and the streets adjacent, as also Golden Square."[75]

The social tensions in St. Martin's, which were both a cause and a consequence of such attempts at social segregation, resulted in the third highest parochial prosecution rates in the west end, after St. Giles and Covent Garden. From the 1693 sample, when the parishes of St. James and St. Anne's can be analyzed separately, prosecution rates were generally higher in what remained of St. Martin's than in the new parishes. Like St. Giles and Covent Garden, the

---

[71] Strype, *Survey of London*, vol. 2, book 6, pp. 67–80.
[72] *The Form of a Petition Submitted to the Consideration and Correction of those Noblemen and Gentlemen who Desire to Subscribe what Sums shall be Necessary for Relieving, Reforming, and Employing the Poor* (1722), pp. 10–11.
[73] *A View of London and Westminster*, p. 8.
[74] Strype, *Survey of London*, vol. 2, p. 69; John Summerson, *Georgian London* (1945; Harmondsworth, 1978), chap. 3.
[75] Strype, *Survey of London*, vol. 2, book 6, pp. 80–81.

older parts of St. Martin's were a focal point of activity against vice. One of the founding acts of the reformation of manners campaign was a petition filed in August 1689, from the churchwardens and overseers of the poor of St. Martin's, complaining that keepers of bawdy houses encouraged the "daily increase of poor" in the parish.[76] In response, justices meeting at the St. Martin's vestry initiated a campaign of committing prostitutes to the Westminster house of correction which continued on and off for more than twenty years.[77] Nonetheless, vice continued to be a problem in St. Martin's, and in 1731, in response to a complaint from eighteen shopkeepers, tradesmen, and other inhabitants, a group of Westminster justices launched a new campaign against disorderly houses in the parts of the parish which bordered on Covent Garden.[78]

The remaining parishes of the west end experienced less social change than St. Giles, Covent Garden, and St. Martin in the Fields, and consequently experienced lower prosecution rates. Although St. Margaret Westminster was home to an even greater mixture of wealth and poverty, its social character did not change significantly during this period. Already in 1664, almost half of its households were not chargeable for the hearth tax, and it is unlikely that the extent of poverty in the parish significantly worsened during the period. In comparison with its neighbors, prosecutions in St. Margaret's were infrequent and informal: almost twice as many recognizances were filed as indictments (Table 10.3). At the other end of the social spectrum, the parishes of St. Mary-le-Strand and St. Clement Danes started the period with very low concentrations of non-chargeable households and appear to have maintained their social respectability over the next sixty years. Although St. Mary-le-Strand suffered somewhat from the westward migration of the aristocracy and gentry, the Strand continued to be an important trading street because of its prominent location between Westminster and the City, and many wealthy merchants and gentlemen continued to live in the parish. As Defoe noted in the early 1720s, the palaces of the nobility on the Strand had been replaced by "noble streets and beautiful houses."[79] The social stability of these parishes may explain why prosecution rates were lower than in neighboring St. Giles' and St. Martin's parishes as well as the fact that recognizances outnumbered indictments by a considerable margin.[80] Patterns of prosecutions in St. Andrew Holborn are more difficult to explain, in part because this large parish had no coherent social character: located immediately north and west of the City of London, St. Andrew's was partly a socially prestigious west end parish in decline and partly

---

[76] MJ/SP/Aug. 1689, no. 10; MJ/SBB/468, p. 6 (Aug. 1689).   [77] See above, section 9.1.
[78] WJ/OC/II, ff. 101d–106 (April 1731).
[79] Brett-James, *Growth of Stuart London*, pp. 381, 389–91; Defoe, *Tour*, p. 297.
[80] One reason for the relative lack of indictments in this area, however, is that nuisance offences in the Liberty of the Savoy were prosecuted in its manor court: see above, chap. 2.

an expanding artisans' suburb north of the City. According to Strype, Holborn had "places good and bad contained in it."[81] Reflecting its mixed composition, prosecution rates in the parish were a peculiar combination of low overall rates (for a west end parish) and, unusually, almost an equal number of recognizances and indictments filed.

Regardless of the differences between them, all the west end parishes had higher prosecution rates than those found in the suburban parishes east of the City. Overall, per capita prosecution rates in the eastern parishes, from Spitalfields in the north to Shadwell along the river at the eastern extreme of the metropolis, were only about one-third those in the western parishes, and indictment rates in the east end were not much higher than those in rural Middlesex (Table 10.1). On more limited evidence, it appears that the eastern parishes provided a very small number of commitments to the house of correction. There are many possible explanations for these enormous differences: while pragmatic considerations such as distance from the courts, the poverty of many inhabitants, and the availability of other methods of prosecuting offences played an important role, a significant cause of the east end's low prosecution rates was the unique social conditions in its parishes.

Not only were prosecution rates lower in the east end, but recognizance rates actually declined by almost half over the five sample periods: while recognizances from the east end accounted for 27% of the county total in 1663–64, by 1720–22 they accounted for only 14% of county business. One possible explanation of this phenomenon is that east end justices adopted the practice of not returning agreed recognizances to sessions, but as stated earlier the nature of the recognizances that were returned suggests this practice did not occur. Neither is the decline likely to have been caused by the unavailability of justices.[82] It is also possible that east end prosecutions were diverted to the Tower Liberty quarter sessions, established in the 1680s by James II. Since this court had jurisdiction over a relatively small area, however, it is unlikely that it caused a significant reduction in the number of east end cases brought before the Middlesex court.[83] It is more likely that the decline in east end recognizances was due to the increasing use of petty sessions during this period.[84] As in rural areas, justices may have found it more convenient to handle minor offences by requiring defendants to appear at petty sessions in lieu of binding them over by recognizance to appear at quarter sessions.[85] In any case, it should

---

[81] Strype, *Survey of London*, vol. 1, book 3, p. 256.   [82] See above, sections 5.2 and 10.1.
[83] John Charlton, ed., *The Tower of London: Its Buildings and Institutions* (1978), pp. 147–50; John Bayley, *The History and Antiquities of the Tower of London* (1825), vol. 2, Appendix, pp. cxii–cxxi. No records from this sessions appear to have survived.
[84] Shoemaker, "Crime, courts and community," Appendix One.
[85] Landau, *Justices of the Peace*, pp. 206–08.

be emphasized that even in the 1663–64 sample prosecution rates by both recognizance and indictment were significantly lower than in the west end.[86]

As we have seen, the poverty of many east end residents provides one explanation of the relative lack of prosecutions. The number of hearths per household in the east end was approximately half that in the western parishes, and from 30 to 70% of the households were judged too poor to pay the hearth tax. It is, unfortunately, impossible to assess the social or economic status of those people who did prosecute offences in the east end, but judging by the status of their defendants, the lowest status groups in the east end used the courts infrequently. Despite the different social compositions of the eastern and western parishes, the proportion of defendants prosecuted from low-status groups in each region was similar; the larger number of low status residents in the east end was not reflected in prosecutions initiated at quarter sessions. The distance east end residents needed to travel to reach the courthouse in Clerkenwell also discouraged prosecutions, especially, as we have seen, commitments to houses of correction. The distance was not great (though the streets through the City were congested), but it was considerably more than that faced by west end residents, especially those resident in Westminster. For prosecutors uncertain about whether a case was worth prosecuting, the additional distance may have been a decisive factor.

Distance and wealth should have had the greatest impact on prosecution rates by indictment, since indictments were considerably more expensive than recognizances and the prosecutor was required to appear in court in order to appear before the grand jury. Yet, prosecution rates by recognizance in the east end were also considerably lower than in the west end. This suggests that, while distance and wealth were important, other factors dissuaded potential plaintiffs from initiating prosecutions in the eastern suburbs. A major cause of this apparent reluctance to prosecute appears to have been the absence of the types of social tensions found in the west end. This is suggested by the fact that it is not simply the volume of prosecutions in the east end, but also their character, which differed significantly from the western parishes. To a greater extent than in other parts of the metropolis, offences against the peace were the most common type of offence prosecuted, accounting for 69% of all east end recognizances (compared to 56% in the west end; Table 10.4). Almost a third of all east end recognizances were simply preventive recognizances to keep the peace, which suggests that the disputes were not serious. Vice offences, on the other hand, were relatively rarely prosecuted in the eastern parishes. Prostitution and other victimless offences account for only 44% of the small number of commitments made to the house of correction, compared with 62% of the much larger number in the west end; in absolute numbers, *seventeen times* as

---

[86] As discussed above, one of the reasons for the high number of recognizances in the east end in 1663–64 was the extraordinary activities of justices Abell and Swalowe.

Table 10.4 *Regional characteristics of urban Middlesex prosecutions*[a]

	West end	East end	Northern suburbs
Recognizances:			
% offences against the peace	56	69	62
Indictments:			
% offences against the peace	45	48	47
% vice offences	15	9	13
House of correction commitments:			
% victimless offences	62	44	48
% female defendants	71	56	48
Recognizances:[b]			
% female defendants	33	48	34
% female plaintiffs	47	55	53
Indictments:[b]			
% female defendants	29	35	20
% female plaintiffs	34	40	23
Recognizances, female defendants:			
% single[c]	47	47	52
% married	40	47	38
% widow	13	6	10
Indictments, female defendants:[d]			
% single	31	23	19
% married	49	53	54
% widow	19	24	27

[a] Non-indicted recognizances only.
[b] Excluding unknowns, and, in the case of plaintiffs, official plaintiffs.
[c] Includes cases where no marital status was given.
[d] Based on 1663–64 and 1720–22 samples only.

many people were committed to houses of correction for victimless offences in the west end as in the east end. Only 9% of east end indictments concerned vice, compared with 15% of west end indictments. Although the east end was the home of the first Society for the Reformation of Manners, the reformers' efforts quickly came to concentrate on the west end. Few of the religious societies that provided supporters for the campaign in the 1690s held their meetings east of the City of London.[87]

Prostitution and bawdy houses no doubt existed in the east end,[88] but it is likely that they were less common than around Drury Lane, and they were

[87] *Antimoixeia: or, the Honest and Joynt-Design of the Tower Hamblets for the General Suppression of Bawdy-Houses, as Incouraged by the Publick Magistrates* (1691); Edinburgh University Library, Laing MS III, 394, pp. 325–28.
[88] See MJ/SBB/732 (April 1715); T. J. G. (Tim) Harris, *London Crowds in the Reign of Charles II* (Cambridge, 1987), p. 82.

clearly not perceived as a threat to the community. It is significant that the narrator of John Dunton's *Nightwalker: or, Evening Rambles in Search after Lewd Women* never visited the east end, and when Ned Ward traveled east in *The London Spy* he described temporary relationships between women and sailors, but little in the way of open prostitution. One observer described Wapping as "the most whorish place about London," but then explained that "the seamen's wives, whose husbands are often long abroad, being very impudent and lascivious, often [have] children to other men."[89] Perhaps because there was less open soliciting and sexual liaisons were longer lasting, there was less fear that sexual immorality would ruin neighborhoods and lead to crime.

The pattern of prosecutions in the east end thus suggests that there were fewer social tensions east of the City of London than in the west end. Offences were mostly minor offences against the peace, and vice was not perceived as a significant social problem. The one type of vice that was prosecuted frequently in the east end, working and permitting tippling on the Sabbath,[90] was the type of vice least likely to result in social tensions; no one argued that working on the Sabbath encouraged crime or ruined neighborhoods. As a consequence of the low level of social tensions, offences were rarely prosecuted formally. Thus, almost twice as many recognizances as indictments came from the east end, and one-third of the justices in the sample who were active in the east end were identified as "mediating" justices in chapter 8. In comparison, less than a fifth of the west end justices were so identified. This apparent inclination to settle disputes informally is illustrated in petitions to the sessions filed from east end parishes, which requested the court to drop prosecutions. When Mary Hall of the riverside hamlet of Limehouse wrote in 1690 asking the court to discharge her from an indictment for a rescue, seven residents of the hamlet, including a churchwarden and a constable, signed the petition.[91]

In comparison with the west end, the east end experienced little disruptive social change during this period. Although the population doubled, the social composition remained stable, and the eastern parishes were far more socially homogeneous. Parishes east of the city were primarily inhabited by artisans and laborers; only about a seventh of the houses had five or more hearths. In particular, the occupational mixture of craftsmen and laborers engaged in trades related to the port in the riverside parishes of Wapping and Shadwell was one of the most socially homogeneous in the metropolis. There was no hierarchy of occupations: the wealthiest inhabitants of Shadwell were relatively

---

[89] [John Dunton], *The Nightwalker: or, Evening Rambles in Search after Lewd Women* (Oct. 1696); Edward Ward, *The London Spy Compleat* (1698–1703; reprint edn, 1927), part xiv; "London in 1689–90," *Transactions of the London and Middlesex Archaeological Society*, new series, vol. 6 (1930), p. 494.

[90] Laing MS, III, 394, pp. 315–22; Bodleian Library, Rawlinson MS D1399, 1401, 1403.

[91] MJ/SP/April 1690, no. 7. See also MJ/SP/Jan. 1708, no. 52.

evenly divided among several occupations. M. J. Power describes mid-seventeenth-century Shadwell as "a society 'writ small' in which people lived and worked in the same small area where they bought their food and met to drink."[92] The sense of community evident in these parishes, a product of the lack of substantial class differences, their stable social composition, and the close proximity of the parishioners' homes, workplaces, and places of recreation, allowed disputes to be settled without the intervention of the courts. Despite the fact that both parishes contained some of the poorest and most crowded dwellings in London, crime was evidently not a problem: on average, only three or four misdemeanor prosecutions per thousand inhabitants were initiated each year, and felony prosecution rates were also lower than average.

Another factor contributing to social stability in the east end was religious dissent. In 1684, it was said that there were "sixteen great and public conventicles" east of the City, and when the Middlesex justices tried to suppress them the local community rallied to their protection, and constables and local juries refused to cooperate.[93] The ranks of the nonconformists were further strengthened by the Huguenot influx after 1685. The common experience of religious nonconformity may have forged a sense of community in east end neighborhoods; the Huguenots formed relief committees and built a hospital to provide care for those in need. Most worked in one of the east end's main industries, weaving, which was still largely carried out in the home. As suggested by their actions in the industrial protests of 1675, 1689, 1697, 1710, and 1719–20, the weavers (both English and Huguenot) possessed a strong sense of collective identity and independence which no doubt helped them to settle their disputes without recourse to the courts.[94]

While the most striking characteristic of east end prosecutions is their low number, one group, women, were proportionally *more* likely to be involved in prosecutions, both as defendants and prosecutors, in the east end than in any other region of urban Middlesex (Table 10.4). As prosecutors, women were responsible for 55% of east end recognizances and 40% of indictments, compared to 47% and 34% respectively in the west end. As defendants, east

[92] M. J. Power, "Shadwell: the development of a London suburban community in the seventeenth century," *London Journal* 4 (1978), pp. 36, 40; and "East London housing in the seventeenth century," in *Crisis and Order in English Towns 1500–1700*, ed. Peter Clark and Paul Slack (1972), pp. 240, 257.

[93] *The Proceedings of his Majesties Justices of Peace at the Sessions of Oyer and Terminer ... September the 6th, 1684, for the Tryal of the Constables ... of the Hamlets of Spittle-fields and Bethnal Green* (1684), p. 2; MJ/SBB/417 (Sept. 1684), p. 56. See also T. J. G. (Tim) Harris, "The politics of the London crowd in the reign of Charles II" (Ph.D. diss., Cambridge University, 1985), Appendix table 1.3; Power, "Urban development of east London," pp. 263ff.

[94] Strype, *Survey of London*, vol. 2, p. 48; H. L. Smith, *The History of East London* (1939), p. 247; Power, "Urban development of east London," pp. 82, 184, 230; C. F. A. Marmoy, "The Huguenots and their descendants in east London," *East London Papers* 13 (1970), pp. 77–82, 88; Robin D. Gwynn, *Huguenot Heritage: The History and Contribution of the Huguenots in Britain* (1985), pp. 167–73; Shoemaker, "London 'mob'", pp. 279–80.

end women account for 48% of the recognizances and 35% of the indictments, significantly more than in the other regions. Either as prosecutors or defendants, women were involved in almost two-thirds of all prosecutions initiated in the east end. Unfortunately, all that is known about these women is their marital status, and for some of the married women, their husbands' occupations. Nevertheless, it is significant that a higher proportion of these women were married, and fewer were unmarried, than in the west end.

It is likely that this pattern is due in part to the fact that fewer single women lived in the east end since demand for domestic servants was lower there than elsewhere in the metropolis. It is also probable, however, that married women were proportionately more likely to become involved in criminal prosecutions in the east end because more of them worked, especially outside the home. Lower-class wives worked more often than their middle- and upper-class counterparts,[95] and, as discussed in section 8.2, this public exposure and independence could lead them to become more frequently involved in disputes and make them less amenable to traditional means of resolving these informally. The low status of these women is reflected in the occupations of their husbands: according to the recognizance evidence by far the two biggest occupational groups were sailors and laborers, and among the other occupations were victuallers, gardeners, tailors, coopers, and weavers, as well as a woodmonger, lighterman, bricklayer, and butcher. Sailor's wives whose husbands were absent at sea were particularly at risk of prosecution because of community suspicions concerning their affairs with other men. Ruth Fry, the wife of a sailor from Ratcliffe Highway in Stepney, was bound over in 1664 by two women who complained that "in the absence of her husband [she] keepeth company with young men [including the son of one of the prosecutors] upon whom they spend whatever they get to their undoing."[96] Laborers' wives were forced to find menial employments such as hawking, washing, and nursing, occupations which provided considerable possibilities for conflicts and disputes.[97] Much the same could be said for the wives of victuallers. The situation of women married to craftsmen depended on the nature of the craft and whether or not the work was carried out in the home; if the wife could not contribute to her husband's business she frequently acquired her own job.[98] Significantly, since weaving was still largely a domestic industry,[99] few weavers' wives were prosecuted, and of those who were, two-thirds were

---

[95] Peter Earle, "The female labour market in London in the late seventeenth and early eighteenth centuries," *Economic History Review*, second series, 42 (Aug. 1989), pp. 337–38.

[96] MJ/SR/1286, R. 63 (April 1664).

[97] George, *London Life*, pp. 170–72; Alice Clark, *Working Life of Women in the Seventeenth Century* (1919; reprint edn New York, 1968), pp. 234–35, 299.

[98] Clark, *Working Life of Women*, pp. 234–35, 294, 299. However, Earle ("The female labour market," p. 338) argues that few women worked in their husbands' occupations.

[99] Power, "Urban development of east London," p. 230.

prosecuted with their husbands. Weavers' wives did not experience the same degree of independence and public exposure as the wives of laborers and sailors.

Prosecutions involving women in the east end overwhelmingly concerned offences against the peace. Of the prosecutions initiated by women, about half of the defendants were also women, a higher proportion than found in the northern and western parishes. Expressed as a proportion of female defendants, female prosecutors in the east end accounted for two-thirds of the prosecutions of women. Women in the east end used the courts to accuse each other of both verbal and physical attacks. Although preventive recognizances ("to keep the peace") were the most frequent type of prosecution involving women, women were both plaintiffs and defendants for significant numbers of riots, incidents involving defamatory words and actions, and accusations of being a common disturber.

Many of these offences, especially those involving defamatory words, were the result of disputes over the sexual reputation of the plaintiffs; such was the incident involving Ruth Fry, the sailor's wife described earlier. Whereas in the west end the people accused of voicing such slander were predominantly men, in the east end it was women who were most often accused of this offence. Sarah Barnett, the wife of a silkthrower in East Smithfield, for example, was bound over in 1664 by Elizabeth Beadle "for most uncivilly and wickedly scandalizing and calling her whore, saying also that she was a bulling whore."[100] Both the defendants and the plaintiffs in these cases contributed to the enforcement of sexual morality. By the act of voicing the defamatory words, defendants attempted to harness public opinion against alleged offenders. Martha May of Shadwell, for example, had her husband bound over for beating her "and then crying her down through the town ... that none might trust her."[101] Plaintiffs, on the other hand, affirmed the existence of moral standards when they contested such allegations by prosecuting the people who defamed them.

Though these examples did lead to prosecutions, most were prosecuted only by recognizance. It seems likely, moreover, that the power of community opinion and informal neighborly chastisement evident in these cases often led to informal resolutions of disputes over sexual behavior (or any number of other issues) in the east end. In contrast, the keepers and frequenters of brothels in the west end were clearly unaffected by the opinions of their neighbors, and the people who prosecuted them chose indictments and the house of correction in lieu of more informal methods of prosecution. The patterns of prosecutions that *were* initiated in the east end thus suggest that strong community ties and a

---

[100] MJ/SR/1294, R. 121 (Oct. 1664).   [101] MJ/SR/1273, R. 88 (July 1663).

general absence of social tensions allowed most disputes to be resolved without recourse to the courts.

The character of prosecutions in the urban Middlesex parishes north of the City of London (St. James Clerkenwell, St. Sepulchre, St. Giles Cripplegate, and St. Leonard Shoreditch) was mixed. Socially, the northern parishes resembled the eastern parishes in the sense that they had a relatively homogeneous lower class population, with high proportions of households excluded from the hearth tax (51–67%) and relatively low proportions of households owning five or more hearths (16–18%). Prosecution rates in the northern suburbs, however, were not homogeneous. Like its eastern neighbors, St. Leonard Shoreditch had very low rates, but Clerkenwell's rate of 5.7 recognizances and 5.7 indictments per 1,000 inhabitants was higher than its western neighbor, St. Andrew Holborn.[102] Per capita house of correction commitments were 5.5 per 1,000 inhabitants, considerably higher than the east end but one-third lower than the rate in Westminster (which had its own house of correction) and 44% lower than the rate for the other west urban parishes. On the whole, however, attitudes towards prosecutions in the northern parishes were lenient, resembling to a certain extent those of the east end. Although recognizance and indictment rates were higher than in the east end, recognizances were more than twice as popular as indictments; the recognizance to indictment ratio of 2.2 was the highest in the metropolis. Indeed, ten of the fourteen active justices in the sample who worked in the northern parishes can be characterized as "mediating" justices, who encouraged prosecutions by recognizance rather than indictment.[103] Perhaps encouraged by the proximity of the courthouse, prosecutors in some northern neighborhoods were quick to file prosecutions, but they were inclined to treat their defendants leniently.

Reflecting the choice of a procedure, the offences prosecuted in the northern parishes were not serious: one quarter of the recognizances were simply "to keep the peace." Here, as in the east end, vice does not appear to have been of particular concern: less than half of the commitments to the house of correction were for prostitution and related offences, compared with 62% in the west end. This lack of concern about vice was particularly evident in Shoreditch, where residents refused to cooperate when a group of inhabitants from east end parishes made an agreement in 1690 to reimburse parish officers for the expenses they incurred indicting keepers of brothels.[104] Similarly, when fourteen inhabitants of Shoreditch were indicted for keeping gaming houses in 1708, several parish officers and "ancient inhabitants" of the parish petitioned the court to drop the prosecutions, pleading that the accused "are very honest,

---

[102] Prosecution rates could not be calculated for St. Sepulchre (because of its small size) and St. Giles Cripplegate (because of a lack of population figures).
[103] Table 8.5 and Appendix III.   [104] MJ/SBB/500, pp. 50–51 (Oct. 1692).

industrious, persons (though but in mean conditions)."[105] Prostitutes are known to have been present in some parts of the northern suburbs, but their activities do not appear to have overly concerned the residents of these parishes. Although a few justices who were active supporters of the reformation of manners campaign lived in the northern parishes, few if any of the religious societies which supported the campaign were based there.[106]

The lack of social tensions evident in attitudes towards vice in Shoreditch suggests that, as in the eastern parishes, the social homogeneity of the parish enabled residents to resolve disputes without filing formal prosecutions. The higher rate of prosecutions in Clerkenwell, on the other hand, may have resulted from the fact that, like the western parishes of St. Giles in the Fields and Covent Garden, Clerkenwell experienced significant social change during this period. Throughout most of the seventeenth century the parish was aristocratic in character, but like its western neighbors it lost many of its wealthy residents in the last decades of the century and by 1720 the parish included "many small lanes and closes with small gardenless houses packed tightly together."[107] The relatively high level of litigation which accompanied these changes may have been a product of tensions between the new inhabitants, who were often poor, and the established wealthy residents of the parish. While social conditions in Shoreditch were similar to those in the eastern suburbs, Clerkenwell social life resembled that of a west end parish.

From this analysis of patterns of prosecutions in their social contexts it is possible to draw conclusions both about the nature of social relations in preindustrial London and about the different perceived uses of each of the methods available for prosecuting petty crime. As we have seen, social conditions in the London suburbs varied considerably. As Dorothy George commented in 1925, "in the eighteenth century the metropolis was made up of a number of self-contained communities to a far greater extent than it is now."[108] Some of those communities, particularly in the west end, appear to have been hardly communities at all, as rapid social change and concern about vice divided neighborhoods and inhibited the formation of social ties. Many east end parishes, on the other hand, possessed a degree of social stability typically found in rural parishes. Despite rapid population growth, these parishes either suffered few crimes or (more plausibly) their inhabitants retained the ability to mediate criminal accusations informally. As Jeremy Boulton concluded from his study of early seventeenth-century Southwark,

[105] MJ/SP/Jan. 1708, nos. 6–9, 53, 54. See also MJ/SP/Jan. 1709, no. 3.
[106] Bawdy houses in Moorfields and Shoreditch were attacked during the bawdy house riots of 1668 (Harris, London Crowds, p. 82). For justice John Fuller's unsuccessful efforts to combat vice in Moorfields, see MJ/SP/April 1717, no. 76, and above, section 9.2. For the locations of the religious societies, see Laing MS, III, 394, pp. 325–28.
[107] Brett-James, Growth of Stuart London, pp. 218–21.   [108] George, London Life, p. 77.

Table 10.5 *Recognizance-to-indictment ratios by region*

Westminster	1.41
West urban	1.78
North urban	2.19
East urban	1.85
Urban periphery	0.96
Rural	0.81

strong neighborhood communities could exist in early-modern London.[109] Unlike Southwark or most rural parishes, however, the east end parishes were socially homogeneous. Although the character of social relations in these parishes needs further research, it is clear that life in this part of preindustrial London was not "anonymous."

Choices of procedures for prosecution in these contrasting social contexts varied widely. Commitment to a house of correction was only convenient from the northern and western suburbs, and the highest rates of commitments were found in the socially unstable west end parishes. Concern about vice and social change in these parishes appears to have resulted in considerable distrust of the poor, leading plaintiffs and justices to commit petty offenders who were poor for immediate punishment in lieu of seeking informal settlements. Despite the fact that the west end parishes had the lowest proportions of poor inhabitants in the metropolis (as measured by exemption from the hearth tax), they had the highest rates of commitments to the house of correction, an institution specifically designed for the punishment of poor offenders. Per capita, the poor in the west end were far more likely to find themselves in a house of correction than the poor living anywhere else in the county. Houses of correction were attractive to plaintiffs who lived in areas where the poor were viewed as a threat to social stability.

The west end was also the home of the indictment. Not only were per capita indictment rates the highest in the county (encouraged, once again, by the fact that distance was not an obstacle), but recognizance-to-indictment rates, especially in Westminster, were the lowest in the metropolis (Table 10.5). Although prosecution by indictment in these parishes was facilitated by the relative wealth of the inhabitants, it is also likely that the same social tensions that led plaintiffs and justices to commit offenders to houses of correction also led plaintiffs to file indictments: prosecutors in the west end appear to have sought convictions and punishments (or expensive out-of-court settlements) in lieu of negotiation and mediation. Relative to the number of recognizances filed, indictments were also popular in rural areas, but for different reasons: the

---

[109] Boulton, *Neighbourhood and Society*.

availability of local informal mediation and the distance from the courthouse meant that only the most serious offences were prosecuted.

Recognizances above all were an urban phenomenon, where they outnumbered indictments in every region. Numerically, recognizances were most common in the northern and western parishes, where the courthouses were located. Proportional to the number of indictments issued, however, recognizances were most popular in the northern and eastern parishes, where stable social relations appear to have encouraged less formal approaches to prosecuting crime. It is significant that many of these prosecutions were initiated by women; recognizances clearly provided an attractive method of addressing disputes between women, many of whom were employed outside the home. Recognizances were also very popular in the west urban parishes (especially St. Giles in the Fields), however, which suggests that they were the most flexible of the procedures for prosecuting petty offences, suitable for both men and women and for areas of social instability as well as stability.

The choice of a procedure for prosecution, therefore, was influenced not only by the nature of the offence or the identity of the participants involved, but also to a significant extent both by practical considerations and by social conditions in the locality in which the offence took place. As the contrasting strategies adopted by prosecutors from different parts of Middlesex clearly demonstrate, each of the procedures for prosecution was particularly suited to a different social context.

11

Conclusion: Law and society in preindustrial England

Even more than in the prosecution of felonies, discretion and flexibility characterized the prosecution of misdemeanors. Potential plaintiffs in misdemeanor cases faced a choice of procedures for prosecution, including three procedures – informal mediation, recognizances, and summary jurisdiction – which were largely unavailable for felonies. Plaintiffs also benefited from the wide range of petty offences subject to prosecution, some of which were very broadly defined. Recognizances for the peace, indictments for assault, and commitments to houses of correction for idle and disorderly conduct, to name just the most obvious examples, could be used to prosecute a wide variety of criminal or quasi-criminal complaints. Punishments for petty offences were also flexible: both the size of fines and the length of imprisonments were easily tailored to the individual circumstances of each case. Finally, individual justices of the peace had considerable influence over the course of prosecutions for petty offences: in most cases a justice, in consultation with the plaintiff, chose the legal procedure, and for informal mediation and summary convictions individual justices determined the verdict and punishment. There was little chance that their actions would be subsequently reviewed; in prosecuting petty crime, justices and plaintiffs possessed a remarkable degree of independence.

How was this discretion used? Informal settlements of disputes were encouraged wherever possible. Informal mediation was intrinsic to the two most popular methods of prosecution, informal hearings before justices and recognizances. Even the most formal procedure, the indictment, was manipulated to provide opportunities for extra-legal settlements. Although the procedures for summary conviction did not allow much time for informal settlements, the evidence suggests that petty offenders were often warned on first offences and only convicted and punished after they repeated the crime.[1] Moreover, by

---

[1] This is evident from the fact that persons committed to houses of correction were often charged with multiple offences, from the attempts to reform offenders by threatening to commit them to a house of correction (referred to in section 7.4), and from the individual case histories in petty sessions minutes. See, for example, GLRO, P79/JN1/214 (Hackney petty sessions; entries

discharging offenders from houses of correction before sessions in response to requests from plaintiffs or respectable friends of the defendant, justices exploited legal ambiguities in order to mitigate punishments and encourage settlements. On the whole, plaintiffs and justices of the peace were far less interested in obtaining formal convictions and punishments than they were in stopping the defendant's offensive behavior and extracting some compensation for injuries the plaintiff had received. By avoiding the cost of defending a formal prosecution and the stigma of a formal conviction, defendants also benefited from informal settlements.[2]

Flexibility in the use of legal procedures, however, was restricted for the poor, the socially unconnected, and women. Because of women's less public social role, the impoverished condition of many single women, and intimidating formal courtroom procedures, women prosecuted relatively few indictments. Because of the costs of prosecution, particularly by indictment, the poor (both male and female) faced substantial disincentives to initiating prosecutions. Recently, several historians have argued that laborers and the poor did file criminal prosecutions, but most of their evidence comes from felony cases in the period after the 1750s, when statutes enabled the courts to reimburse the expenses of prosecutors of felonies.[3] Peter King has demonstrated that laborers in Essex frequently prosecuted assaults, where expenses were never paid, but per capita they were less likely to do so than their social superiors.[4] Similarly, the geographical distribution of prosecutions in London shows that the residents of London's poorest neighborhoods initiated significantly fewer prosecutions than elsewhere in the metropolis. Even the indictments the poor did file were thought to be unnecessary; a Middlesex grand jury presentment suggests that grand jurors believed indictments were an inappropriate method of dealing with assaults committed by the poor. Characterizing such cases as arising "from scolding, backbiting, and reproaching," the jurors recommended that such cases be punished with "the old legal way of a ducking stool" instead of by indictment, since the "money which they spend at law" should be used "to clothe their families."[5] On occasion the poor were able to use indictments to their advantage, but they

concerning Mary Scott: 7 Oct 1738 and 21 July 1739). In cases where justices chose to discharge suspects brought before them without further legal action, the justice could charge a discharge fee as an informal punishment if he felt that the person had misbehaved: MJ/OC/I, ff. 111–112d (11 Jan. 1721).
[2] This conclusion applies equally well to the church courts (Ingram, *Church Courts* p. 50).
[3] For the role of the poor in prosecuting felonies, see Peter King, "Crime, law and society in Essex, 1740–1820" (Ph.D. diss., Cambridge University, 1984), p. 181, and "Decision-makers and decision-making in the English criminal law, 1750–1800," *Historical Journal* 27 (1984), p. 32; Beattie, *Crime and the Courts*, p. 47; Jennifer Davis, "Prosecutions and their context: the use of the criminal law in later nineteenth-century London," in *Policing and Prosecution*, ed. Hay and Snyder (Oxford, 1989), pp. 400ff.
[4] King, "Crime, law and society," pp. 181–82.   [5] MJ/SBB/408, p. 47 (Oct. 1683).

faced considerable obstacles, including possible juror prejudice, when attempting to do so.[6]

In theory informal mediation was available to all, but the ability to achieve significant results from informal negotiations depended to some extent on whether the plaintiff was able to threaten the defendant with a formal prosecution. Where the defendant was in no such position, it was less likely that informal mediation would prove satisfactory. Furthermore, a sympathetic justice had to be found who was willing to hear the case. Although there is insufficient evidence concerning the extent to which the poor availed themselves of informal judicial mediation, it may be significant that the strongest evidence of this practice comes from rural areas.[7] Some urban justices appear to have actively sought the respect and custom of the poor, but it was alleged (though there is little hard evidence on this point) that some of these justices, "trading justices," exploited the poor.

Turning to those accused of crimes, not everyone was equally liable to be suspected of petty crimes: among Londoners it was the unemployed, the unconnected, the newly-arrived migrant, and young, single women who were particularly liable to be brought before justices of the peace. The subsequent treatment of the accused depended very much on the philosophy of the justice handling the case, but because such people were least likely to be trusted, it was less likely that complaints against them would be resolved informally. With its offer of immediate corporal punishment, justices and plaintiffs in urban areas often found commitment to a house of correction to be the most attractive option. In any case, people who were unable to find socially respectable acquaintances to serve as sureties could not enter into a recognizance for the peace or to try an indictment. Defendants who were required to appear in court faced incarceration at their own cost until sessions. For those poor defendants who were indicted, the high cost of defending oneself in a jury trial and the prospect of receiving a less than sympathetic hearing from the jurors were strong incentives to plead guilty. Not only were the poor less likely to benefit from the flexibility of informal mediation and recognizances, they also rarely experienced trial by jury.

It is in the prosecution of victimless offences, or "police-defined"[8] offences, where judicial and prosecutorial discretion was widest, and where discretion worked most directly to the disadvantage of the poor. Prosecutions of offences such as "idle and disorderly" conduct, nightwalking, prostitution, and keeping or frequenting an unlicensed or disorderly alehouse (offences which were thought to be the roots of serious crime) fluctuated as public and official concern about these offences waxed and waned. As victimless offences, they

---

[6] Douglas Hay, "Prosecution and power: malicious prosecution in the English courts, 1750–1850," in *Policing and Prosecution*, ed. Hay and Snyder, p. 367.
[7] See above, section 8.1.   [8] This term comes from the work of Jennifer Davis.

were most likely to be prosecuted at the instigation of parish officers or informers, and both had many reasons not to apprehend or report offenders. When justices or the respectable inhabitants of a neighborhood demanded action against these offences, however, the fact that most such offences could easily be prosecuted summarily facilitated concerted campaigns of arrests and prosecutions of the community's underclass of vagrants, beggars, and unemployed. A campaign against crime and immorality in the socially unstable area around Drury Lane in 1731 illustrates the prosecutorial strategies informers, officers, and justices adopted in such contexts. In response to a petition from eighteen shopkeepers, tradesmen, and other inhabitants, a group of justices met weekly in the vestry of Covent Garden and issued search warrants for the arrest of keepers of disorderly houses, rogues, sturdy beggars, and other "idle and disorderly" persons. Nine months later, the justices reported that they had bound over forty-eight persons for keeping disorderly houses and committed sixteen more to prison for want of sureties. Of these, twenty-four were indicted. Fourteen more people were either bound over or committed for want of sureties for assaulting the constables in the execution of their office. In total, seventy-eight people were referred to quarter sessions for these offences. A larger number of offenders, however were dealt with using the justices' powers of summary conviction: ten were convicted of profane swearing and cursing, one was convicted of selling liquor without a licence, and 127 were committed to the house of correction for having been apprehended in disorderly houses or as people "who infest the streets in the night time."[9]

The number of cases dealt with summarily thus far outnumbered those indicted, and those who were bound over or indicted were the people most likely to have some wealth and local roots, since most were accused of keeping disorderly houses. Those who frequented their houses, many of whom were poorer, were committed to the house of correction. It could be argued that the choice of legal procedures was determined by the nature of the offences (one could not, for example, be indicted for "infesting the streets in the night time"), but plaintiffs and justices possessed considerable discretion in choosing which offences to prosecute. Those accused of keeping disorderly houses or assaulting constables, for example, could have been accused of having been apprehended in a disorderly house and sent to a house of correction. Similarly, those committed to the house of correction for "infesting the streets in the night time" could easily have been bound over by a recognizance for good behavior. By manipulating the offence charged, plaintiffs and justices of the peace acquired considerable flexibility in their choice of a method of prosecution, and the evidence suggests that when prosecuting public

[9] WJ/OC/II, ff. 101d–105d (April 1731); WJ/SP/April 1731, no. 17.

order offences they targeted "disorderly" and suspicious behavior among the poor, and punished the offenders in houses of correction.

Commitments to houses of correction increased dramatically in London in the late seventeenth and early eighteenth centuries primarily because houses of correction were thought to be suitable for the types of offenders apprehended around Drury Lane: people accused of minor victimless crimes who often lacked respectable social connections. At a time of growing concern about the growth of poverty, crime, and disorder in the metropolis, houses of correction provided a place for punishing people whose behavior threatened to undermine social stability. As we have seen, the Societies for the Reformation of Manners were responsible for a significant proportion of the house of correction commitments in the second half of this period, and it is significant that the frequency of their prosecutions fluctuated to a certain extent in tandem with concerns about the level of serious crime in the metropolis.[10] Although the reformation of manners campaign collapsed in 1738, the next reformation of manners movement surfaced less than twenty years later – during the next period of serious concern about crime in the capital.

Although there is little direct evidence on the subject, it is necessary to consider the implications of these findings for our understanding of popular attitudes towards the law in preindustrial England. It seems clear that for many people the law of misdemeanors provided a practical and flexible method of settling disputes. Judging from the large number of cases informally mediated by justices, or recognizances that did not lead to further action, and of indictments which were dropped (and presumably settled informally) before reaching a final verdict, many plaintiffs achieved satisfactory results from resorting to the law. And judging from the number of counter-prosecutions initiated by defendants of all social groups, many of which were vexatious, the law was perceived as a useful method of pressuring one's antagonists when an informal settlement was rejected.[11] After he was bound over in 1721, Thomas Jefferys told the justice that "if he could not have law here he would go where he could have law,"[12] a statement which exhibits confidence that the law could be made to work to his advantage. Nonetheless, as Douglas Hay has suggested, it is unlikely that people who filed malicious prosecutions believed that the legal system promoted justice.[13] Rather, such people appear to have viewed the law in instrumental terms, in the sense that the judicial system provided useful

[10] Section 9.1.

[11] Above, section 6.3; Hay, "Prosecution and power," pp. 343–95; Ruth Paley, "Thief-takers in London in the age of the McDaniel gang, c. 1745–1754," in *Policing and Prosecution*, ed. Hay and Snyder, pp. 301–40.

[12] MJ/SR/2358, R. 71, 72 (Jan. 1721).   [13] Hay, "Prosecution and power," pp. 389–95.

tools for pressuring one's antagonists. But the law was not the only available instrument for that purpose – litigants also committed riots or assaults to advance their causes.[14]

Victims of crime clearly felt no obligation to resort to the courts. Indeed, there is some evidence that filing a formal prosecution was regarded as antisocial unless informal mediation failed.[15] Moreover, victims could easily be dissuaded from prosecuting by practical obstacles such as the distance to the courthouse, the court fees, and the difficulty of finding a justice willing to act. While the Middlesex sessions were heavily used by people living near the courts, rates of prosecution from more distant parishes were considerably lower. As suggested by the large number of small-scale riots and incidents of defamation which took place in late seventeenth- and early eighteenth-century London, there were other ways of addressing disputes besides bringing them before the courts.[16] Those who did prosecute, moreover, felt no obligation to carry the case through to a final verdict; there may even have been community pressure not to do so.[17] Even in felony cases, where informal settlements were illegal, victims were often willing to settle out of court, a willingness which Jonathan Wild and others exploited by profiting from the returning of stolen goods.[18] Thus, the courts did not provide the only methods of responding to crime. Even in the late nineteenth century when the greater availability of the police, summary jurisdiction, and state payment of costs made prosecutions considerably easier, informal methods of confronting offenders were still popular.[19]

The attitudes of those people whose access to the courts was most limited are even more difficult to determine, but it is important to consider the implications of the fact that many people benefited only partially, or not at all, from the flexibility of the law. Potential prosecutors who could not afford to initiate a prosecution by recognizance or indictment must have doubted whether the judicial system could work in their interests. Indicted defendants who were

[14] MJ/SBB/575, p. 48 (August 1700); MJ/SP/Oct. 1708, no. 32.
[15] J. A. Sharpe, "Enforcing the law in the seventeenth-century English village," in *Crime and the Law: The Social History of Crime in Western Europe since 1500*, ed. V. A. C. Gatrell *et al.* (1980), pp. 111–12; Martin J. Ingram, "Communities and courts: law and disorder in early seventeenth-century Wiltshire," in *Crime in England*, ed. Cockburn, p. 127. The Middlesex grand jury in 1683 thought that if indictments for assault filed by the poor could be prevented, it "would beget amity and kindness among neighbours": MJ/SBB/408, p. 47 (1683).
[16] Shoemaker, "London 'mob'". Defamation cases account for about 7% of the recognizances issued to attend the Middlesex and Westminster sessions, and they were also prosecuted in the church courts.
[17] J. A. Sharpe, "'Such disagreement betwyx neighbours': litigation and human relations in early modern England," in *Disputes and Settlements. Law and Human Relations in the West*, ed. John Bossy (Cambridge, 1983), pp. 180–81.
[18] Gerald Howson, *It Takes a Thief. The Life and Times of Jonathan Wild* [formerly published as *Thief-Taker General* (1970)] (1987).
[19] Davis, "Prosecutions and their context," p. 426.

forced to plead guilty in order to avoid the cost of a jury trial must have had an even more skeptical view of the law. And what was the attitude of defendants committed to houses of correction, often on the basis of weak evidence? Reactions in these circumstances must have varied, from passive acceptance to aggressive hostility. It is the hostility towards the representatives of the judicial system, in the form of insults directed towards justices of the peace, that has been recorded. Thus, as we saw in chapter 7, a woman complained that sending people to Bridewell was not "justice."[20] Similarly, justices who supported the enforcement of unpopular laws risked losing popular respect in some neighborhoods. In 1709, Thomas Evans insulted justice Nathaniel Blackerby (a supporter of the reformation of manners campaign) by "calling him hellfire son of a bitch and saying he would not do him justice."[21]

Jennifer Davis has argued that in late nineteenth-century London the poor who were subject to oppressive treatment by the police were nonetheless willing to initiate prosecutions against others in the police courts.[22] In the early eighteenth century, however, justice was less institutionalized and the evidence suggests that in neighborhoods where the poor were subject to commitment to houses of correction residents did not bring their complaints before the justices who were most active in making such commitments. Evidence on the wealth of plaintiffs is thin, but it was shown in chapter 8 that "social control" justices, who committed large numbers of poor women to houses of correction for morals offences, attracted fewer private plaintiffs in their house of correction business and issued fewer recognizances on behalf of female plaintiffs than other justices. Whether in such circumstances potential plaintiffs brought their cases before another justice depended no doubt in part on the availability of a sympathetic neighboring justice, but the fact that women were less likely to prosecute by recognizance and indictment in London's west end where house of correction commitments were highest (and 70% of the prisoners were women) suggests that poorer women simply did not trust justices of the peace in areas where the house of correction was in frequent use.[23]

By extension, the overall decrease in per capita indictment and recognizance rates in urban Middlesex during this period may have been caused in part by the concurrent substantial increase in house of correction commitments. Although this phenomenon was to some extent caused by the transfer of prosecutions from recognizances to summary jurisdiction, the per capita decrease in indictments and recognizances may have also been caused by declining

---

[20] See above, section 7.4.   [21] MJ/SR/2136/R. 19 (Sept. 1709).

[22] Davis, "Prosecutions and their context," p. 418; and "A poor man's system of justice: the London police courts in the second half of the nineteenth century," *Historical Journal* 27 (1984), pp. 319–21.

[23] Tables 8.6 and 10.4.

popular confidence in the judicial system.[24] Judging from the insults levelled at individual justices, and on occasion justices of the peace as a whole, there was an undercurrent of serious lack of respect for representatives of the judicial system. In 1720, a carpenter insulted justice Alex Hardine, "deriding him as being a justice and giving him abusive language." In 1709, a group of rioters including one Joseph Robinson broke into a room where two justices were conducting a petty sessions and violently assaulted the justices and insulted them by "often bid[ding] them kiss his backside and [he] told them they were not justices but two old women and that he did not care a fart for all the justices in England."[25] There is no systematic way of measuring popular attitudes towards justices, but cases like this suggest that declining respect, possibly caused by the increased use of summary jurisdiction, may have been a cause of the per capita decrease in the number of cases brought before the Middlesex justices during this period.

Whether as plaintiffs or defendants, people experienced the legal system differently in preindustrial England depending on their gender and social class, and for this reason it would be wrong to assume that attitudes towards the law were uniform. Because women and the poor faced numerous obstacles when they used the judicial system, they are unlikely to have believed that the law would always treat them justly. But these were not the only people who were reluctant to bring their disputes before the courts. People of all social classes appear to have used the law as only one of several possible methods of confronting people with their misdeeds, not as the only legitimate arbiter of criminal accusations. Not only did the judicial system not have a monopoly on methods of prosecuting crime, but not all laws were regarded as legitimate: some activities defined as misdemeanors (such as attending conventicles, prostitution, or violations of the game laws) were viewed as legitimate by many people. As Peter King has observed, "individuals and communities were highly selective in their approach to the law and its institutions, taking advantage of, assenting to or revering certain parts while attempting to ignore, flout or oppose others."[26] While there may have been a consensus among the propertied section of the population concerning the proper judicial treatment of felons (characterized by Cynthia Herrup as the responsibility to preserve "the common peace"), there was certainly no consensus concerning the proper response to petty offences.

In explaining the remarkable social stability of both London and the country

---

[24] Compare Figure 3 with Figures 1 and 2; see also Table 10.1. The decline in indictments was also caused by the declining number of nuisance and regulatory offences prosecuted by indictment.
[25] MJ/SR/2349, R. 148 (July 1720); 2136, R. 208 (Sept. 1709).
[26] King, "Decision-makers and decision-making," pp. 33–34.

as a whole at the beginning of the eighteenth century, the widespread impact of the law (either as arbiter of disputes or as instrument of social control) is, therefore, not a sufficient explanation. To explain the apparent stability of rural parishes or London's east end, where relatively few people resorted to the courts, for example, requires analysis of the role of other institutions such as the family, the church (both established and dissenting), employment practices, and local government. In fact, it was in the most socially unstable part of London, the inner west end, that the law of misdemeanors had its greatest impact. Yet prosecutions in these parishes frequently took the form of indictments and commitments to houses of correction, procedures which were as likely to aggravate tensions as resolve them. Just as the flexibility of the judicial system frequently facilitated satisfactory informal settlements of disputes, the discretion it accorded to plaintiffs and justices allowed the law also to be used aggressively to seek the punishment of adversaries (or to attempt to control an underclass) whose activities were not necessarily criminal. From the vantage point of the prosecution of misdemeanors, the law does not appear merely as a service industry,[27] but neither was it a bulwark of social order. For those with access to it, the judicial system provided a useful set of tools for advancing their interests.

[27] As suggested by John H. Langbein, "Albion's fatal flaws," *Past and Present* 98 (1982), p. 119.

Appendix I
Sampling procedure and significance[a]

The enormous volume of cases heard by the Middlesex and Westminster sessions during this period necessitated sampling of recognizances, indictments, and house of correction commitments (Table 3.3 lists the average annual number of prosecutions for each procedure). For statistical reasons, it was more appropriate to sample short time periods intensively rather than to extract a proportionally much smaller sample of the entire sixty-five year period of this study. For indictments and recognizances, five sample periods comprising a total of seven years were selected for sampling: 1663–64, 1677, 1693, 1707, and May 1720 to April 1722. The proportions sampled were as follows:

	Recognizances	Indictments
1663–64	20%	40%
1677, 1693, 1707	20%	33%
May 1720–April 1722	17%	25%

As explained in Table 7.1, the less complete survival of house of correction calendars dictated a somewhat different sampling method and choice of sample years: 1670 and 1673 (four Middlesex rolls), 1680 (Westminster), 1693 (Westminster), 1697 (four Middlesex rolls), 1712, and 1721. The sampling proportions were 50% for the years up to and including 1697, and 50% thereafter. The results from these samples can be considered accurate *for the sample periods* within the confidence intervals (C) calculated by the following formula, with a 95% chance that the actual proportion of prosecutions falls within the confidence interval. The confidence interval is calculated as the sample proportion (p) plus or minus a few percentage points:

  p = the proportion of the sample with a given characteristic
  n = the sample size
  N = the total number of cases, including those not sampled

$$C = p +/- 1.96 \times \sqrt{\frac{p(1-p)}{(n-1)} \times (1 - n/N)}$$

Confidence intervals for each sample[b] (95% certainty)

	Recognizances		Indictments		Houses of correction	
	1693	Total sample	1693	Total sample	1721	Total sample
Total defendants[c]	2,341	15,546	1,293	8,382	1,425	4,813[d]
Sample size[e]	468	2,936	434	2,751	488	1,913
Proportion sampled[f]	20%	19%	34%	33%	34%	40%
Confidence interval						
for 5% result	+/−1.8%	+/−0.7%	+/−1.7%	+/−0.7%	+/−1.6%	+/−0.8%
for 10% result	+/−2.4%	+/−1.0%	+/−2.3%	+/−0.9%	+/−2.2%	+/−1.0%
for 50% result	+/−4.1%	+/−1.6%	+/−3.8%	+/−1.5%	+/−3.6%	+/−1.7%

[a] For advice on this issue I am grateful for the help of Dr. B. Blight of the University of London and the Stanford University Statistics Department. For more information, see W. G. Cochran, *Sampling Techniques*, 3rd edn (1977), chapter four.

[b] Where one sample year is given, confidence intervals for the other sample years were less than or equal to those presented here.

[c] The total number of cases for each period has been multiplied by the average number of defendants per case, as calculated from the overall sample. For recognizances, the multiplier is 1.11 and for indictments it is 1.55. No multiple was needed for the houses of correction, since the total number of defendants was counted.

[d] Includes an estimate of the number of defendants for a year in the early 1670s to correspond with the rolls sampled from those years (for no year in the 1670s do calendars survive for the entire year).

[e] In some cases the size of the sample actually analyzed was slightly smaller as the result of the exclusion of cases connected with another procedure: recognizances connected with indictments were often excluded from the recognizance sample, and commitments to houses of correction for want of sureties, for punishment after conviction on an indictment, and for "safekeeping" were always excluded from the house of correction sample.

[f] Sampling was carried out by examining every nth case, depending on the sampling proportion. Thus, for the 20% 1693 recognizance sample, every fifth case was included. For the early years of the house of correction sample, a different strategy was used to account for missing calendars. See above, Table 7.1.

For example, in Table 6.6 it is reported that 8% of the defendants in 1693 initially pleaded innocent and subsequently changed their pleas to guilty. Taking the closest row in the table, for a 10% result, this table demonstrates, with 95% certainty, that the actual proportion of defendants who pleaded in this manner was between 5.7% and 10.3% of all the defendants indicted in 1693. Similarly, in Table 8.2 it is reported that women account for only 27.2% of the indicted defendants in the entire sample. Using the confidence interval for a 50% result (which somewhat exaggerates the size of the interval for 27%), one can say with 95% certainty that *in the seven sample years* the actual proportion of indicted defendants who were women was between 25.7% and 28.7%. Where a result is based on only a portion of a sample, such as when recognizances connected with indictments are excluded from the recognizance sample, or the unit of analysis is the crime instead of the defendant, the confidence intervals are somewhat larger.

Appendix II

Profiles of the cases heard by active justices[a]

Recognizances[a]

	Estimated no. of recognizances per year[b]	Area of activity[c]	Offences vs peace %	Official plaintiffs %	Female plaintiffs %[d]	Low status defendants %[e]	Indictment rate %[f]	Ratio of recognizances to house of correction commitments[g]
1663–64 sample								
Abell, Richard	240	EU	68	16	58	47	11	
Blomer, Francis	80	N	70	none	45	41	7	
Byde, Thomas	50	EU	70	8	67	70	none	
Geery, William	65	WU	27	25	25	67	27	
Godfrey, Edmund	75	W	40	5	28	37	N/A	
Jegon, Robert	387.5	WU,W	39	11	40	26.5	13	
Lucy, Thomas	47.5	N	53	8	42	75	10.5	
Newman, Richard	37.5	W	60	none	40	37.5	N/A	
Pitfield, Charles	52.5	N	48	36	43	50	10	
Powell, Richard	112.5	N	58	21	63	37	5	
Smith, John	70	N	39	38.5	25	50	4	
Snape, Nathaniel	42.5	WU	53	9	50	22	12.5	
Swalowe, Thomas	180	EU	68	17	60	35.5	24	
Weld, Humphrey	50	W	45	none	40	27	15	
1677 sample								
Bowles, William	125	N	52	33	60	50	22	
Dewey, James	95	W	74	none	71	18	none	
Forster, Reginald	110	N	54.5	27	27	38.5	5	

Godfrey, Edmund	130	W	54	17	27	15	9	
Parry, Simon	215	WU	60.5	9	52	5	18	
Ricroft, Josiah	200	EU	55	9	38	63	19	
Rosewell, William	80	WU	31	none	33	50	50	
Sabbs, Peter	185	WU	59.5	15	77	43	26.5	
Underwood, John	225	EU	64	13	41	48	13	
1693 sample								
Allestree, William	95	WU	58	20	50	57	35	
Bohun, George	95	EU	63	none	43	40	33	
Buck, Samuel	105	WU	38	12.5	57	50	25	
Chamberlaine, Hugh	75	W	60	10	22	22	N/A	1.0
Cole, Michael	125	W	72	10	28	8	N/A	5.4
Constable, Robert	205	EU	76	4	61.5	31	26	
Eyton, Theophilus	135	All	59	44	67	60	12.5	
Johnson, Launcelot	95	N	42	25	33	36	6	
Marshall, Ralph	105	W	62	none	65	33	N/A	3.4
Railton, Thomas	100	W	50	10.5	41	43	N/A	2.2
Smith, Thomas	90	N	44	18	78	50	29	
Wilson, J.	75	N	47	13	31	29	N/A	11.25
Withers, William	90	N	72	8	58	60	12	
1707 sample								
Chamberlayne, John	80	W	22	29	20	62.5	8	
Constable, Robert	140	EU	86	6	75	50	40	
Crosbie, John	75	N	93	8	54.5	78	21	
Ellis, Thomas	80	WU	81	8	75	N/A	6	
Ireton, George	195	WU	46	10	50	32	29	
Negus, Francis	130	W	23	25	47	75	26	
Smith, Roger	280	EU	62.5	10.5	62	44	41	
1720–22 sample								
Blackerby, Nathaniel	69	W	52	27	45.5	20	N/A	2.8
Boteler, Thomas	69	W	48	none	50	85	N/A	1.1
Conne, William	102	W	68	4	41	70	N/A	1.0
Ellis, John[h]	111	WU	65	17	35	31	20	1.7
Fuller, John	45	N	73	4.5	60	71	10	1.1
Hewitt, Matthew	189	N	78		67	71	11	1.8
Johnson, Bastwick	81	EU	63	14	58	67	N/A	3.1

Kyrby, Robert	90	EU	90	none	46	50	12	4.0
Mercer, John	60	WU	70	18	67	33	17	3.25
Michel, D'Oyley	54	EU	72	none	47	12.5	10	0.9
Moore, William	45	W	60	25	33	30	N/A	28.0
Parry, Simon	204	WU	78	6	57	43	25	3.8
SaintLo, Lawrence	54	W	61	none	45.5	27	N/A	3.0
Saunders, Jeffery	150	W	64	11	55	32	N/A	3.0
Tillard, Isaac	45	N	40	none	60	50	N/A	2.0
Ward, Alexander	117	WU	69	3	48	67	12	2.5

N/A: Insufficient information available

a   Active justices are defined as those who issued more than fifteen recognizances in the sample. Recognizances to answer existing indictments are excluded.

b   Calculated by multiplying the number of sample recognizances issued by the justice by the inverse of the sample proportion.

c   EU: east urban; N: north urban; W: west urban; WU: Westminster; WU: west urban. These areas are delineated in Figure 10.1.

d   This calculation excludes official plaintiffs and unknowns.

e   Defendants in low status occupations and those who were unable to risk bail. Because their status is difficult to determine, this calculation excludes apprentices, servants, officers, and women. Also excluded are defendants prosecuted by officers of the peace.

f   See note a.

g   The average number of recognizances issued for each commitment to the house of correction.

h   Of Denmark Street, St. Giles in the Fields.

House of correction commitments[a]

	Estimated no. of annual commitments[b]	Victimless offences %[c]	Private offences %[d]	Most frequent offence	Ratio of recognizances to house of correction commitments[e]
1680 sample (Westminster)					
Cutler, James	60	50	50	theft	
Dewy, James	164	91.5	7	LIDP[f]	
1693 sample (Westminster)					
Brydall, Walter	30	53	47	prostitution	1.3
Langley, Roger	32	44	56	theft	2.2
Railton, Thomas	42	43	52	theft	2.2
Tully, John	36	22	72	theft	1.7
St. Martin's vestry[g]	70	89	11	LIDP	N/A
1712 sample (Middlesex and Westminster)					
Bealing, Richard	69	52	48	prostitution + theft	
Hanway, John	45	47	53	theft	
Lavigne, Peter	54	94	6	prostitution	
Peter, Charles	225	68	32	prostitution	
Stewart, John	147	37	63	theft	
Ward, Alexander	81	37	56	theft	
1721 sample (Middlesex and Westminster)					
Boteler, Thomas	60	95	5	prostitution	1.1
Colthurst, Thomas	69	74	26	prostitution	0.5
Conne, William	123	73	27	prostitution	1.0
Ellis, John (Middlesex sessions)[h]	63	33	67	theft	1.7
Haynes, Joseph	57	89.5	10.5	prostitution	0.2
Hewitt, Matthew	111	47	51	theft	1.8
Newton, Richard	45	100	—	prostitution	0.9
Parry, Simon	54	61	39	prostitution	3.8
Saunders, Jeffery	66	64	36	prostitution	2.0

(*cont.*)

N/A: Insufficient information available.

a   Active justices are defined as those who made more than fifteen commitments in the sample.

b   Calculated by multiplying the number of sample commitments made by the justice by the inverse of the sampling proportion.

c   Prostitution; loose, idle and disorderly conduct; other vice; and vagrancy.

d   Theft, offences against the peace, master/servant disputes, and miscellaneous offences.

e   Ratio of the number of recognizances issued to the number of house of correction commitments in 1721.

f   LIDP = loose, idle and disorderly person.

g   Committed by a group of justices meeting in "private sessions" of the vestry of St. Martin in the Fields. Unfortunately, it is not possible to identify the names of these justices.

h   There were two justices active at this time with the name of John Ellis. One lived in Denmark Street, St. Giles in the Fields, Middlesex, and the other lived in Pall Mall, Westminster. On house of correction calendars, it was not possible to determine definitively which justice was responsible for which commitments, but it was assumed that each justice was responsible for the commitments made to the house of correction connected to his own sessions: thus it is assumed that the Middlesex commitments, documented above, were made by the Ellis of Denmark Street.

Appendix III

Population estimates used in calculating prosecution rates

	Persons per household[a]	1664[b]	1676[c]	1694[d]	1708[e]	1720s[f]
Westminster						
St. Margaret	4.3	13,205	13,708[g]	14,212	14,375	17,631
St. Paul Covent Garden	4.3	2,085	[2,580]	2,232	2,365	2,639
St. Martin	4.3	13,210	17,118	15,656	17,846	22,439
St. Anne[h]	4.3			5,207	7,095	[5,720]
St. James[i]	4.3			9,864	14,190	16,339
Westminster total		28,500	33,058	47,171	55,871	66,143
West Urban						
St. Andrew Holborn[j]	4.4	8,070		13,244	14,128	15,239
St. Clement Danes and St. Mary-le-Strand[k]	4.3	7,834		9,920	10,486	10,796
St. Giles in the Fields	4.4	6,706	7,842	12,087	[14,520]	14,355
West urban total		22,610		35,251	36,701	40,390
North urban						
St. Leonard Shoreditch[l]	4.2	6,040		8,978	9,240	10,124
St. James Clerkenwell	4.4		[4,347]	3,485	5,547	7,358
St. Sepulchre	4.4			1,760	[1,738]	2,505
St. Giles Cripplegate[m]	4.4			3,960	8,231	12,503
North urban total				18,183	24,778	32,490
East urban						
St. Mary Whitechapel	4.4	10,921		11,439	[9,079]	12,153
St. Katharine by the Tower	2.2	2,039		2,614	[2,057]	[2,079]
St. Botolph Aldgate	4.4			4,906	[4,840]	5,324
St. John Wapping[n]	3.7	[5,609]		5,530	[5,258]	5,623
Stepney	4.6	34,814		39,375	48,708	65,659
(Spitalfields)	7.4	(7,015)		(10,335)		(15,430)
(Shadwell)	5.4	(7,349)		(7,891)	(9,909)	(10,146)
East urban total		53,304		63,864	73,197	91,373
Urban periphery						
Bethnal Green[o]				5,585		
Bow				772		
Mile End				3,288		
Poplar and Blackwall				2,255		
Chelsea	4.4			1,267		

	Persons per household[a]	1664[b]	1676[c]	1694[d]	1708[e]	1720s[f]
Islington	4.4			2,319		
Hackney				2,896		
Hampstead	4.4			748		
Kensington	4.4			898		
St. Pancras	4.4			1,043		
St. Marylebone	4.4			132		
Paddington	4.4			88		
Urban periphery total				21,291		
Rural Middlesex						
Ashford		104	124			
Friern Barnet			262			
East Bedfont		177	180			
Bromley			315			
Chiswick		945	[900]			
Ealing and Old Brentford		1,427				
Edmonton		1,609	2,125			
Endfield		2,196	2,250			
Fulham		1,118				
Greenford		246	[213]			
Monken Hadley		331	340			
Hammersmith		1,503				
Hampton		616				
Hanwell		177	[157]			
Harmondsworth		440	[372]			
Harrow		1,366	[1,000]			
Hayes			350			
Heston[p]		549				
Hillingdon		754				
Hornsey		779				
Isleworth[q]		1,403				
Kingsbury		200	211			
South Mimms			750			
Norwood			226			
Pinner			300			
Staines		909	[831]			
Willesden		470	[457]			

Note: Figures in brackets represent totals which are lower than earlier estimates or higher than subsequent estimates. In each case, this figure was not used in the calculations and was instead replaced as follows: for figures from 1676, the 1694 figure was used where available, otherwise the 1664 figure was used. For figures from 1707 and the 1720s the next earliest figure was used. For Wapping in 1664, the 1694 figure was used.

[a] These are the uncorrected figures calculated by Gregory King in the 1690s, as reported by D. V. Glass, "Gregory King and the population of England and Wales at the end of the seventeenth century" and "Gregory King's estimate of the population of England and Wales, 1695," in *Population in History* (Chicago, 1965), pp. 117, 195 and 198. King corrected his figures by adding 10% for underenumeration; this modification has been left out in this table because King's figures are for the number of persons per *house* and most of the tax figures are for *households*. P. E. Jones and A. V. Judges discovered that the number of households was between 7 and 21% more than the number of houses in the City of London, so the error of

underenumeration is approximately cancelled by the error of multiplying by households instead of houses ("London's population in the late seventeenth century," *Economic History Review* VI [1935–36], pp. 45–63).

b From the hearth tax assessment lists for 1664, multiplied by the number of persons per household in the first column. Figures are from M. J. Power, "The east and west in early-modern London," in *Wealth and Power in Tudor England*, ed. E. Ives *et al.*, (London, 1978), p. 181; and "The urban development of east London, 1550–1700" (Ph.D. diss., London, 1971), p. 23. Population estimates based on hearth tax assessments for the rural parishes are from L. Martindale, "Demography and land use in the late seventeenth and eighteenth centuries in Middlesex" (Ph.D. diss., University of London, 1986), pp. 21–22.

c From *The Compton Census of 1676: A Critical Edition*, ed. Anne Whiteman (1986), pp. 36–67. Figures were used only when it was possible to determine (by comparing the figures with the hearth tax assessments) whether it was the whole population, adults, male adults, or households that were counted (pp. xlix–lxxvi). As recommended by Whiteman, the multipliers used were 4.25 for households, 3.0 for adult men, and 1.5 for adult men and women.

d From figures for the four shillings in the pound tax, generously supplied to me by James Alexander. For all but the east urban parishes the figures were for the number of households and consequently were multiplied by the number of persons per household in the first column.

e Based on estimates of the number of houses from E. Hatton, *A New View of London* (1708), listed in George, *London Life*, pp. 408–12. The number of houses in each parish has been multiplied by the number of persons per household in the first column, plus 10% to account for the fact that there were slightly more households than houses, as explained in note a.

f These figures are derived from the average of the estimated number of houses in 1708 (see the previous note) and the average of the estimated numbers of houses in 1732 and 1737 (from *New Remarks of London by the Company of Parish Clerks* [1732] and F. Maitland, *History of London* [1739]; both are listed in George, *London Life*, pp. 408–12). Where either the 1732 or the 1737 figure was missing, I used whichever figure was provided. Where no figure was given in 1708, I took the average of the 1732/37 figures and subtracted the average percentage increase between 1708 and 1732/37 from all parishes where both figures are known. The figures for the number of houses were then multiplied by the number of persons per household as explained in the previous note.

g This figure was calculated simply by splitting the difference between the estimates for 1664 and 1694.

h Formed from St. Martin in the Fields in 1678.

i Formed from St. Martin in the Fields in 1685.

j Includes the Liberties of Ely Rents, Saffron Hill, and Hatton Garden for all but the 1664 figure.

k Includes the Liberties of the Savoy, Rolls, and Duchy of Lancaster.

l Includes Norton-Folgate Liberty.

m Middlesex portion.

n Formed from St. Mary Whitechapel in 1694.

o Bethnal Green, Bow, Mile End, and Poplar and Blackwall were all hamlets of Stepney and consequently were also included in the figures for Stepney under "east urban".

p Including part of Hounslow.

q Including part of Hounslow.

BIBLIOGRAPHY

MANUSCRIPTS

BODLEIAN LIBRARY, OXFORD

Rawlinson MSS
  D129 Reformation of manners documents
  D1396–1404 Register of accusations and convictions kept by the reformation of
  manners campaign

BRITISH LIBRARY

Additional MSS
  32,512 Dudley North, "Some notes concerning the laws for the poor" (ff. 124ff)
  35,601 Hardwicke Correspondence (ff. 260–75)
  35,979 Cases tried before Sir John Holt (ff. 66–73)
  35,994 Cases tried before Sir John Holt (ff. 94–100)
  38,856 Reports and petitions concerning conditions in Middlesex prisons
  (ff. 138–56)
Portland MSS
  Loan 29/185–6 Harley correspondence, 1691–92
Stowe MSS
  228 List of changes to the Middlesex commission of the peace, 1715 (ff. 205–205d)

CAMDEN LIBRARIES, SWISS COTTAGE BRANCH

A/SF/30 Journal of William Woodehouse, j. p., 1699–1709

CORPORATION OF LONDON RECORD OFFICE

Lord Mayor's Waiting Books, volume 3, 1664–68
Mansion House Charge Book, volumes 7–8, 1686–95
Sessions papers, 1675–1723
Sessions rolls, 1664, 1675, 1690, 1693, 1718–23

EDINBURGH UNIVERSITY LIBRARY

Laing MSS
  III, 394 Copies of reformation of manners documents, 1691–95

GREATER LONDON RECORD OFFICE

Accessions

70/123–145 Miscellaneous sessions documents
203/11 Petition of neighbors against Richard Bradbery for disturbing the peace (n.d.)
890 Brentford petty sessions minutes, 1653–1714
1379/23 Isleworth Syon manor roll

Archdeaconry court

AM/1 Archdeaconry of Middlesex, papers in causes, 1671, 1689, 1728
AM/36 Archdeaconry of Middlesex, acts and exhibits, 1670, 1672–78

Consistory court of London

DL/C/144 Allegations, libels and sentence book, 1685–88
DL/C/329 Act books, office, 1684–1706
DL/C/625–6 Act books, office, 1664–71

Middlesex and Westminster sessions

MJ/EB/1–14, 22–25, 32–34, 49–57 Estreat books 1689–97, 1702–03, 1707–08, 1720–25
MJ/GSP/1663, no. 2 Gaol delivery sessions papers, 1663
MJ/OC/I–IV Orders of the court, 1716–43
MJ/SBB/187–836 Sessions books, 1660–1725
MJ/SBP/4–12 Sessions process books, 1660–1725
MJ/SBR/8–9 Sessions registers, 1663–64
MJ, WJ/SP Sessions papers, 1642–1727
MJ/SR/1205–2453 Sessions rolls, 1660–1725
MJP/CP/14 Middlesex commission of the peace, 1691
MJP/L/1–2 Alterations of the commission of the peace, 1714–15
WC/R1 Westminster clerk of the peace, miscellaneous entry book, 1665–1708
WJ/EB/4, 14–15, 32–33, 45–46, 56–58 Estreat books (Westminster), 1663–64, 1677–78, 1693–94, 1707–08, 1720–23
WJ/OC/I–II Orders of the court (Westminster), 1720–31
WJ/SBP/1 Sessions process books (Westminster), 1660–79
WJP/CP/15 Westminster commission of the peace, 1691
WJP/L/1–10 Lists of justices and alterations to the Westminster commission of the peace, 1689–1721

Other records

M79/X/I Notebook of Henry Norris, j. p., 1730–41
P79/JN1/214 Minutes of Hackney petty sessions, 1731–53

HAMPSHIRE RECORD OFFICE

Coventry MSS
   1M53/1373–74 Notebooks kept by James Dewy, j. p., 1692–1703

HERTFORDSHIRE RECORD OFFICE

Cowper MSS
  D/EP/F54, 57, 152–54, 157 Correspondence and papers of William Cowper, Lord
  Chancellor

HOUSE OF LORDS RECORD OFFICE

Main Papers

20 March 1704 List of justices put out of the commissions of the peace since 1700
16 February 1705 List of changes to the commissions of the peace since 1704

MANCHESTER CENTRAL LIBRARY

MS F347.96 Diary of Nathaniel Mosely, j. p., 1661–72

PUBLIC RECORD OFFICE

Chancery records

C231/7–8 Crown Office docket books, 1660–99
C234/25 Crown Office fiats for justices of the peace (Westminster)

King's Bench records

KB1/1–2 Depositions, 1716–23
KB10/7, 17 London and Middlesex indictments, 1693–94, 1719–20
KB33/13 Precedents, summary convictions

State Papers

SP 35/12–67 Domestic, George I, 1718–25

SOCIETY FOR THE PROMOTION OF CHRISTIAN KNOWLEDGE ARCHIVES

Papers of Moment

WESTMINSTER CITY ARCHIVES

E2554 St. Margaret's petty sessions minutes, 1719–23
H803 St. Paul Covent Garden vestry minutes, 1711–21
WCB 3–5, 7 Minutes of the Court of Burgesses, 1705–24
WCB 29 Court of Burgesses register book

WILTSHIRE RECORD OFFICE

Accession 118, Notebook of recognizances and informations taken before Edward
  Smyth, j. p., 1664–1666

PRINTED PRIMARY SOURCES

NEWSPAPERS

Athenian Mercury (1691)
London Journal: or, the Thursday's Journal (1720–23)
Original Weekly Journal. With Fresh Advices, Foreign and Domestic (1719, 1720, 1723)
Universal Journal (1724)
Weekly Journal: or Saturday's Post (1719, 1720, 1723)

BOOKS, PAMPHLETS, ETC.

An Account of the Endeavours that have been used to Suppress Gaming Houses (1722)
Alcock, Thomas, *Observations on the Defects of the Poor Laws, and on the Causes and Consequences of the Great Increase and Burden of the Poor* (1752)
Antimoixeia: or, the Honest and Joynt-Design of the Tower-Hamblets for the General Suppression of Bawdy-Houses, as Incouraged by the Publick Magistrates (1691)
[Baston, T.,] *Thoughts on Trade, and a Public Spirit* (1716)
Blackerby, Nathaniel, *The Justice of the Peace his Companion, or a Summary of all the Acts of Parliament, whereby ... Justices of the Peace ... are Authorized to Act ... Begun by Samuel Blackerby ... and Continued ... by Nathaniel Blackerby* (1723)
Blackerby, Samuel, *Cases in Law: Wherein Justices of the Peace Have a Jurisdiction ... Being the Second Part of the Justice of Peace's Companion* (1717)
Blackerby, Samuel and Nathaniel, *Reports of Cases Adjudged in the Courts of Westminster* (2nd edn, 1729)
Blackerby, Samuel and Nathaniel, *The Second Part of the Justice of Peace his Companion; or, Cases in Law (Wherein Justices of Peace have a Jurisdiction)* (1734)
Blackstone, William, *Commentaries on the Laws of England*, 4 vols. (Oxford, 1765–69)
[Bohun, Edmund,] *The Diary and Autobiography of Edmund Bohun, Esq.*, ed. S. Wilton Rix (1853)
Bohun, Edmund, *The Justice of the Peace, His Calling and Qualifications* (1693; first published anonymously in 1684 as *The Justice of Peace, His Calling: a Moral Essay*)
Bond, John, *A Complete Guide for Justices of the Peace* (3rd edn, 1707)
Bray, Thomas, *The Good Fight of Faith ... Exemplified in a Sermon Preached the 24th of March 1708/9 at the Funeral of Mr. John Dent* (1709)
[Bullock, C.,] *The Per-Juror. As it is Acted at the Theatre in Lincoln's Inn Fields* (1717)
Bulstrode, Whitelocke, *The Charge of Whitelocke Bulstrode, Esq.; to the Grand Jury, and other Juries of the County of Middlesex* (1718)
[Bulstrode, Whitelocke,] *Laws Concerning the Poor* (4th edn, 1720)
Bulstrode, Whitelocke, *The Second Charge of Whitelocke Bulstrode, Esq.; to the Grand Jury, and other Juries of the County of Middlesex* (1718)
Bulstrode, Whitelocke, *The Third Charge of Whitlocke [sic] Bulstrode, Esq.; to the Grand-Jury, and other Juries of the County of Middlesex* (1723)
Burn, Richard, *The Justice of the Peace and Parish Officer*, 2 vols. (1755)
Calendar of State Papers, Domestic Series, for the years 1660–1704 (1860–1924)
[Carter, Samuel,] *Legal Provisions for the Poor* (1710)
The Case of the New Parish in Bloomsbury, Intended to be Taken out of St. Giles's in the Fields [1716?]

The Case of the Parish of St. Giles's in the Fields, as to their Poor and a Workhouse Designed to be Built for Employing Them [1722?]

Coke, Edward, *The Fourth Part of the Institutes of the Laws of England* (4th edn, 1671)

Coke, Edward, *The Second Part of the Institutes of the Laws of England* (1642)

The Complete Constable. Directing Constables, Headboroughs, Tithingmen, Church-wardens, Overseers of the Poor ... in the Duty of their Offices (1724)

The Compton Census of 1676: A Critical Edition, ed. Anne Whiteman (1986)

Cowper, William, *The Charge of William Cowper, Esq., to the Grand Jury of the City and Liberty of Westminster ... October the 7th, 1719* (1719)

Dalton, Michael, *The Countrey Justice, Containing the Practice of the Justices of the Peace out of their Sessions* (1618, 1635, 1661, 1677)

[Defoe, Daniel,] *Augusta Triumphans: or, the Way to Make London the Most Flourishing City in the Universe* (1728)

Defoe, Daniel, *Everybody's Business is No-Body's Business* (1725)

[Defoe, Daniel,] *The Great Law of Subordination Considered; or the Insolence and Unsufferable Behaviour of Servants in England Duly Enquired Into* (1724)

[Defoe, Daniel,] *Parochial Tyranny: or, the House-keeper's Complaint Against the Insupportable Exactions, and Partial Assessments of Select Vestries, etc.* [1727]

Defoe, Daniel, *Reformation of Manners, A Satyr* (1702)

[Defoe, Daniel,] *Some Considerations Upon Street-Walkers* [1726]

[Defoe, Daniel,] *Street Robberies Considered: The Reason of their Being so Frequent* [1728]

Defoe, Daniel, *A Tour Through the Whole Island of Great Britain* (1724–26; Harmondsworth, 1971)

DeVeil, Thomas, *Observations on the Practice of a Justice of the Peace* (1747)

Disney, John, *A Second Essay upon the Execution of the Laws against Immorality and Profaneness* (1710)

[Disney, John,] *An Address to Grand-Juries, Constables, and Churchwardens, Representing their Power in the Suppression of Vice and Profaneness* (1710)

Disney, John, *An Essay upon the Execution of the Laws against Profaneness and Immorality* (1708)

Dolins, Daniel, *The Charge of Sir Daniel Dolins, Kt. to the Grand Jury and Other Juries of the County of Middlesex* (1725)

Dolins, Daniel, *The Second Charge of Sir Daniel Dolins, Kt. to the Grand Jury, and Other Juries of the County of Middlesex* (1726)

Dolins, Daniel, *The Third Charge of Sir Daniel Dolins, Kt. to the Grand Jury, and Other Juries of the County of Middlesex* (1726)

[Dunton, John,] *The Nightwalker: or, Evening Rambles in Search after Lewd Women* (Sept. 1696–April 1697)

English Reports, 178 vols. (1900–32)

Fielding, Henry, *Amelia* (Dublin, 1752)

Fielding, Henry, *The Coffee-House Politician; or the Justice Caught in his own Trap* (1730)

Fielding, Henry, *Covent Garden Journal*, no. 16 (25 Feb. 1752)

Fielding, Henry, *An Enquiry into the Causes of the Late Increase of Robbers* (1751)

A Foreign View of England in the Reigns of George I and George II. The Letters of Monsieur de Saussure to his Family, ed. Mme. van Muyden (1902)

The Form of a Petition Submitted to the Consideration and Correction of those Noblemen and Gentlemen who Desire to Subscribe what Sums shall be Necessary for Relieving, Reforming, and Employing the Poor (1722)

[Fowler, Edward,] *A Vindication of a Late Undertaking of Certain Gentlemen in Order to the Suppressing of Debauchery and Profaneness* (1692)

[Fuller, William,] *Mr. William Fuller's Trip to Bridewell* (1703)

Gonson, John, *The Charge of Sir John Gonson, Kt. to the Grand Jury of the City and Liberty of Westminster* (2nd edn, 1728)

Gonson, John, *The Second Charge of Sir John Gonson, Kt. to the Grand Jury of the City and Liberty of Westminster* (1728)

Gonson, John, *The Third Charge of Sir John Gonson, Kt. to the Grand Jury of the City and Liberty of Westminster* (1728)

Graunt, John, *Natural and Political Observations . . . made upon the Bills of Mortality* (1662)

A Guide to Juries: Setting Forth their Antiquity, Power, and Duty (1699)

Hanging, Not Punishment Enough, for Murtherers, High-way Men, and House Breakers (1701; reprint edn, 1812)

[Hare, Hugh,] "A charge given by Hugh Hare, Esq., J. P., at the general quarter sessions for the county of Surrey, holden at Dorking, 5 April 1692," *Surrey Archaeological Collections* xii (1895), 109–44

Harvey, J., *A Collection of Precedents Relating to the Office of a Justice of the Peace* (1730)

Hatton, E., *A New View of London* (1708)

Hawkins, William, *A Treatise of Pleas of the Crown*, 2 vols. (1716)

Hitchen, Charles, *A True Discovery of the Conduct of Receivers and Thief-Takers in and about the City of London* (1718)

[Ilive, Jacob,] *Reasons Offered for the Reformation of the House of Correction in Clerkenwell* (1757)

[Ilive, Jacob,] *A Scheme for the Employment of all Persons Sent as Disorderly to the House of Correction at Clerkenwell* (1759)

The Jurisdiction of the Court-Leet: Exemplified in the Articles which the Jury of Inquest for the King in that Court is Charged (1791)

The Justice's Case Law: being a Concise Abridgment of all the Cases of Crown Law, Relating to Justices of Peace (1731)

The Justicing Notebook of William Hunt 1744–49, ed. Elizabeth Crittall, Wiltshire Record Society, vol. 37 (Devizes, 1982)

Keble, Joseph, *Assistance to Justices of Peace for the Easier Performance of their Duty* (1683)

Lambard, William, *Eirenarcha: or of the Office of the Justices of Peace* (1582, 1599, 1614)

[Lambard, William,] "An ephemeris of the certifiable causes of the peace, from June, 1580, till September, 1588," *William Lambarde [sic] and Local Government*, ed. Conyers Read (Ithaca, New York, 1962)

A Looking-Glass for Informing Constables: Represented in the Tryals . . . for the Murder of Mr. John Dent (3rd edn, 1733)

Mandeville, Bernard, *An Enquiry into the Causes of the Frequent Executions at Tyburn* (1725)

Mandeville, Bernard, *Fable of the Bees* (3rd edn, 1724)

Memoirs of the Life and Times of Sir Thomas DeVeil (1748)

Meriton, George, *A Guide for Constables, Churchwardens, Overseers of the Poor* (1669)

Middlesex County Records, ed. J. C. Jeaffreson, 4 vols. (1886–92)

"Middlesex County Records. Calendar of the Sessions Books," ed. W. J. Hardy,

21 vols. (typescript, 1911–23; available at the Greater London Record Office and British Library)

Middlesex County Records. Calendar of the Sessions Books 1689–1709, ed. W. J. Hardy (1905)

[Middlesex Sessions] *An Alphabetical List of Persons who are Reputed to be Common Bail, whose Recognizances, by Suffering the Same to be Forfeited, have been Divers Times Estreated into the Court of Exchequer* [1730]

Middlesex Sessions Records (New Series) 1612–18, ed. William Le Hardy, 4 vols. (1935–41)

Midd'ss Ad general' quarteral' session' pacis [Proceedings of the justices of the peace of the county of Middlesex in relation to the reformation of manners] (10 July 1691)

Misson, Henri, M. *Misson's Memoirs and Observations in his Travels over England* (trans. J. Ozell, 1719)

N., S., *A Catalogue of the Names of All His Majesties Justices of the Peace ... According to the Late Alterations* (1680)

Nelson, William, *The Office and Authority of a Justice of the Peace* (1704, 1710, 1715)

North, Roger, *A Discourse of the Poor* (1753 [written c. 1688])

"Notebook of a Surrey Justice [Bostock Fuller]," ed. Granville Leveson-Gower in *Surrey Archaeological Collections* 9 (1888), 161–232

Nourse, Timothy, *Campania Foelix; or, a Discourse of the Benefits and Improvements of Husbandry* (1700)

The Oath of a Constable, so far as it Relates to his Apprehending Nightwalkers, and Idle Persons, and his Presenting Offences Contrary to the Statutes Made Against Unlawful Gaming, Tipling, and Drunkenness, and for Suppressing of Them (1701)

The Office of the Clerk of the Assize ... together with the Office of the Clerk of the Peace (1682)

Powell, Thomas, *The Attorney's Academy* (1647)

The Proceedings of his Majesties Justices of Peace at the Sessions of Oyer and Terminer ... September the 6th, 1684, for the Tryal of the Constables ... of the Hamlets of Spittle-fields, and Bethnal Green (1684)

The Proceedings on the King's Commissions of the Peace, Oyer and Terminer, and Gaol Delivery of Newgate, held for the City of London, and County of Middlesex, at Justice Hall in the Old Bailey (1715–21) [title varies]

Proposals for a National Reformation of Manners (1694)

Reasons, Humbly Offered for a Bill to Rebuild the Parish-Church of St. Giles's in the Fields [1717?]

Ryder, Samuel, *The Charge to the Grand Jury of the City and Liberty of Westminster, at the General Quarter Sessions of the Peace, held in Westminster Hall, October 6, 1725* [1726]

S., P., *A Help to Magistrates* (1721)

Shaw, Joseph, *The Practical Justice of Peace: or, a Treatise Showing the Power and Authority of all its Branches*, 2 vols. (1728)

Sheppard, William, *The Justice of the Peace, His Clerk's Cabinet* (1660)

Sheppard, William, *A Sure Guide for his Majesty's Justices of the Peace* (2nd edn, 1669)

Shower, John, *A Sermon Preached to the Societies for the Reformation of Manners* (1698)

Smith, William, *The Charge Given by Sir William Smith, Baronet at the Quarter Sessions of the Peace held for the County of Middlesex* (1682)

[Stephens, Edward,] *The Beginning and Progress of a Needful and Hopeful Reformation* (1691)

[Stephens, Edward,] *A Plain Relation of the late Action at Sea ... and upon the present State of the nation. Together with ... a Specimen of a Bill for a Reformation of Manners* (1690)

Strype, John, *A Survey of the Cities of London and Westminster ... By John Stow*, 2 vols. (1720)

A True List of the Names of the Good Men of the County of Middlesex, summoned to be of the Grand Jury in the Quarter Sessions, begun at Westminster 6 October 1681 (1681)

A View of London and Westminster: or, the Town Spy, etc. By a German Gentleman (1725)

Ward, Edward, *The London Spy Compleat in Eighteen Parts* (1703; 5th edn, 1718)

Warwick County Records Volume 9: Quarter Sessions Records Easter 1690, to Michaelmas, 1696, ed. H. C. Johnson and N. J. Williams (Warwick, 1964)

Watts, Isaac, *A Sermon Preach'd at Salters-Hall, to the Societies for Reformation of Manners, in the Cities of London and Westminster, October 6, 1707* (1707)

Whiston, James, *England's Calamities Discovered* (1696)

Woodward, Josiah, *An Account of the Rise and Progress of the Religious Societies in the City of London, etc., And of the Endeavours for Reformation of Manners* (4th edn, 1712)

Woodward, Josiah, *An Account of the Societies for Reformation of Manners, in England and Ireland* (5th edn, 1701)

SELECTED SECONDARY SOURCES

Amussen, Susan D., *An Ordered Society. Gender and Class in Early Modern England* (Oxford, 1988)

Archer, Ian, "Governors and governed in late sixteenth-century London, *c.* 1560–1603: studies in the achievement of stability" (Ph.D. diss., Oxford University, 1988)

Bahlman, D. W. R., *The Moral Revolution of 1688* (New Haven, 1957)

Baker, J. H., "Criminal courts and procedure at common law 1550–1800," in *Crime in England 1500–1800*, ed. Cockburn, 15–48

Baker, J. H., "The refinement of English criminal jurisprudence, 1500–1848," in *The Legal Profession and the Common Law: Historical Essays* (1986), 303–24

Beattie, John, *Crime and the Courts in England 1660–1800* (Princeton, 1986)

Beattie, John, "The criminality of women in eighteenth-century England," *Journal of Social History* 8 (1975), 80–116

Beattie, John, "London juries in the 1690s," in *Twelve Good Men and True: The Criminal Trial Jury in England, 1200–1800*, ed. Cockburn and Green, 214–53

Beattie, John, "The pattern of crime in England 1660–1800," *Past and Present* 62 (1974), 47–95

Beier, A. L., and Roger Finlay, eds., *London 1500–1700* (1986)

Boulton, Jeremy, *Neighbourhood and Society: a London Suburb in the Seventeenth Century* (Cambridge, 1987)

Brett-James, N. G., *The Growth of Stuart London* (1935)

Brewer, John, and John Styles, *An Ungovernable People: the English and their Law in the Seventeenth and Eighteenth Centuries* (1980)

Bristow, Edward J., *Vice and Vigilance: Purity Movements in Britain since 1700* (Dublin, 1977)

Brooks, C. W., "Interpersonal conflict and social tension: civil litigation in England,

1640–1830," in *The First Modern Society*, ed. A. L. Beier, David Cannadine, and James M. Rosenheim (Cambridge, 1989), 357–99

Burke, Peter, "Popular culture in seventeenth-century London," in *Popular Culture in Seventeenth-Century England*, ed. Barry Reay (1985), 31–58

Bushaway, Bob, *By Rite: Custom, Ceremony, and Community in England 1700–1880* (1982)

Clark, Peter, "Migrants in the city: the process of social adaptation in English towns, 1500–1800," in *Migration and Society in Early Modern England*, ed. Peter Clark and David Souden (1987), 267–91

Clark, Peter, and Paul Slack, *English Towns in Transition* (1976)

Cockburn, J. S., *Calendar of Assize Records: Introduction* (1985)

Cockburn, J. S., ed., *Crime in England 1500–1800* (Princeton, 1977)

Cockburn, J. S., "Early-modern assize records as historical evidence," *Journal of the Society of Archivists* 5 (Oct. 1975), 215–31

Cockburn, J. S., *A History of English Assizes 1558–1714* (Cambridge, 1972)

Cockburn, J. S., "Trial by the book? Fact and theory in the criminal process," in *Legal Records and the Historian*, ed. J. H. Baker (1978), 60–79

Cockburn, J. S., and Thomas A. Green, eds., *Twelve Good Men and True: The Criminal Trial Jury in England, 1200–1800* (Princeton, 1988)

Corfield, P. J., *The Impact of English Towns* (Oxford, 1982)

Craig, A. G., "The movement for the reformation of manners, 1688–1715" (Ph.D. diss., Edinburgh University, 1980)

Cressy, David, *Literacy and the Social Order: Reading and Writing in Tudor and Stuart England* (Cambridge, 1980)

Curtis, T. C., "Some aspects of the history of crime in seventeenth-century England, with special reference to Cheshire and Middlesex" (Ph.D. diss., Manchester University, 1973)

Curtis, T. C., and W. A. Speck, "The Societies for the Reformation of Manners: a case study in the theory and practice of moral reform," *Literature and History* 3 (1976), 45–64

Dowdell, E. G., *A Hundred Years of Quarter Sessions* (Cambridge, 1932)

Earle, Peter, "The female labour market in London in the late seventeenth and early eighteenth centuries," *Economic History Review*, 2nd series, 42 (August 1989), 328–47

Elliott, V. B., "Mobility and marriage in preindustrial England: a demographic and social structural analysis of geographic and social mobility and aspects of marriage, 1570–1690, with special reference to Middlesex, Kent, Essex, and Hertfordshire" (Ph.D. diss., Cambridge University, 1978)

Elliott, V. B., "Single women in the London marriage market: age, status, and mobility, 1598–1619," in *Marriage and Society. Studies in the Social History of Marriage*, ed. R. B. Outhwaite (New York, 1982), 81–100

Finlay, Roger, and Beatrice Shearer, "Population growth and suburban expansion," in *London 1500–1700*, ed. Beier and Finlay, 37–59

Fletcher, Anthony, *Reform in the Provinces* (1986)

Fletcher, Anthony, and John Stevenson, eds., *Order and Disorder in Early Modern England* (Cambridge, 1985)

George, M. D., *London Life in the Eighteenth Century* (1925; reprint edn, Harmondsworth, 1966)

Glass, D. V., "Socio-economic status and occupations in the City of London at the end of the seventeenth century," in *Studies in London History Presented to P. E. Jones*, ed. A. E. Hollaender and W. Kellaway (1969), 373–89

Glassey, Lionel K. J., *Politics and the Appointment of Justices of the Peace* (Oxford, 1979)

Goodacre, K., and E. Doris Mercer, *Guide to the Middlesex Sessions Records 1549–1889* (1965)

Green, Thomas A., *Verdict According to Conscience. Perspectives on the English Criminal Trial Jury 1200–1800* (Chicago, 1985)

Harris, T. J. G. (Tim), *London Crowds in the Reign of Charles II* (Cambridge, 1987)

Hay, Douglas, "The criminal prosecution in England and its historians," *Modern Law Review* 47:1 (1984), 1–29

Hay, Douglas, "Poaching and the game laws in Cannock Chase," in *Albion's Fatal Tree*, ed. Hay *et al.*, 189–253

Hay, Douglas, "Property, authority and the criminal law," in *Albion's Fatal Tree*, ed. Hay *et al.*, 17–63

Hay, Douglas, "Prosecution and power: malicious prosecution in the English courts, 1750–1850," in *Policing and Prosecution*, ed. Hay and Snyder, 343–95

Hay, Douglas, "War, dearth and theft in the eighteenth century: the record of the English courts," *Past and Present* 95 (1982), 117–60

Hay, Douglas, Peter Linebaugh, John G. Rule, E. P. Thompson, and Cal Winslow, eds., *Albion's Fatal Tree: Crime and Society in Eighteenth-Century England* (Harmondsworth, 1975)

Hay, Douglas, and Francis Snyder, eds., *Policing and Prosecution in Britain 1750–1850* (Oxford, 1989)

Hecht, Jean, *The Domestic Servant Class in Eighteenth-Century England* (1956)

Herrup, Cynthia, *The Common Peace: Participation and the Criminal Law in Seventeenth-Century England* (Cambridge, 1987)

Hitchcock, T. V., "The English workhouse: a study in institutional poor relief in selected counties, 1696–1750" (Ph.D. diss., Oxford University, 1985)

Holdsworth, William, *A History of English Law*, 12 vols. (1923–72)

Howson, Gerald, *It Takes a Thief. The Life and Times of Jonathan Wild* [Formerly published as *Thief-Taker General* (1970)] (1987)

Ignatieff, Michael, *A Just Measure of Pain: The Penitentiary in the Industrial Revolution* (1978)

Ingram, Martin J., *Church Courts, Sex and Marriage in England, 1570–1640* (Cambridge, 1987)

Ingram, Martin J., "Communities and courts: law and disorder in early seventeenth-century Wiltshire," in *Crime in England*, ed. Cockburn, 110–34

Innes, Joanna, "Prisons for the poor: English bridewells, 1555–1800," in *Law, Labour, and Crime*, ed. Francis Snyder and Douglas Hay (1987), 42–122

Innes, Joanna, "Social problems: poverty and marginality in eighteenth-century England" (unpublished typescript, 1985)

Innes, Joanna, "Statute law and summary justice in early modern England" (unpublished typescript, 1986)

Innes, Joanna, and John Styles, "The crime wave: recent writing on crime and criminal justice in eighteenth-century England," *Journal of British Studies* 25 (Oct. 1986), 380–435

Isaacs, Tina Beth, "The Anglican hierarchy and the reformation of manners 1688–1738," *Journal of Ecclesiastical History* 33 (1982), 391–411

Isaacs, Tina Beth, "Moral crime, moral reform, and the state in early eighteenth-century England: a study of piety and politics" (Ph.D. diss., University of Rochester, 1979)

Kellett, J. R., "The breakdown of gild and corporation control over the handicraft and retail trades in London," *Economic History Review*, 2nd series, 10 (1958), 381–94

Kent, D. A., "Ubiquitous but invisible: female domestic servants in mid-eighteenth century London," *History Workshop Journal* 28 (Aug. 1989), 111–28

Kent, Joan R., *The English Village Constable 1580–1642* (Oxford, 1986)

King, Peter, "Crime, law and society in Essex, 1740–1820" (Ph.D. diss., Cambridge University, 1984)

King, Peter, "Decision-makers and decision-making in the English criminal law, 1750–1800," *Historical Journal* 27 (1984), 25–58

King, Peter, "Gleaners, farmers and the failure of legal sanctions in England 1750–1850," *Past and Present* 125 (1989), 116–50

Knafla, Louis A., " 'Sin of all sorts swarmeth': criminal litigation in an English county in the early seventeenth century," in *Law, Litigants and the Legal Profession*, ed. E. W. Ives and A. H. Manchester (1983), 50–67

Landau, Norma, *The Justices of the Peace 1679–1760* (Berkeley, 1984)

Langbein, John H., "Albion's fatal flaws," *Past and Present* 98 (1982), 96–120

Langbein, John H. "The criminal trial before the lawyers," *The University of Chicago Law Review* 45 (Winter 1978), 263–316

Langbein, John H., *Prosecuting Crime in the Renaissance: England, Germany, France* (Cambridge, Mass., 1974)

Levine, David, and Keith Wrightson, *Poverty and Piety in an English Village: Terling, 1525–1700* (New York, 1979)

Lindert, Peter, "English occupations, 1670–1811," *Journal of Economic History* 40 (1980), 685–712

Linebaugh, Peter, "(Marxist) social history and (conservative) legal history: a reply to Professor Langbein," *New York University Law Review* 60 (1985), 212–43

Linebaugh, Peter, "Tyburn: a study of crime and the labouring poor in London during the first half of the eighteenth century" (Ph.D. diss., Warwick University, 1975)

MacFarlane, Stephen, "Social policy and the poor in the later seventeenth century," in *London 1500–1700*, ed. Beier and Finlay, 252–77

MacFarlane, Stephen, "Studies in poverty and poor relief in London at the end of the seventeenth century" (Ph.D. diss., Oxford University, 1983)

Marshall, Dorothy, *The English Poor in the Eighteenth Century* (1926)

Martindale, L., "Demography and land use in the late seventeenth and eighteenth centuries in Middlesex" (Ph.D. diss., University of London, 1968)

Milsom, S. F. C., *Historical Foundations of the Common Law* (2nd edn, 1981)

Morrill, J. S., *The Cheshire Grand Jury 1625–1659* (University of Leicester, Department of English Local History, Occasional Papers, Third Series, no. 1, 1976)

Munsche, P. B., *Gentlemen and Poachers: the English Game Laws 1671–1831* (Cambridge, 1981)

Pearl, Valerie, "Change and stability in seventeenth-century London," *London Journal* 5 (1979), 8–27

Pearson, Geoffrey, *Hooligan: a History of Respectable Fears* (1983)

Portus, Garnet V., *Caritas Anglicana* (1912)

Power, M. J., "The east and west in early-modern London," in *Wealth and Power in Tudor England: Essays Presented to S. T. Bindoff*, ed. E. W. Ives, R. J. Knecht, and J. J. Scarisbrick (1978), 167–85

Power, M. J., "Shadwell: the development of a London suburban community in the seventeenth century," *London Journal* 4 (1978), 29–48

Power, M. J., "The social topography of Restoration London," in *London 1500–1700*, ed. Beier and Finlay, 206–22

Power, M. J., "The urban development of east London, 1550–1700" (Ph.D. diss., University of London, 1971)

Radzinowicz, Leon, *A History of the English Criminal Law*, 4 vols. (1948–68)

Rappaport, Steve, *Worlds within Worlds: Structures of Life in Sixteenth-Century London* (Cambridge, 1989)

Roberts, Michael, " 'Words they are women, and deeds they are men': images of work and gender in early-modern England," in *Women and Work in Preindustrial England*, ed. Lindsey Charles and Lorna Duffin (1985), 122–80

Rogers, Nicholas, "Popular protest in early Hanoverian London," *Past and Present* 79 (1978), 70–100

Samaha, Joel, "The recognizance in Elizabethan law enforcement," *American Journal of Legal History* 25 (1981), 189–204

Schofield, R. S., "Sampling in historical research," in *Nineteenth-Century Society: Essays in the Use of Quantitative Methods for the Study of Social Data*, ed. E. A. Wrigley (Cambridge, 1972), 146–90

Sharpe, J. A., *Crime in Early Modern England 1550–1750* (1984)

Sharpe, J. A., *Crime in Seventeenth-Century England* (Cambridge, 1983)

Sharpe, J. A., "Enforcing the law in the seventeenth-century English village," in *Crime and the Law: the Social History of Crime in Western Europe since 1500*, ed. V. A. C. Gatrell, Bruce Lenman, and Geoffrey Parker (1980), 97–119

Sharpe, J. A., "The people and the law," in *Popular Culture in Seventeenth-Century England*, ed. Barry Reay (1988), 244–70

Sharpe, J. A., " 'Such disagreement betwyx neighbours': litigation and human relations in early modern England," in *Disputes and Settlements. Law and Human Relations in the West*, ed. John Bossy (Cambridge, 1983), 167–87

Shoemaker, Robert B., "Crime, courts and community: the prosecution of misdemeanors in Middlesex county, 1663–1723" (Ph.D. diss., Stanford University, 1986)

Shoemaker, Robert B., "The London 'mob' in the early eighteenth century," *Journal of British Studies* 26 (1987), 273–304

Souden, David, "Migrants and the population structure of later seventeenth-century provincial cities and market towns," in *The Transformation of English Provincial Towns 1600–1800*, ed. Peter Clark (1981), 133–68

Stone, Lawrence, "The residential development of the west end of London in the seventeenth century," in *After the Reformation. Essays in Honour of J. H. Hexter*, ed. Barbara C. Malament (Manchester, 1980), 167–212

Styles, John, "Embezzlement, industry and the law in England, 1500–1800," in *Manufacture in Town and Country Before the Factory*, ed. M. Berg, P. Hudson, and M. Sonenscher (Cambridge, 1983), 173–210

Thomas, Keith, "The double standard," *Journal of the History of Ideas* 20 (1959), 195–216

Thompson, E. P., "Eighteenth-century English society: class struggle without class?" *Social History* 3 (1978), 133–65

Thompson, E. P., "Patrician society, plebeian culture," *Journal of Social History* 7 (1974), 382–405

Thompson, E. P., *Whigs and Hunters* (Harmondsworth, 1977)

Webb, Sidney and Beatrice, *English Local Government from the Revolution to the Municipal Corporations Act: The Manor and the Borough* (1908)

Webb, Sidney and Beatrice, *English Local Government from the Revolution to the Municipal Corporations Act: The Parish and the County* (1906)

Wrightson, Keith, *English Society 1580–1680* (1982)

Wrightson, Keith, "Two concepts of order: justices, constables and jurymen in seventeenth-century England," in *An Ungovernable People*, ed. Brewer and Styles, 21–46

Wrigley, E. A., "A simple model of London's importance in changing English society and economy 1650–1750," *Past and Present* 37 (1967), 44–70

INDEX

Cambridge Studies in Early Modern British History

Titles in the series

* Also published as a paperback